LIVES AND LETTERS

A series of diaries and letters, journals and memoirs

LEFT HAND, RIGHT HAND!

SITWELL, Sir Osbert, 5th Bt., *cr.* 1808; C.H. 1958; C.B.E. 1956; C.Lit. 1967; Hon. LL.D. St. Andrews, 1946; Hon. D.Litt. Sheffield, 1951; Hon. Associate of A.I.A.L., 1950; Hon. F.R.I.B.A. 1957; F.R.S.L.; poet, essayist, novelist, and writer of short stories and art criticism; a Trustee of the Tate Gallery, 1951-58; *b.* 3 Arlington Street, W., 6 Dec. 1892; *e.s.* of Sir George Sitwell, 4th Bt., and Lady Ida Emily Augusta Denison (*d.* 1937). *d.* of 1st Earl of Londesborough; *S.* father. 1943. *Educ.:* during the holidays from Eton. Grenadier Guards, 1912-19. For the past 30 years has conducted, in conjunction with his brother and sister, a series of skirmishes and hand-to-hand battles against the Philistine. Though outnumbered, has occasionally succeeded in denting the line, though not without damage to himself. Advocates compulsory Freedom everywhere, the suppression of Public Opinion in the interest of Free Speech, and the rationing of brains without which innovation there can be no true democracy. Chm. Management Cttee., Society of Authors, 1944-45, 1946-48 and 1951-52. Received the first Annual Award of the Sunday Times Prize and Gold Medal for literature for 1946-47. Has lectured extensively in public and private. *Publications:* Twentieth Century Harlequinade and other Poems (with Edith Sitwell), 1916; Argonaut and Juggernaut, 1919; The Winstonburg Line, 1919; Who Killed Cock Robin?, 1921; Out of the Flame, 1923; Triple Fugue, and other Stories, 1924; Discursions on Travel, Art and Life, 1925; Before the Bombardment, 1926; England Reclaimed, 1927; All at Sea (a play, with Sacheverell Sitwell), 1927; The People's Album of London Statues (with illustrations by Nina Hamnett), 1928; The Man who lost Himself, 1929; Sober Truth (with Margaret Barton), 1930; Dumb Animal and other stories, 1930; Victoriana (with Margaret Barton), 1931; Portrait of Michael Arlen, 1931; Collected Poems and Satires, 1931; Winters of Content, 1932; Dickens, 1932; Miracle on Sinai, 1933; Brighton (with Margaret Barton), 1935; Penny Foolish, 1935; Those Were the Days, 1938; Trio (with Edith and Sacheverell Sitwell), 1938; Escape with Me, 1939; Two Generations, 1940; Open the Door, 1941; A Place of One's Own, 1941 (Filmed Gaumont British, 1944); Gentle Caesar (a play, with R. J. Minney); Selected Poems, 1943; Sing High! Sing Low!, 1944; A Letter to My Son, 1944. Autobiography: Vol. 1, Left Hand, Right Hand!, 1945; Vol. 2, The Scarlet Tree, 1946; Vol. 3, Great Morning, 1948; Vol. 4, Laughter in the Next Room, 1949; Vol. 5, Noble Essences, 1950. The True Story of Dick Whittington, 1946; Ed.: A Free House (The Writings of Walter Richard Sickert), 1947; Demos the Emperor (Poems); Death of a God (short stories), 1949; Wrack at Tidesend (Poems), 1952; Collected Short Stories, 1953; Four Continents, 1954; On the Continent (Poems), 1958; Fee Fi Fo Fum (modern Fairy Stories), 1959; Tales My Father Taught Me, 1962; Pound Wise (Collected Essays), 1963; Portraits of People, of England Reclaimed, 1965; and innumerable contributions to newspapers. *Recreations:* listening to the sound of his own voice, preferably on gramophone records, and not answering letters. [Died 4 May 1969]

Patrick Taylor-Martin was born in 1953 and read history at Hull University. His first book, *John Betjeman: His Life and Work*, was published by Allen Lane in 1983. He is currently working on a study of the writers of the twenties and thirties.

LEFT HAND,
RIGHT HAND!

AN AUTOBIOGRAPHY BY
OSBERT SITWELL

ABRIDGED BY
PATRICK TAYLOR-MARTIN

PENGUIN BOOKS

Penguin Books Ltd, Harmondsworth, Middlesex, England
Penguin Books, 40 West 23rd Street, New York, New York 10010, U.S.A.
Penguin Books Australia Ltd, Ringwood, Victoria, Australia
Penguin Books Canada Ltd, 2801 John Street, Markham, Ontario, Canada L3R 1B4
Penguin Books (N.Z.) Ltd, 182–190 Wairau Road, Auckland 10, New Zealand

The Cruel Month first published by Macmillan 1945
Copyright © Frank Magro, 1945

The Scarlet Tree first published by Macmillan 1946
Copyright © Frank Magro, 1946

Great Morning first published by Macmillan 1948
Copyright © Frank Magro, 1948

Laughter in the Next Room first published by Macmillan 1949
Copyright © Frank Magro, 1949

This abridged edition first published 1984
This abridged edition and Introduction copyright © Patrick Taylor-Martin, 1984
All rights reserved

The biographical details on the first page have been taken from *Who Was Who 1961–70*,
published by A. & C. Black Ltd.

Filmset, printed and bound in Great Britain by
Hazell Watson & Viney Ltd,
Member of the BPCC Group,
Aylesbury, Bucks
Set in 10/12pt VIP Bembo

CONTENTS

DEDICATORY NOTE

The original volumes of this autobiography were dedicated to the author's brother and sister, Maynard Hollingworth, Field Marshal Lord Alexander of Tunis and David Horner.

I should like to dedicate this abridgement to the memory of Sir Osbert Sitwell and to Mr Frank Magro.

INTRODUCTION

The three Sitwells – Dame Edith (1887–1964), Sir Osbert (1892–1969) and Sir Sacheverell (b. 1897) – were born into a rich landed family. It was an unusual background for writers and explains some of the hostility – as well as some of the sycophancy – which they encountered in their lives.

The first Sitwell (or Cytewel) was recorded in north-east Derbyshire in the fourteenth century though, in fact, this Sitwell line died out in the eighteenth century with William Sitwell, a rich bachelor, whose property passed to his nephew, one Francis Hurt. Francis reverted to the Sitwell patronymic and called his son Sitwell Sitwell as if to drive the point home (thus provoking Evelyn Waugh's malicious speculation that Sir Osbert, his hyper-sensitive descendant, might have been better called Sir Hurt Hurt).

Though the Sitwells' wealth had originally come from iron-founding, they were, by the late eighteenth century, also substantial landowners with a large rent roll. Sir Sitwell Sitwell (the baronetcy was created in 1808) was the typical Regency buck, a keen sportsman and an acquaintance of the Regent, who transformed Renishaw, the family home in Derbyshire, from a solid seventeenth-century yeoman-squire's house into a large and imposing mansion, complete with the fashionable gothick appurtenances of battlements and pinnacles as well as follies in the park and a huge classical stable-block to house his racehorses and packs of hounds.

After this halcyon period of building and ennoblement, a cloud appeared. Sir Sitwell's son, Sir George, suffered partial financial ruin as a result of the combined effects of a sharp fall in land prices after the Napoleonic wars, embezzlement by his solicitor and the failure of a Sheffield bank into which he had just deposited a large sum. Sir George's son, Sir Reresby, was forced to shut up the house and sell land as well as chattels. The family fortunes were revived, however, by the skilful management of his widow, Louisa, Lady Sitwell, and the fortunate discovery of large coal deposits on the estate in the 1870s. Sir Reresby's son, the redoubtable Sir George Sitwell, father of the three Sitwells, succeeded to a secure inheritance at the age of two though he was haunted, all his life, by the prospect of another descent into relative penury.

The strange character of Sir George dominates his son's autobiography as it did, in different ways, the lives of his three children. Despite his many talents, however, he made more of an impression on his family than he did on the world at large. For instance, during his two periods in the Commons, he spoke only four times. Indeed, his most significant public achievement was to have exposed a fraudulent medium while still an undergraduate and he continued to list this battle honour – 'captured a spirit at the headquarters of the Spiritualists, London, 1880' – in *Who's Who* to the end of his life. Though he may have dreamed of the grand imperial and political achievements of a Curzon, who had been his contemporary at Eton, his restless intellect rather found expression in extensive genealogical researches, sporadic forays into commerce, cranky inventions and manic building and landscaping activities. His monument is the superb garden he created at Renishaw as well, of course, as *Left Hand, Right Hand!* itself in which his eccentricities are immortalized.

On the whole, despite his passion for making life difficult for those around him, Sir George emerges from the pages of *Left Hand, Right Hand!* as a comic figure. There were, perhaps, sides of Sir George's character which his son chose not to explore just as there were of his own. Indeed, a note of discretion amounting at times to blandness is one of the faults of the book. However, the constant play of Osbert Sitwell's wit animates the book's stately progress, giving life to the spacious anecdotes in which it abounds and adding a little salt to its lush descriptions of fashionable life. For all its faults, it remains a remarkable achievement and the portrait of Sir George places him securely in the distinguished company of English eccentrics.

This eccentricity, by which he was genuinely consumed rather than which he consciously deployed for effect, came at times dangerously close to madness. He suffered some sort of breakdown in 1902 and from then on became increasingly removed from reality, the lonely inhabitant of an ivory tower of which the Castello di Montegufoni, the Tuscan villa-fortress which he bought in 1910, became the material embodiment. According to Anthony Powell, who met him in the twenties, 'there was something "wrong" about Sir George Sitwell, badly wrong'. This 'wrongness' manifested itself in sounds of maniacal laughter coming from his room at night as well as in his treatment of his children and, above all, of his wife.

He had married a daughter of the extremely rich Lord Londesborough, a beautiful, frivolous, impulsive and empty-headed girl of seventeen. Lady Ida Denison could scarcely have been more ill-matched than with this strange man with his scholarly tastes, aloof manner and hatred of society. The marriage began unhappily and continued unhappily. The three Sitwell children were brought up, therefore, in an atmosphere of extreme domestic tension. Human warmth came from the servants in whose company they spent much of their time rather than from the austere Sir George or from Lady Ida who, despite a willingness to indulge and pet her sons, had a violent and unpredictable temper. The misery of the Sitwells' family life reached a tragic climax in 1915 when Lady Ida was involved in a lawsuit which resulted in her imprisonment.

The events leading up to 'this, our private calamity' are treated rather sketchily by Osbert though they have been brilliantly illuminated in John Pearson's indispensable *Façades* (Macmillan, 1978). Briefly, Lady Ida, who had landed herself in debt, was put in touch, by Osbert, with a man called Julian Field who was believed to be able to arrange loans discreetly. Unfortunately, he was a crook who, having arranged a first loan of £6,000, drew the hopelessly naïve Lady Ida into a web of financial intrigue. She was persuaded to take out further loans and to get other people, anxious to have her help in getting them into society, to back her bills. Osbert's help was enlisted to 'get hold of' suitable backers and she retailed her attempts to do so in letters of the wildest indiscretion to Field. If she wanted to extricate herself from the arrangement, Field had only to mention the possibility of talking to Sir George to convince her that she must, at all costs, avoid such an outcome. Eventually, her debts stood at £12,000, though most of this had stuck to Field's fingers, and she was reduced to borrowing from servants ('I owe my butler £125, the brute,' she told Field, 'I want to get out of his clutches.').

It was only when the clamour for repayment became so strong that it could no longer be ignored that Sir George was let in on the secret. Even then, he may not have been told of the full extent of Lady Ida's indiscretion, particularly of the letters which she had written to Field. He promptly settled Osbert's affairs and arranged for his transfer to the Guards from his hated cavalry regiment (Osbert is rather mysterious about this transfer). He also repaid some £5,000 of his wife's debts but he refused to settle the original debt – which now stood at more than £7,000 – as he believed that here Field could be proved to have acted fraudulently. In this he was right, though by bringing Field to justice he also precipitated his wife's imprisonment. In one sense, Sir George acted public-spiritedly in ending Field's career and saving other families from similar disgrace. His own children took a somewhat less generous view of his actions. Whether he acted maliciously remains a mystery. Certainly, he tried to persuade the Home Secretary to have the sentence revoked. Almost certainly, he did not expect a jury to convict a woman who could scarcely count let alone conspire to defraud. Nevertheless, this 'sordid' (Edith's word) episode transformed the embattled state of family life into something little short of open war. It forced the three Sitwells, already close, to assume a united front in opposition to their father.

Sir George's relationship with Osbert, as his elder son and heir, was particularly fraught. Osbert's own reckless spending on food and clothes and wine disgusted and alarmed him. ('I think men who spend profusely on their bodies are really swine', he told him in a letter which Osbert did not use in *Left Hand, Right Hand!*) Whether he suspected Osbert's homosexuality, about which in his autobiography as well as in his life he maintained a pose of absolute concealment, is not clear. What is clear is that Sir George inspired fear as well as hatred in his son. This fear may have been what impelled Osbert to turn him into a figure of fun, a sort of running joke for the amusement of his friends. Sir George was a formidable and steely man who was far from sympathetic to any weaknesses other than his own. Denied a wider stage on which to exercise himself, he delighted in tyrannizing his family and Osbert was pathetically dependent on him. Siegfried Sassoon, who stayed at Renishaw in the summer of 1921, caught the strange atmosphere of the house:

> But all this incessant wrangling about money, Osbert trying to snatch money from Ginger (Osbert's nickname for Sir George), etc. Why does O. let himself be under G.'s thumb? A complete break would be more dignified, surely? But O. is too fond of luxuries and prestige to sacrifice a single square meal. So they go on with their skirmishings about 'pay and allowances', and wait for somebody to die off.

In *Left Hand, Right Hand!* these 'skirmishings' are treated in *opera buffa* terms. The idea of 'a complete break' was unthinkable. Sir George was an indispensable part of the personal legend which the Sitwells had created and round which their lives revolved. In Edith and Osbert – Sacheverell having married and had children of his own was less involved – this sense of isolation and absorption in some private black comedy was pronounced. D. H. Lawrence, who met them both in Italy, was profoundly affected by it:

> I never in my life saw such a strong, strange family complex: as if they were marooned on a desert island, and nobody in the world but their own lost selves. Queer!

Although the passage of time was to separate them, at the beginning of their careers they confronted the world, in Sir Edmund Gosse's words, as that 'delightful but deleterious trio', united in the determination to shock and to praise each other's work. Despite his dignified and reserved exterior – Gertrude Stein thought that, even in his thirties, he resembled 'the uncle of a king' – Osbert Sitwell was a lover of controversy and publicity all his life. Indeed, all three Sitwells – but particularly Edith and Osbert – were so regularly in the public eye that one of their enemies, F. R. Leavis, contemptuously dismissed them as belonging to 'the history of publicity rather than to that of poetry'. In part, the hostility they engendered was a reaction against the Sitwells' own overestimate of their importance as writers and their absurd pride in their ancestry which they seemed to think should have insulated them from the 'impertinent' criticisms of 'pipsqueaks' and 'upstarts'. However, their readiness to cross swords with any detractor, no matter how insignificant, only served to make them more tempting targets: Sitwell-baiting became a popular sport.

But all three Sitwells were professional writers who took their work seriously. Though Wyndham Lewis felt that they would have been better advised to support artists than to set up as artists themselves, they cannot be dismissed as mere amateurs; as the sheer volume of their work alone testifies. Osbert Sitwell, however, was a patron and a collector as well as a writer and, together with his brother and sister, was generous in his welcome to young artists, composers and writers. His collecting was confined mostly to the works of eighteenth-century masters such as Magnasco though he also bought some distinguished modern works and commissioned the Futurist, Severini, to fresco a whole room at Monte-gufoni, having failed to persuade Sir George to meet Picasso's price for a similar project. In the nineteen-forties, he gave John Piper, who regarded him as 'quite the ideal patron in the way he would suggest a subject but never interfere', the task of producing a vast number of drawings of Sitwellian locations in England and Italy, many of which were used to illustrate the autobiography. It was the family's decision to take up the young William Walton, however, which was their most inspired act of patronage. As well as enabling Walton to develop his talents without interference and allowing him to live and travel with them, it resulted in the producion of *Façade*, an entertainment of music by Walton with words by Edith Sitwell, which, in the popular mind at least, established the Sitwells as bywords for modernity in the arts. As moulders of taste, Osbert and Sacheverell were also prime movers in the rehabilitation of the despised art and architecture of Baroque Spain and southern Italy.

Osbert Sitwell's courtly manner made him a favourite of all the great hostesses of the day, notably of the grotesque royalty-snob ('One wears out *so* many red carpets in a season'), Mrs Ronald Greville, as well as of Queen Mary herself. To the generation of writers led by Evelyn Waugh, he was urbane enjoyment personified: wit, raconteur and dandy, proving, in Cyril Connolly's words, 'that it was possible to reconcile art and fashion'. His literary output was extensive and embraced poetry – of which the bitter anti-war poems still retain their hard satirical edge – novels – of which the best is *Before the Bombardment* – short stories, travel books, plays and essays. *Left Hand, Right Hand!* was his finest book and became a bestseller, bringing him much prestige and many honours both here and in America where, with Dame Edith, he made a number of successful lecture tours.

Although he wrote relatively little after the appearance of the last volume in 1950, he was able to bask in his success. Sadly, Parkinson's disease, which had been diagnosed when he was still in his fifties, made him increasingly an invalid. In 1965, he retired permanently to Monte-gufoni where he died in 1969.

The curious reader may be interested to know what he will be missing in an abridgment less than half the length of the original. I have excluded all the family history, much merely anecdotal material, all the footnotes and appendices, a rather overblown account of the author's part in the ending of the General Strike, some bland accounts of society hostesses and many of the exercises in fine writing in which the author liked to indulge whenever the opportunity presented itself. I have not altered the sequence of the material, moving backwards and forwards in time being the essence of the book. Although I have sometimes broken up sentences and paragraphs, I have inserted words only when the sense absolutely requires it. Readers of the original text will be aware that Osbert Sitwell was addicted to a particularly irritating form of punctuation, viz. . . . not to mention . . . , with which he liked to pepper his long paragraphs. This entire rash of dots has been eradicated, firstly, because they are redundant and, secondly, since they might lead some readers to suppose that they indicated passages blue-pencilled by the present editor.

Left Hand, Right Hand! – the title derives from palmistry, the left hand carrying the marks of heredity and the right charting what we have made of our lives – chronicles high society and high art in a prose of conscious magnificence. It is an elegy for the world which perished in 1914 and a celebration of a life devoted to the arts, both as champion and practitioner. Though its style and its mood of remembrance of things past lead, inevitably, to comparisons with Proust, one is more often reminded of Dickens in the great set-pieces of portraiture with which the book is filled. Sir George and Henry Moat, his Rabelaisian foil and majordomo, are but the leading players in a huge cast of eccentrics and human oddities who move against a variety of backcloths – storm-wracked Scarborough, the haunted beauty of Renishaw, islanded in industrial squalor, and Montegufoni brooding on its cypress-clad hill. It is not just the portrait of a writer against the background of his times but a sort of *tableau vivant* suggesting something of the vast extent of human oddness.

Left Hand, Right Hand! is no exception to the rule that inside every good long book there is an even better shorter one trying to get out. By throwing some of the ballast overboard, I hope I have succeeded in keeping the ship afloat and in persuading some hitherto reluctant passengers to come aboard and sample the delights.

Patrick Taylor-Martin

ACKNOWLEDGEMENTS

I should like to thank the following: Mr John Denny of Penguin Books for going through the proofs with exemplary care; Mr John Guest of Allen Lane for supporting my proposal for this book, Mr Bruce Hunter of David Higham Associates for his help and encouragement, Mr Frank Magro for permission to make the selection and Mr Reresby Sitwell for allowing me to visit Renishaw.

BOOK ONE

THE CRUEL MONTH

PROLOGUE

The garden would be beautiful – and is beautiful – with no flower blooming there. Though this lovely country teems with industry, every prospect is idyllic, and chimneys in the distance become tall obelisks. Its architecture does not consist so much in stone walls and paved walks, as in green walls of yew and box. If you stand with your back to the large old house and face due south, on your left, behind and below the formal arrangement of beds and statues and fountains and yew hedges, lies the Wilderness, part of a wild garden surviving from the eighteenth century, with dark, mysterious cut glades, and at the end of them, far away, a golden cornfield in which in August and September you can just descry the turreted sheaves. Here in spring, when the trees are burgeoning, the ground is covered for three weeks at a time with the azure snow of bluebells and later, in the summer, you find the tall, over-weighted spires of wild Canterbury bells, no doubt descended from flowers escaped long ago from older enclosed gardens of monasteries and manors. On your right hand towers up the Avenue, a piece of formal planting, old elms alternating with limes, surviving, it is said, from 1680. To the south, in front of you, the garden descends by level terraced lawns and green platforms, each with its piece of water, pool or fountain, to the outer green terrace, which commands a wide view of the lake, lying far below, and of a sweep of beautiful country rising up beyond it.

The gimcrack, tangled battlements of Barlborough, that have yet stood so long, show near at hand among the green mounds of the fat-leafed tree-tops, while, on the horizon, you can distinguish the lofty stone keep of Bolsover, jutting like a cliff, its windows burnished every evening by the setting sun, and, upon a clear day, the three tall towers of Hardwick, perhaps the most beautiful Elizabethan house in England, a sky-scraper of glass and golden stone. A little to the right, the view ascends towards the Peak, so that in the distance are the shimmering faint outlines of what, for England, are mountains. On each side of flights of steps, stone statues of Neptune and Diana, and of two giants, gaze outward from the house towards this superb and romantic prospect bound together by the glint of water, – pool and lake and fountain.

Often you would wonder which is the most beautiful moment in this garden; at noon, on a hot summer day, when the light reflected from the water quivers in dazzling patterns upon statues and walls, and upon the warm velvet of the lawns, or on spring mornings when in their mist the trees are towers of crystal, each twig a glittering vein in it, or later, when whole rival choirs of birds practise within them, and every twig is unfurling a golden and transparent pennon; on summer nights when you feel its mystery as at other times you feel its joy, – for in the manner of all gardens it is a little haunted, with the mystery of stillness and space and silence, a rustling sense of expectancy that, though alarming, is not disagreeable, – and then, a miracle that can only occur in this neighbour-hood, the whole sky flames out from the furnaces, and the sighing, tall summer trees and the dark walls of the hedges smoulder in the fierceness of this light until, after a minute or two, the flares subside and the world settles to darkness again, the white owl snores once more in her moated grange, the hollow tree upon an island, and the startled bats fly home in arching, segmented flight; or in the early mornings of October, when the mists and cobwebs natural to a Derbyshire fine morning at that season are being brushed away by the sun, which, nevertheless, all day long, seems a little tarnished, so that everything, every stone and trunk and dying, gilded leaf, takes on a hue of deeper and decaying gold.

But this is the pompous month of August – a month of an unnatural length ordained by the pride and caprice of an Emperor eighteen centuries ago – and the early, the very early, morning. Already, however, the light summer mists have evaporated, the distances are visible, and at the end of the long, sombre aisles of the trees, upon the sides of the hills at which they are pointing, the pale yellow glint of cornfields twists in and out of the nearer pattern of green leaves like the Arabesque by Schumann. And already, too, a tall man, fair and with a curious air of isolation, is out there upon the terraces.

My father is very fond of walking, extremely rapidly, in these gardens he has made. All day long he can be found in them: and this year, into which I lead you, he is there for a longer time than ever, because to him the Middle Ages are the model for all life to follow – hence the isolation you noticed, for he lives behind invisible barriers of pedigrees and tourneys and charters and coats-of-arms, and all round him hang its shields and banners, all round him sound its discordant trumpets and the battle-cries of armoured men – and since every medieval romance opens in a garden at the hour of sunrise, he has, this summer, chosen to be called every morning at five. But, though he has his share of the proselytizing spirit and is anxious that others should benefit from the same experience, he is still alone. But this, in itself, in no way irks him.

He walks up and down, surveying his work, which will never be finished, his head full of new projects of sun and shade, but never of flowers, measuring the various views with a stick to his eye or a pair of binoculars. Sometimes he is planning a boat of stone upon the lake, or a dragon in lead, writhing for a quarter of a mile through its level waters, or a colonnaded pavilion upon another island, or a Roman aqueduct in counterfeit to frame the prospect with its elongated arches, or a cascade to fall down a stone channel for a hundred and fifty feet, from the water to the garden below: and, for projects such as these, though most of them never materialized, he would cause wooden towers, built up of planks and joists and beams – like an early machine for siege warfare or a drawing by Piranese – to be erected here and there at the right points of vantage. In the summer he would spend many hours aloft on these platforms, with a large grey hat or grey umbrella to shield his light-coloured skin and eyes from the sun, and with a telescope to his eye, enjoying the air and also, perhaps, the feeling of command which such an altitude above the ground affords. Then he descends, preoccupied, recognizing, if it is by now the hour of social activity, no one whom he passes, and walks up and down the terraces again, pausing occasionally to contemplate a vista lately cut. If it is past eight-thirty in the morning – for to his sorrow he 'cannot induce the fellow to follow the right plan and be here by six' –, he will stop occasionally to talk to his agent, ever and again asking, after surveying the model for some new box-edged, formal beds or the possibility of a new perspective, 'How much can we twist this, without being found out?' . . . All my life these have been his ways, in one place or another. He made the great garden lay-out at Renishaw just before I was born, and I grew up, year by year, with its yew hedges. I never remember a time between the ages of three and seventeen when we were not the same height, though now they overtop me, and this is a privilege and rare experience for which I have him to thank. Indeed, though he has written many books – of which, perhaps, the best and best-known is, happily enough, a volume of essays entitled *On the Making of Gardens* –

it is as an artist in levels and lawns and vistas and lakes that he lives and will survive.

At any rate, one fine summer morning, when the yew hedges were about four feet high, and I was about nine years of age, he raced me at a tremendous pace up and down the Avenue, telling me of various relations of his in the past. I can see now the wide expanse of lake and woodland – nowhere else in England can you find such contrasts in the sky, such dramatic effects of cloud and sun and smoke –, high over which flew the proud streamers from the mines. Suddenly he stopped talking of these dead lives, and said, as though to himself – and, indeed, I had not been paying much attention:

'It's quite evident, if you read the family letters, that we've been working up towards something for a long time, for well over a century.'

He did not, I think, realize fully the implications of what he said – though as he said it, I experienced a slight lifting of the heart –, for his mind, though in many directions so very unconventional and gothic, displayed certain strata of intense conventionality, and he did not think of writers when he made this pronouncement – because writing was to him only an incidental accomplishment, part of the general make-up of a cultured man – and doubtless in his heart he dreamt of colonial governors and proconsuls, supreme over the wastes and teeming cities of an empire, shining somewhere among his descendants, among his great-grandchildren – since he was interested more in ancestors and descendants than in fathers and sons.

CHAPTER ONE

On the 7th of December of 1892, at Scarborough, my Aunt Florence entered in her diary the following words:

'Yesterday morning a telegram to Mother announced the birth of a son to George and Ida. Rejoicing in the town, and bells ringing. Today, in a letter to Mother, Lady Londesborough describes the little boy as healthy, lively, compact and plump – also pretty.' And, three months later, she notes: 'Wednesday the eighth of March was the day when little Francis Osbert Sacheverell was "received into the church" here at St Mary's. I was so sorry, not being well, to be unable to attend the service. Such a crowd, I heard . . . Mother says the baby kept his blue eyes fixed on the coloured glass window, or on the lilies that decorated the font. When the service was over, one woman in the crowd rushed forward and kissed him before anyone could prevent her.'

The preceding account of my christening, together with the fact that, so I have been told, I gave during the ceremony a violent tug at the beard of the Bishop contains all the precocious indications of appearance or character of which I have been informed. Even now, however, were I to sit for long in church, my eyes would wander toward the coloured glass or the decoration of flowers round the altar; and no wonder, besides, that I rebelled and tore wildly with my hands at the iconic countenance of the Bishop, for, being a delicate infant, I had already once been baptized, by the son of the same dignitary, in London, so that 'the pomps and vanities of this wicked world', which have always been so dear to me, had ere this been forsworn on my behalf, and were now doubly prohibited. As for the crowds of people, and the general and pleasant attitude of welcome recorded, this was, alas, in no way due to infant merit or virtue, but the result of my father being Conservative member for the old borough of Scarborough, and of the popularity of my mother and himself in a day when personal enthusiasm still supported party politics. For my names, too, my father was responsible, Francis being, like George, a name borne by the Sitwells in succeeding generations for many centuries, and that, in addition, of my uncle and sponsor, Lord Raincliffe; I was called Osbert, after an ancestor through the Reresbys of whom we are the heirs, Sir Osbert Fitz Osborne, and Sacheverell to celebrate another ancient family, now extinct, from whom the Sitwells are descended, and whose portraits and many of their belongings they inherited. The name Sacheverell is a corruption of Saute de Chevreuil, the home of the Sacheverells in Normandy.

I had come into the world in London, rather unexpectedly and with nothing prepared for my reception, on a very cold December afternoon, and the place of my birth was 3 Arlington Street, opposite to where the Ritz Hotel now stands; described contemporarily, I find, as a 'nice house with electric light', which my father had taken for a year or two in order to attend his parliamentary duties. Perhaps London, a year or two subsequently, is the first place I remember. Exploring dim recesses of memory, I seem to have a recollection of being wheeled down Piccadilly, of the trees of the Green Park and the old wooden gates of Devonshire House opposite, and of my mind being occupied with the polysyllabic music of the word 'Piccadilly . . . Pic . . ca . . di . . lly', which seemed to me then, as it does today, a very strange and beautiful name. But London did not then occupy an important place in my existence; the two backgrounds of my childhood were Renishaw and Scarborough. In any case, though, being a slow rather than a quick child, it is places more than people, and words more than thoughts, that remain to me from my earliest days. The first words I learnt were 'Rags and Bones'.

At Scarborough the night nursery was at the top and back of the high old stone-pillared house we then occupied, and looked out above a narrow alley. When the rushing and bellowing winds of the winter ceased for a moment to roar down this passage made for them, tearing the words from the throats of the speakers right away into the void, and only the background of tumultuous seas remained, you could hear very distinctly what was said below. In the winter dawn, before it was fully light, these houses resounded with the loud cry, 'Rags and Bones! Rags and Bones!' And so it came about that these words were the first I learned, and who knows that such countersigns to mortality, pronounced at an impressionable age, may not have influenced my mind, making me seek behind the flattering disguise for the mortal and immortal core. It served, maybe, as a warning not to take too seriously the comfortable life of the senses developing round me, and emphasized the same lesson to be learnt in my favourite nursery rhyme:

Hark, hark, the dogges doe bark,
The beggars are coming to town.

'Rags and Bones!,' the old man used sometimes to shout, sometimes to insinuate slyly, in a voice that was between a song and a whine, into the frozen air, beneath where the fleeces of the sky were now showing their flayed and bloody edges, 'Rags and Bones!' And so, since I associated him with the first words I had taught myself to utter, I took an interest in him and can still see very clearly his figure as he was a few years later, his bearded face crowned by a battered top-hat – the survivor, it seemed, of innumerable orgies, just as it had been the witness, too, of countless interments –, vacant and smiling eyes full of an ineffable crankiness and guile, his whole impression and his jerky movements as he pushed his barrow along, giving a little the flustered yet inanimate air of a scarecrow subjected for many seasons to the force of an intolerable wind. My curiosity concerning him made me, too, watch the other gesticulating figures on the perimeter of the circle, so that my eyes in their observation of people moved from the outside towards the centre, towards those nearest me, rather than in the usual and contrary direction; torn figures in grotesque and appalling attitudes, like those of Callot's etchings, with a sinister and legendary panache, who stand on walls under the fierce short polar light of white foam from enormous storms and of the immutable, shadeless, cold flashing of seagulls' wings.

Of such human beings, feckless, unable to extricate their weighted limbs from this terminus in which they found themselves, Scarborough in those days offered an inexhaustible supply: the negro, locally known as 'Snowball', who limped with a pitiful exoticism through the winter streets, trying to sell flowers, bunches of violets and button-holes, a figure from a warm Italian picture strayed into these prim, northern streets, with their frozen gutters and their roofs saw-edged with icicles; the bearded and witless tramp, known as Lousy Peter, ever tormented by various gangs of small boys, who would hit him when he fell asleep, warm in his rags, in the deserted squares at the hour which for everybody else was the dinner hour, or throw buckets of water over him – and then run away; or experiment upon him daily with a new booby-trap of their own skilful invention; the Cat Man who mewed to himself on the sands; the cretinous cherubs, children of the rich, but no less fantastic than the beggar contingent, and the more ordinary, but yet alien, players of the hurdygurdy, now extinct, with their pleading, broken English, and their coated and capped attendant monkeys, decked out in the remnants of a brighter age. (How well I remember being allowed to throw down coppers to them, as they played, from the nursery window: two or three pennies, I recall, were always screwed up in a piece of paper, whether to secure them or to disguise the smallness of the gift, I do not know.)

At the time of which I write, people still scarcely existed for me; the cry, the song, the tune on the barrel-organ, but not those who uttered or produced them. Indeed it is a question whether I did not see and remember a ghost before I could pin down any human being in my mind, since a giant and spectral figure was seen one summer morning, just as it was growing light, a figure, immense, gaunt and grey like a shadow, that rushed round the room, its rhythm faster and faster, but making no sound. We all saw it, my nurse, my sister and myself – or so it was supposed, for I first called the attention of my two sleeping companions to it, by yelling, loud and long. Our nurse got up, and the figure, nine or ten feet high, rushed like a wind through the door, which it must have left open, into nothingness, no sound, no trace, no sign. There was no one there, and I have no solution of the mystery to offer. The event, or the hallucination, or whatever it may have been, remains inexplicable.

When next I woke, it was full daylight, and I was saying 'Rags and Bones, Rags and Bones' to myself. It was a cry that announced the day, and I welcomed it, for it kept me safe from the beings that had escaped out of the darkness of which they were part and had, thus isolated, assumed a visible substance until the light drove them back. Perhaps partly it was the memory, a faint stirring of memory, of that ghost which made me look forward to hearing the words spoken outside in the bitter green light of the next day. The hours of sleep would be finished. Nowhere as well as here, in the wintry north, situated in a frozen white cocoon of spray and fog and rain and cloud, could one watch the unending and gigantic battle that swayed, though its rhythm was undeviating, first this way, then that, between day and the victorious night. The night was hollow and of immense size. Nor was it invariably unfriendly, though it was always sad, and always frightening. It possessed two faces, one kind and one unkind. Very occasionally, when the day had been a disaster, the hollow night offered its numberless caves as a refuge into which you could creep, and hide the voice that spoke within you – that voice which was the enemy of all authority – and wherein you could hide yourself too, and not be found. But more usually, on the other hand, it would unleash against you the dead, and its army of the monstrous, giants and dwarfs, contorted faces that floated past, who made their lair in these derelict dark quarters.

'Rags and Bones' was thus a cry of delivery, and I repeated it rather indistinctly but none the less to the continual dismay of dear old Davis, who always tried to prevent these particular attempts at articulating and would no doubt have preferred me to lisp more reputably 'Gentle Jesus, Meek and Mild', than such words of ominous suggestion.

With the mention of Davis we come to the first person who can be seen clearly through the vanishing darkness. Gradually from the chaos of wide-eyed incomprehension and blind instinct, various figures begin to present themselves in the pale green light, cool as the sound of a hunting horn in the first hours of the morning. I see a group, Davis and Edith and myself, beneath a tree bearing golden fruit, gleaming in the bright armour of the sun; an apricot tree, I imagine, but I know not where it grew. Davis is in her grey alpaca dress and straw hat, and has her usual expression of kind and puzzled patience, while Edith is dressed in blue, pale blue, and under a hat like a mushroom, her curved eyelids, lank golden hair and sweet, musing expression, all give her an air of dreamy determination.

We must pause now to examine the most important member of this small group, both because of the force of her personality even at such an early age, and because of my affection for her. Five years older than I when I first remember her, in this respect unlike most other members of her sex with whom I was acquainted in my infancy, and who are today younger than myself, she has remained so ever since. She first comes on the scene when just over two years old, in an entry in my grandmother's diary: 'George's little daughter paid me an early visit, and was wildly excited when I offered her a bit of garden, exclaiming "E dig and plant flowers. E go to sleep, and wake up and flowers all grown." ' And, from the later journals of my Aunt Florence, I am able to give a more detailed and vivid picture of this unusual child and of her surroudings at the age of three and a half. In June 1891 she writes: 'Baby is just like a child in a story book in appearance, with fat cheeks, sometimes like pink campions, blue eyes and fair curls, a dear little person, touchingly devoted to her dog, Dido. She seems very young . . . to have visited Venice, but has quite a memory for her tour abroad.' Three weeks later, she gives us a delightful family group at the station, rather reminiscent of an Academy picture of the period. My grandmother had gone to see them off by the night train to Scotland, and had subsequently described the scene to my aunt. 'She told us of George at the station, with his many books of historical research under one arm, and the *Spectator, Lancet, Athenaeum* and the architectural journals under the other, embracing her, regardless of onlookers, of Baby, who declared "No little 'gell' has had so many night journeys as I've had – but, oh, how I've had to sing and repeat things to amuse the grown-up people!", and of her little dog, Dido, waking the station with her cries, thinking she would be parted from Baby and left behind – but she went, too, with the family.'

My father considered sons, especially elder sons when they were small, as a valuable extension of his personality, and my mother preferred small sons to small daughters, and the newest arrival to the earliest, and so my birth caused Edith to be relegated to a second place in the nursery, a position which her nature forbade her to occupy anywhere, even at that tender age. It never altered, I believe, her feeling for me, but all the same it must have constituted, like an inoculation, a first experience of the cruelty and fickleness of men and women. In consequence, it was only a few months after my birth that this little creature tried to run away from home, making an escape from our house in Scarborough so far as the outskirts of the town. Only the fact of her being as yet unable to lace her own boots, and of their being, as a result, so loose that further walking became impossible, was responsible for her capture and enforced return after an outing of three or four hours. Davis herself was angry with her. As for my parents, they were furious: for where she was concerned, a sense of humour, usually so noticeable a trait in both their natures, entirely deserted them. They had produced, instead of what they had expected – a 'charming' toy reproduction of themselves in fifty-fifty proportion –, a changeling, a small being with an intensely individual character and appearance, quite unlike those nearest her, with an aquiline nose instead of the straight one for which my father had been prepared, and (it became clear in time) with no love of sport, as my mother had hoped – worse, a small creature with an alien and immortal soul, difficult to bend or mould to the comfortable, late Victorian conventions of her class. No, their sense of humour, and even of pity, completely vanished when in contact with her.

I doubt whether any child was ever more mismanaged by her parents; they failed entirely to comprehend the sort of being who was in process of flowering before their eyes, they mistook nervous sensibility for awkwardness, imagination for falsehood, and a capacity for throwing the cloak of drama over everyday events – often the sign of an artist – for 'being affected'. As she grew older, instead of allowing her to find her own range, in the same manner that she had taught herself to read, they tried to force her to comply to their own measurements. Her seriousness, and an attitude of criticism which gradually developed in her concerning current class beliefs (such as that the poor deserved to be poor, and the rich, rich, or that sport was of more value to life than art) terrified my mother, albeit she enjoyed, and always more with the passing years, the immense sense of fun that my aunt had noticed in the child so early, and which continually developed. My father, on the other hand, insisted on her admiring the things which he, with a taste held to be infallible, himself admired. If she wanted to play the piano, no, it must be the 'cello instead, for he, profoundly unmusical though he was, had in his own mind decided that the 'cello was the finest of all instruments. Then, where poetry was concerned, Swinburne must be bad for her to read, for he had not read him, and therefore could not like him: she ought to be content with Tennyson for beauty, Austin Dobson for charm and Kipling for strength. Besides Swinburne was not the sort of poet to read; my mother agreed. 'Morbid', she pronounced, with some lack of conviction, for she never read a line of poetry of any sort – or, rather, 'morb', for she clipped her words.

Davis and my sister, then, compose the first group. But, soon now, the background becomes recognizable, the figures clearer and more plentiful, – Edith, Davis, the nursery-maid, Martha or Emily or Mary, Mother and Father, aunts and uncles, grandfather and grandmothers, ranged one behind the other in their generations, building themselves up into a concrete image of the past; and servants, above all in those days, servants.

The traditional upbringing of children in a family such as mine, implied, before the present nursery days of vitamins and orange juice and the use of Christian name between the employed and the children of the employer, a frank acceptance of the situation. Parents were aware that the child would be a nuisance, and a whole hedge of servants, in addition tò the complex guardianship of nursery and schoolroom, was necessary, not so much to aid the infant as to screen him off from his father and mother, except on such occasions as he could be used by them as adjunct, toy or decoration. Thus, in a subtle way, children and servants often found themselves in league against grown-ups and employers. The female child sought shelter with nurse and housekeeper and cook, the male in the pantry. Certainly I learnt more, far more, from talking to Henry and Pare in the pantry, from their instinctive wisdom and humour, than from more academic sources. They prevented the atmosphere from becoming too rarefied or refined. Their expressions nourished the writers hidden within the children, just as the food which Davis favoured on special occasions, when my father was, for some reason or other, not likely to interfere, nourished our bodies. For though she held boiled mutton and rice pudding to be the correct everyday food, and though she thought bananas 'common', she often added winkles, bought as a treat on the sly (because of my father's fear of ptomaine), to our diet for tea, or shrimps, measured out in an enamel mug at the fish-shop or dragged, sandy and recalcitrant, from the pools along the shore, by ourselves. It would be vulgar for ladies and gentlemen to indulge such tastes, but children were children.

In the days when I first remember the pantry, it contained as its permanent figures Jones, Henry and Pare. Jones was in charge, a lean individual, who had been my father's scout at Oxford, and possessed an extraordinary physique, thin and long-chinned as the meagre type favoured so often by Rowlandson: it was, really, a memorable chin, all the more so because, contrary to the usual reading of such a feature, it spelt indecision and lack of organizing power. Under him served Henry, who later became butler, and Pare, while a few friends or ex-retainers like James Broadbent, my grandmother's fat and jovial coachman, then retired – or, rather, discharged – would look in, especially late at night. But Henry Moat, even before he superseded Jones, was always the chief personality there. How often he used to imitate for me some guest, to whom I had taken a childish dislike, or talk to me about 'Sir George's latest idea', or tell me stories about the sea, or sing in his handsome bass bellow, which resembled the singing of a whale – could a cetacean be induced to sing –, that won him, I found out later, so many female admirers; his atmosphere was always of the sea, for he came of a long line of sailors, fishermen, and whalers. His humour was in no way esoteric, but belonged to the genius of the race. Stephen Pare was his foil, intensely appreciative of Henry's jokes and general character, but sad himself – and not without reason, for his wife, whom I only remember dimly – though she was often mentioned in my hearing with a lowering of the voice – and to whom he was devotedly attached, had gone mad, and he was losing his sight through having been struck by lightning. Thus he introduced a contrary and bibilical element of Job-like patience into the happy and robust eighteenth-century atmosphere of the pantry.

Henry first came to us as footman in 1893, as his signature, cut with a diamond on a window-pane of the pantry at Renishaw, still testifies, and remained with us, on and off, for forty-two or forty-three years. His absences were caused by his giving notice to my father, usually because of the introduction of some new idea of which he disapproved. But, as Henry used to complain to me, you 'never knew what Sir George would do next'. He lacked continuity, it seemed, in the smaller items of behaviour, though, regarded in another light, each fresh contradiction seemed hall-marked with his personality. 'There's only one certain thing, and that is, you can't do right.' Thus, at the age of one and a half to two years, I had unknowingly provoked a crisis, for while if Henry broke anything, or allowed it to be broken, he was always severely taken to task for it, yet on this occasion, when he had grabbed a valuable wine-glass from me, just as I had smashed one, and was evidently going to smash another, my father's esthetic theories were disturbed, and he reproved him sternly, in the words, 'Don't do that, Henry! Leave him alone, or you will spoil the boy's sense of touch.' And there were his innumerable other theories, or 'Sir George's fads', as Henry called them. New ideas or, indeed, ideas of any sort, were a great trouble, for servants, even the most unusual, always like their master to be conventional. In spite of his antiquarian attitude towards life my father, for example, was fond of reading the latest scientific treatises and of trying to keep up with modern inventions. (He considered he had made some discoveries himself on occasion.) 'Henry,' he called one day to the great man, 'I've a new idea! Knife-handles should always be made of condensed milk!' (I must explain that a substance derived from milk, a sort of paste in various colours, had lately made its appearance.) Henry looked particularly disgusted at the idea and very worried at its application. Then, with emphasis, and with an unusual air of correctitude, he countered, 'Yes, Sir George . . . But what if the cat gets at them?'

At other times he left because it was a tactical move in the lifelong strategic game which he and my father played together, or, again, he disappeared in a trail of mystery and disapprobation, because his enjoyment of sensual pleasures had been too pronounced.

Sometimes Henry would ask to come back, sometimes my father would invite him to return; but one thing was certain, whatever the cause of the break had been, however permanent it might have appeared for the moment, or for the month, back he always came in the end. He and my father, though mutually critical and at the same time appreciative, never failed to gravitate towards each other again, as if influenced by the working of some natural law. My father always referred to Henry as 'the Great Man', and Henry for his part, mixed with feelings of the utmost disrespect, cherished towards him, as well, sentiments approaching veneration. He realized his quality, both mental and physical, and that he was an uncommon, if difficult, character.

Yet though, as I say, all these persons played so large a part in my childish life, and though I saw more of them than of my parents, yet the atmosphere for all of us was distilled by my father and mother; by my mother's unusual beauty and strange temperament, her kindness, indulgence, and furious, sudden rages, my father's cleverness and determination, and a view of life, a plotting of detail, of each move in the countless games in which he was engaged, which seems to me more Chinese than European. The atmosphere they provided was unmistakable.

I was in the happy position as a small child of being my mother's favourite. I played on her bed, and upset everything with impunity. I adored her. Yet there were two things about her which I could not understand. The first time she lost her temper with me (I forget about what, but now I deeply sympathize with her), the whole world temporarily assumed a more tragic tone. I had been so sure of our relationship, now growing out of darkness into light, in which neither could do wrong for the other. I would not have believed that such a thing as this could happen, that so radiant and lovely and considerate a creature, always gay and gentle, could contain so dark a shadow within her. Moreover, though we were on such equal terms – for she treated every child as a friend and contemporary, never let him see that she was laughing at something he had said (and this no doubt was the secret of the easy influence over children, the affectionate intimacy with them, which all her life she was able to establish) – I had not until that moment suspected its existence. But the dreadful day at last ended, and by morning, time had restored the old relationship.

I used to wander in and out of my mother's room as I liked. I upset everything, as I have said – that was my privilege. I used to lie for hours in the morning on her bed, which was a drift of every newspaper published, of letters, and of cards, for she had been playing patience. I knew so well every familiar object, the flat, folding, leather card-tray upon which she had arranged her game, the clock like a huge watch in a green morocco case, the vases of flowers, the bottles of scent, the handkerchief laid on top of one of them ready for the day, the pincushions, with every size of hat-pin in them, always with black shiny tops, pins that had continually to be rescued from me by my mother's prim and patient maid, who would edge into the room, holding a newly arrived or newly brushed dress at arm's length, as though it were a corpse, instead of an object of pride to her. But she would always have to drop it, and remove the pins from me before irretrievable harm was done. I recognized the use of all the detail on the table, the diamond and ruby horseshoe brooch, the gothic pendant that had been made for an ancestor to give his wife, with its fantastic shape and its black pearls, the silver hair-brushes, the innumerable photographs, the bottles and jars: but I did not understand one thing, a loop of thick rope, a foot or two long, twisted in a knot round the head of the bed. Eventually, after many implorings, I was told what it was. 'It's a bit of a hangman's rope, darling. Nothing's so lucky! It cost eight pounds – they're very difficult to get now. Old Sir William got it for me.' And, suddenly, I was back again in a world, instinctively comprehended, of Hogarth and Gay.

Now a barrel-organ struck up outside a tune called 'Queen of My Heart', and the sunshine was pouring in at the three wide windows, which showed an expanse of light-blue sea, of a sparkling gaiety that was imbecile. A German band, also, was playing at the corner of the Crescent, and a voice somewhere was singing 'Linger Longer, Lucy, Linger Longer, Lou!' The gardenias my mother had taken off the previous night were lying on the dressing table and were scenting the room, and competing with the fragrance of tuberoses and sweet geraniums that stood in a vase. It was nearly noon, and she must begin to get up, for she was going to play a game of croquet before luncheon, and at the same time to rehearse with her partner and opponents a conversation – for a man, who had the reputation of being 'most amusin' ', was going to show her and three friends how to make a phonograph record, and they were to pretend to have a quarrel over a croquet match.

Shut up in his study that smelt of strong Egyptian cigarettes, of which he smoked from twenty to thirty a day, my father was meanwhile, though quite unaware that an expensive phonograph had been imported into his house, reading a paper that had just appeared in a scientific journal upon the more recent discoveries of Edison, with especial reference to a machine – apparently called a phonograph – which recorded voices. (It was an interesting idea, but what a pity, he reflected, that he did not know Edison; he might have offered some valuable suggestions to the inventor, if only he had been consulted!) Then, he must run through a thing in the *Athenaeum* on 'Modern Modifications of the Theory of Evolutional Survival'. But, alas! he could not spend so much time upon it as he would have liked, would have to leave making notes on the subject until another day, for he had also to think out a scheme for the discomfiture of 'the other side', and he must work, too, at the pedigree of the Sacheverells, the origin of part-singing (a subject in which, except that it *had* an origin, he was not really much interested), make notes for a speech that he was to deliver to a large audience the following evening, ending with the quotation of a couple of lines from Byron, and consider the decorative motives employed in the leaden jewellery of the Middle Ages. The household bills were again too high – such a mistake to entertain all these friends, people never did it in the thirteenth century, but were content to live modestly and quietly within the castle except on some great occasion! He must send for the cook about them, and also explain to her about the making of that sauce, she did not do it right. Henry polished boots the wrong way, and he must show him how to set about it. He must enter in his architectural note-book what he had found out about the origin in the East of Romanesque architecture. He must write to Turnbull, to say that the yew hedges were not being properly planted, and that he wanted all the levels taken again in the Eckington Woods for the new twelve-mile drive. He must send a letter to that new shoe place, pointing out that he refused to pay more than 18s. 6d. for a pair of shoes, and send a cheque to an architect, whose name he had temporarily forgotten, for £346 6s. 11d. He must revise, since seeing that last exhibition, his notes on 'Greek Sculpture of the Golden Age'. The editor of the *Scarborough Post* ought to bring the leading article to him every day, so that he could approve it: he must think out a letter to him at once. (Sometimes he felt he would never get all these things done!)

Then he shut his note-books and went to his solitary luncheon, with Henry in heavy and dignified attendance. He always had luncheon by himself except on special occasions. People distracted him, and their company prevented 'the gastric juices from following their normal course'. An hour later, my mother and her friends would have an enjoyable meal, full of laughter and fun, and I would be in attendance under the table. Several of the guests were staying in the house, others came from the town or the country houses round. (There were sixteen to luncheon, but my father did not know that, and I was not to tell him. He made such a fuss about the household bills. 'But whatever one may say about him, there's no one else like him,' she would add.) Some friend would admire a bracelet, and she would say 'Take it, darling,' and give it to her. She would also give away, in the same manner, several dresses after luncheon. Ada, or Ethel, or Amalia or one of my mother's other devoted friends, would try to prevent her from this folly. But it was no use; if anyone liked anything she had, she must give it to her.

In the evening my mother and father would both come to say good-night to me: it was the high moment of the day, a reception! My father would tell me a story, but his attitude was very different from that of my mother, – it was thought-out. He was considering my good, not my pleasure. It would be something about the Crusades, though he was in no way stiff with children, but they existed to be improved, and in the meantime to amuse and interest him with their curious point of view. My mother stayed on with me while I fell asleep, which even then, when I was a very small child, I found difficult because of a fear of not sleeping. She kissed me, and I remembered nothing more until morning came and I heard the cry 'Rags and Bones, Rags and Bones!' But the full tide of spring was washing the town, and the urgency and meaning, tragic and implicit, of the cry was lost beneath the surge of flowering trees in backyards, hawthorn and apple and pear and lilac and laburnum, and the brilliance of the sky, a hard northern brilliance reflected in the sea.

CHAPTER TWO

To me, my home always meant Renishaw; and the summer took me there, so that it meant the summer, too; summers that from this distance all merge into one. I remember, every year, directly I arrived, running through the cool, pillared hall to the low, painted door a little taller than myself, opposite, and standing on tiptoe, so that the smell of the garden should come at me over it through the open window; the overwhelming and, as it seemed, living scent of stocks and clove carnations and tobacco-plant on a foundation of sun-warmed box hedges, the odour of any component of which to this day carries me back to infancy, though never now do I obtain the full force it drew from that precise combination. I remember, too, the pleasure with which I always arrived at the house, and my sorrow at leaving it, for though we spent much time in Scarborough, and paid long visits to London and to grandparents, Renishaw was my home. I felt this with peculiar intensity, experiencing a curious attachment to the soil, a sympathy with the form of the country, with its trees and flowers, the frail blue spires of the bluebells in May, or the harebells and toad-flax of August, which has never left me and has made me wonder at times whether my ancestors, in the building-up of an estate through so many hundreds of years, and by the hunger and passion for this land which must have inspired them – for it was an estate gradually accumulated, not obtained by huge grants or the purchase of church property – had not bequeathed to me something still very real and active in my nature; this love seemed to me so much older than myself and so much part of me.

Again, it may have been due to the sombre but vivid charm of the country, so unusual in its appeal. On one side is Hallamshire, from which we spring, once a kingdom stretching across England, and from which during the passing of the centuries – for coal was dug here in Roman times and iron was exported to the Bahamas, Bermuda and Virginia before the Civil Wars – has been born a great industrial district, a conglomeration of cities, Sheffield and Rotherham and Chesterfield, situated in wild and splendid scenery of which the famous crooked spire of Chesterfield Church, whether bent by wind or lightning, or, as a legend says, kicked by the Devil as he flew over it, is the soul and symbol; on the other, the hills and dales of Derbyshire, with their druidical remains, with their quarries of bluejohn and of grey marble, with their gushing and mineral waters and petrifying streams, with their thousand lingering traditions of Sherwood Forest – which not so long ago extended into our countryside as far as Chatsworth – and of the Peak, where the playing of the bagpipes lingered on until the sixteenth century.

Moreover, at the time of which I write, when the light first sculptured for me the outlines of ridge after ridge, misty and tree-tufted, stretching away toward the heights, distant and unattainable, the landscape and its inhabitants possessed even more character than they do today. Then, as now, in the distance beyond the park, the great plumes of smoke would wave triumphantly over the pyramids of slag, down which, every now and then, crawled writhing serpents of fire, as the cinders were discharged from the trucks. After dark, this process at conjecturable intervals lit the whole night with a wild glory, so that, my father told me, standing on the lawn, he could read his watch by the light of Staveley flares three miles away, and in the woods this sudden illumination gave an added poignance to the sylvan glades that it revealed, causing the rabbits to be frozen for an instant into immobility, their eyes reflecting the glare and the terror within them, showing a shape, which might be that of an otter from the lake below, scudding through the long wet grass, and making the great owl hiccup uneasily in the trees where formerly he had hooted with assurance. As the golden surge diminished, so did the uneasy stirring of the minute but multitudinous life beneath the tall bracken.

In this *chiaroscuro* world, the gangs of miners returning from their work would tramp along the roads, wearing stuttering clogs, cord trousers and scarlet tunics, the cast-off tunics of a happy army, then still dressed in musical-comedy uniforms, which the colliers bought regularly; a costume which set off the blackness of their faces and their scarlet lips. Where else could you see such colour in the clothes of the working people at this period? Even the roads were different, bordered with tall trees, not cut down by councils eager in their triple quest of tidiness, uniformity and standardization, and the lanes of the countryside, and the drives through the park, were more vivid, I believe, than others anywhere – for their surface was laid with clinker, a vitreous substance, turquoise-blue, marine-blue and sea-green, which, if it had been a natural product instead of having been cleaned out of the vast furnaces of the neighbourhood, would rank, such is its beauty, as a semi-precious stone.

In the hot summer the house, standing above the world on its wide table-land, threw its battlemented and spired shadow, uncompromising and stark for all its fantasy, as far as the tall beech trees at the hills' edge, while down below, in the north park, the golden mist still lay melting. On this side, the house makes no gesture to the graces, but is a stout-built, machicolated screen with but a few shallow breaks in the hundred yards of its façade. Here is no garden, only the grass and the old trees, of great girth; in spite of its austerity, it is rustic and pastoral, cows and horses come out of the Palladian stables into the park, and in their seasons buttercups and mushrooms grow among the green tufts of the turf. But on the south side, the atmosphere changes dramatically, is no longer pastoral but romantic. The house with its deep recesses, the fountains and pools and hedges set so fast among their surrounding woods that in the distance from the south the building appears to rise from a forest, the vistas to which lead every alley and every green court, are all part of the great romantic movement; and water provides the link which binds them together, water dripping from fountains and flashing from pools and culminating in the expanse of lake below, that swoons in a summer ecstasy of sun-born mist and still green leaves to the nostalgic rhythms of Mendelssohn, Weber, Chopin and Tchaikovsky.

People, except those very near me, were still strange and stiff from first sight as those figures, full of latent movement, seen in a pointillist picture, female figures in wide skirts and angular sleeves and straw-hats, resembling those portrayed by Toulouse-Lautrec or Beardsley, figures just learning to ride bicycles, men in round caps and cricket blazers and white trousers. Then there were the rustics, bearded or bonneted. But, more easily, I remember *occasions*; those aquatic afternoons for example.

How delicious were those long picnics on the lake, in the wide, flat-bottomed boat, blue-painted, that yet rots somewhere in the disused stables; those long, hot, calm, drowsy, sun-spangled afternoons of childhood spent on that mirror-flat, cool surface, the slow movement and the sound of the rowlocks as Davis listlessly plied the oar, the hours in which we drifted, yet never wasted our time, for if Edith and I leant over the thick blue wall of the boat, we could watch the fish flickering in their chequered mail through trailing avenues of weeds. And sometimes my father would appear and carry me off for a swift darting journey in a canoe, while his spaniel flopped and splashed after us in the water or, after shaking himself in the sun on the bank, until his dangling ears flapped wildly and a smell of hot wool ascended from his steaming body, then tried, if we were near enough, to jump upon our prow, and, missing it, fell into his other element again.

Edith and Davis would be watching us from the boat, now moored by the island under the light shadow of a grove of young trees. At four-thirty a footman would come down with a hamper, and we would begin collecting dry wood to make a fire upon which to boil the kettle. The twigs crackled and burst, and the kettle began soon to hiss. Presently my mother and her friends would join us, and their grown-up laughter – laughter at things hidden and beyond our sight – would sound among the tea-cups. But my mother, with her own children and with others', but especially with her sons, was like a child herself, absorbed in their interests. Her friends, however, were thinking of themselves and how they looked; their air was patronizing in its unnecessary and false kindness. Soon my mother would light a cigarette to keep the midges away. (In those times, women who smoked usually did so to be daring, but she smoked for pleasure.) But time was passing, and soon we would climb the steep sun-baked hill to the house, entering the garden, sweeter than ever in those hours of dwindling light.

In the lamp-room, under the heavy fumes of paraffin, the sightless Stephen Pare – with his vast and hollow eyes, that now I understand resembled the gaping eyes of an antique mask of tragedy – was already lighting the wicks, which, by an unhappy irony, were to make clear for everyone else the exterior world, to him so dim, and indicate the shape and corners of chair and table, blurred to him and fading. Indeed he was the only person to gain no benefit from the process; he could not read at all, even, and he felt his way by instinct through the lofty, darkening rooms. But never, during the many years I knew him, did he make a mistake; he placed things down more softly than would any man who could see. Many of the rooms were now beginning to glow with a light forgotten today, for we belong to the last generation of children brought up by candlelight, and the smell of snuffed wax lay heavy on our nostrils as we went to sleep. There was, however, though it was already time for bed, still a grateful hour or two before we must go to sleep, for I hated darkness here, was frightened in this large, rambling old house, haunted and haunting, and counted every moment until my mother came upstairs after dinner to bid me a second good-night – a custom strictly forbidden by my father –, bringing with her the comfort of her warm and, to me, loving presence, and the scent of the gardenias and tuberoses she was wearing, and usually – which was also prohibited – a peach, strawberry water-ice, or some delicacy of that sort. She would bend above me, standing close to me, talking to me as to one of her own age, telling me how her cousins, who were staying with us, had behaved at dinner, of how Henry, still a footman, had suddenly laughed at something that was said, and of how difficult my father was being, with all his new ideas – probably he would alter them all again, tomorrow.

My mother, who looked so beautiful in her light-coloured evening dresses, pale pink or yellow, would say good-night, and unless already I was in an almost trance-like condition of fatigue, I would struggle to prevent her going. With her, as she walked out of the door, she took the last remainder of all the light that the day had held. The lingering breath of strong scent she affected, and of the warmth of a physical presence that, as with other members of her family, was Italian in its radiance and, at first sight, apparent simplicity, only made the night still darker than it had been before she arrived. There was nothing now except darkness, out of which substance ghosts are spun and torn. Through the door, however, left open on purpose, I could, if I removed the sheet from over my ears, hear the monotonous, grating tone of Davis's voice as she talked to the nursery-maid in the day nursery. It was a dull sound, but I loved it, because it supported me on its safe wings, even the smell of cheese and beer which accompanied it – for they were having their supper –, though at other moments it made me feel sick, now seemed pleasant to me, exhaling a human warmth and animal coarseness. A piece of garlic hung outside the window, says the folklore of South-East Europe, secures a sleeper against vampires, and, equally, I can testify that the scent of bread and cheese can dispose of ghosts for children. I would listen to the voices, and then, the next thing I knew, it was morning and the blinds were being drawn up in our room level with the highest tree-tops.

Sometimes, I would be taught to fish in the lake, the hook being baited with a maggot, chosen by an attendant, with the eye of a connoisseur, from a loathsome tin box that contained all writhing hell within its putrid compass, or I would watch my mother fishing for pike in Foxton Dam (Foxton, the Wood of the Little Folk, is near by, through meadows full of dark-blue scabious a-flutter with small blue butterflies). After fishing in the Dam, there was always tea with old Mrs Stubb, wife of a farmer, who lived by the edge of the wood in a large stone cottage hidden behind a huge espalier apricot; and when we had eaten home-made scones and cakes and jams, she would, on being pressed, favour us with – in, if the truth is to be told, a rather cracked and hollow voice – part of the Hallelujah Chorus. She loved to display her gift, but it was a treat that always reduced my mother, partly, perhaps, because of our obvious enjoyment of it, to helpless though carefully hidden laughter. And finally, towards the end of August, came the climax of the summer, a flower-show, held in the park on the highest ground where there is a flat stretch bearing the biggest and oldest trees. Here was every possible attraction. Besides the tents – filled with a crowd that surged round mounds of fruit and vegetables, in an atmosphere laden with the heated scent of prize flowers and of prize onions mingled together –, besides purple potatoes in their Assyrian armour, besides giant cauliflowers like rustic faces and mammoth dahlias, and huge gooseberries, over-ripe, sticky and melting like cheap sweets, there was a military band playing Waldteufel waltzes, simple tunes pursued by fat, moustached bandsmen down serpentine instruments into an eternity, an infinity, in which nevertheless every vista was clearly defined and obvious. At the gallop, green-clad Lancers would tilt at wooden Turks'-heads and there were Punch-and-Judy shows within the natural stage formed by the seven branches of a vast old elm known as the Seven Sisters, there were marionette shows and displays by midgets, while in the hot seclusion of small, red-lined tents rustic professors foretold the future from the lines of sweaty hands. I was held to be too young to consult them, though several times I ran in a determined manner towards the entrance.

From my infancy in Scarborough, I can remember incidents more clearly than people; incidents better forgotten. Thus I recall only too well how I stole an apple at the age of three from the market – not so much 'stole' perhaps as 'took', for all children are born communists. The next episode is hardly less discreditable. On a hot summer day I was taken down by Davis to the sands to bathe. I very much resented the squalor of the old bathing machine but when I stepped out, and was led into the water, my fury knew no bounds. I hated crowds, communal life and obedience as much as I do now and regarded the whole proceeding as unnecessary and undignified. Accordingly, when for a moment Davis looked behind her, I lay down resolutely under the foot or so of receding water and with determination held my breath, until I was hoiked out, dressed, and began to roar at the top of my voice as I was conveyed home in a cab.

I made my first excursion into the outer world when I was three years of age. Davis's father was a cobbler in a small village near Newbury in Berkshire, and she was going home to spend a few days with her parents, who were both very old. Since I refused to be parted from her for an instant, she – though it must have spoilt her holiday – nevertheless, in accordance with the principle of appeasement which she had adopted where I was concerned ('Anything for peace, Master Osbert!'), arranged to take me with her. How clearly it comes back to me! Perhaps I remember it so well because that the visit took place at all, constituted, I even then realized, a personal triumph; my mother was jealous, my father disapproved, my sister would like to have gone too, and the governess was frankly furious; by the sheer power of my plaguing I had obtained, almost for the first time, my own way.

Certainly every detail of my stay lives in my memory; our arrival, very tired, at the cottage on an evening of timeless June, the long shadows of the trees on our way there, and how I woke up the next morning, very early, because of the excitement of the change, and how at that hour the light of the sun still lay flat as feathers along the ledges of the windows. Presently the rays slanted downwards, and there were signs of activity. Life seemed very intimate and enclosed here, after the larger houses to which I was accustomed; warm and compact and lacking in any sense of fear. There were no creaking boards, no inexplicable rustlings, no feeling of interruption if one ran into an empty room. Every noise here made explicit its meaning. I heard now, as I lay there beside Davis who was still fast asleep, the sounds that accompanied her father's getting-up, the washings and splashings and crinkling tug of clothes being put on, then his going downstairs, moving about, lighting the fire and washing the dishes. Soon after, I heard the sizzling of bacon as he crisped it on a fork before the fire for my breakfast – for, I do not know why, he, not his wife, did this part of the cooking –, and then there reached me the talking of rustic voices below.

From contrast with the surroundings I had left, the primitive conditions of this cottage existence seemed to offer a new kind of idyllic comfort, composed of warmth and simple ease. Everything I saw, I touched, I ate, possessed a new value for me. Even the waking-up so early was in itself a joy, I comprehended, as I lay there in bed, touching the warm reality of Davis's body, for I stretched out a foot against her leg. The shafts of light now entered the windows, and I watched happily the gay vibrations of their dancing motes.

After I had been dressed and had eaten the bacon, so crisp and delicious, I was allowed to sit in the workshop, full of the smell of leather, and watch the old cobbler hammering at his last and listen to him talking through the din to his friends. Then, after that, there were the walks, accompanied by the angelic host – fair-haired and round-eyed – of Davis's numerous nephews and nieces, through the flat, flowery meadows so different from the abrupt, dramatic country to which I was used. As a rule shy of other children, with these I was at my ease, for I loved all beings and all things belonging to Davis.

My next, my second, visit was of a different kind, accompanied by my entire family and paid to my grandfather and grandmother at Londesborough. And it must have taken place, I think, in the late May of the following year, for I remember that the hawthorns, grafted pink on white or red on white, were carrying their chequered banners, exhaling their curious and alluring perfume – not so much sweet as enticing, making you want to smell the blossom, so as to make sure of what it smells – over the hilly, beautifully shaped park.

They were whole continents apart, these two houses; this was a different world, given over to those pomps and vanities which, in their own day so overwhelming, notwithstanding, leave no shadow behind them – unless they are fortunate enough to catch for a moment the attention of a Rowlandson or a Constantin Guys, and so remain fixed in the eye of time –; a world of horses, carriages and liveries, an immense machine, producing little, unless it were the love given it for its own sake, scarcely, even, rewarding with smooth working, still less with any pleasure, those to whom it ministered. Here there were major-domos, grooms of the chamber, powdered footmen, wearing velvet knee-breeches on the right occasions, grooms, gamekeepers, the cool and ordered processes of the dairy, and stables full of haughty and glossy gods, well tended. In their fragile glass were caged the steamy fragments of Africa and Asia, orchids and rare, strong-smelling flowers, while, in their seasons, ripe peaches and grapes and nectarines and melons flourished within their crystal orchards.

The park, I remember, contained groves of immense dead trees, as well as living, for my grandmother, though in other directions of by no means so soft a disposition, would not allow them to be cut down, because to see an old tree felled always made her cry. In consequence, these gnarled, gigantic skeletons, standing in groups, seemed to preserve, within the general leafy paradise, their own bony deserts of winter, and in their antique desolation, contrasted with the well-drilled, even ranks of trees of the young plantations which soared up the hillsides, and then swept down again as sharply. Every branch in them seemed to shelter a cock pheasant that, giving its Chinese cries, flew whirring like a rocket out from it as we passed. A whole army of men looked after the domestic life of these birds until the time came for their slaughter. How tall they seemed, both trees and men; for my uncle – my mother's only brother – was six foot six inches, and my grandfather but an inch or two shorter.

As a rule, however, all day long the men of the party were out, only returning for their meals. In the mornings, Edith and I would wait with some trepidation for our summons to an audience with our grandmother – not so much that we were frightened or had cause to be, as because it was plain that our parents, our governess and nurse quailed before the ordeal. Then, afterwards, tension having relaxed, we would spend the rest of the sun-streaked hours before luncheon sitting with Davis in the pleasure-grounds, as they were called, which lay some distance from the house.

In the afternoon we walked by the side of our grandmother's Bath-chair, accompanied by our mother and her tall sisters, in slow progress round the red-walled kitchen gardens, full of every sort of sweet-scented leaf, myrtle and geranium and verbena. And, at tea-time, we fell back into the rhythm of the nursery. This life went on for some time, until I let my parents down by developing that mysterious 'summer cold', an ailment which so frequently afflicts children, and which, in the houses of relatives as opposed to one's own home, always carried with it a suggestion of disgrace. No doubt in my case this *congestion*, as it would aptly be termed in France, had been caused by over-indulgence in the most delicious chocolate-cake in the world, a speciality of the house. The taste of it, as I write, I can still recall vividly as the varying flavours of the old-fashioned remedies made in the still-room, such as black-currant tea, to which my consequent indisposition and confinement to bed rendered me for some days subject.

CHAPTER THREE

My grandfather Londesborough was devoted to children and had a fascinating manner with them. He liked to take Edith or me – or sometimes both of us, though there was scarcely room – for a drive in his buck-board, a then fast and dashing equipage (there were of course no motors in those days), balanced precariously on two enormous wheels and drawn by, one would have said, a permanently bolting horse. My grandfather chose this vehicle, because it could be driven over the countryside, without following a road, and could actually cross ditches without its occupants incurring any mishap worse than a severe shaking. But he was a famous whip, the president of the Four-in-hand Club, and we trusted him implicitly even when the drive became unusually exciting. As a rule we first went through Raincliffe Woods, to the beautiful and celebrated Forge Valley, where a groom would be waiting to take the reins. My grandfather would give him orders to meet us in some other valley, while we walked up one of the steep hills, thickly covered with trees, and down the other side. Or he would take us to see where the sea-birds nested, or to some other of his domains, for the cliffs belonged to him as well as the woods. Indeed he was still in those days one of the largest landed proprietors in England – Scottish land-owners possessed, of course, bigger estates, but they were usually somewhat barren. He could ride, it was said, from Scarborough to Londesborough, sixty miles away, without leaving his own ground; and the estate included whole towns, such as Selby.

When the family descended to the Spa, by way of the private bridge which crossed the main thoroughfare that led to the sands, red carpets, literal as well as metaphorical, had to be put down for them; almost a mile of red carpet. It was, indeed, an atmosphere of the hill-tops – though not mentally, I am afraid: but it was pleasant, welcoming, luxurious, and the thought never occurred to many of those living in it that it might not be deserved. Moreover, the genuine good-feeling which lay under what some people might have thought the sycophancy evinced in various directions, had, in truth, been earned by the kindly qualities of the principals.

Nobody, however, dared to interfere with my grandfather. Occasionally, I am told, he would suffer from hours of exaggerated depression over his money affairs and exaggerated abnegation, hours in which he believed himself to be utterly ruined, and would refuse to spend a farthing: but they were quickly followed by a reversion to his normal lavish moods of spending money, and of his intense pleasure in doing so. A great deal had, of course, already gone. Yachts, races, coaches, carriages, sport of every kind, especially shooting, speculation and the stage were the chief channels he had found for ridding himself of his earthly burden.

His daughters adored him, and my grandmother was in her own way, a protective way, devoted to him; while he – I think there can be no doubt about it – was terrified, even though fond, of her. The whole world trembled when she spoke, for her words, which she could inspire with an infinite and indefinable charm, partly from the sound of her voice, warm and luxurious, could also perform the most expert incisions upon conceit and self-importance grown dropsical.

To her young grandchildren she was invariably charming. Well shepherded by – in the background – a circle of nurses with restraining hands and cautioning voices, we would raid the breakfast table at The Lodge at about 10.30 every morning, to be rewarded or bought off with a peach or nectarine (and fruit seemed particularly delicious in those days). Our tall uncles and aunts would be sitting round the table, trying to eat a little – and breakfast then meant cutlets and cold grouse, as well as such things as fish and eggs – in order to fortify themselves against the fatigues of the hours before luncheon: but this, owing to the bullying and cajolery of their young relatives, who, now entirely out-of-hand, worried them after the manner of so many gypsies or the whining beggars of Spain and South Italy, was a difficult process. The pack of children was numerous, composed of Raincliffes, Codringtons, Westmorlands, Ogles and Sitwells. Behind us the nurses looked pale, showed in their features clear evidence of strain: for my grandmother with the compact, feminine adaptation of the Wellington profile, her features powdered very white, almost floury, and revealing through this make-up a small blue vein above the bridge of the nose, and one on each temple, with her deepset, tragic eyes of brown velvet peering from this mask, and with her velvet voice, so slow and emphatic, with her beautifully-shaped, decisive hands – which carried on their fingers, besides the wedding ring, only one other, bearing an enormous square-cut emerald – was, most clearly, not a person to be trifled with.

Meanwhile my grandfather would be thinking out some way of amusing himself and us. The treats provided for us – that is to say for his grandchildren – were many and diverse.

Chief of the treats (though never, alas, for me) was the Cricket Week, when Scarborough broke out into its greatest display, and there was feasting in the hot tents of the rich at the ground's edge. The tents blazed with the ties of the cricketing clubs and the port-wine-coloured faces of the *aficionados*, and between the rounds of cold salmon and cold chicken that were dispensed, we would have to sit solemnly and watch the progression – if such it can be called – of this, to me, always unattractive and lengthy game. But my grandfather loved it and, guided by intuition, had formed, from the first moment of my appearing, extravagant expecations of my future prowess at it. In myself, out of all the family, he had divined the cricketer, and so had arranged with 'W. G.' to enter my name for the M.C.C. on the very day of my birth.

Alas, already, at the age of four, I was disappointing him, and early afforded, indeed, some evidence of the devil within me by falling asleep during what was, for others, one of the most thrilling moments of a County Championship match, and hurtling off my chair with a crash like a falling meteor. I shall never forget the sense of shame when I woke up bruised and on the ground, and realized by the wooden repartee of bat and ball, and by the expressions of shock and displeasure on the faces of my elder relatives and attendants, the execrable taste of the manner in which I had failed them.

Sometimes we would be permitted to stay up to see the fireworks which accompanied 'Gala Nights' at the Spa, and from the windows of The Lodge would watch the rockets proffering their golden or tinsel-starred bouquets towards the empty and uncaring heavens, the lines of their stalks, before they burst into flower, momentarily incised in gold upon the darkness. Or, best of all – for the strain of staying up to see the fireworks was considerable, the excitement flagged and one was apt to grow sleepy –, word would be brought round in the long summer evenings, just as we were preparing for an ordinary and unexciting end to the day, that 'His Lordship was going to the circus'. Tremendous excitement would ensue in the various houses that we occupied, as all his grandchildren were hurriedly decked out in their best frocks and suits, before congregating at The Lodge and driving thence to the circus. There, in the pointillist mist created by the clouds of sawdust and the miniature explosions of the arc lamps, we would find a quarter of the circus reserved for us, and the gangs of tufted and conventionally painted and powdered clowns waiting specially to sell us the programmes and to give my Uncle Raincliffe a welcome, for he was a patron and amateur of the circus.

In the fullest spring, when the tardy flowers of Yorkshire decked every hill and garden, my other grandmother would come from Gosden to stay at Hay Brow, a small property she now owned about three miles outside the town. (Her house in Scarborough stood empty during these years.) Bringing her daughter, my Aunt Florence, and various retainers, she would spend a month or two there every summer, in order to be near both her eldest sister, Lady Hanmer, and my father. By no means a rich woman, with little more than her jointure to support her, she possessed a remarkable head for business, and her enterprise and power of organization enabled her to extract an almost incredible value from every pound spent. She maintained in Scarborough at her own cost a small hospital (there was then no public hospital), a home for fallen women, and a club-room. All these were under the care of trained sisters, and everything was most methodically controlled. Even her smaller charities were imaginative – including, in former years when she had resided in the town, a breakfast of great local celebrity, given in her house to the Scarborough postmen during the early hours of Christmas Day before they started on their rounds. In addition to all this, she ran her own two houses, which were usually full of people, friends and relations.

How well I remember the collection of old servants! Leckly, who at the time of her death had been with my grandmother for sixty-three years, a gnarled and characteristic figure from the background of a piece of Flemish tapestry, keys at the waist, and on her wise but not agreeable face, somewhat fanatical in a common-sense way, a tinge of blue (her jaws fumbled always, as though one were trying to meet the other, in some indigestive prayer); Wilkinson, the cook, grey-haired and good, whose life passed in a dream of orange jelly, and who was with her sixty years; Hill, the coachman, who insisted on mending and, if possible, re-gilding the furniture in his spare time, which, so slow a driver was he, one would have deemed insufficient for the task; Jane, who had been there twenty years, the delightful, lanky housemaid from Suffolk, so kind and rustic, with a bump on her forehead, about which she often used to confide to me, as though it were a treasure, that 'the doctors wanted to take it away'; Frank, the grave, humorous, grey butler; and the hot, white, furry Samoyed dogs – one of which had been the first of its kind to be brought to England.

Hay Brow charmed its every visitor. The garden, with its little lake and rare trees – a lake so still and deep, so embosomed in its trees, that it seemed to reflect them better than any water I have seen – imparted a sense of infinite, remote, yet well-ordered peace, a little comparable, perhaps, to that which must have prevailed in the Garden of Eden; all men and women who entered here, it seemed, were innocent, all creatures tame, all birds engaged solely in the practice of their choirs. The clusters of blooms seemed ever in full flower, and smelt of honey. Even in the height of summer, a deep peace and eternal coolness dwelt here, as dew dwells, even on the hottest day, in the heart of the rose.

The beauty of the flowers was in part due to my grandmother, and the interest she took in them in part to the gardener, Ernest de Taeye, a Fleming. Ernest was the son of one of the chief gardeners in a famous azalea nursery near Ghent; the old man, when over seventy, had been given notice by his employers, and the shock of the prospect of being separated from these plants which he had so long tended was such that he had committed suicide. My grandmother heard of this curious tragedy, for she knew the nursery in question, and was informed, too, that his son, a boy of twenty or so, wished to find a place abroad. Feeling very sorry for him, and thinking, too, that the great love of flowers to which this suicide testified might be hereditary, she engaged him for Hay Brow. Thus this quiet, clever, sensitive man, a born gardener, with the secret of growing things in his hands, large but delicate, came to England, and remained in her service for many years until her death in 1911, when he came to us at Renishaw. When first he arrived at Hay Brow from abroad, he was still depressed by the death of his father, and for several years the only English word he knew was 'No': which rendered conversation difficult and non-conductive, though it did not prevent him from courting and marrying the daughter of a neighbouring farmer. In appearance he was a huge man, with the look of a portrait by Van Eyck; a similarity heightened, singularly enough, when in middle age he caught a rare disease from handling a plant in a hothouse, and lost in consequence all his hair, becoming completely bald, even of eyebrow and eyelash: after which he laid it down as a condition of his employment that he need never take off his hat of fine, amber-coloured straw in an unusual shape (in winter he wore a cap); so that even when arranging flowers or watering large-leaved plants in the house, he wore it, a badge of his green office.

At Hay Brow, the garden was lovely, but the house was negligible, the exterior, even, being rather ugly, but my grandmother, with her very individual taste and with the various fine objects she possessed, had made it into a charming summer residence, so that it appeared to be but an annexe of the garden, a series of tents pitched for hot weather, since the rooms were lined with *mezeries*, printed designs in light colours on a cool white cotton background, made in Genoa about a hundred years before – and the scent of the garden drifted in at the wide open windows or through the Venetian shutters, to join the perfumes exhaled by huge bouquets of flowers, roses and sweet peas, and by more exotic blossoms from the hot-house, their pots concealed in very Victorian china bowls, china of brightest blue and pink, her two favourite colours.

Here, in this house and garden, the activities of the inhabitants were very different from those that prevailed at Londesborough Lodge, three miles away. No two backgrounds could have been more dissimilar than my father's and my mother's. At Hay Brow, theatre and circus, actresses and clowns had no part, for Lady Sitwell's interests were of an intellectual, but more especially of a devout order. Her whole life had been spent in carrying out, as she saw them, the Christian principles. Religion and charity had engrossed her every thought. Her upbringing had been of the orthodox pious type of the period, but in the course of time evagelical fervour had come to tinge strongly her outlook. Yet to a certain degree she could enter into the views of others, and would certainly have rather that faith took any form than none.

Lady Sitwell's appearance and personality, though they made a profound impression on all those that met her, are not easy to reproduce. As a girl she had been considered beautiful, and her features, in their aquiline mould, were symmetrical and distinguished. But radiance is a better word to match her quality, I think, than beauty, and a certain sad radiance still clung to her. The cast of her face was unusual and mysterious and sweet in its aspect, and she possessed a rare dignity of carriage and demeanour, and a grace of movement that I have never seen in another woman of her age, and which helped me to understand what I was told, that in her youth she had delighted in dancing and riding; pursuits that seemed now so far removed from her. As you could see in the decoration of her houses, she loved bright colours, though she now no longer wore them, but black in the day-time, and dark-hued green or brown or blue velvet in the evening. She liked to wear ornaments, brooches, necklaces and bracelets, and even when in mourning she would wear long heavy chains of onyx, jet or ivory.

Her habitual expression of sweetness, sympathy and resignation – the first thing you would notice – masked, however, an iron will, and disguised with a semblance of calm the fires of her temperament. She was never happy except in bestowing, both of her energy and her possessions, yet she was, and must be, the dominant influence in her house, and an absolute ruler. She would tolerate no least evasion of propriety or respect, either due to herself or to others. All the members of her household must feel themselves to be part of one concern, and must think nothing of the trouble to which they were put. Her orders on all points had to be strictly carried out, and her old servants firmly supported her (except that Leckly allowed herself some laxity in that she would go to church where and when she wanted, and nothing could ever persuade Hill to stop re-gilding the furniture – but these were time-honoured idiosyncrasies). Otherwise there would be little effort to spare, – and all effort must be given over to religious causes.

From this quiet spot was generated the power which galvanized the good works of Scarborough and many other towns and villages. Here were founded the charities for the relief of those sins fostered by the love of pleasure, so evident in the other side of my family: here, as I discovered in after years, were thought out those various plans that resulted in the removal of the inebriate from his drink and in the conversion of sirens into Magdalene washerwomen. And whereas even the most eminent member of the stage, Sir Henry Irving himself, would have been received at Hay Brow – if at all – with suspicion, almost any curate could be sure of a welcome, and treated to long and intimate hours of conversation. They circled round my grandmother like flocks of crows, and, when we visited her, we were obliged to listen to their cawings – unless my mother came with us and dispersed them. The best flowers would be reserved for their invariably sick mothers, the best peaches and grapes and melons – at the growing of all of which Ernest de Taeye excelled – for their invariably sick friends. A continual manna descended upon them in generous measure. This was the weak, or at least the soft, spot in her ardent, compact, clever character. For them, she evinced a special kind of esteem, which included, perhaps, in its components a little of that kind of regard later exhibited by members of her sex for film stars, Gary Cooper or, in his day, Rudolph Valentino.

As for her grandchildren, she would give us flowers also, but I believe children tired her, for she was growing old and had never been strong since she had injured her spine in a railway accident. In consequence she was obliged to rest a great deal now. She would show us, too, coloured plates in the fine old books which she collected, flower-books with illustrations of cactuses that coiled serrated green tentacles after the manner of squids, of orchids, lolling their tongues, and of pagoda-like blossoms, tier upon tier, from Mexico and China. Other volumes were devoted to birds, shells, volcanoes and the Wonders of the World. All were stimulating to the imagination. When I was a little older, I became more and more fond of her, and grew increasingly to appreciate the particular qualities of loyalty and intelligence, and of fascination, which she embodied.

In the various causes I have mentioned, in the various technical processes she and her friends invented for separating the vicious from their vice, she was wearing herself out, no less than her daughter – that mild and trustful character, a Fra Angelico saint in type, who seemed to have tumbled accidentally into this century from the days of the early Church or from the age in which prevailed the gothic seclusion of women, and to have remained somewhat dazed from the impact of the alien civilization in which she now found herself.

In the early days of which I am writing, though my aunt was always kind to us, and though my grandmother was devoted to Edith, I am inclined to think that she regarded me with some distrust. In my character, the fondness, for example that I evinced for dancing and for the clichés of the barrel-organ, gay and tawdry, showed the most clearly defined imprint of the cloven hoof. She had been the mother of only one son, and had had four sisters but no brother, and, in consequence, unused to the young male, expected less self-will and more resignation in him than is usual. In spite, therefore, of her kindness and charm, it was then a greater pleasure to me to visit my more hedonistic relatives on the maternal side.

CHAPTER FOUR

Meanwhile my father was watching, waiting for me to betray those symptoms of extravagance, weakness and self-indulgence which from my family history he so confidently – and not without considerable justification – expected. He blamed me for resembling members of my mother's family, while, rather unreasonably, he entered a judgement on a contrary plea against my sister; because he thought she resembled members of his own mother's family. He had always hoped that a daughter of his would have a straight, Grecian nose, and here she was at the age of eight or nine, already provided with an aquiline! Most provoking and inconsiderate.

As a child I was slow as my sister was quick of apprehension. And in each of us this was wrong. She should have been slow, being a girl – dedicated, as girls of her class then were, first to a life of Infanta-like seclusion and then to marriage. On the other hand my childish difficulty in pronouncing certain consonants was regarded as downright original sin.

The development of my character for which my father was looking was not the only trouble that existed between us. There was, for example, my misunderstanding of the nature of humour. This discordant theme continually recurred to perturb him and – to go forward in time again – I remember very well, when in London, at the age of eighteen or nineteen, being taken out for a walk by my father so that he could speak to me upon, as he said, 'a serious subject'. I had the usual 'sinking feeling' which the thought of such a process entails: but eventually we sat down on a bench in St James's Park and he told me what the trouble was. He was very much afraid, he said, that there must be something wrong with my sense of humour. He had often noticed that I laughed at things in which he could see no joke, while at other times when he said something extremely amusing, I apparently saw nothing funny in it.

Well, the same rankling trouble was at work even in this early period. We were in the middle of one of the great practical-joke epochs (it must have been about '97, when I was four years old). One morning I went with my father into the dining-room before luncheon. He was expecting as a guest at this forthcoming meal a supporter of his in politics, an alderman, mighty in stature, a very heavy man, and he now placed ready for him at the table a Chippendale chair, the seat of which collapsed when you sat down on it. As a matter of fact, over this particular incident my sense of humour at that time coincided entirely with my father's. I remember thinking it an extraordinarily funny joke. And so, after he had left the room, I changed this chair – with tremendous labour, for I was very small at that time – with his own, and then hid under the table to watch the effect. My father sat down, rather slowly, waiting for the alderman's collapse, and then fell through his own chair with an expression of intense amazement and consternation, while my merry laughter rang out from under the table. He was not in the least amused, but got up, very red in the face, remarking at the same time, 'I might have most seriously injured my back.' My laughter soon changed to tears and it was some time before I was forgiven. All the same, I had meant no harm.

On the other hand, my father was always helpful and sympathetic about such things as nervous symptoms or health generally – though, with illnesses that might prove contagious, himself would go to any length to avoid possible infection. (Thus, for example, when subsequently at the age of eleven I was very seriously ill, in bed for four months, and the doctors did not quite know what was the matter with me, he never once came near me, never even to the door.) He would be extremely kind to me, however, about my fear of the dark, a fear which I suppose all children have, but which I suffered in an exaggerated form. For this I daresay many things are responsible, including heredity and a sensitiveness to atmosphere. I forget at what precise age I was first made to sleep by myself, but it was a moment which I dreaded, and my father was most sympathetic.

In such ways, even Davis could not help. Her character was too simple. Besides, she and my father disliked each other very thoroughly. She thought him 'too clever for a gentleman', opinionated, abrupt and irritable: he thought her stupid and old-fashioned. Further, she had been in the service of my mother's family, and this seemed in itself reprehensible to him.

The darkness begins now to clear with more coherence. Birth and death entered my life about this time and together, and with them came the sense of mortality. Mortality, a spectre, peered at me first through a conversation that I heard murmured between my nurse Davis and a female assistant in a toy-shop; who was dressed, after the manner of her calling in late-Victorian days, in very voluminous, tightly-waisted black clothes that smothered her body from foot to chin, while a fringe draped her naked forehead. For a long time they discussed something in undertones, as if it were a matter to which no reference could be made in public, and then, out of the words, I pieced together the fact of a dreadful operation on some unmentionable part of the unmentionable human body. An atmosphere of intolerable and muffling sadness envelops this incident for me in the memory; for it was only then that I realized that we were all condemned to death in a world of swathed dejection and faint voices. And soon after this initiation, my Aunt Lilian died. I did not know her very well, but I had been a page at her wedding the year before and could remember that ceremony and the excitement of it. And now the bitter weeping of my mother made me comprehend the existence of a world of sorrow beyond the world I knew. All this Davis emphasized – for she possessed a naïvely morbid mind – by taking Edith and me every Sunday afternoon when in Scarborough for a walk in the municipal cemetery, to admire the white marble angels, with a touch of green mildew on their wings, and the damp-clotted, mouldering chrysanthemums that adorned the graves of which they smelt. My father would have been furiously angry with her for leading us on these mournful expeditions under dark, grey-blue northern skies, with the wind howling round the sharp-edged headstones: but he never found out.

Then birth came, a miraculous baby from the void – but for some reason this seemed to me no more strange than the truths of revealed religion as I was learning them. If one had to believe one, why not believe the other? At the age of nearly five I became an elder son: for a great event in the family occurred with the birth of my brother Sacheverell, from his earliest years my chief friend and companion. I suppose that when he was a very small child I understood him better than did anyone else, I instinctively comprehended what he wanted to say, before others could: and on this foundation our friendship was soundly based. He was a particularly fascinating and genial child, as well as exceptionally good-looking, and – to anticipate – when he was three or four years of age, his love of life and of people was so intense that if Davis and I were not looking, he would often run up to strangers and say to them, 'My Mummy and Daddy would be delighted if you would lunch with them tomorrow.' The stranger would easily find out, if he was not already aware of, our identity, and the most amazing raggle-taggle gypsy crew would thus occasionally assemble to be entertained in response to his invitations. It made things difficult for my poor father, who was either candidate or member at the time, and on whose part it would therefore have been most impolitic to turn constituents away. This love of life, shown in his earliest days, this curiosity, was undoubtedly the root of my brother's subsequent search for knowledge, and perpetual eagerness to know the ways of humanity in every part of the world.

It can be imagined that some of the guests, thus hospitably gathered from highway and byway, were surprising in the extreme to my parents: and among them they included one or two of the untouchable class, known to us as 'People At Whom You Must Not Look'. This diverse regiment existed only, of course, at Scarborough – and not at Renishaw with its industrial and rural background: these were the eccentrics in behaviour and morals, blown hither on some wind of curiosity and misfortune, and here stranded, listless, unaffected by life outside the town. As the light grows stronger, it reveals this strange population against the background of a world, stippled and very pale in tone, with the glitter of the sea about it on the fronts and the roofs of the houses and in the sky itself. Even the ordinary people – the men in their bowlers, boaters, close-fitting caps and with their carefully trained or trailing moustaches, the women with their narrow-waisted bodies, like continents, their huge hats feathered and contaminated with milliners' flowers, decaying in purple and deep pink – walking, riding horses, riding bicycles, driving in varnished shells of wood, were strange enough, looked back upon; but how do justice to these other capering figures at the world's edge, on the faces of whom the light plays with the same trembling power of emphasis as a mirror flashed in the sun upon the features of an unsuspecting person by some small child? There was, for example, Count de Burgh. A tradesman, retired and prosperous, who had bought a papal title, he always wore, over tightly laced stays, a frock-coat, and to the rim of his top-hat he had attached a row of curls, so that as he walked down the middle of the road – he generally seemed to be advancing from a broad cul-de-sac into the main street – and doffed his hat to his acquaintances, in a gesture reminiscent of the court of old France, his hair swept off with it. He seemed ever to be acknowledging the homage of the crowd, gravitating with certainty to the middle of every picture.

The same light that shows me these faces, wry and contorted, also illuminates for me the countenances of those I loved dearly, such as Miss Lloyd who, until her death in 1923 or '24, remained a great friend of mine. Her background was a little mysterious and we knew little of it except that she was related to Sir Charles Wyndham, the actor, who used to come and see her, and that she was partly of French extraction, – but her gifts were plain to us all. She was, for an old lady, exquisitely pretty, with small beautifully chiselled features and a round mass of long white curls spread all over her head, on which, when she went out shopping, – after the manner of a Frenchwoman, with a basket on her arm – she put a sort of black poke-bonnet. Her fingers were the nimblest in the world; she painted flowers, did feather-work and embroidery, designed and baked china, embroidered and painted in a thousand different ways and as well and delicately as she cooked. I have never eaten chicken or cutlets that were so delicate and fragrant, or bread that was as delicious as the many different kinds she made. She lived in a tall red house full of the things she had created, and the window-boxes were always a-flutter with the feathers of birds, so that they seemed an extension of the room itself and of herself too, as they darted with their quick, neat movements and bright, woven wings. But though fond of all three of us, she constituted herself from the first especially my champion. And since – for she was intensely practical – my father valued her advice on many subjects, she was able, as I grew older, to exert, from my point of view, a very valuable influence on him – that is to say, to the extent to which he could be influenced, which was not very considerable. But she had, as well as this practical ability, a romantic side to her life. She did not see things in the tones in which others saw them and she was capable of exaggerating to their limit incidents which occurred, so that they possessed a grotesque and interesting distortion. All through my early life – and, indeed, until I was thirty or more – she was an important figure, frequently staying with us at Renishaw, while when in Scarborough we would always go to tea with her and often to luncheon.

She used on many occasions when I was a small boy, to give me presents, things she made, and I remember my grandmother Sitwell warned me against selfishness in this respect, and that, in consequence, an ethical difficulty assailed me thus early, for I, too, used to give Miss Lloyd small presents, bought with my pocket-money in return, as often as I could, and soon discovered that I preferred the pleasure of giving to that of receiving. Was it not, therefore, still more selfish on my part to give? And I remember my father, unintentionally, did not help me in the matter, for I heard him remarking, apropos of some member of the family, that it was 'easy to be generous with other people's money'; an aphorism which caused me much reflection. Nevertheless, I liked receiving as well as giving, and that brings me to my great-aunt, Lady Hanmer – Aunt Puss, my grandmother's sister; the most worldly member of an unworldly sept.

I went to see her every week when I was in Scarborough, and later took my brother with me, and four times a year she would give us a tip. The suspense for some weeks before each of these occasions was considerable, the atmosphere carefully worked up. Miss Lloyd would say to us, 'I think your aunt has a present for you.' Our visits to her would consequently become more frequent and anxious in tone, but the gift that had been prophesied would not materialize. When eventually it did, the procedure was always the same. The old lady would ring the bell. Alfred, her harlequin butler, would alight on the drawing-room rug – an Aubusson – for her commands, and then conduct us away into another room. After a few minutes she would ring once more. This time, it would be to summon us. Alfred would leave the room, and she would bestow upon each of us a golden sovereign wrapped in a neat piece of tissue paper. We would then, as it were, kiss hands on relinquishing office, and be ushered out by Alfred, who would be waiting discreetly behind the door with a slight smile of congratulation, but not enough to give offence. He would make no allusion in words to our good fortune. At her death in 1908 or 1909, she left her property to my father, with appointment to Sacheverell and myself, and in her drawing-room, inside a cabinet, with ormolu mounts, and with a Dutch flower-piece for front (it faces me now as I write) – a cabinet made for her father in Paris, when he was with the English troops in their occupation of that city in 1814 – were found fifteen hundred golden sovereigns, done up in tissue paper in ones and twos and threes, ready to be presented to us in the course, as it were, of the next three hundred and fifty years: for we received them as I have said only four times a year, and my sister because of her sex was never given a sou.

I see two other figures, not such constant landmarks through our childhood, but going back to very early days and then disappearing. These figures, contrasting so violently one with the other, are nevertheless bound together; they belong precisely to the same epoch, and their antithesis is so strong as almost to present a likeness. One of them was Sir Henry Pennell, a magnificent old soldier, brave and handsome in his old age, gay, even when he suffered, and altogether charming, who had earned great distinction in the Crimean War; the other was 'Old Charles', a deserter from the same conflict. These two old men, so different in their styles and virtues, though contemporary, constituted to Edith and me an insoluble puzzle; because, while my grandmother Sitwell and my mother, whose points of view were often divergent from one another, both of them encouraged our loving veneration for Sir Henry, Davis never failed to solicit and to claim our sympathy and respect for 'Old Charles'. Secretly my sympathies were – and still are – with Old Charles. 'Think of him *daring* to desert!' Davis used to say with the light of wonder and simple love in her eyes. Certainly, these two contrary currents of opinion worried us: yet, looking back, I think I understand them and that between them can be discerned a very ancient rift, a difference of mind due to status. In Davis's attitude can be distinguished that common-sense view of war which prevailed in England among the working classes from the time of the Norman invasion until the end of the nineteenth century (an outlook similar to that of the Chinese, which saw in soldiering a low and disgraceful profession), the same which in medieval times had made the villeins shake their sides with laughter as they saw their ridiculous masters strutting off to the wars; while in the opposing attitude of my grand-mother and mother could perhaps be seen the survival of that same fire that had caused the nobles to kill each other off for no reason, except an exaggerated sense of honour and loyalty, during such struggles as the Wars of the Roses.

Sir Henry I see always sitting, muffled up, in a garden under the faint sunshine of the first spring days, the sea showing distant, misty and fitful glints of blue. His heavy, rugged limbs seemed to be sinking with fatigue into the earth, cruelly sprinkled with the shrill, unheeding cups of the crocuses, insistent for attention: he was too old for the spring to do anything for him but tire him further. When he saw us, though, he would rouse himself, and throw round him the old fiery garment of his courage and gaiety, and tell us stories. Old Charles was not nearly so attractive a character as Sir Henry. He appeared to be connected by analogy, as well as by profession, with milk. He delivered it, and everything about him was milky. Always faintly splashed with milk, in addition, his hair and beard were milky, and his face had the milky complexion of a baby's. If you pricked one of his veins, this opalescent liquid would most surely have run out of it. He was very badly paid for his work, it appeared, and, being a veteran deserter, as it were, could obtain no Poor Law Relief, because – or so Davis led us to believe – if he demanded it and gave his name (which incidentally he could not write, being only able to make a mark), the authorities would instantly recognize him and claim him for the Army.

At Renishaw I see many more people. Maynard Hollingworth, for example, the agent at Renishaw, who first emerges in my memory when I was aged seven, and he came to the house to try to teach me how to take a large clock to pieces and put it together again: (for my father, I do not know under what inspiration, at the time believed this to be an essential part of a child's training): alas, my native lack of sympathy with the machine in all its forms triumphed over his every effort to instruct me. I was much more interested in talking to him about other matters, and in finding out what a delightful being, decisive, ingenious and unusually versed in the lore of animals, flowers and trees and yet with a rare comprehension of character in human beings – hence his long friendship with Henry –, was screened by his reserved manner and great height.

Alas, many others from those days have gone back into the darkness; the old bearded woodsmen, Topham and Kirton, for example. When at Renishaw I would pass them nearly every day, and even now, on Sunday's, Kirton, with his bearded Elizabethan face, and sombre clothes and cap – so permanent a part of this landscape did he appear – still seems, in my mind's eye, to sit on the rugged knot at the base of an enormous old elm between the house and the stables, keeping watch to be sure that nothing comes to harm. These I saw frequently, but I also catch sight occasionally of a face that I have seen only once, modelled by the light of that distant decade, the nineties: old Staniforth, for instance, one of the family of farmers who are our oldest tenants – having been, indeed, established in the district as long as we have, from at least the thirteenth century. When I was very young and he was very old, he came to tell me of how he remembered being present at the festivities that attended my grandfather's christening. The Bachelor Duke was the godfather, and came over from Chatsworth, there had been skating – it was hard, frosty weather – and a ball in the evening, and an ox roasted whole in the park. I can still see the rather delicate face of the old man as he talked to me, and hear his quavering voice.

The light of hills and sea shows in these faces: and my first Dionysian or rhapsodic experience was, too, connected with light; light which has always meant so much to me, its quality even affecting my writing. I was about five years old, and had been involved in what seemed at the time irretrievable misfortune. It was a Saturday afternoon in June, the first real exquisite day of summer that year, and I was doing some of my first lessons; but so much did I long to be in the golden air outside that it became an obsession. From my high child's chair I could obtain a view of sea and sky and, lured by their temporary but seemingly ineffaceable gaiety, I resolved to make a dash for freedom. Accordingly, I hurled my copy of *Reading Without Tears* down upon the floor and ran out of the room, a screaming Swiss governess in pursuit after me. But I had obtained a good start and hid under the billiard table in a room in the furthest part of the house. Extricated with some difficulty, I was carried upstairs by my father, who had been summoned by the governess, and in the course of the journey kicked him very hard in the belly. Naturally he could not let that pass, and fearful scenes ensued. I felt disgraced and humiliated for ever. My mother had been out at the time but, when she returned, may have divined the original source of the trouble, because she took the same exaggerated delight in fine days as I did, and felt the same depression over those that were black and foggy: – at any rate she rescued me, restored my self-respect, told Davis to give me tea and, though it was by now rather late for my usual promenade, for it was about six, sent me out alone with Davis.

We went a little further than usual, to the gardens on the north side;

flat, level lawns, broken off above the sea (the gardens there had slid into the water about ten years before), which were usually lacking in charm. On the edge of sea and sky great, white, furry clouds, golden-tinged, wrestled and tumbled like Polar bears clumsily in the summer wind. But tonight, skilfully eluding Davis, I ran to the edge of the precipitous cliff and stood there looking straight in the face of the evening sun. The light bathed the whole world in its amber and golden rays, seeming to link up every object and every living thing, catching them in its warm diaphanous net, so that I felt myself at one with my surroundings, part of this same boundless immensity of sea and sky and, even, of the detailed precision of the landscape, part of the general creation, divided from it by no barriers made by man or devil. Below me and above me stretched the enormous merging of blue air and blue water with golden air and golden water, fathomless, and yet more and more fervently glowing every moment, the light revealing new vistas and avenues up into space or out towards the horizon, as though the illimitable future itself opened for me, and, as I watched, I lost myself. All this must have endured only an instant, for presently – but time had ceased to exist – I heard Davis calling. The eye of the sun was lower now. The clouds began to take on a deeper and more rosy hue, and it was time for me to return home: but this strange peace, of which poetry is born, had for the first time descended on me and henceforth a new light quivered above the world and over the people in it.

CHAPTER FIVE

My first contact with the worlds of art and literature occurred a year or two after this early experience of Dionysian or creative emotion. My father, gifted though he was, spent his life apart, alone. Indelibly stained with gothic darkness and its accompanying colours, pure and soft in tone, his mind inhabited that ivory tower of the thirteenth century, complete with every convenience of the time – cross-bows, battlements, oubliettes and thumbscrews – that growing unhappiness had obliged him to construct for his protection against the exterior and contemporary world. Like an elephant, he carried his castle on his back, or, after the manner of a snail, could retire into it for dark hours and a hard winter.

More and more he came to frequent his solitary refuge, until just as Pirandello's Henry the Fourth finally declined to emerge from the imperial character part for which he had cast himself, so my father played almost continuously his lonely rôle. Occasionally, he would lower the drawbridge and make a sortie; but these forays became rarer and rarer. The ivory tower, within its magic circle and protected by the stout stone fortifications of a Harrison Ainsworth castle, grew more and more fantastic, and, with each passing year, he spent a longer time in it until, gradually, he was able to produce within himself even the views obtainable from the loopholes of his fastness, and began to be unwilling to contemplate reality at all.

Even in these days of which I write, when he was a comparatively young man, he inclined to shun the company of living human beings, for they disturbed his ideas, forced him to adjust them with so much violence that slabs of ivory would fall from the tower, exposing its furniture to the light of the outside world. And this he disliked, becoming shy and paralysed under its vibrations. But, though he felt no sense of anachronism in sitting in his thirteenth-century retreat, reading the latest scientific theories by electric light, at all other times he liked to be surrounded with archers, bowmen and servitors. For the rest, if my father *must* meet the living, to him as insubstantial as were the dead to others, he preferred them to be in a trance-like condition of subservience and astonishment.

Thus, in spite of his respect for artists and men of learning – a quality he most certainly possessed – he was acquainted with very few, and although he intended to see a great deal of them in some ideal and nebulous future, and, indeed, boasted of getting on well with them in a visionary present, in fact he seldom met them, and always remained apart, though not without an effort to impose his will upon the two or three antiquarian soul-mates who from time to time crossed his path. Before, however, proceeding further I must illustrate his genuine reverence for these beings, together with his attitude of aloofness, even from those to whom his temperament most nearly related him, by two anecdotes picked at random out of time. When I was eleven years old, my health compelled my parents to take a villa at San Remo for the winter, and during that period Mr Horace Round, the great authority on heraldry and genealogy, came for a few days' visit. In appearance he was hirsute and solid, in the manner of the late nineteenth-century Englishman. Just before he left, he suddenly asked 'Are the young people interested in genealogies too?', and then, before there was time to answer him, slid with abandon down the whole length of the banisters. This unexpected behaviour on the part of one who was normally dignified, and by no means young, made us children laugh, and my father subsequently reproved us, saying 'Don't laugh! These Great Men have their Little Idiosyncrasies.'

The other incident took place some time in the insouciant twenties of this century. Our dear friend Arthur Waley was staying with us at Renishaw, and my father very much admired his translations of Chinese poetry. My father's manners are later in period than himself – about the time of Charles II, but with a touch, too, of the Meredithian baronet, Sir Willoughby Patterne or Sir Austin Feverel, clinging to them; or again they might belong to the eighteenth century, as seen through the pale amber spectacles of one of his favourite artists, once so famous and now so greatly neglected, Orchardson. But, formal, exquisite and elaborate though they are, they could scarcely be more beautiful than Arthur Waley's. Upon a Sunday morning, then, my father was walking round the lake which he had caused to be created, regretting that he had not moved the old river-bed further back, and thinking out possible fantasies in stone, torrents to fall through the hanging woods above, pavilions upon islands and decorative effects generally (a few years before, he had determined to have all the white cows in the park stencilled with a blue Chinese pattern, but the animals were so obdurate and perverse as in the end to oblige him to abandon the scheme). The lake is shaped like an hour-glass or a figure-of-eight, and a bridge spans its waist. On this bridge my father met Arthur Waley advancing towards him. Each took his hat off ceremoniously and said to the other, 'How much I wish we were going in the same direction!' and passed on. Half an hour later they met again at the same place, having pursued their contrary courses as though they were planets whose goings and comings are immutably fixed by the sun, and repeated the salutation.

This aloofness, which hedged my father ever since I can remember him, possessed its own beauty and interest. Yet, how remote he was! For example, in those days of house-to-house canvassing, he had personally visited each dwelling in the borough of Scarborough several times, but he seldom remembered any single constituent when he met him. (He has frequently in later years passed me by in the street, looking at me without recognition.) Often at Scarborough, when I was a small boy returning from a winter's afternoon walk with Davis, just as we entered the hall, he would open the door of his room, which was on the ground floor, and call me in to talk to him. (He loved children until they were old enough to reason, express their views and show a will of their own; he loved their originality and the amusing, naïve things they said.) He would talk – always interestingly. But, looking back, I realize how little he told me of himself. My mother for example would, when I was with her, tell me of incidents from her childhood, and of her brother, her sisters, her mother, her adored father who could do no wrong in her eyes. She enabled me to enter into her childish life as she had lived it. But my father, I suppose because it had not been happy, never mentioned his childhood. His range was wide, and intentionally instructive. It touched inevitably at some point or other in history, geography or art, with, occasionally, the wonder of an elementary conjuring trick, with pennies disappearing from between the fingers, for amusement and to hold wandering attention. Even this, I have sometimes thought in later years, was really designed in order to prove that magic could not exist, and that everything that occurred possessed a material explanation. Then he would veer to medieval times, tell me a story he had read lately about a knight or a minstrel, or lift me up to look at a painting – a painting brought from Renishaw.

It was by George Morland, a picture of the Westminster Election, and represented Georgiana Duchess of Devonshire kissing the butcher, or about to kiss him, in an attempt to win his vote for Charles James Fox. On each side of the butcher's are the usual Morland sheep, the foreshortened face of a farmer's boy, the usual thatch and trees, and the rather horrifying concomitant detail, the meat hanging up in the open shop, the dingy, mangy collie running out of it with a sheep's head in his mouth, all this was painted with, for all its convention, an extreme realism, so that my father had chosen it out of the other pictures, very skilfully for his purpose. Its story was easy to explain, and it was precisely the painting to arouse a child's interest and hold his attention at an age when the greatest work of Titian or Raphael or Michelangelo would to him signify nothing. Thus it would ensure an early inclination towards noticing pictures, and looking at them. From the time, therefore, when I was four or five, I remember *The Westminster Election* much more vividly than the lovely Copley group of *The Sitwell Children* or *The Fruit-Barrow* by Henry Walton: but, notwithstanding, it may be that the intense pleasure I have derived from seeing works of art all over the world, and the influence they have exercised upon my mind, are due, at any rate to some degree, to this ruse of my father's; for he was very anxious that, when I grew up, I should care for pictures – though, of course, only for the pictures himself admired. At any rate it became a regular turn, a treat, and I was constantly worrying him to 'show me the butcher's shop'.

My first impression of a great artist – I do not mean a great painter – dates from the age of five, when Edith and I went to spend Christmas in London with my Londesborough grandparents, and without my father or mother. Looking back to that time, it seems to have been a season of primrose-yellow fogs and of snow, of brilliantly-lit shop windows, full of toys and flowers and sweets, and from the distant darkness of the nights that followed I recall – so that our nursery must have looked out on the square – the occasional clip-clop-clop of the horses, their hoofs muffled by the snow. Very clearly, too, I see the carriages, (who, that has known it, can ever forget the peculiar smell, mingled of oats and beer and leather, which haunted every four-wheeler, and accorded so well with its speed, and the face and voice of the driver?). In my ears still vibrates the tinny whistling that went on desultorily through the night; another London sound that has vanished, a whistling all the more shrill and forlorn because the world of the nineties was so quiet. As it died upon the thick night air, it left behind it, you would have said, a trail of sadness, of disillusionment; while the very hopefulness of its original start, until the break came in its voice, was as though someone were seeking a needle in the haystack of the enormous night. That sound, so typical of the city to which it belonged, was killed by the coming of the telephone – though it continued until forbidden at some period during the war of 1914–1918. And, accompanying it, I see the face of the crossing-sweeper under the gas-lamp as he limps to open the door.

The culmination of our visit was the opening of the Drury Lane Pantomime on Boxing Day, to which our grandparents were escorting us in state. All through the afternoon which preceded the performance, Edith and I were made to rest in bed, in a darkened room; that kind of resting which during childhood makes those subjected to it so much more tired than would the perpetual running about which both their limbs and spirits crave. We were mad, drunk, drugged with excitement. Drury Lane on Boxing Day had been a subject of conversation between our nurse and her friends ever since we could remember. It had seemed an ideal, visionary and beyond attainment. Outside the drawn blinds, the yellow murk was deepening into a thick and nearly palpable darkness and the whistles that sometimes pierced the silence sounded lonely and choking. (Perhaps the fog would be so bad that we should be unable to leave the house?)

At last, the climax arrived; we climbed into the carriage, and after half an hour arrived at the immense portico, got out, were conducted to the stage-box, sat down on our chairs, our chins just resting on the dusty red plush of the curving ledge that hemmed us in. The curtain went up. Already our grandparents were watching us, with the strained and anxious attention which elderly people reserve for children, to see if they are enjoying themselves. Alas, right at the beginning, just as the devil had appeared in a red enveloping cloud through a trap-door, the accumulated feelings, the long-drawn-out sense of expectation and, above all, the total exhaustion resulting from so protracted a period of resting, overwhelmed me and my nose began to bleed. Hastily I was taken out, to the little room at the back of the box, and told to lie down, flat, upon the gilt sofa.

Fortunately, I recovered early enough to see Dan Leno as the Beautiful Duchess, wearing a hooped dress and a large picture hat with a feather flowing from the brim, fall through the harp he was playing. I can still remember vividly that supreme representation of artistic abandon, and also, before it, his virtuoso plucking at the instrument, the strings of which were made of elastic. I even recall a fragment of Dan Leno's dialogue with Herbert Campbell. I believe it took place in the same pantomime, though I saw him subsequently more than once. At any rate on this occasion his appearance contrasted violently with that of his former rôle. Gone were the Gainsborough costume, the wig and the plumes. Instead of them, he wore a tattered white silk dressing-gown: and a little tail of hair, screwed up at the back of his head, together with a curl-paper or two, completed a masterpiece of slatternly *ensemble*. His face looked unmade-up and wrinkled. He was, temporarily, a pantomime Queen interviewing her cook in the morning. Herbert Campbell, Leno's large and wonderful foil, acted the part of the cook. The Queen was finding fault with the household accounts.

'Cook,' she was saying, 'the bills for the Palace are far too high. Look at them! Onions, onions, onions, always onions. I don't understand. Did we give a garden-party?'

'No, Your Majesty, you forget. Onions repeat.'

Such jokes may not sound funny – though this still seems funny to me –, but Dan Leno's personality in effect raised everything he did or said on to a plane of its own, for he possessed a sense of comedy that transcended comedy and became tragic, just as his face, one of the most sad and individual masks that any actor ever presented to the public, went beyond laughter and placed him on a level with the most famous clowns who have ever lived.

The next of the arts to come my way – though I was not aware of it at the time – was music, and a year or two later, in the person of Rubio, the well-known 'cellist. I saw him in London, where he came to teach, or try to teach, my sister the 'cello, till the whole house echoed with wooden groans, melodious certainly, but formless and inchoate as the singing of the choirs of fallen angels; or at Blankney during the English Saturnalia, when there were always a great many foreigners in the house, friends and governesses and teachers of the various generations.

If Rubio represented for me the birth of music, my earliest recollection of an author, and of the impression such a being is apt to create, goes back to the same year, when I was seven.

Renishaw was full of guests, mostly relations of my mother's; poor relations who spent a shadow-like existence silhouetted, at discreet intervals, upon the walls of great house after great house. They were said – and proudly they bore their label – to be 'such fun'; though, somehow, one never gathered precisely how or why. Nor did my Sitwell and Hely-Hutchinson relations ever seem to enter into this ambiguous, esoteric category: serious-minded, their every thought tinged with religion, no one attempted, or dared, to say it of them. Though they prided themselves upon the possession of a sense of humour, they would have been the first, I think, to resent being dismissed as 'such fun'. No, these relatives of whom I am talking were in the main distant female cousins of my mother's or 'connections', spinsters for the most part, though they included a few married couples. If they could think of nothing to say, they just laughed, which kept things going, and compared with saying things to make the others laugh as treading water does with swimming. It kept them afloat, and just maintained their reputation for gaiety and humour.

At such moments the children regarded them with a horrid, round-eyed wonder. Indeed, they hated the children in every house at which they stopped, and the children returned the feeling. But though the young were so great a trial, experience had taught these relatives that it was usually necessary to mask their animus, because the mothers never really seemed to *like* a show of it and one pleasant place of resort had already disappeared from circulation owing to a piece of over-enthusiastic and too hastily improvised mischief-making. In so far as the members of my own family were concerned, they had already detected the existence in Edith of some germ of poetry, which had made them single her out as an object for spite, pretending to be pity, and had soon found that the game was safe. I was an 'elder son', so, quite apart from the fact that my parents would have resented criticism of me, it was wiser to pet and to take trouble; you never knew; this treatment might pay a bonus later on. They did not, I apprehend, care much for my father either. He had the reputation of being 'clever', and if you were 'clever' that somehow or other cancelled out 'fun'.

Fortunately, in those worlds apart of child and adult, except upon a picnic or outing of some sort, we saw little of the fun contingent. One such occasion presented itself, however, when an old elm, at the near end of the avenue, was cut down. We were all of us, fifteen or sixteen persons it may be, taken out to see the giant fall, for this is a process that most of humanity loves to witness. And it proved, indeed, an interesting spectacle, because, as it fell, a cloud of bats, hundred upon hundred of them, flew out into the, to them, impenetrable daylight, and wildly sped and spun and circled, squeaking in their voices that are so high-pitched as to be felt rather than heard. With shrieks of terror, as though they had just witnessed the landing of Mr H. G. Wells's contemporary Martians, the women of the party, clasping their piled-up masses of hair tightly with their hands, so as to protect it – for a myth persisted that bats loved to become involved in those nests of crowning glory –, fled towards the house. It was an extraordinary scene, such as I now see might have inspired the brush of Nicholas Poussin, the flight, the stricken faces, the gestures of despair, the eyes round and welling with terror.

Even at so early an age, I found this rhythmic flight of women towards the house impressive: I scarcely expected to witness again soon such a classic scene of anguish. But I was wrong, for a few days later Miss de Rodes, the heiress of the beautiful Elizabethan house of Barlborough, brought over to tea at Renishaw the members of her house-party. When, arriving on the lawn, she introduced one of them as 'Mr Augustus Hare, the writer', her words created obvious panic. There ensued, metaphorically, the same tragic rush of women, away, off stage, holding their hair and, this time, crying, 'He may put *me* in a book!' It was then brought home to me for the first – but alas! not the last – time, the universal horror in which the writer is held in England, in elegant circles no less than among the common men. The lurking, inexpressible, awful fear haunted each of their hearts, like that which, were it sentient enough, would haunt the mind of a butterfly about to be netted, anaesthetized, killed and pinned out upon a square of cardboard. The prejudice was immense. Each man – though my father's attitude, of course, was exceptional, for he was interested – and each woman felt sure of being herself the quarry. Perhaps, also, beneath the horror, sprang up a certain feeling of self-importance, in the same way that it had been, in a sense, self-flattery in each woman to have been so convinced that the bats wished particularly to snuggle in *her* hair. But then, writers, in addition, were *clever*. Even bats were not *that*! Again, the victims recoiled.

This, then, was my first glimpse of a writer. My initial contact with a painter, on the other hand, began during the following spring, when with the rest of the family I sat for a portrait group to John Sargent.

CHAPTER SIX

In order to make a living in England during the late-Victorian and the Edwardian ages, every portrait painter had, to a certain extent, to become a faker of old masters, because the clients who could afford to patronize him demanded, 'Give me the sort of Gainsborough that my grandfather had,' – or, more usually, that somebody else's grandfather had, and which the grandson had sold – 'but not so old-fashioned!': that was the clamant cry. Sargent, by supplying old masters, to which was added the skin-thin glint of the French Impressionists, novel to the English public, precisely met this demand. His portraits are usually good period-pieces, *de luxe*, and bearing the same relation to the portraits of Gainsborough or Sir Joshua, that the Ritz Hotels in the ruined capitals of Europe present to the Place Stanislas in Nancy. But they will always retain their own charm; a charm often founded in the repulsiveness of their subjects. For to light upon a fashionable painter who knows how to paint at all is a rarity, and

Sargent knew how to make – or, rather, fake – his obvious effects better, even, than did Winterhalter.

Moreover, Sargent matched the Edwardian Age to a nicety; he was entirely occupied with outward and superficial effects. Money, one would hazard, bore for this painter the identical Edwardian sanctity that it possessed for the City magnates, sporting peers and old-clothes and furniture dealers whose likenesses and those of their wives he was obliged to perpetuate. Yet the fact that he was so plainly more interested in the appurtenances of the sitters and in the appointments of their rooms than in their faces, from which he sought refuge in the tilted top-hats, with their sombre but water-light reflections, the cravats and fur coats of the men, or in the tiaras, flashing, stiff but uneasy, above the heads of the women, or in the brocades and velvets they were wearing, in no way detracted from his popularity with them. To the whole age which he interpreted, these values were true values, and so could not be resented: sables, ermine, jewels, bath-salts, rich food, covered every lapse or defect. Sargent remains the painter of Pêche Melba, the artist who exalted this dish to the rank of an ideal.

Sargent agreed to paint a picture of the dimensions and kind desired, for fifteen hundred pounds: a charge by no means excessive, for, though not yet at the height of his vogue, which reached its climax in about 1910 when his prices ranged from two to three thousand pounds for a single portrait, he was already receiving large sums for his work.

The sittings began on 1st March, as planned, and I remember the day because we heard in the morning that Ladysmith had been relieved. Every second day for five or six weeks we posed to the famous portrait painter in his studio, and no picture, I am sure, can ever have given the artist more trouble, for my father held strong views concerning the relationship of the patron to the painter, who ought, he inwardly maintained, to occupy the same position as a bone to a dog – or, as for that, of a mouse to a cat –, being created and placed before him to be worried, gnawed and teased. That my father believed this painter to be a great artist at his greatest in no wise relieved him of his duty as patron, which was to offer an opinion upon every matter, whether of taste, of feeling or of technique, with an air of absolute and final authority, and to distract him by starting a new theory every instant, and then swiftly abandoning it or, alternatively, by suddenly behaving as though it were Sargent's theory and not his own at all, and by consequently opposing it with startling vigour just as the artist had agreed to accept it. At moments that became steadily more frequent as the picture progressed, he played a very strong hand and became positively dictatorial.

In some ways a man of gentle temperament, despite his full-blooded, energetic, resolute appearance, Sargent exhibited under this treatment a remarkable mildness and self-control. Notwithstanding, albeit difficult to provoke, there were enacted from time to time considerable scenes, though, even then, the sudden outbursts of the artist, his rushing bull-like at the canvas and shouting, were in reality the expression more of tremendous physical vitality than of rage. And, in any case, my father himself enjoyed these exhibitions very much, for, according to his code, a show of temperament was expected of every artist – who ought, indeed, to be goaded daily by the patron until he gave it, that being part of the contract, as it were, existing between them, and a guarantee that the work would be of the highest quality.

My father, who only admired in a female small du-Maurier-like features, pointed out to the painter that my sister's nose deviated slightly from the perpendicular, and hoped that he would emphasize this flaw. This request much incensed Sargent, obviously a very kind and consider-ate man; and he showed plainly that he regarded this as no way in which to speak of her personal aspect in front of a very shy and super-sensitive child of eleven. At any rate, he made her nose straight in his canvas and my father's nose crooked, and absolutely refused to alter either of them, whatever my father might say.

Certainly the artist had shown forbearance, had even been indulgent. He had permitted my father to have a considerable say in the action of the picture, and had, further, allowed him to choose the clothes, curiously and significantly unrelated to each other, in which the figures were painted: my sister, then still a child, in her scarlet dress, my father in his riding kit (he rode very seldom), my mother in her hat and evening gown, myself in a sailor suit, with white duck trousers, while Sacheverell wore a silk dress suitable to his age – perhaps the only sitter who did. My father's brown riding-boots, at least, stood for something; they were, I am sure, an assertion of independence in a world that had grown drab. Edith's red dress was calculated to set off his grey clothes; while the silver embroidery on my mother's gown was no doubt thrown in as a sop to Sargent; the rendering of it would keep him quiet and prevent him from interfering with his patron's picture, for he would enjoy painting it, and it would give him an opportunity of indulging in the particular, 'clever', texture-technique in which he specialized.

A child of seven is granted very good chances of observation, for he is old enough to notice a considerable amount and, so long as he behaves himself, grown-up people are usually unselfconscious, thinking that he is too young to understand their characters. Thus, if he is much with them, he can for the most part watch them being their natural selves, without any attempt at disguise, except, occasionally and only with certain individuals, for a special show of friendliness and condescension. I was privileged in this manner to watch at his work this tall, taurine figure, with his large, rather shapeless but forceful torso and strong arms, his head, small for the body supporting it, and his flushed face with its little beard, and prominent, bulging blue eyes. He was always dressed in a conventional blue-serge suit, for in those times fashionable portrait painters never indulged in the overalls or semi-fancy dress which they would adopt today, and no doubt the tight, starched white collar was responsible for the rather plethoric appearance of his face as he painted, for work of an aesthetic and intellectual order is as difficult as manual labour in such constricting fetters. I can still see him now, if I shut my eyes, as, when something he had done displeased him, he would lower his head and, as it were, charge the canvas with a brush in his hand to blot out what the minute before he had so rapidly created, bellowing, at the same time, in his deep voice, the words, 'It's pea-green, pea-green, pea-green – it's all pea-green!'

I think Sargent must have liked children – or perhaps he only found them a pleasant change from the usual, more sophisticated occupants of his studio, public monuments of men, proconsuls and generals, grave and portentous mouths through whom spake spirits, the infinite army of the banal dead, or fashionable beauties, with psyches that resembled air-balloons, inflated, light and highly coloured. Certainly he was very patient, would go to almost any trouble, consistent with being allowed to paint, to amuse us. When the first fascination of watching him at work, a conjurer drawing effects out of the void, had worn off, we became restless – especially Sacheverell who was only two years old. After a quarter of an hour, it would be impossible for either Davis or me any longer to restrain his childish impatience, or to cajole him into posing: but Sargent could always contrive to hold his attention for a few extra minutes, either by indulging in a peculiar and elaborate whistling he had cultivated, like that of a French *siffleur* upon the music-hall stage, or by incessantly intoning a limerick, which ran:

There was a Young Lady of Spain
Who often was sick in a train,
Not once and again,
But again and again,
And again and again and again.

As the evenings grew longer and finer, my mother would sometimes come to fetch us in an open carriage, so that we could have some air. We would usually cross the Suspension Bridge that spanned the enormous river, and drive in Battersea Park, through idyllic groves of young trees, now fringed with the shrillest of golden and transparent leaves, until the light changed, as though a slide had passed over it, from that of golden afternoon in early spring, through the blazing and splendid smoky drama of a London sunset, when a thousand fleeces catch fire and smoulder in the sky above, down to the cool and tender dim green light that follows it. Then we would return to the mauve, brightly-lit interior of Chesham Place. The footman would open the door, and I would quickly dash through it into the dining-room, to turn on the electric fan before anyone could stop me.

Altogether, I liked London. The atmosphere of this city was exciting – though this, indeed, made the length of the sittings more dreary – and there was – oh, so occasionally! – a theatre to visit, and the Zoological Gardens, living continuation of Noah's Ark, were open to us on Sundays. But, besides, there existed the fascinating pleasure-round of every day: one could always go to Hamley's to look at the latest and most enchanting tricks and toys; brightly lit shops that put to flight the yellow fogs outside. Or I could tease Davis till she took me to Harrods' Stores – 'Anything for Peace!' and, once there, while she was not looking, make a dash for the escalator; (the earliest, I believe, in London, not so much a moving staircase as a moving inclined-plane). Even out walking, treats were plentiful. We might meet a battalion of one of the regiments of the Brigade of Guards, with its red coats and enormous bearskins, lighting the grey streets like fires, as they passed with drums and fifes, or even occasionally accompanied by the regimental band. Or we might see persons or personages at whom we were actually *encouraged* to stare, in order that we might never forget having seen them, and how they looked.

Thus, one cold spring morning, when grey clouds clustered round the sky as grey feathers round a sea-bird, Edith and I were walking with Davis along the Mall – then an unpretentious street, and not a processional road modelled by elephantine Edwardian taste upon the Sieges-Allee in Berlin. Suddenly a clatter and scraping of hoofs told us that a body of Life Guards was approaching, and behind them, in an open carriage, sat a small figure, in black, with a black bonnet, bowing with a regular swaying motion to right and left, as the people thinly lining the road cheered her. She liked the air, and her face was rather red with exposure to it. 'The course of the Boer War must be worrying the Queen,' I heard my father say subsequently at luncheon; but she showed no sign, even at her great age, of strain or emotion and, still bowing, had driven through the gates up to the old front of Buckingham Palace, with its chocolate-brown façade by Blore, and a skyline, crowded as the roof of a roundabout, with stucco shields and lions and trophies and a great effigy of Britannia; a façade that was part of London architecture, and lacked the sterilized rigidity of the present Portland stone front. As she drove in to the courtyard, my sister and Davis were talking of how, once before, they had seen the Queen. My parents had spent a winter at Cannes when my sister was three, and one morning this plump small child had been walking with her nurse along the pavement of a straight dusty road lined with palm trees. They had been the two figures in all its deserted length, when they noticed from the distance a carriage rolling toward them down this straight perspective of painted villas with green Venetian shutters, and cobbles, and green palms, high up, and waving gently in the sun. As the horses neared them, Davis called out 'Miss Edith! The Queen!', and my sister had accordingly stopped in her walk and had dropped a low but uncertain curtsey, which Queen Victoria had most ceremoniously returned with a bow.

At last, the picture was finished; at last the moment came when we no longer had to go to Sargent's studio.

At Scarborough the following January, a tolling of bells at seven in the evening announced the death of the old Queen. 'What *shall* we do now?' I heard people say in perplexity; for the loss was something in which no man, born and brought up in that long reign, could altogether believe. The people mourned sincerely: but perhaps a few inwardly rejoiced at the overthrowing of the prim barriers of the Victorian conventions. Now it would be possible to live in the shell of these, in the space hollowed out behind them, as a wasp lives in a peach.

The ageing heir to the throne had at last inherited it. Within a few years it was boasted that nothing remained of the Victorian Age! But the Rich

Man's Banquet, which was to last for a decade, had now begun: the feast, it was recognized, went to the greediest. And Sargent was to be the recorder of it in paint, as Veronese had been of the Age of Opulence in Venice. But Beauty, today, was not everything – indeed, anything. The Venetians had lavished their fortunes upon the building of palaces and gardens, upon brocades and jewels in lovely settings, upon masques and entertainments of an exquisite loveliness: the Edwardians squandered their accumulated riches at the shrine of the strange new goddess Comfort; they spent them on the gilding of pathetic but vulgar dreams from South Africa and the Ghetto, on the installation of bathrooms, electric light, and radiators.

Soon we were back at Renishaw, in a life that somehow one knew had the patine of time upon it. The very nursery atmosphere itself was impregnated with that of other epochs; one of the blankets on my bed bore the date 1801 on it, the rooms were full of plain oak chairs of the time of Charles I, and long, long ago a hand that was now dust had scratched a phrase in French, with a date, upon one of the window-panes. Outside, in the passage, stood the large old rocking-horse upon which a former generation of children had been painted in 1836. It had lost one ear, so that it was more difficult to climb on to, but its rocking was as satisfactory as ever.

The world today was kind, and comfortable, it seemed: and padded, well padded, yet Renishaw, though luxurious in an old-fashioned way, was bare. You could see its shape. The bones were there, and you could feel them. And we were, as I have said, the last generation to be brought up by candlelight. At night the house was immense, and the rooms were caverns.

That year the autumn came early, and the afternoons had an unusual length. The leaves of the tall trees in the avenue that stood like masts above the garden assumed a peculiar air of glossy well-being that hid their approaching dissolution, and the flowers glittered in the autumn light. We would walk quickly through the gardens, and then run in the baking heat down the steep hill – so steep that it was impossible to stop running, and the momentum swept one inexorably down – to the lake. On that mirror, which reflected feathery golden clouds and cloudy golden clumps of trees, Edith and I would be rowed slowly in the blue, flat-bottomed boat by Martha, the nursery-maid, trailing our wrists in the water, so that over the beating pulses would flow a cool, slow tide. Or the girl would stop rowing, and we would drift listlessly toward the large yellow cups of the lilies, and their patches of green leaves, like stains upon the surface of the water. Once among them, and it was difficult to disentangle the oars. Meanwhile Davis would be sitting, nursing our small brother, near the boathouse, while the tea was being prepared for ourselves, and for the party, who were coming down to join us.

It seemed hotter upon the water than on the bank. It was September now, early September, the sepia and gold cylinders of the bulrushes were splitting open to show their lining of buff cotton, and the water-birds seemed heavy-winged, as though the thought of migration weighed them down already. On the shore was a faint odour of decomposition, and on the water mists began to rise, cloaking the end of every perspective, or causing, as it were, false quantities in the metre of the surrounding landscape, by suddenly obliterating one familiar feature. Or, again, in places, the evening being so calm, the mist lay like layers of disintegrating water, one above the other. Davis called out, saying that it was getting chilly, we must wait for my mother no longer. There must be a mistake. Martha could pack up and the boy could come down and bring the hamper back.

So we climbed the hill; this time we went up the straight path by the side of the kitchen gardens. As we passed them, we could see through a window in the brick wall, the peaches, with skins of rosy and green-white velvet ripening within their tents of glass. Up here there was no mist, the sun glowed on the hill-top with a deeper and more burnished gold. And now, as we topped the steep path and neared the gardens, we could hear voices and laughter, and the sound of mallets and croquet balls. They had forgotten all about us.

BOOK TWO

THE SCARLET TREE

CHAPTER ONE

It was the following year. A shadow had come to live among us, and it was
growing thicker and darker. Suspicion, conjecture and fear now plainly
took substance to themselves. A vein of indefinable sorrow and uneasiness
threaded the air of the rooms, and affected the persons in them. The air, I
say, was disturbed and jarring, with hints of dire futures more than of a
lengthy and tragic past, but old talk revived that the house was haunted, and
the maids, white as milk, walked hand in hand down long corridors. To us,
it was difficult to trace the outline of the shadow, for it was still ill-defined,
if opaque, bearing about it something loutish and lumpish, yet it was
showing more audaciously every day, coming out into the light, altering
and distorting the outlines of familiar things so that they could be seen
through it but dimly. It seemed to be there all the time, the shadow, the
forerunner, mixing itself up now with the beauty of what it was trying to
obscure and degrade. Though we loved the house, we were yet eager to be
out of it and beyond reach. Thus we would choose now the longer, cooler
way to the lake below, through the wooden gate between the stone warrior
and amazon, whose plumy, characteristic images floated, glittering upon
the surface of the leaves, with a kind of melancholy and solemn panache.
Then we would run along the sheltered alleys of the Wilderness, with their
tall holly hedges caught in dewy cobwebs, on through the parabolas made
by the young trees, and down under the high vaulting of the old beeches,
their pillars grey like smoke, down the steep paths, that lay, narrow strips,
deep in leaf-mould, upon the rocky sides of the hill, past cliffs and clefts,
down precipices, as they seemed, and stony chasms, towards the water.
Looking up, the sides of the hills were lighter and more blue than the sky,
for the hyacinths were out, and their breath, sweet, evasive, unlike any other
scent, permeated the entire countryside.

Up on the hill, the house stood in a sullen dream, and the clustered
blossom of apple and pear showed pink and white clouds, very pale and

strange in their illumination, against a sky darker than the stone, for a Sheffield blight was passing over, and the light seemed to come from the ground of the blue glades, odorous and idyllic. Indoors, my father was superintending the general rearrangement of the pictures occasioned by the arrival of the Sargent group. It was difficult work, and he was determined not to make it less difficult – *everything* must be moved. But it was dark – it looked as if there was going to be a thunderstorm, he said to himself, for though Sheffield blights were proverbial as Sheffield steel, and came our way several times a year, he would not admit their existence; they had not occurred in 1341 – or, at any rate, had not been mentioned –, so why allow their presence? Such a mistake! Yes, there it was! They were carrying the Sargent past him now; but the coming storm was making it impossible for him to see the picture clearly – one thing, though, he could see: they were carrying it all wrong, so he called out in an exasperated voice, 'No, no, no! Put it down!', and then added, 'Not like that! Of course not!'

Yes, it was a fine thing, he thought, as he gazed at it. How right he had been to go to Sargent – a pity, of course, that the painter had not consulted him more often, but artists were notoriously pig-headed and always thought they knew more about their own work than anyone else could tell them. Self-opinionated. All the same, it was an interesting group. And looking back, I, too, am obliged to allow that this portrait focused and summed up personalities and things, and the ways to which life had been pointing. It cut across our lives. After it was finished, everything, so far at least as I was concerned, was noticeably different.

Now that I was a little older, I began to comprehend more fully the world round me; people said, and I understood what they said, though even now saying and understanding were only the brittle crust that formed over the deep chasms and gullies of feeling. But the surfaces of the earth were cooling for me; the sunrise, with the mysterious hints which it had carried from the darkness out of which it came, was over, and its intimation of a glory beyond the ken of man was fading. The light, though still strange and beautiful, and peculiarly clear, was fast becoming daylight.

It was possible to perceive now that the childish impression of permanence as a thing in itself was false; it proved to be but a slow-motion section of something in progress. Even the Boer War, and the British disasters that had seemed the enduring part of it, were drawing to their close. Then there were illnesses, too, and my grandfather Londesborough had died, and there were the lawsuits in which my father was engaged, against the lessees of the coal-mines. Large sums of money were at stake in these, and though I did not understand the facts, I understood what they portended. One case had already been lost and, consequently, talk of poverty had for months fallen, like a miraculous shower of pebbles, among the peaches and the silver. My father spoke both of personal privation and of a doubtful future for Englishmen – and though this latter view, in such utter contradistinction to the popular forecast of a golden age of Empire, may at the time have been ill-founded, yet the future for our race, which included two major wars within forty years, was indeed harder than any fate he can have foreseen.

As for our new-found indigence, to me – and I often felt bothered about it – it seemed to be of an odd sort. I had not known poverty, but I had seen its face very clearly as a child. I had heard the bitter whining, 'Rags and Bones! Rags and Bones!', insinuated against the glare of the winter dawn by the battered scarecrow who slunk down back alleys; later I had examined the collections he made. I could, from him and from the tattered clothes and mouldering goods he piled upon his barrow, deduce the gesticulating automatons whom want drove to every action, to thieving and every kind of crookedness and crankiness, even to killing themselves or the slaughter of others. I had beheld the poor in London, that other nation that lived pressed into the narrow spaces between the houses of the rich. But this brand of poverty I could neither recognize nor comprehend; though now I can see it possessed the same sort of reality as pertained to those problem pictures that so fascinated the public of the same epoch every year at the Royal Academy: a man, let us say, sat sighing at a table in his study, with his head in his hands, and a pile of bills – yes, they were bills, they *must* be bills – on the table in front of him, where also were depicted the plush interior of an empty jewel-case, an overturned silver mustard-pot, a silver-backed hair-brush, a pawn-ticket and an empty bottle, labelled 'Sleeping Draught'. Just outside the window, a tree was being cut down; and in the room itself, a pet spaniel, so thin as to appear afflicted, was endeavouring to eat a mouse.

Our poverty, then, signified chiefly that we were no longer allowed to throw down pennies, done up in screws of paper, to the conductors of German bands, in their peaked caps, or to the Italians, childishly gay and childishly melancholy, who turned the handles of barrel-organs, and that Stephen Pare's wages were cut down to a figure I cannot bear to think of; indeed, how furnished with sadness was his life, with his wife, to whom he was devoted, mad, and himself condemned to a lifelong solitary confinement in darkness.

The chief difference, however, which my father's alleged loss of fortune made to us was that in future, so our governess told us, we were only to be given 'useful presents'. This deceptive phrase formed cover for a device which, even then, I considered as unworthy, and which Davis character-ized as 'downright mean'. It meant that, when it became plainly necessary for us to have new hair-brushes, or a piece of soap, these articles now reached us, not as a natural fulfilment of our needs, but disguised as a Christmas or birthday present. No self-respecting child could possibly like to have his stocking on Christmas Eve filled magically with such prosaic objects as toothbrushes and bootlaces, instead of tangerines done up in silver paper, chocolates and toys. My mother, with the indulgence and generosity of her temperament, tried always to circumvent such prophetic experiments in austerity, but my father, his relations and the governess were in league, and now Davis, who had always stood ranged on the other side, behind my mother, was suddenly snatched away from us after a violent quarrel with my father.

It took me many months to recover from losing our old friend, and to forget my jealousy of the fortunate children upon whom she was now attending. It seemed, too, as though, with her going, all instinctive wisdom had been withdrawn from us, and that 'trying to do the right thing' had taken its place. It was at about this period, too, that there entered into my life that round collar-box made – I recollect the strong feeling of inner repulsion I had to master on first being told of this derivation – of pig-skin. Upon its smug face it bore, in the large compromising writing of our governess, my full initials, F.O.S.S.; initials belonging, as it were, to my left hand, as opposed to O.S., my sign manual, belonging to my right hand and to my life as I have made it. Always – even then – I have felt a stranger to my full initials, and, in addition, I much resented the large full stops, placed in so forthright a fashion after each letter. This hard-featured, unprepossessing box later seemed to me to have constituted a sort of foretaste of school; from it could have been deduced the horrors lurking there, the boredom, the bullying, the want of all except sadistic imagination; a time during which I was lost in the initials F.O.S.S., marked, under fear of punishment, so clearly on everything I owned, playbox, books, clothes. But throughout boyhood, though I lost everything else that belonged to me, I could never get rid of this unattractive chattel: nor could I ever catch sight of it without being reminded of that process of a pig being killed to which it owed its existence. Far into adult life, it dogged – or should I write pigged? – my footsteps. A hundred times I hid it and lost it, but always it would appear in my room again, whether I was abroad or in England.

Besides, then, the new kind of presents that were given us, many other changes in our intimate lives had come in the interval since Sargent had finished the family group; changes which, in their turn, affected the way in which I regarded my fellow men. Thus the consequences of my grandfather's death certainly altered my view of life, because I observed that the sycophantic reverence and adulation which had hitherto been reserved for my grandmother Londesborough was now transferred suddenly to her daughter-in-law and successor. Not only did the old lady lose her husband, but, in addition, nearly all her belongings, being obliged to pursue hereafter the dolorous manner of life decreed by tradition for an English dowager; not only were horses and carriages and grooms and gardens and houses and jewels and plate, and, indeed, the whole luxurious decoration of life by which she had been so long surrounded, snatched from her at a single grab, but she also forfeited – commensurately, it seemed, – the love of the majority of those who had pretended to be her friends. She felt, I apprehended, peculiarly desolate, though as a rule she would not admit it. Few people now went to see her. Especially, I noticed, the younger members of the fun brigade, mentioned in *The Cruel Month*, deserted her in a body. Their extravagantly expressed infatuation ceased with the last notes of the funeral march, for it transpired now that, without their having been conscious of it, it had really been to my aunt, and not to my grandmother, that these people, with their easy, affectionate natures, had the whole time been devoted! No longer did the air resound with their tittering denunciations of this same aunt's extravagances, their diatribes against her style in dress or the ways of her house. No, they had fallen in love with them, as much as with the woman herself.

The singular twist, which had come upon life since the portrait was finished, applied most of all to those depicted in it. Edith had withdrawn, as it were, still further to one side and into the background. With a room of her own and a guardian governess to teach and guide her, she was receiving the peculiar education reserved for young girls of her time and class. My father, of course, would have liked her to learn typewriting and prepare for a business career; she evinced a considerable disinclination for it and lack of ability in that direction, which was the main thing, for one must always, he said, concentrate on the things one was bad at, try to make up one's weak points, and do at least one disagreeable thing each day: (he had been reading Nietzsche). But my mother, weak in so many ways, was here a rock. She insisted that Edith should have the usual 'advantages', or what would people say? So they compromised by agreeing to cut off some of the time she gave to the piano – she seemed to like playing it –, and it was decided for her that, after the manner of a geisha, she must learn to charm by means of esoteric accomplishments, such as 'cello-playing – there were others who thought the guitar would be more effective –, scarf-dancing, water-colours, recitation and small-talk.

My sister's hours and days were most fully taken up by her dedication to these attractions of long ago; to them she was obliged to add the prevalent rites of the gymnasium, the antics in which would, she was told, be as useful to her as the obsolete dances, lancers and the rest, which she was learning: ('Nothin' a young man likes so much as a girl who's good at the parallel bars'). To this curriculum was also added, in the name of health and beauty, a good deal of plain physical torture, invented by my father in consultation with a children's surgeon, who had been introduced to him by my Aunt Grace and specialized in such things. Dr Grabbe – for such was his name – designed and planned his own orthopaedic devices, thumb-screws, nose-slams, ankle-twisters and all sorts of boards, flat or sloping, on which the young patients could be bound, a thousand little clever dodges for giving pain and taking money. Alas, my sister's nose was still not of the shape for which my father had bargained, so the reign of iron and manacles began. The harm inflicted both on her nervous system and her physique proved to be costly though fortunately not irreparable; a few years later it took many months to break down by electric treatment the adhesions that had formed as a consequence of the use of these instruments. It was the result, on my father's part, of good intentions, coupled with a belief that he could understand the principles, and advise on the practice, of any art. Meanwhile, Dr Grabbe had been let loose upon the family in general; our cousins were martyred as much – or nearly as much – as ourselves. Already the same enterprising doctor was looking forward to slicing me about as well, – and to the fresh fees he would obtain for it. No trouble or expense – and certainly no pain – was to be spared. Very soon he had snatched from me my tonsils, which I have missed ever since.

In general, I was not nearly so far advanced as Edith, and was only just beginning to be instructed in the masculine counterpart to feminine accomplishments, riding and cricket and tennis and, even, rounders and ping-pong. Ping-pong was, in a sense, the very opposite of the obsolete attainments which I have discoursed upon; it had only just made a triumphant appearance in the world, but was deemed to have arrived for ever, so that I remember my father expatiating to me on what a big part it must of necessity play in my life. He talked in a strain of great seriousness about it, and wound up with the words, 'Unless you learn to play ping-pong properly, you can never hope to be a Leader of Men.'

The sole accomplishment that Edith and I learnt jointly was dancing: but of a form, again, that made no attempt to compromise with reality. The classes, which we regularly attended at Scarborough twice a week for several years, were held usually in the morning, and were rather small, being composed of the children of the local *noblesse*, Willoughbys, Cayleys, Ledgards and Johnstones, who drove in from the countryside with their parents, come to do a day's shopping. All of these children were, superficially, of the same type as ourselves; they had the same straight fair hair, the same fair skin and blue or grey eyes, and yet between them and us was set some difference for which I could not, at the time, account.

Sometimes the mothers of the children taking part would come and sit on chairs placed round the edges of the room, watching our ceremonious and rhythmic convolutions with that sort of uneasy-eyed concentration that parents show when they want in reality to talk to one another and yet have to pretend to follow the actions of their children with at least a modicum of pride and pleasure. How much I was delighted with the surprise visits of my mother, who would come in unexpectedly and sit behind me at the side of the room! I could always detect her arrival, even if I did not see it, by the scent of the gardenias or tuberoses she would be wearing, and her presence afforded me a warm feeling of support in the ordeal that classes, pleasant though they were, constituted. I suffered this feeling of being cut off, divided from those round me, without being able in any way to understand it; but my mother seemed to act as a link, for I realized how well and easily she got on with the other mothers, and that they all admired her beauty, and were glad to see her and talk to her, as she sat there, with her short astrakhan coat and a hat with a mauve feather in it.

CHAPTER TWO

My father had decided to give up politics. He showed symptoms of being unwell, and he and my mother and a friend went to Germany for a holiday that year, hoping that a sojourn in the ancient cities of Nuremberg and Rothenburg, with their gothic character, their toys and torture-chambers, would soon put him right. For a while he seemed better, but the improvement did not last. The effort of finding a balanced hanging in one room for the three large family groups of himself, his grandfather and great-grandfather – and consequently of being obliged to shift every picture in the house – was making him more irritable than he had ever been in his whole life. He admitted to himself that he was not feeling well; it had begun two days before, when there had nearly been that thunderstorm, and he had been trying the pictures in their various places –, as he was doing again today.

Generally, this sort of thing suited him: but now he had to confess he felt overdone. In addition, as he had decided to leave Belvoir House, there was all the furniture from Scarborough to arrange, for he had moved it hither. But the hanging of the pictures must be settled first. Three joiners were on duty all day, carrying the various things. He still had not found the proper place for the Sargent. Almost before the picture had been hoisted tentatively, and with difficulty, into the space he had last chosen for it, he would shout, 'No, no, no!', and give orders for it to be held up once more in the position from which the men had just brought it. Backwards and forwards they tramped, seeming figures come to life from an Assyrian frieze of conquest, plodding slowly, their backs bent.

My father had other troubles, besides; he had called in allies. He had asked an old friend, Major Viburne, to 'keep an eye on the household bills', and had imported him to Renishaw for that purpose. We children had made his acquaintance the previous summer in Scarborough, when there had broken out one of those recurrent attacks of charity matinées, which always afflict towns of this sort in times of national emergency.

As for his 'keeping an eye on the household bills', nothing could have been more disastrous. To begin with, his knowledge of them was entirely theoretical; himself was always on a diet. The regime varied but it could usually be summarized by a medieval formula, such as

> Shun things that run,
> Eat things with wings,

or

> Foot and fin
> Go ill within,
> Fruits of earth
> Will prove their worth.

(Usually these inane little rhymes had a catch concealed in them; for example, with reference to the first, the Major could eat partridge, but not French partridge, because that bird *runs* for long distances in the stubble.) At the moment, moreover, he had, as it were, altogether lost touch with his teeth, being confined by his doctor to a total diet of Plasmon biscuits, a health food which, though altogether admirable and sustaining, was one that, as an only form of nourishment, no medieval couplet or quatrain could romanticize. My father, however, had formed the opinion that he was a *bon vivant*, and had run an army mess, and, in the face of every evidence to the contrary, always consulted him on the ordering of dishes and of wines for the cellar, as well as on the paying of the bills, a subject upon which he was no less ignorant. In reality Major Viburne had never held a commission in the Regular Army, though for a time he had been in the Volunteers, but this only rendered him the more military, ideally military, in bearing and outlook. In a year or two, he became Sacheverell's tutor, and after that, when we were both at school, he always came to us for the holidays. Indeed he was the best possible foil that could be found for an imaginative boy, and with us would always be good-tempered and, in his way, amusing. Sacheverell would continually ask him questions that seemed impossible to answer: 'Do people live on the moon?' and 'Why not?', or 'Where did the Greeks come from?', or 'Why is the sun larger than the earth?', and would always receive in reply a concise, polite and matter-of-fact – though no doubt often a wrong – answer. While making these inquiries, in which he was genuinely interested, Sacheverell would none the less be engaged in drawing pictures with an indelible pencil on the flat scarlet surface of the Major's head. It would always take the old man a long time to discover the trick played upon him; nor would he be angry, for he was conscious that we liked him. And he knew he could lull us into quiet by recounting his military experiences to us. We used, both of us, immensely to enjoy listening to his braggadocio stories of the sixties, of how formerly he had commanded at Scarborough Castle, and quelled a mutiny, or how the War Office experts had consulted him, while he was still a boy, on the running of the Crimean War.

At the moment of which I am writing, my father had brought over to Renishaw from the office of the local Scarborough paper, which he owned, his chief printer, Stubble. Stubble printed books, therefore books were his territory, and my father accordingly set him to the uncongenial task of cataloguing the books in the library. I liked the man, for, since he did no work at all, he spent much time in talking to me, and he was, indeed, a lively companion. I remember when I said one day to my mother, 'I like Stubble. He seems to enjoy himself so much,' she laughed and replied, 'Yes, that's just his trouble.' I wondered at the time what she meant, but I found out later. My father, however, observing Stubble's idleness, would grow very angry at finding himself obliged to pay him for doing nothing, and would decide to send him away. Accordingly he would give him his journey-money and tell him to go home to Scarborough. But it was obvious that Stubble regarded his journey-money, literally, as *pourboire*. He would catch the local train to Sheffield, where he was obliged to change, and in that black but riotous city would spend on drink every single shilling he possessed, and would then proceed to roar his way back to Renishaw on foot – eight miles at least – in the early hours. The look of him, back in the library again the next day, plainly suffering from what we have since learned to call a 'hangover', enraged his patron. But it seemed no good giving him his journey-money again and so he would be there for another two days, until once more he obtruded his lack of energy too clearly, and once more my father dismissed him, and the whole jolly process would repeat itself.

Last night had been the sixth time it had happened. There he was, in the library again! Better not to look at him, my father thought, it would only annoy one. Where were the joiners? And where was Hollingworth? There was a lot to do, such a lot, things that *had* to be done. All the furniture from the ball-room at the far end of the house must be taken to the upper drawing-room, and all the furniture from the upper drawing-room moved down to the ball-room, and then, if it did not look right – and he was by no means convinced that it *would* look right –, back again. There the Sargent was, being carried past once more. But he had never told them to do that! And why must they carry it upside-down? And why weren't they doing it as he had instructed them? How often had he ordered them never to touch the frame without wearing gloves? So inconsiderate. What was that? No gloves? *Certainly not.* Why should he pay for them? He had never heard such a suggestion. (It was extraordinary the way that nowadays people expected one to do everything for them, though the income tax was a shilling in the pound.) Very sorry, *he* couldn't afford it. (That reminded him, he must tell his secretary to write to the lawyers about raising money on mortgage, and Viburne must insist on a contract for jam! The catering ought to be run on the same lines as an army mess.) There was the Sargent again. No, no, of course not. That would never do!

It was not only the intense activity of my father's mind, and the amount and variety of tasks that he set himself, which rendered him just at this time in a peculiarly exacerbated condition of irritability. These traits were his, as they are mine, by heredity and nature, but ordinarily his temperament could cope with them. Now, however, he was unhappy in his own life. The great political career for which, conscious of his own remarkable talents, he had hoped, did not materialize of itself, and he seemed unable to command it. He saw, instead, fools preferred. The second lawsuit had been lost, though himself had been in the witness-box for two days, a very great strain. In addition, he was crushed, he felt, by a mountain of debts for which there was nothing to show, neither reason nor result, since my mother bought objects because she liked them, or, at any rate, liked buying them; then she would give them away – or she would buy them in order to give them away. With her, spending money was an expression both of the enjoyment of life and of its opposite: if she felt well and happy, she would order every sort of thing, that neither herself nor anyone else could want. If she felt miserable, then she chose things at random in order to cheer herself up.

I do not know how long my father and mother had been married before he realized the extravagance of her nature. Perhaps the episode of The Learned Pig may have put him wise to it. Certainly this had been one of her earliest and most ill-fated purchases. A few months after her marriage, when she was not yet eighteen, she had been asked to open a Conservative bazaar at Scarborough. There she had seen an animal known as The Learned Pig, which told fortunes, and had been greatly impressed by its uncanny knowledge of character and grasp of the future. I am not sure by what method, whether by horoscope, tea-leaves, palmistry, clairvoyance or rapping on tables with its cloven hoof, the creature made its prognostications, nor how it published them to its clients or the world. At any rate my mother had been unable to resist bidding for the remarkable creature when it was offered for auction at the end of the bazaar. Sure enough she obtained it, but for a very considerable amount of money. This was bad enough, but once the erudite porker was on her hands, its psychic gifts deserted it, and at the same time she realized she dare not tell my father what she had bought. Nor did she mention it to *her* father; but, since she could not let the poor brute starve, she arranged for it to be boarded at one of his farms, and told the farmer on no account to divulge the animal's existence. However, after a year or two, the farmer, finding that he was not paid, rendered an enormous account for feeding and grooming the beast to my grandfather. Though he was furious at having to pay, my mother succeeded in persuading him not to mention the matter to my father. My mother agreed that the pig must be killed, but the idea of killing such an unusual animal – or, as for that, of killing any animal at all – upset her so much, that secretly she took steps to have it sent, instead, by rail to Renishaw. Here she contrived for it to be farmed out again – on this occasion, of course, on one of my father's farms, and again it refused to tell fortunes. This time, after a long period, the farmer wrote to the agent to demand payment, the agent, not understanding at all what had happened, forwarded the letter to my father, and the true story came out. My father paid the bill, not with the best of grace, and ordered the animal to be destroyed. But The Learned Pig could never be mentioned in front of him, for not only was he annoyed at having to find the money for it, but in addition he was angry because, hating superstition as he did, he found that he had become a vicarious victim of it.

I do not know whether this opened his eyes at all, but, in any case, in spite of his strength of character, he appeared incapable of preventing or putting a stop to such expenditure. He would never recognize any fact which he did not want to recognize, neither the tendencies of the time, nor even the more visible processes of nature, least of all the actions of human beings. We were having luncheon one hot August day at Renishaw, and there had been a silence of some minutes, when my mother suddenly said, across the table:

'George! . . . The mountain ash berries have turned already . . . It means an early autumn.'

'Well, I haven't seen them.'

'That doesn't prevent their being there, George.'

To which my father replied finally, and with an air of triumphant virtue:

'I don't *allow* myself to see things like that!'

This last remark was particularly true. He had learnt to mask his sensitiveness and to barricade himself behind the multiplicity of his interests, so that he would only see the end of a process, when, indeed, it naturally, by the appearance of violent change that it offered, since he had noticed none of the intermediate steps, forced itself upon his attention. Then, when he could no longer avoid seeing, he could still nevertheless avoid comprehending; and, further, what he now saw, suddenly, he perceived far too large – an exaggerated vista of ruin, of empty, desolate houses and penniless children. 'If it were not for me,' he would sometimes remark, with an air suitable to the pathos of the situation, 'we should all be living in lodgings on three thousand a year!'

Notwithstanding, it was true that he exhibited in his character streaks of intense foresight, and was undoubtedly a clever business man, though apt to want to strike too hard a bargain. Immensely extravagant after his own fashion, he knew the value of money, but he could never understand or excuse extravagance in others. If only people would come to him for his advice! If only, *if only*, Ida would consult him about her clothes, instead of getting those expensive fashionable dresses! He could put her on to something interesting at a tenth of the price! Or he could order the dresses himself – she should make more use of his taste –, pay for them, and then deduct the money every other fortnight from her quarterly allowance (it was called an allowance, but was, in fact, the income from her own small capital). Or he might give it her; let her pay for it, and then let her have the money back, so much every ten days. He had a passion for rather complicated transactions of this kind. Such a mistake to leave him out of it, he could so easily run her up one of those charming medieval things. It would be original and friends would want to copy it. He had lots of notes somewhere, for the reformation of clothes. It was only necessary to get back to the old lines (they understood these things so much better in the Middle Ages!). There was, for example, that delightful old leper's gown at Naples, a thing anyone would be glad to wear! Probably, if he asked him, the curator, Professor Roselli, would be only too pleased to lend one a piece of it, so as to have the pattern copied. And himself would give her a necklace or pendant to go with it; perhaps one of those beautiful old bits of lead jewellery. He could easily have it imitated, if he could find the right person to do it. It was just as beautiful in design as any piece decorated with emeralds or diamonds, and far less expensive; and it would look splendid with a sackcloth jerkin! If he decided on a pendant, he could have it copied from one of the examples

in the Musée Cluny in Paris. He had made full notes on them when he
was there, with little drawings, rough but serviceable enough.

By this time he had worked himself up and was growing really excited
about the idea (though underneath, somewhere deep inside him, lay the
haunting, bitter certainty that his advice was not wanted, would not be
asked for and, if it were, most certainly would not be taken: but he did not
allow this knowledge to come to the surface). Where was that book? *The
Beauty of Dress at the Time of the Black Death*: it bore its name on its back in
large letters. No, that was not it! Where could it be? No, nor that. (These
housemaids would tidy everything up! Or it might be Henry, though he
pretended never to move anything.) It was annoying that he could not find
it at the moment, but the real beauty of the system he had evolved for
keeping such things was, that though you might not find a particular note
when you looked for it, you would be sure to find it some other time. Of
course it might be in one of the boxes upstairs in his study, together with the
loose notes. He went up to search for it. The boxes of notes, all with their
names pasted on the front, were arranged in a wooden case he had designed
for them. He ran through the list of names:

> *Schedules for Re-settlement (. . . no, it would scarcely be in that)*
> *Reresby and Normanville*
> *The Young Pretender's Court in Rome*
> *Sacheverell Miscellaneous*
> *Design in Brocades*
> *The Origin of Surnames*
> *Rotherham in the Dark Ages*
> *Lepers' Squints* (could it have got in there by mistake?)
> *The Romances*
> *Sweet Preserves in the Fourteenth Century*
> *Wool-Gathering in Medieval Times and Since*
> *The Eckington Dump*
> *Court-Life in Byzantium*
> *Estate Miscellanous*
> *Heraldry*
> *Introduction of the Peacock into Western Gardens*
> *John Brown & Co.*
> *The History of the Fork*
> *Landscape Notes*
> *On the Colours of Flowers*
> *Sheffield in the Eighteenth Century*
> *Nottingham Guilds* (1328–1384)
> *Trust Accounts*
> *Heber – Hiccock – Hely-Hutchinson*

No, it could be in none of those. He would look for it again tomorrow. Disappointed, his mind reverted to what had originally started the trail of thought. *What* a pity Ida did not consult him! It was especially difficult to curb these oubreaks of extravagance in London, for, when there, he worked much at the British Museum, had business to do, with lawyers and banks, and so he only saw her in the evenings. The source of all this trouble, he deduced – and in this perhaps he was right –, was to be traced to having friends.

Now, however, all these various interests and worries and troubles came together and coalesced to overwhelm him, and by their timing appeared to quadruple their power. And the final touch was added, I was always given to understand, by the literary strain imposed upon him by the writing of an essay, entitled 'The Origin of the Word Gentleman', for a quarterly of luxurious format called *The Ancestor*. His serious illness came on with great suddenness.

At the end of May, he felt he would like to return to Scarborough, though previously he had just decided to leave it. Accordingly, having a few months before given up his old house, he took from his brother-in-law a lease of Londesborough Lodge. There, in the following month, he fell alarmingly ill; presumably with a nervous breakdown, though people scarcely knew the term then, and certainly did not understand the misery that it connotes. Whatever the nature of his affliction, it entirely prostrated him, so that he could attend to no business. He became convinced that he was a dying man, and the knowledge that his father had died at precisely the same age – a fact of which his mother kept reminding him by inference, saying to him, for example, 'You look just like your poor father did, today' – persuaded him of it still more surely. And members of the medical profession could do – or at any rate did – little to help him.

Just as my father's illness began, preparations were in progress throughout the land for local displays of loyalty to the throne, for King Edward VII was to be crowned on 26th June. Not least did our loyal borough resound with shouting and hammering, which must have been most trying for a nervous patient. It was impossible to escape the noise and bustle. And even for us children, who loved this sense of bustle and happy energy, nevertheless the bright colours of the bunting outside and the general feeling of cheerful anticipation only served to emphasize the atmosphere of illness and unhappiness within the house. Moreover, there were other contrasts to be observed; although the keenest sense of patriotism and rejoicing seemed to inspire everyone, so that even the strange being from whose example I had first learnt to speak, the whining, hoarse-voiced collector of rags and bones, this summer, sported a miniature union-jack in the buttonhole of his scarecrow's frock-coat, and although, indeed, I could not help wondering what particular cause he found to be thus jolly and excited, for a kind of mad sense of frolic now gleamed from his eyes, nevertheless I noticed that others were absent or had disappeared. Yet another and more enormous form was to replace them, at any rate temporarily. It was this very summer that a whale, the first I ever saw, was stranded upon the shore, on the sands near the old harbour. A colossal, shapeless and primeval carcase, it reared its useless bulk there for weeks, and seemed in its immensity, that was yet lost against the golden sweep of the bay, to hold in it some symbolism difficult to seize upon; to herald, perhaps, the wrecking of an empire or of a civilization.

Ill and sleepless as he was, nevertheless the intense activity of my father's mind remained unabated, and – for was I not his eldest son, soon due to go to school? – he was much occupied with the problem of education. It was wrong, all wrong (they had managed these things so much better in the Middle Ages; archery was splendid training). It should be different. He did not feel well enough now to think it out, but if he survived the present year, which he doubted, and when he had time, he would turn his attention to it and try to get it right – at any rate in theory. However, he could not get on with the matter now, so the system remained unreformed and it was understood that I should have to put up with it as best I could.

The winter before his collapse, he and my mother had succeeded in picking out a school that they thought suitable for me, and one which was known to pay much attention, by means of the generally accepted combinations of brutality, boredom and slow torture, to preparing its pupils for their time at Eton.

My father was as full of original theories as ever – indeed they tended to grow still more erratic – and I was now, alas, doomed to become the victim of one of them. Before going to the place of trimensual internment they had chosen for me, he decided that I had better attend a day-school. Herein, no doubt, he was right, for I had encountered few children except my cousins. I preferred the company of people older than myself, or of my sister and brother, and had always detested boys of my own age. The school, however, which he chose, was situated in Scarborough and mainly supported by superior tradesmen and rich farmers.

Accordingly, one heartless, sunny morning, I experienced when I was called the sinking feeling in the pit of the stomach that always accompanies for the imaginative a new adventure of this order, for Henry was in two hours' time to conduct me to the school and there hand me over to the headmaster. All too soon we arrived, Henry left me, and the headmaster, a bearded man with the happy but puzzled expression of a resolute and vigorous bore, spoke 'a few words' to me in an absent-minded way, as though occupied with affairs of moment. But the few words increased like the Israelites in the land of Canaan, and it seemed a long time before he had finished, and had sent for a boy to take me to the dreary asphalt torture-yard, known euphemistically as 'playground'.

Not a blade of grass, not a leaf, broke the grey-mauve monotony of asphalt, stone walls and slates. Only a few odd instruments, bits of rope and wood clamped to the wall by iron rings and joints, and suggestive of torture, fair and square, stood in one corner; though, as I found out later, they were in fact the furnishings of a poorly stocked outdoor gymnasium. At this moment, however, I had no time to examine the yard, or indeed anything but the jostling, screaming mob that occupied it, for it teemed with shouting, whistling, roaring schoolboys of different ages and sizes, though all covered with spots, and all wearing caps with the same skull and crossbones proudly blazoned upon them. I looked round, and felt rather out of it – but not for long. Evidently I had been expected, for about half of the larger boys, directly they saw me, set on me with whirling fists and yells of *'Don't think you're everybody just because your father's a bloody baronet!'* Now this was, as matter of fact, something which had not occurred to me heretofore, because my mother made no secret of her view that a baronetcy was a disgrace, and that she regarded baronets in general as the Ishmaels of the British race, and no one else had ever mentioned it to me. None the less, I returned from my first encounter with victorious British Democracy suffering from two black eyes, an aching body and a sore heart. And I fear, too, that I gave a very poor account of myself, since I did not know how to fight, hated pain and was tremendously surprised by the onslaught.

My family pretended not to notice the black eyes, and said nothing about them, except that I 'looked tired'. Perhaps, indeed, they were proud of them, saying to each other, 'The boy will go far, he begins fighting the very first day he goes to school.' I went back every morning to the school, where I displayed no ability, no aptitude of any sort for work or play. Even when I was shown how to play rounders, a game confined to the youngest boys – that is to say to those of my own age –, even at that

I was a failure. Perhaps a precocious instinct for words and their meanings may have been at the root of it, for I felt that the word *play* denoted something you enjoyed, and since I did not enjoy these dull runnings to and fro, I did not expect to have to go on with them. At other times, while the bigger boys were listlessly continuing their studies within, we smaller ones, eight to ten of us, were turned into the yard to play by ourselves, with no master present. Then my companions were wont to indulge in an exhibitionistic and obscene game, known by them as 'horses'; rites perhaps akin, by some strange atavistic trait, to the hobby-horse exploits of primitive races such as the Mongols and Manchus, who staged this same kind of orgy in yourtals and even in the great courts of the Imperial Palace, on the marble platforms, beneath the immense shadows of yellow-tiled roofs. Perhaps these miniature orgies, also, would have been of interest to the anthropologist; but, unfortunately, the scene was neither so savage as in the one place, nor so splendid as in the other. Here the setting was appropriate to the squalor of the game. I refused to take part in it, and grew still more unpopular in consequence.

Moreover, I was now unhappy at home as well as at school. My nights, occupied with my private problem, with my picturings of hell flames, my efforts to overcome my terror of them, or to think, equally, of some way of avoiding them through virtue, became an absolute torment. Eventually, since my mother and the governess both saw that I was learning nothing, and in danger of losing what little I knew and of deteriorating generally, I was withdrawn, after about a fortnight or so, from the scene of my father's experiment.

Even the short span I had endured at the day-school had been sufficient to inspire me with a well-founded distrust concerning the traditional 'happiest time of my life', now fast approaching. My mother, noticing this, used to tell me how sure she was that I should enjoy my time at the boarding-school they had chosen for me, and in which I was to be incarcerated the following year. She knew the parents of many of the boys, and I should find them quite different; their fathers were sportsmen, and several of them were friends of my uncle's – the highest award of praise that she could bestow on anyone. My father, though I saw him so seldom, when we did meet, went further and drew positively enchanting pictures of the life before me, and of how deeply I should enjoy it; a real, fine, healthy life which put one in a glow. Schools had, apparently, improved beyond recognition since his day. Then the boys had learnt nothing except bad language and bad habits, and had been beaten and half starved; all that bad old tradition had been swept away. He only wished he could have my time in front of him, as his own, all over again.

Alas, though, this source of comfort diminished, for I saw him less and less. He was growing no better, it appeared. The doctors continued to arrive, and each of them recommended at least one new cure, and more probably returned, after its failure, to prescribe a further experiment. The invalid tried them all, one after the other, in good faith and in swift rotation: continual fresh air (he was sent lumbering round the woods in heavy old cabs), no fresh air, to lay his head on hop pillows, to take exercise, to give up exercise, to stop smoking, to smoke special cigarettes, to live on meat, to touch no meat, to give up alcohol, to drink champagne and port, to walk, to run, to sing, to lie down for long periods without moving, never to keep still, to take up golf, and to abandon it, 'not to use his mind', and to 'think of other things'. For all these pieces of advice the doctors charged ample fees, and his payment of them aggravated the financial worry which had largely caused his illness, and so rendered his condition yet graver.

Nobody seemed, even now, to know what was the matter with him or just how ill he was. Finally, as he showed no sign of mending, the general practitioner who had first attended him asserted himself, and got him away from the other doctors. He advised change. He must travel with a friend. But *where* was the friend to be found? In the end, the doctor himself went with him. Thus it was that my father began to spend so much of his life abroad in France and Germany and Italy, but chiefly in Italy, and that we children came to hear so much of it, of Italian houses and gardens and ways of life. At first, my mother would only occasionally, or for part of the time, go abroad with him, and, in her absence, an acquaintance of his mother's, or 'somebody suitable', of whom she or my mother had heard was chartered to keep him company; but Henry, of course, was always in attendance as well, and soon learnt to talk Italian, though with a broad Yorkshire accent. He was much struck, I recollect his confiding in me, by the palpable resemblance between the languages of Whitby and Italy, respectively: for example, in Whitby, the ordinary greeting in the streets, when you passed a friend, was ' 'Ow ist tha?': while in Italy the counterpart was *'Come sta?'*

★

While my father flitted so erratically from house to house, my mother, as a rule, remained at the Lodge, for it was too much of a strain on the household if she also were to move her home every day.

In spite of her real concern for my father, I think that at the same time she rather appreciated the immunity from criticism that her expenditure enjoyed now that his constant wish to economize had brought on a costly illness, which necessitated a complete rest from all business. Scarborough would be more full than ever of visitors this year. Lawyers could not – though they did – argue with her about household bills, so there were many parties at the Lodge, until she moved to the new house my grandmother was preparing for us.

But the worst domestic effects of his illness were to be experienced in the future; although his direct influence on my mother, headstrong and impulsive, had always been small, his indirect influence had been considerable. By his preoccupation with the gothic age and consequent aloofness from the day, by his formal, frosted manner, he always, even perhaps without wishing it, exercised a chilling process of restraint upon those friends of hers who sought to live upon her. Her many genuine and devoted friends, it was to be noticed, liked my father; but the others were frightened of him, for, besides his alleged 'cleverness', of which they were not in a position to judge, their sense of guilt, their inner knowledge that they were out for all they could get, made them mistake his remoteness for percipience, and his unsureness of himself, caused by his ignorance of the times in which he lived, for a thoroughly justified mistrust of themselves. Now that he was temporarily no longer to be reckoned with, now that there were, even, some doubts existing in their minds concerning the likelihood of his recovery, this control was removed. They behaved just as they liked. They encouraged my mother in every folly. They led her in any direction that could harm her, by flattering her in every way possible, by urging her on to lose her temper, telling her that she had been 'splendid', and by trying to make her do it again, by persuading her to insult some of my father's relations who disapproved of them, by leading her on to find fault with my sister in public and to mortify her, but, above all, by plundering my mother and sponging upon her.

All this while, in the new house, my mind was more than ever occupied with the struggle I have mentioned earlier in this chapter; my lone tussle with the idea of a conventional hell. After all, if the Christian religion was true, then hell existed; and if hell existed, as it was so elaborately and even exultantly described in various passages in the Bible, and if I was as wicked as I was frequently told I was by my mentors, then I ought to take the whole matter with the utmost seriousness. Yet none of those round me – except my Aunt Florence – seemed to be excessively worried about it. Alas, the more I thought of it, the worse became the torments of my nights, and the worse, in consequence, my conduct, willy-nilly, the following day. I was treated continually to a review of my sins, my temper and selfishness – and could not, and did not want to, explain my difficulties.

Before many months had gone by, we were living in my grandmother's house, Wood End, which she had prepared for my father and given him. To me, the house had always something rather evil about it, and I was often frightened there at night. My bedroom was cut off from the main body of the house by the conservatory, through which you had to pass to reach the library – which had been built by my father on the model of the library at Renishaw, some twenty years before – and then climb up a small staircase to the room over it. I was so nervous at times, and felt so distant and alone, that I often used to creep quietly out of bed at ten or eleven, and stand in my night-clothes on this staircase I have mentioned, so as to hear the companionable sound of the voices in the room downstairs, in which it was customary for our governess and tutor to sit after dinner. Usually I could not hear what they said, and I certainly did not want to; I heard enough of their talk in the daytime. But on one occasion I, in fact, overheard what they were saying, when they were discussing my father and his illness without much apparent sympathy, and remarking how extraordinary it was to have a nervous breakdown just because you could not get your own way in everything.

In those days, I suppose, I was really devoted to my father, and possessed great faith in him and his wisdom. As I have said, he played for this and the following year or two a rather indirect part in our lives, affecting us more by the atmosphere induced by his illness than by the little we saw of him. But it was, notwithstanding, he who rescued me from my purgatory of religious fear. One day, when he happened to feel better, he sent for me and took me out for a drive. We had not met for some weeks, and though he was so ill himself, he noticed, directly he saw me, that something had gone wrong, and contrived to persuade me to tell him my secret agony. And I have always been grateful to him for the triumphantly clever and subtly imaginative manner in which he dealt with it. He realized at once that it would be no good to enter upon long theological discussions with a small boy, and that the whole matter must be tackled from a different angle and with a different point of view. On the other hand, it would not do to dismiss the matter too lightly. So he said, in serious tones, 'My dear boy, if you go to hell, you'll certainly find all the people you most admire there already – Wellington, Nelson and the Black Prince –, and they'll discover a way of getting you out of it soon enough!'

This answer completely disposed of my childish terrors, and every night I would think of my favourite heroes organizing the powers of hell, disciplining their ranks, and in the course of eternity recalling them – if only in a moderate form – to virtue.

CHAPTER THREE

With an insuperable repugnance I face, in writing about it, the prospect of going to school for a second time. As I am thus obliged to concentrate my mind upon it, the sensation amounts almost to physical nausea, to the feeling of being lost, isolated, of waking up in a strange place and wondering who and where you may be, of being utterly disorientated and confused in the world of the senses, so that what you touch and see is not what your neighbours touch and see, your north is not their north, nor your south their south.

I see in my bedroom, for a week or so beforehand, that terrible play-box (how ironical a name!) of white wood, with – painted on it, plainly and immensely in black – as if it were tarred and feathered upon it – those impersonal initials F.O.S.S. I see the preparations, the fussy packing and consequent unpacking; I hear the worried, excited voices, rather pleased but argumentative, crying, 'I can't have forgotten the soap, can I? The only thing is to see . . . We shall have to unpack again', or discussing the various essential items of clothing and impedimenta, figuring in the printed list issued by the authorities for the help of the parents, and classified in the cant terms of the school.

I see, too, the badges of my degradation, the hideous garb laid out; and the things intended to compensate one for it in the imagination, the supplies of oranges, biscuits, Suchard chocolate in slabs, – all, again, purchased strictly in accordance with rules laid down in the encyclical. Then I remember nothing more, until the afternoon of the day itself, when I found myself somehow or other in my mother's sitting-room in a hotel in London, and an elegant, perhaps rather cynical friend of hers – a rich young man, who was a sybarite, and possessed his own hansom-cab, both horse and vehicle polished from head to foot, and driven by a personification of every smart hansom-cab driver of the time, with a hoarse voice, and a red, smiling face, a top-hat, and a red carnation in his buttonhole, – was pressing a sovereign into my hand. As he accomplished this conventional act of tipping a schoolboy, he also, however, gave me a piece of unconventional advice for which I have always been grateful to him. 'Don't believe what everyone tells you, that school is the happiest time of your life. Or you'll be miserable. It isn't. You'll hate every moment of it.'

Then follows a lapse, again, until my mother and I were getting into the train that afternoon. In the darkness, we only knew which station it was because the masters and school officials were bouncing up and down the stained, damp platforms, barking questions, and asking names. Then followed a drive through wet darkness in a rolling cab. We arrived: a bright maid, in a white apron and a cap shaped like a petrified blancmange, opened the door and ushered us into the drawing-room.

I do not know how long we were in the room. I could feel the talk, but no longer hear it, for I knew the moment was drawing near. My mother got up to leave, in order to catch her train back to London. Suddenly she began to cry. I felt this in a thousand different ways. I could not comfort, or attempt to comfort, her in front of the other four new boys – unknown quantities – or in the restraining presence of the headmaster's sister. My mother was the only parent who cried, and I perceived that the rest of them disapproved of it. Indeed I appreciated that, had she possessed the ordinary modicum of common sense, she would not have broken down at all, and I was profoundly grateful to her for not putting herself in such a category. Her sobbing was something that, long after she had left, I could remember. Now the headmaster entered, to say good-bye, and it was plain that he and his sister both despised us for our softness. But, though I suppose there was never technically a bigger 'cry-baby' than myself, I courageously, or more probably, obstinately, refused to weep.

Dry-eyed, I faced my weeping mother. Now she was at the door, had left. That moment was here, that moment which, in its solemnity and terror, only death can rival. The headmaster's sister turned towards the boys, and said, 'Now, dears, I'll take you through into the school.'

She led the way from her comfortable, rather overcrowded room – outpost of civilization – to a heavy red-baize door that blocked the passage. She opened it, and we were in a different world. The air was full of an astounding clamour, as loud with cries and yells and clatter as any madhouse in the eighteenth century. We saw a vista of bare corridors, and of class-rooms with bare floors, reformatory benches with inkstains, inkstands and iron clamps; it was scented appropriately with the aroma of rusty iron pipes and the sour smell of ink and clothes from the lockers. Boys of various ages were milling round the rooms, shouting, screaming, singing and hitting. A calm fell, as Miss Wolfe was seen.

'Cornwallis,' she cried, 'act as shepherd for Sitwell.'

This injunction sounded comforting in a biblical way. But no sooner had the door clanged behind her than the din started again, and I was surrounded by a mob of small boys, who bore down on me like a cloud of locusts, to devour my self-esteem. This *was* the moment; the moment that has always, since that time, made me dread arriving in any place strange to me, mess-room or country-house, hotel or lecture-hall, hell, or heaven even. (How was it possible to learn, for example, to identify the faces glaring round me?) Already the air resounded with heartening shouts of 'Here's a new scug'. The word was not familiar to me as yet, but it was plain, from the very sound of it, that its application could not be regarded as complimentary. 'What's your name?' 'Your *name*, baby . . . ooo! Who's a cry-baby? – not your Christian name.' 'What's your pater?' 'I bet he's a scug like you are!' – all this punctuated by hundreds of little kicks and punches, token payment of what was to come in due course. As for my shepherd, he appeared to be resting from his crook. Indeed, at moments, he took a leading part in the inquisition.

The fashionable private school where I was sent bore the reputation of being a very good school, among the best of the period. The parents felt, I believe, that so long as they had to pay a great deal of money to keep their boys there, it must be a good school. They spared no expense. There was not within these precincts, so far as I am aware, any case of lice, impetigo or of the other complaints that arise from living in dirty conditions. Cases of severe illness were comparatively few, because small boys are tough, nor do I recollect, during the terms I was there, a single instance of an inmate dying. But the conditions to which we were submitted would not for an instant have been tolerated in a State school. The long line of closets, with no open doors, and only flushed once every few hours, were a typical feature of this life so revolting to civilized beings. When we had baths, only once a week, the boys, eight or nine in number, of a dormitory would have to wash their heads and bodies in the same thick, viscous, warm water. As for the minds of the boys, they were scatological, certainly, but free of any knowledge of sex. The good points that they showed, such as their manners, except to other school-boys, were due to the homes from which they came, rather than the school to which they were sent.

To give the reader an idea of it, this place could be regarded as a miniature model prison, essentially middle-class, with all the middle-class snobbery and love of averageness, but lacking the middle-class comforts. The whole system, the meals, the ways of speech and thought were middle-class, and in this manner – for I was used to a different background – strange to me.

It was too late for me to suffer a religious crisis; that had passed for ever. Therefore, I was debarred from the enjoyment of imagining the tortures that in due time would so rightly be inflicted on several, indeed, the majority, of my small companions. And if the reader has seen how it was that my belief in a conventional hell – I dare say, quite wrongly – was dispelled, I must explain, too, that it was the conception of heaven that I derived from reading the Book of the Revelation according to St John – the girdles and crowns of gold, the glass seas and harps and harmoniums – which convinced me that this region also would provide no desirable residence for me – nor for anyone else. The opulence, the abundance of opal and chrysoprase and jasper and cedar-wood, offended my taste then, as later did their recurrence in Oscar Wilde's *Salome*. These slabs of semi-precious stone were too material in the beauty they offered. The saints were content, it seemed, to cast pearls to the starving; better a crust now. Notwithstanding, I felt the appeal of Christianity more strongly than ever before. And the works, too, of Charles Dickens, that champion of the oppressed, though I had always loved them since I first began to read, came to have a new splendour, as well as their abiding attraction.

There was not much time, though, for reading Dickens: whereas the hymns belonged to every day. As I heard the rolling, pious voices of the masters, I often wondered how they ventured to join in them. I hated them – with one exception: the music-master, who happened to be Cecil

Sharp, and only visited the school at intervals. No doubt unjustly, I saw them as so many uninterested and mentally lazy men, who tired themselves out with physical exercise, to such a degree that they were fit for little else. They would return from the football field, drenched and dripping with green sweat, panting and hollow-eyed, and with an incipient death-rattle in their knotted throats. Naturally, they were not inclined to exert themselves again until the following afternoon, when they would play once more: even their pipes, in the masters' room, could not bring them solace. A few Latin tags, a knowledge of the more reputable parts of the Bible, an aptitude for footer and cricket – and, of course, fives; that, they knew, was what got most gentlemen comfortably through life. But while, of course, they liked every boy to be of the same mental height, and with nothing odd, or 'weird', as they would have said, about him, yet they did not actually *want* unusual boys to be beaten to death in the dormitories, for that, too, would have been unconventional, and would interfere with the games: and so to a certain extent they exercised a watchful attitude, at first sight apparently kindly, but really very impersonal, over their charges. Nor, except for the headmaster – and he, only for flagrant offences –, did they flog their pupils themselves. Perhaps they were too tired.

The days went on: that was the sole comfort to be pressed out of them. Perhaps the end of the week was of slightly better colour than the beginning, and Sundays had about them a tinge of their own, undeniably more pleasant than that of the others.

To begin with, one got up an hour later in the morning, and the hard-boiled eggs bore upon their shells a date more recent than was usually the case. After breakfast, we lounged about a little, and everybody was in an amiable mood. Indeed, I recollect the hour before church as always being sunny, and invariably associated with flowers, because on that morning we were allowed to wear buttonholes.

Sundays offered protection. In the mornings, you were safe in church – unless, better still, your cold proved too bad for you to go out. We walked in the afternoon, returning in time for tea, and had then to write our letters home – though these were subject to censorship by the school authorities. They afford certain clues to my character, as it was developing, indicate my backwardness in some respects, such as spelling, while they provide, too, evidence of my intense love for my mother, shown by patient remonstrances with her concerning her bad – indeed almost indecipherable – handwriting, and by the way I teased her about her feminine horror of rats and mice and insects, no less than by the more direct pleadings with her to come and see me.

I lived for her visits, and she, with her violent and uncontrolled nature, responded and came to see me, no doubt more often than was good for me; in the sense that it was difficult for me to 'settle down', as the matron said, or, to put it in another fashion, to acquiesce in my own misery. I was fortunate in being her favourite child, and in thus obtaining much of the love of which my sister was deprived. And though I saw the sufferings of this young creature, it was difficult for me to realize the extent of them; for I was privileged to the degree that she was penalized. Edith still remained in the schoolroom, and so was seldom as yet allowed to come down to see me.

If my mother were late, either because she had taken the wrong train, or because the trains were delayed by fog, which seemed always to be present, I had to wait, sometimes an hour or more, in the small room in which the boys met their parents. The matron, with her white cap, tied under the chin, and her sallow complexion that seemed designed to draw attention to her curative systems, her salves and boluses, would look in from time to time, and say, with a certain acerbity coating her native kindness, for she believed in 'hardening' the boys – 'Fussing again, Sitwell, I suppose. You *are* an old crock!' And then she would hurry out, because she had to dispense continually the various, but sparse and Spartan, remedies of her eighteenth-century pharmacopoeia: iron, castor oil, licorice, and Gregory powder – and, of course, there was always rhubarb, an immense shadow in the background. Even the matron's abruptness could not depress me for long. I paced up and down, and stopped to listen intently. And sooner or later, I would hear my mother's footsteps – I did not like to open the door and look down the passage, because such a show of feeling inevitably would constitute Bad Form. At last she would come in, bringing the fragrance of tuberoses and sweet geranium, kiss me and take me for a drive. (I think that she felt, as I did, the necessity of getting right out of the place.)

The last few days of the term brought with them a sense of longing so intense that each night it seemed incredible that one could continue to live, to breathe until the next morning. Even the examination at the end of the term became dear to one, as being the final obstacle interposed between school and home. Nevertheless, the last day, known as *Pay Day*, was singularly – to a new boy, surprisingly – horrible: more so, perhaps, because the name suggested something pleasant. But it transpired now that all through the term the masters had been keeping the sum of each pupil's trifling offences – untidiness, bad handwriting, answering back, laughing in class, upsetting inkpots, or flicking paper darts about in school hours. On that morning they totted them up inexorably, awarding the evil-doers so many bad marks – known technically, in the prison-jargon they encouraged, as 'scug-marks'. These they made you pay off in the afternoon, by keeping you in, and at work; a more severe punishment, when the prevalent state of excitement and, even, train-fever is taken into consideration, than it sounds at first. *At work*, I have written: but I must modify this statement by substituting the words, *by making you work as far as you were able* – since it was difficult to see out of two black eyes, or to concentrate with a head so confused. Because there was a corollary in the junior world of the system adumbrated above. The morning, while the masters were reckoning the crimes, had been left free for physical torture. Vague and rather menacing references to Pay Day during the previous few weeks by their older school-fellows had yet in no way prepared the new boys for the treat to come: they entertained no idea of what was in the wind, since their elders of every kind had been careful not to tell them. For the bigger boys had all through the term been preparing their own, and much more fanciful, scores. The new boy, in the highest of spirits at the idea of returning home the next morning, his head full of friends, meals, favourite amusements – in fact, fun –, would emerge from the buildings to cross the yard. Suddenly four or five bullies would bear down on him. He would find himself being led off into some quiet corner of the playing-ground, at the far edge, as it were, of the whole concentration camp – to one of the fives courts for choice, since the enveloping configuration of them enabled the masters not to notice what was going on (if they had seen, they would have been obliged to stop it), and served also to muffle the cries.

As for the small victim himself, he knew that the next day he must go back to his home, revealing plainly, by various contusions and discolor-ations, his unpopularity, the little esteem in which he was held, both by the masters – in spite of their mealy-mouthed assurances that he was 'quite a popular little feller' – and by the boys. He was, in fact, left to find what pleasure he could in the reflection that in two or three years' time he too would be able to vent a senseless spite and rage upon those smaller, weaker, and sillier in a childish way, than himself.

My holidays were spent at Gosden with my grandmother, for my mother had gone abroad to join my father. My grandmother never alluded to my black eyes, for she was a wise old woman who understood the secrets of both pride and humility.

I remember little of these, my first holidays. I was, perhaps, a little lonely, for my parents had taken Edith with them. Everyone round me seemed so old: yet, when to myself I appeared to miss the society of those of my own approximate age, I reflected philosophically that, so far, I had not much cared for the company of such of them as I had met. Yet I liked to be treated as being old myself, and I recollect, when my grandmother asked me to help her choose a governess for Edith how much flattered I felt by such a tribute to my years, and to my understanding of human nature. We interviewed together many applicants, and in the end our choice fell upon Helen Rootham, then a very young woman of the most vivid character and temperament. With dark hair, and eyes of almost Spanish vehemence, she possessed a passion for truth and justice, together with a love and understanding of the arts, and especially of music, which was of the greatest service to my sister and, indeed, to all three of us. Helen was undoubtedly super-sensitive, apt, even, to be censorious, but she was the first person we had ever met who had an *artist's* respect for the arts, that particular way of regarding them as all-important – much more important than wars or cataclysms, or even the joys of humanity –, without which it is impossible for a painter, writer or composer to achieve anything. Moreover, at the moment, my sister, whose character was fast developing, found it harder than ever to please my parents: but in Helen Rootham she found a champion, and we all gained a friend. She was a pianist of the most remarkable quality, perhaps the finest woman pianist it has ever been my good fortune to hear. There was no mistaking the fire and magnificence with which she played. And from the moment she came to us, during my next holidays, the music of Chopin and Schumann, Brahms and Debussy, flowered as a constant background to our hours of leisure, and became associated at Renishaw with every expanse of water, every vista seen through green trees. The rooms there were filled with her fine and sensitive interpretation of this music, into which she poured her fervent spirit.

As the first holidays swept, at an increasing tempo, nearer to their end, a tremendous depression enveloped me. My grandmother must have noticed it, since she allowed Jane, the housemaid, to conduct me for an evening to a delightfully rustic and rather slatternly circus, held in an enormous tent on a neighbouring common. In the darkness outside, you could see animals tethered by the tents, a few goats that belonged to the villagers perhaps, while the elephants trumpeted from near by. The arc-lights spluttered under the dingy white canopy, and Gypsies and clowns lolled about without much discipline, equivocal, belonging in part to the audience, in part to the ring. The spangled ladies pirouetting on the broad backs of their horses had, for all their sparkle, a soiled vagueness, almost a sadness underlying it.

When I returned, the faces round me had grown the more threatening because of the rest and refreshment their owners had enjoyed. Bullying was no longer stale sport, and they entered with zest upon a further, and longer, period of it. The very horror of this life rendered the few freakish escapes from it as enchanting as is a fine day in the English summer. One such spell of freedom occurred soon after I had gone back to school, and once again I welcome the combined force of northern gales and southern breezes that for a single day it brought me. My mother and my father – and him I had not seen for over a year – had arrived in London from abroad, and had expressed the wish for me to spend a day with them in London. The school prospectus stated plainly that no exeat was allowed during the term – except, of course, for the Eton and Harrow match. It was most irregular – but in view of the circumstances, it was decided to make an exception in this case, and accordingly my father was sending his servant to fetch me the following morning.

I could hardly sleep for excitement, and at 7.30, while the boys were still getting up, I went downstairs in my best suit – even that fact brought a sense of escape – and there in the drawing-room, amid the fretting decoration and accumulated and detailed furnishing, among the delphin-iums, shedding dry blue heads on the parquet floor – chrysanthemums were over for the moment and it was too early, still, for sweet peas –, I found Henry, looking unusually sunburnt, and as congruous in this setting as a whale in a china-shop. We started off at once towards the station, across the golden meadows of the morning.

He told me that my father was 'quite himself again', though he would not admit it. Nevertheless, he still suffered from relapses and, as it happened, that very morning, when I arrived in London, he proved to be too ill to see me, except for a few minutes. I found him lying listlessly in a darkened room, with a look of such extreme dejection that it saddened me for the day. I spent the rest of it with my mother and Edith, and was taken to drink chocolate at Charbonnel & Walker's in Bond Street, then the chief place where children of the richer sort were conducted for a treat.

Henry accompanied me back to school in the evening – but I recall nothing of the journey. The light had gone out of the day. Fortunately, as soon as I arrived, it was time to go to bed.

The grand fête of the school year took place in the summer: the exeat for the Eton and Harrow match. I would really have preferred to go home, but it was recognized by boys and parents alike, that this, albeit officially permitted, in order to placate those pariah-fathers who could not easily afford such treats for their children, entailed an inevitable loss of caste. But in the end I went to stay with some cousins, and so was able to attend the festival. One had to sit there, clad in Eton suit and top-hat, for hours, watching the cricket or pretending to do so. For the rest, I observed with interest the smug-faced crowds, the happy families, that promenaded in the intervals, keeping in clumps, across the ground.

Soon after this break came the first summer holidays, and we spent that lovely, long spell of hot weather at Renishaw. Freedom would have been complete, except that I found myself provided with a tutor, who followed me everywhere, and prevented Sacheverell and myself from ever going out alone. Beyond that, I could not help feeling that it was unfair that I should be plagued with lessons in the holidays, too. I wanted to go for a drive in the pony-cart round the woods, to walk with my mother in the gardens, to listen to Edith playing the piano, to fish, to catch butterflies with Maynard Hollingworth, to eat fruit in the orchards – and here I was, doing sums again, or hitting a ball with a bat. I complained: but my father countered by pointing out how woefully bad I was at my work, and how shameful a lack of interest I displayed in games. Within doors, puff-ball had now succeeded ping-pong as the recreation of master minds – but even for that I showed no aptitude. How could I wonder that he had felt himself obliged to find a tutor for me? He was sure he only wished it had not been necessary; it was a very grave expense.

The real advantage of engaging a tutor consisted, of course, in the fact that his employment by parents of a certain fortune enabled them to continue to evade the responsibilities of parenthood, during the holidays as well as during term. But from the point of view of the children, it was a detestable arrangement. Somehow or other, no walk was ever so nice, no game ever so enjoyable, in the company of a tutor, whereas things you disliked became to a similar degree more hateful. Nevertheless, a tutor attended us during every holidays, except for the Christmas vacation, which we spent regularly for several years at Blankney; where, as will be seen in the next chapter, there were enough resident and visiting spoil-sports to regiment a whole pack of children.

Sometimes Sacheverell and I would spend a whole morning in the pantry; where Henry now reigned. Stephen Pare, fixing his large, melancholy, nearly sightless eyes upon a silver bowl, which he held up to the light, so as to catch its glint, would be polishing it and acting as chorus for the great man. He did not talk much, but would chuckle quietly, as he drew Henry out, prompting him and leading him on, but when a footman entered, they would both look solemn and disapproving. From where Henry stood, near the window, with his name incised on the pane, he could see everything that was going on outside. The St Bernard, in his large kennel, would gaze back at him with an equal stubbornness, and sometimes a workman or farmer would call a greeting to him through the open window. Pare said to him – for Henry, though now promoted to be butler, still called my father in the morning –

'And how is Sir George today, Henry? I haven't seen him.'

'Well, when I called him this morning at five o'clock, 'e was laughing fit to kill 'imself. He was, really, Master Osbert. He laughed and laughed – never seen 'im so jolly. He 'as all sorts of good jokes up there by 'imself. Only 'e doesn't let on to us.'

At this moment, my father's resonant, rather thin voice could be heard echoing down the stone passages:

'Henry, have you seen Master Osbert?'

'No, Sir George . . . I thought I heard him just now. He'll be at work, I expect.'

Or he would be heard asking for the agent or the clerk in the office, or answering in pained, patient tones, 'Yes. Wha-a-at is it?' or demanding that more workmen should be sent to help with the erection of the two statues he had bought in Italy, of Neptune and Diana. He was, indeed, beginning to be himself again, and the garden was cobwebbed with ropes and full of pulleys.

He had gone now, to the library, or to one of the seven rooms in the house which he used for writing, covering chairs and floors and tables with a thin layer of business letters and notes of antiquarian interest. 'You see, with my system, I can put my hand on anything I want . . . Let me see; where have I put it? . . . Just for the moment, I can't find it.' But perhaps the housemaids, who had strict orders never to touch the papers or attempt to tidy them, had been dusting, for almost immediately a bell rang. As Henry remarked, it was difficult to talk with any enjoyment when the bells never stopped ringing. You couldn't settle down to a subject. 'Sometimes,' he added, 'I wonder what would happen, if ever they had to do anything for themselves. There's Major Viburne, ringing again for those primrose-coloured boots of his. He wore them at Balaclava, and the socks go with them. Not a bit worn-out. Only been to the wash once or twice; that's what wears things out – that, and putting them on and taking them off . . . There's Miss Vasalt's bell. It always rings like that. "Would you mind bringing me a biscuit and a glass of port, Henry?" or "Aren't there any peaches yet? . . . How late they are!" The doctor's frightened about her health this year, she says, and's given her a diet. 'E told 'er it's dangerous for her to have anything but peaches and a glass of champagne between meals – every hour, she ought to have it. No wonder she's hungry, poor lady, and not a penny to bless herself with . . . O Jericho! That's Her Ladyship's bell – and hell to pay, by the sound of it. I'd be happier if I was a nigger slave!' When he came back – for he thought it best to answer that bell himself – I remember he told me about one of the gardeners, John Thurtle, who, like Ernest de Taeye after him, lost all his hair as the result of touching some plant. I do not know whether it was the erecting of Neptune or Diana in the garden, or the fact that he had lately visited Matlock, about twelve miles away, and watched bowler hats being turned to stone by the process of being thrown down a well, that gave him the idea, but he suddenly said: 'Have you seen John Thurtle, Master Osbert? Lost every 'air on 'is 'ead, and even his eyebrows and eyelashes. Not one left . . . My word, 'e looks peculiar! Something like an Ancient Greek.' Then, after a pause, he added, reflectively: 'I wonder Sir George doesn't 'ave 'im petrified and turned into a garden statue.'

CHAPTER FOUR

Blankney stood, a dead weight in the snow, pressing it down with a solidity pronounced even for an English country-house. For us it loomed large at the end of each year, and the roads of every passing month led nearer to it, an immense stone building, of regular appearance, echoing in rhythm the empty syllables of its name. The colour of lead outside, its interior was always brilliantly lit, its hospitable fires blazing, flickering like lions within the cages of its huge grates, so that it seemed to exist solely as a cave of ice, a magnificent igloo in the surrounding white and mauve negation. What was the purpose of these spacious, comfortable tents of snow, that appeared all the more luxurious because of being pitched in so desolate and empty a whiteness, and that were full of a continual stir? Ease, not beauty, was their aim; for beauty impeaches comfort, disturbing the repose of the body with questions of the spirit and, worse still, pitting the skeleton against its encasing flesh. The Saloon, chief sitting-room, was long and rather high, full of chairs and sofas, piled with cushions (the aim of which was plain, to get you to sit down and prevent you from getting up and so to waste your time), with tables with many newspapers lying folded on them, and the weekly journals, and green-baize card-tables, set ready for you to play. The light-coloured, polished floor had white fur rugs, warm enough and yet suggesting the pelts of the arctic animals that must prowl outside: but to counterbalance such an impression, there were tall palm-trees, and banks of malmaisons and carnations and poinsettias, a favourite flower of the time, a starfish cut out of red flannel, and the standard lamps glowed softly under shades of flounced and pleated silk that mimicked the evening dresses of the period. There were writing-tables, too, and silver vases, square silver frames, with crowns in silver poised above them, containing the photographs of foreign potentates, posing in their full panoply of flesh as Death's Head Hussars, or with flowing white cloaks and firemen's helmets, their wives, placed, with folded hands – silver inkstands and lapis paper-weights, and near the fireplace, two screens, cut out of flat wood, and jocularly painted, a hundred or so years before, to represent peasants in costume. On one wall hung a portrait by a fashionable artist, of my aunt balancing her second son in an easy position near or on her shoulder. There were many silver cigarette-boxes, ash-trays and boxes of matches of every size from giant to dwarf. Certainly the rooms had a supreme air of modish luxury, and no quality so soon comes to belong to the past – for the skeleton outlives its flesh. What more do I recall: the broad, white passages – out of which led the bedrooms –, so thickly carpeted, and the white arches, on one side of the corridors, looking down on hall and staircase? What else? The warmth, the fumy, feathery scent of logs and wood ash, and a lingering odour, perhaps of rosewater, or some perfume of that epoch, a fragrance, too, of Turkish cigarettes. And for a moment, I see the women, their narrow waists and full skirts, and the hair piled up, with a sweep, on their heads, or surrounding it in a circle. Above all, I hear the sound of music.

Sometimes a string band would be playing in the Saloon – Pink or Blue Hussars insinuating whole Hungarian charms of waltzes, gay as goldfinches – but more often the tunes would be ground out by innumerable mechanical organs. There seemed to be one or two in every passage. You turned a handle, and these vast machines, tall as cupboards – objects which, since they have been superseded by gramophone and radio, would today constitute museum pieces –, were set in motion, displaying beneath their plate-glass fronts whole revolving, clashing trophies of musical instruments, violins that shuddered beneath their own playing, frantic drums, tambourines that rattled themselves as at a séance, and trumpets that sounded their own call to battle. I scarcely recollect the tunes they played, overtures by Rossini and Verdi, and – of this I am sure – some of the music of Johann Strauss's *Fledermaus*. The warm golden air of these rooms trembled perpetually to martial or amorous strains, yet they are not in memory more characteristic of the place than are the sounds of the family voices, variations, that is to say, of the same voice. For this house was the meeting-ground of all the generations surviving of my mother's family. I hear, too, something scarcely less typical, the quarrelsome, rasping voices of packs of pet dogs, demanding to be taken out into the cold air, their bodies surrounding the feet of the women of the house, as they walked, with a moving, yapping rug of fur, just as in frescoes clouds are posed for the feet of goddesses. And as, at last, these creatures emerge into the open air, they bark yet more loudly, jumping up, lifting their ill-proportioned trunks to the level of their mistresses' knees.

The house, the church, the stables, the kennels formed a dark and solid nucleus, a colony in this flat landscape that did not exist: the village was somewhere near, yet out of reach as the equator – perhaps it was interred under the snow. For an hour at midday the cold yellow daylight poured down, else always it was mauve against the electric light. Snowflakes scurried past on the east wind, that lived so conveniently close, in the sea, just beyond the edge of the negation; of which all one knew was that somewhere in it, about eleven miles away, stood the ancient city of Lincoln. This town shone, indeed, in my imagination, as a kind of Paris, a *Ville Lumière*, beckoning across the plain. But until it was reached, there was nothing, neither hills, nor mounds, nor mountains, nor trees – nothing except stretches of flat whiteness for hounds to run over, or occasional gates or barriers of twigs for red-coated, red-faced men to set their horses at.

Nearer, in the park, and in what must have been the meadows beyond – but until a few years ago I never saw Blankney at another season, so could form no idea of the country buried under this enveloping white shroud – were many enormous pits, containing whole armies of Danish invaders. Of this my father informed me, for, to tell the truth, he found himself, had he permitted the existence of such a word, bored, in a house where all the interests were of a sporting nature, and, in consequence, called his bluff. Moreover, it was made worse for him by the fact that the remainder of the guests enjoyed themselves to the same extent as he was miserable. Pure self-indulgence. But he could always find solace, he was thankful to say, in thinking over historical associations – so long as they were of the correct period. And here he was fortunate, for the great slaughter, of which these pits were – if only you could see them – the abiding sign, had taken place between AD 700 and 800, and nothing much had occurred in this district since then to spoil the idea of it.

In fact, my father shone at these family gatherings with a lonely and peculiar lustre, since he was the only man of intellectual pursuits who appeared in the small court centring round my aunt and uncle. (On the other hand, my uncle admittedly knew more about music than my father could ever begin to comprehend.) But, in general, I realize, now that I have read *The Chronicles of Clavijo*, that most of the other male guests of his age would have probably felt more at home at the court of Tamerlane the Tartar than in the contemporary world, and would have formed the most appropriate leaders for a new Golden Horde. They were scarcely at ease out of the saddle, and tended to fall asleep if they entered a house and sat down for a moment, except at meals. They were all tall: for height was an ideal in this circle; everyone, especially the women, despised the undersized as elsewhere the talented look down on the half-witted – and it may be that this natural response was not so stupid as it would seem, since, for example, big men are more sure of themselves, less disposed to want to force their wills upon those with whom they live. Further, with an exception or two, they were good-looking, with the gloss and ease – and the generous outlook within narrow limits that accompanies these particular qualities – of those whom the world has always treated well. But, though in their fashion they were most kind, yet if during the daytime a spare moment not already occupied with slaughter occurred, it, too, must necessarily be devoted at once to killing: otherwise they would consider they had wasted their time. No small creature on four feet, no feathered thing with wings, as it ran over the snow, was safe; neither the fox – but that was a lengthy business and very ritualistic – nor hare, shrieking its soul out like a human being, nor pheasants, designed so splendidly for a brief autumn, nor partridges, more discreetly clothed than those who shoot them, nor the dank, long-beaked birds of the marshes, snipe and woodcock, nor the ducks, with their hints of water in white and blues and greens, their bright feathers that might, when wet, so well be scales – none of these could hope for much mercy: while as for rabbits, they were collected by the attendants, put in sacks, and emptied out of them at a moment when there was no other killing to be had, so that tweed-clad hordes of men, and the women, many of whom accompanied them, could set their dogs on these confused, bolting creatures, and knock them on the head with sticks. Should these amusements fail, ratting could always be improvised through cellars or in lofts. Yet if the leaders of the Horde appeared to be consumed by some divine fury against the fowls of the air, and the soft, furry beings of the wild creation, perhaps in their own minds they compensated for it by their fantastic devotion to horses, their insane passion for dogs; the horses constituting, as it were, the gods, the dogs the angels or patron saints.

The men of the Golden Horde were almost as kind to children as to horses and dogs – though, naturally, they regarded them with less reverence –, but to any male of the species who did not run true to type, they could show an equal cruelty in many directions. For example, this was a generation that had been much addicted to practical jokes. Here the custom survived, and the chosen butt, recurrent every year, was a middle-aged, quarter-witted cousin, comfortably below the level of the stupidest fellow guest. He talked as though his mouth were full of sugar-plums, with a voice pleasant enough in sound, yet carrying the family voice beyond the characteristic to the pitch of anomaly and caricature, as, let us say, Charles II of Spain carried the Habsburg chin; moreover, he was wont, when in the grip of trivial misfortune, to bellow like a calf, accompanying the ludicrous inflections of his voice with angry but similarly absurd gesticulations.

The repertory of tricks played upon him every Christmas by the elect was simple enough; consisting of booby-traps of every kind, pails and sponges full of water balanced above doors or just behind them, fake telegrams sent and delivered, messages concocted, apple-pie beds, hens tethered under the bed and lobsters let loose in it. Most of the fun was physical. At dinner, while he was enjoying the food, the flowers, the flow of champagne, his face would be seen to be assuming gradually a curious shade, as though he were in the grip of some secret dolour – and so he was, the explanation being that as usual, each year, a mustard plaster had been sewn into the seat of his evening trousers. Though the children of the Golden Horde inherited a taste for practical jokes, and, albeit that it was, I regret to say, funny, this was not my sort of fun. The artist, like the idiot or clown, sits on the edge of the world, and a push may send him over it; there, I felt in my bones, but for the grace of God, went Osbert Sitwell. Edith, as the most sensitive person there, naturally hated the entertainment; nor, either, did my father much care for it; he too felt sorry for this poor buffoon, and, I think, secretly preferred his company and conversation to those of many others present. 'An interesting survival,' he used to explain to me, 'the type of medieval court fool.'

It was not possible here to find Henry, as at home, and relieve one's feelings by talking to him. His every moment was occupied, but more in amusement than in duty, for he too was a guest. He would be engaged in taking a lady's-maid out for a walk in the snow, in talking, singing, dancing – he was one of those elephantine men who are born to dance beautifully. The visiting servants lived in style, and were always addressed, ceremoniously, it was said, by the names of their master and mistress. Thus, Henry was translated into 'Sir George'. It would be no use my trying to grumble to the servants of the house, rank on rank; they were too impersonal and well-trained to talk. Only my uncle's former valet, Midwinter, a man of great charm, who knew everyone and could supply sufficient tact to furnish out a Foreign Office, who had something of Tweedledum in his composition, both in physique and character, something of an ambassador, something of the Italian Comedy, and a touch, perhaps, of Figaro, possessed individuality – only he, and Fat James, an enormous footman with powdered hair, who was apt to fall asleep while handing round the dishes.

What made luncheon particularly trying was this: it was the Edwardian mode of the moment for a large party to break up for this meal, and re-crystallize at little round tables for four or six, rather than sit at one long table as at dinner ('It makes it so much less formal,' people said; 'and more fun,' echoed the brigade, 'more fun'). And so it was far from easy for a child to know where he should sit or be sure whether he was wanted. As in all houses of this kind, the food, however delicious, carefully thought-out and elaborate, must nevertheless be bolted, the plates swept from the table, as course replaced course, with the greatest speed: this constituted the reaction against the lengthy Victorian meals, which the ruling generation was always deriding, referring to them as 'those awful Lord-Mayor's-Banquets'. But to the greedy the meals of the day must have proved a banquet of Tantalus; and I have often thought that, with this same set of people, the growing popularity of restaurants was due to the fact that in those places they were not chivied over their meals. The time, then, given to luncheon was short. Soon those who feasted must be at their killing again: it got dark so early – or, indeed, was hardly ever light –, and so those of the ruling generation wanted for these few minutes to engage in its own talk, to discuss the current or probable divorces of the time, which must not be mentioned in front of the children – nor, as for that, in front of the old, who were wont to look down their formidable noses at the mention of the word: whereas the Edwardians, though they did not smile on those who had been through the divorce court, fawned on those whose conduct should have entailed the process, according to former standards.

As for the old, though they would try to be amiable to the young, by now crossness had settled in their bones. The women seemed always to live on for ten years or more after their husbands, and dowagerdom possessed its own very real attributes. Moreover, they made their age felt through the medium of many devices. It was not, after all, merely that they *looked* old; on the contrary, they gloried in their age and the various apparatus of it, and indulged in a wealth of white wigs and fringes, sticks, ebony canes and Bath-chairs, while, as for strokes, these were *de rigueur* from sixty onwards. In fact, it was a generation which, unlike the next one, did not know how to grow young gracefully. Thus, my grandmother Londesborough was seldom now to be seen out of a Bath-chair, though she was still able to exercise her charm on us without effort, and equally to deliver the most portentous snubs when she wished it. Nevertheless, her world had changed. She possessed a stricter outlook, a more severe sense of duty, and all the rather naïve, unsophisticated courage of the Victorians, as well as sharing their genuine belief in the conventions.

In general, each Christmas the representatives of the older generation were the same, invariably numbering in their company my grandmother, her brother-in-law and sister, Lord and Lady Ormathwaite, and Sir Nigel and Lady Emily Kingscote. Lord Ormathwaite was even then over eighty – he lived to be ninety-three. Both he and his wife were of a deeply religious nature (it was very noticeable how much more devout were the old than their sons and daughters), and one of the favourite amusements of the children, I remember, was to hide in the broad passage outside the bedroom of this old couple, and listen to the vehement recitation of their lengthy and extremely personal prayers.

I do not know how much the old or the young enjoyed the parties – scarcely as much as the members of the ruling generation, I should say; to the old, certainly, these Christmas festivities brought a feeling of sadness, of deposition. Among the children, I am sure that the child who felt least happy, an alien among her nearest grown-up relations, was my sister. Acutely sensitive, and with her imagination perhaps almost unduly developed by the neglect and sadness of her childhood since she was five, she could find no comfort under these tents. She loved music, it was true, but the music of this house meant little to her, and the formal conversation between children and grown-ups, even if they were trying to be kind, frightened and bored her; while she did not care for the machinery of the life here; the continual killings seemed to her to be cruel, even insane. And, if anything, my father's inclination to nag at her on the one hand, my mother's, to fall into ungovernable, singularly terrifying rages with her, on the other, because of her non-conformity, seemed stronger when there were people, as here, to feed the fires of their discontent, and other children to set a standard by which to measure her attainments. But while my father was angry with his daughter for failing to comply with another standard – his own –, for not having a du-Maurier profile, a liking for 'lawn-tennis', or being able to sing or play the zither after dinner (it did not affect him that his wife's relations would have been very angry if she had attempted to play the zither at them), he was also disappointed on another score. She seemed far less interested than I was – or even Sacheverell who was only six or seven – in his stories about the Black Death (a subject he had been 'reading up' in the British Museum), and she seemed to have no natural feeling for John Stuart Mill's *Principles of Political Economy*. The Victorians, I think, appreciated Edith more than did the Edwardians.

Another permanent feature of these festivals, held, as it were, for the re-creation of the family spirit, was the number of governesses present: French and German governesses, governesses old and young – for governesses –, outdoor governesses and indoor governesses, governesses militant and governesses civil; the cause of this sensational plethora being that my uncle and aunt, hospitable equally by nature and tradition, invited hither for Christmas those who had instructed their own youth. None of these old ladies of assorted nationality ever went home to their own countries to live; they preferred to exist in subsidized, rather angry retirement in the suburbs; where, out of the faded splendour of their anecdotes, they peered unseeingly at their neighbours, as fish in glass cases look at you from their background of dried grasses. But these visits revivified both them and to a certain extent their anecdotes, and this brief spell now constituted the annual event to which, more even than to their three weeks by the sea, they most looked forward. It afforded them an admirable opportunity for criticizing the work of their successors, as well as to renew past friendships and, still more, to rekindle ancient feuds. For it, they prepared their richest wigs and most royal fringes, polished their beads, shook out, free of dust and camphor, their most splendid, but always discreet, dresses. Here, too, the oldest generation of French and German governesses fought again the well-remembered battles of Metz and Sedan. And the fact that none of their former pupils could speak any of the languages in which these ancients had been hired to instruct them (the members of the ruling generation were patently less cultivated than their parents), plainly by no whit lessened self-esteem.

Usually – to the rage of the servants, who hated them, and counted the consequent extra trouble to their score – they feasted upstairs; whence often their voices could be heard rising in shrill dispute. They descended to the dining-room, however, for special occasions; when, too, the children were allowed to sit up late. On such evenings, the guest governesses were determined to quell their successors by a show of suavity and a mood of high reminiscence, more than by open warfare.

One dreaded going out. The country on the other side of the long sheets of glass, some of which caught the light of the fire and so interposed a false glow, as of sunrise or sunset, between us and the snow, looked colder, much colder, than that round Renishaw even at this same season. It was impossible to tell the shape of it, what lay under the various blurring masses and deposits of white; white mounds, white tufts, white slabs, white undulations, the roads being only recognizable by dirty brown streaks in the snow. White roofs, white trees, these alone were to be identified. No snowdrift, however deep, was vast enough to prevent one from having to walk across – or, rather, above – the lawn to church. A path was swept, and, holding our prayer-books, we proceeded through this snow lane; for the weather was not allowed ever to spoil the sombre magnificence of our elders, no longer clad in the usual tweeds of the morning, but decked in the semi-sacred splendour that belonged to the late Victorian and the Edwardian Sabbath. The grooms and estate workers we passed were also dressed with care and a sort of smothering respectability. They wore, beneath their bowler hats, and protruding bangs of hair upon their foreheads, a look of ox-eyed and almost aggressive unwatchfulness, and they walked with a special, slow, Sunday gait. As we entered the church and sat down, there would be a little whispering among the congregation, and the governesses were particularly observant, to see how we children were behaving. Nudging or smiling was barred. My uncle took his watch out of his pocket, and placed it on the ledge of the pew, with his prayer-book, for he carefully timed the sermon, which he would not permit to last for more than ten minutes. But the whole service was short, and it was the half-hour which came after it that I really dreaded, since it had to be passed in the stables, under the almost professional eye of sporting relatives. They noticed with disapproval the repulsion I felt from these creatures to whom I was obliged to offer a carrot and pieces of sugar, and how I shrank from their slobbering over my outstretched hand.

We attended stables, as we attended church, in our best clothes, thereby no doubt showing the degree of respect due to horses no less than to the deity: but afterwards, before luncheon we changed into ordinary clothes. Though children object strongly to changing and especially to washing their hands, yet on these occasions, how hard, and with what delight, I used to scrub them, seeking to rid them of the horses' slaver. Nevertheless, we could not shed Sunday with our clothes; it remained an awkward, bad-tempered day. There was the sense of relief that church was over, and meals, it is true, were more delicious than ever, and tended to be longer than on week-days. But what damped the spirits of sportsmen and sportswomen alike, what rankled, was that convention forbade the killing of animals on this day. It was waste, sheer waste.

Looking back at those days, with their formality and ritual, there are several features of them that arouse amazement: the quantity of creatures killed every day, for instance, and the comfort in which the sportsmen went to the massacre. They fed, even when out shooting, as though preparing their strength for armed combat against a mortal foe. Another matter for wonder was, of course, the continual changing of clothes that I have mentioned; the guests always changed before tea, as well as before dinner. And though, as I have said, the children objected, the women no doubt took pleasure in it. There were always present here at Christmas certain famous beauties of the day – and the beauties of the Edwardian reign undeniably looked their best displayed in evening dress, by artificial light. They needed and enjoyed every inch of finery, every aid to allurement.

Little knots of maids and clumps of housemaids – phantoms who, in the next generation, were to inherit the earth – would be grouped together, like so many Cinderellas, under the arches above the staircase, to watch the party go down to dinner, noting, with envious feminine acuity, the silks and velvets, the huge puffed sleeves, the wreaths, the flowers, the jewels, the furs, the fans, the fringes and puffs. Many of these women, descending the stairs, already bought their clothes in Paris. The great fashions of the time, the moment when once again they became consciously fantastic, would not arrive for another few years, for we are yet in the first years of the reign. These dresses, for all the richness of their material, still possessed on the surface a kind of tasteless and disfigured naturalism, allied to musical-comedy standards, to the pink-and-white paper trees that do service for fruit-trees in the spring, and to the bumpy tunes. The favourite colours were mauve and violet and rose. As for the figures to show off these dresses, the fashions of the day aimed at particular but not general slimness. The thin woman, like the ugly woman, hardly aspired to be a *femme fatale* until Léon Bakst had introduced her as paragon into Western Europe. The waist, alone, had to be slim, the body must jut out in front and behind. The stay-maker, rather than the costume-designer, appeared to be fashion dictator of that time, and, though the waist had not to be as minute as formerly, a good deal of constrictive torture, comparable to that caused in the contemporary Chinese Empire by fashionable binding of feet, still existed. As for the rest, every adjunct must be conventional and costly; the dresses must be cut very low, while on the contrary the white kid gloves without which at dinner the women would have deemed themselves naked, and which could only be worn once, must reach as high as possible above the elbow.

It seemed as though this world, new born, would last for ever. One thing alone in this panorama might have suggested – though only then to those prescient to an almost prophetic degree – its coming disintegration. (Not, perhaps, that many of these people would have taken the threat very seriously, had they been able to foresee it, for the political doctrine of the Edwardian generation, as well as its altruism, was expressed very aptly in their favourite apophthegm – 'Never mind! It will last our time.') One object alone might have given them a vision of a civilization falling to chaos, and of the cities they loved, laid waste: the motor which sometimes tinnily vibrated and steamed in the frost outside the door; for this was the first appearance of the internal combustion engine which was to destroy them. A few of the older generation, it is true, fought the very idea of their ultimate destroyer, but this was because of the novelty of the conveyance, not because of any instinct for their own protection.

The news that my mother and I were going for a drive, had to be kept from my grandmother as carefully as from my father, so many years her junior. As for her contemporaries in the house-party, they could not help hoping, I conjecture, that one afternoon, this rare machine, puffing outside, would fail to return, and the audacious passengers with it. Further, it must be admitted that the accidents in which the motors of those days were continually involved, occurred as frequently, and often proved as fatal, as the bicycle accidents of ten years before or the aircraft accidents of ten years later.

This particular motor-car had inherited its features from horse-drawn carriages; a black, oblong creation with the seats facing each other sideways, with a top that opened and shut – I was going to say at will, but at any rate, under pressure, for it had first to be fought, and then knocked out and strapped down, as if it were a dangerous lunatic. This arduous combat was entered into on our behalf by François, the driver; a Frenchman who, wearing a dark coat and a black cap – for chauffeur's hats had not yet been invented –, sat at the wheel, in order to control his luxurious frisky machine. Just as the French tongue was acknowledged to be the language of diplomacy, since it offered the fullest scope for entering into the crafty devices and subterfuges that were necessarily the chief of any diplomatic business, so too, French, it was recognized, would constitute the medium between driver and motor, could it talk – in short, English for horses, French for motors. No Englishman could be found tricky enough to manage such a novel and temperamental contraption; a prejudice that is now history, crystallized in the English language by the word *chauffeur*.

Often I would accompany my mother and Sybil Westmorland when they went for a drive. Usually they would go just as far as Lincoln, in order, as they said, 'to get the air'; but these excursions at that date were also in essence romantic, similar to the night drives of King Ludwig of Bavaria, and an instance, too, of that passion for speed without purpose which members of their and the ensuing generation – including, I may say, myself as a motor-addict – were to develop to so intense a pitch that they could not be happy except at sixty miles an hour, or over: a passion which perhaps had begun in the attempt to escape from themselves; if only they could go far and fast enough, how different they thought the world would be!

At Blankney, I watched the Edwardian Age ripen. After 1905 or 1906, we stopped going there for Christmas and, though often the guest of my aunt and uncle elsewhere – for my aunt, despite her vagueness, possessed a very strong sense of family and tried to be kind to all her husband's and her own young relatives –, it so happened that I never saw it again until one summer's day, over thirty years later, when my cousin Hugo was to be married. This was in fact the first time that I had seen the country taken, as it were, out of cold storage. Then only was I able to form an idea of the configuration, of woods and meadows glowing now in a splendour of light, contained in that vast radiance held between sea and sky. All these things had been hidden by the snow, which at last had melted to reveal the surroundings, in the same way that the passage of time, flowing behind us, had revealed in the interval the trend of events, the fall of empires, the rise in their place of atrocious tyrannies. Now one could see the ground itself, but not the people it hid: my uncle and aunt were dead, Raincliffe, their eldest son, was dead: all the old were dead long ago: even the laughter of the fun brigade was silent. The kind of life itself which had been led here was rare today; Russia, Austria, Germany, in all three of which it had flourished, were empty of it. To live in that way would seem lonely, now. Looking back at it was like regarding some previous existence of which we had once been part. The house was just as it had been, though some of the rooms had grown smaller, while the various objects that a generation before had been responsible for evoking such an impression of luxury, now meant nothing, had attained a period air that made them almost seem to belong to a museum. Even the large portrait of my aunt and her son – the bridegroom of the day –, a picture which had formerly seemed so intensely of the present, had retreated into a vanished past.

CHAPTER FIVE

After my first term at school, I settled down – as it seemed for life – in a dunces' class, under a dunce master. Before long, I had reached a state of dunder-headed despair, out of the depths of which I could not rise. I could, for instance, pass no examination, since, in order for me to do my best, or even tolerably well, at anything, I had then – as I have today – to be congratulated very warmly and at frequent intervals upon my performance. I knew that I *could* do better, but the conditions governing such a hypothetical improvement did not exist. It was a cruel predicament, because I could find no way of escape; being comparable in that respect to the religious crisis in which I had earlier found myself involved, and wherefrom the reader has seen my father deliver me. For over a year I dwelt in so dark a valley, lived in so deep an abyss of spiritual misery, that the physical collapse ensuing at the end of it should have offered no matter for wonder to parents or masters. Illness, however, did eventually come to my aid. It freed me.

During my second summer term, a mysterious and novel epidemic, said to be of pleurisy, broke out. Since cases continued to occur, we did not again reassemble after the customary exeat for the Eton and Harrow match. My mother decided to take me to Scarborough, where, as our arrival was unexpected, I for once found no regular tutor in ambush for me. Major Viburne had, therefore, hurriedly to mobilize himself and his faculties, and come, every morning, a military figure, in his thin, primrose-coloured leather boots through the sunshine that lay in pools upon the asphalt paths, black and white like spotted dogs in reverse, that were such a feature of the town, to Wood End, some mile and a half away, so that he could teach me once again the rudiments of those things that I had forgotten at school. It would be true, I think, to state that both he and I possessed a genius for making my lessons dull. For myself, I had completely lost interest in work – and never found it again until I stumbled into my profession. I repelled with alternate attacks of fury and baffling dullness every attempt to instil knowledge into me. I made it plain that I knew nothing, and was determined at all costs to defend my sacred ignorance. In consequence, I became almost as unpopular at home as at school. Edith, accompanied by her new governess, had just gone to live for some months in Paris, in order to perfect her French, and my chief companion was Sacheverell. To everyone else – even to my mother, who did not pretend to any respect for learning – my conduct during the fourteen days or so that followed must have brought a sense of frustration.

The hours of liberty that I spent at this time possess, as I look back at them, a singular atmosphere, surcharged, perhaps because of my approaching illness, with feelings and impressions. In the East Riding, hot weather is rare enough, but now, for the short space, the whole town sweltered, though its green summer seas appeared so cool. A curious heat, veiled but glowing, brooded over the northern streets, flicked into life again at morning and evening, or at the change of tides, by a breath, brief and salty, of cold air. In spite of the mist, which compelled short perspectives, the parti-coloured shirts, with their pellucid yet aqueous tints that looked as if seen through clear, deep water, and the peaked caps of the jockeys, astride the ponies that drew the carts, quivered and shone as they rode by. Soon these light and rapid vehicles were to vanish from this scene, their only home, to which they lent so unique a charm, obscured by the dark clouds of the petrol fumes generated by the conquering motor-car. Already a little of the splendour had departed.

I did not often go into the town this summer. I suppose I felt too ill to stray far in the heat, and Sacheverell and I used for the most part to play inside the grounds of Wood End. The garden stretched in terraces down a hillside. Its most characteristic features were the rugged old elms at its boundaries, an ilex or two, their thick, sombre but glittering leaves projecting over the terraces, and offering the best possible shelter from the sun, and, at its western edge, in a far corner, built in the identical style as the house, and of the same stone, a square, four-storeyed tower. Everything about this lofty erection with its stone balconies and outside staircase and colonnaded cupola, level with the sunny green mounds of the tree-tops, was rusty, forlorn and derelict. The windows, smeared and dusty, and the locked doors creaked in a dark breeze that only blew within, and for no reason.

Through the misty panes of the bottom storey of the tower one could perceive nothing of the interior except the blowing, silken banners, tattered and grey, of the spiders' old triumphs, but, if one climbed the narrow stone steps to the first floor, one could distinguish the shapes of a number of large jars, and of ovens, that inevitably recalled Ali-Baba and the Forty Thieves, whose adventure I had lately followed in a pantomime, or the experiments of medieval alchemists: in fact, a perfect playground for small boys. We forced the door. The room appeared to have been deserted for a hundred years. But the apparatus, though it seemed to serve no purpose in the modern world, had actually been installed by my grandmother some thirty years before, in order that Miss Lloyd might bake there the china she made, and taught my grandmother and aunt, and later my mother, to paint. These objects, when thus embellished, used to be sold at bazaars, either in support of the Conservative Party, or in maintenance of a Home for Fallen Women which my grandmother had founded.

After a fortnight at home, it was discovered suddenly that I had developed a high temperature, and had evidently become afflicted with the same illness responsible for the early disbanding of my school. Now the whole tenor of life changed; everything was done for me, every desire, if its execution was conformable to my state of health, granted almost before I had expressed it. I lay in bed for nearly three months, in a large room cut off from the rest of the house. No longer did I suffer here at night from feelings of terror, for three nurses attended me, and one of them had to sit up all the time in the room with me. Nevertheless, the nights and days were distorted, and tinged equally with dreams, so that now they were difficult to disentangle. Certainly, however, this short period was the most important of my whole childhood, because it gave me that which is granted to so few children: time – apparently endless time – in which to think and still more to feel. In my mind the whole perspective of this illness and the months to follow is immensely magnified, no doubt because of its moment to me. Yet I inhabited no pleasant or comfortable world, though at any rate it was one in which the imagination could flourish without hindrance, was, on the contrary, helped and forced on. During the day, if I were not asleep and the room were not darkened, I lay watching through the broad windows the flights of charcoal-winged rooks flapping their way over the tree-tops into the sky, where, in a splendour of golden light, existed those cloud-continents that one so seldom for long examines, for, in health, the eyes prefer a world that is on their own level. But now I looked at them until, when I turned my glance back to the objects in the room, I could see little of these; I gazed at the shifting and melting castles, the fulgent towers and palaces, shapes that in their turn revealed processions from times past, antique and plumy triumphs of arches and spears and helmets and cars drawn by wild-maned horses, or, with a sudden change of scale, dissolved into superhuman torsos, their golden muscles rippling in the wind, or into the likeness of gods and furies, all these being brought to life by the flickering and hispid sun. I visited countries and kingdoms I was never to see again, equatorial vistas of sand, and snow landscapes with an organization of their own, more wild in architecture than the forms to which even limestone can lend itself, floating alpine heights built up in a golden flame that was like a lion's steadfast glare, vast cities washed by huge seas, that undulated in answer to the moon's call, through a mist of prismatic spume – metropolises of a thousand spires, a thousand belfries from which, very occasionally, I caught the sound of the solemn but brassy peals rung for immense victories I could not fathom, and then, my eyes dazzling with rainbows, I was forced for a moment to shut them, and so was asleep again.

During these many weeks I saw no one but my mother and the nurses, for Edith, as I have said, was abroad, and my father, with his neurotic dread of germs – perhaps a consequence of the long illness from which at last he was beginning to recover –, refused even to approach the door. Sacheverell, too, was forbidden to venture near the room, though he often surreptitiously made attempts to visit me. On the other hand, my mother came in to see me continually. Moreover, I made a new friend in the devoted chief nurse who looked after me, and this friendship, following on a period when I had acquired nothing but enemies, inspired me with a fresh confidence. In every direction, it was felt that the only thing to do was to let me have my own way: I could, for example, be induced to eat nothing I did not like, and every day I was brought either claret, burgundy, champagne or port, in the hope that I might drink them and that they would restore my strength – but no, though I tried them all, I disliked them and the blurred sense that they induced of all being well with the world for no particular reason. Indeed doctors then supplicated me with as much vehemence to partake of these wines, as, since I have been afflicted with gout, they adjure me, in equally old-fashioned style, to lay off them.

Convalescence was slow and trying, and the local doctors were in some doubt as to the nature of my illness, but they agreed in advising my family to take me to spend the winter in a milder climate. After long correspondence, and making inquiries of friends, a suitable villa was eventually found in San Remo.

San Remo is no more romantic than Margate, but it is, in landscape and people, Italian. And the very first morning that I woke on Italian soil, I realized that Italy was my second country, the complement and perfect contrast to my own. As I looked out of the window of my room, I knew that this was how I had always hoped the world would appear. There are painters who allege that the light in France or Holland – or even in England – is more beautiful, or at any rate better for painting: but this was the light I needed and in which I thrived. Here there was no necessity to struggle for breath with an encompassing and enveloping fog: here, on the contrary, was serene and aromatic air, scented on the mountains with herbs and in the valleys by orange-blossom, here was not the occasional, savage, polar light of the north, to which I was used, but light that was hyaline and yet varied, and such – I came to know later – as had given birth to the most perfect works of art in Western Europe. Light! Light was everywhere, spattering ceilings, walls and floors, even through the narrow slats of the green Venetian shutters, which were kept closed throughout the middle of the day, light from the sky and light from the sea – but how different a sea from that of Scarborough –, trembling, moving, affording an infinite richness of texture to every plain, dull surface. The whole landscape was made alive by light, even when deserted: though, when inhabited, the human being held to it so different a proportion from that comfortable importance which he maintains in relation to every part of our islands. Light vivified everything, there was no need for defiant colours. Since every stone glittered as though it were of gold, and every patch of lichen, even, swam in almond-husk green or rose, the vegetation here was darker, more grey than green, so as to afford contrast to the flowering skies and to the Mediterranean, with its tessellations of wine-colour and azure and copper, holding its hints of gold, and of a green more intense than that which clothed the land. And, as if the life-giving, creative light, besides calling out this entire range of colour, this wide vision of form, penetrated, too, to the heart of every human being, purifying it, I discovered the simple and unspoiled nature of the people of Italy, who laugh and cry and sing – or sang in those days – so easily. Moreover, though this town seemed comparatively new, something told me that existence here, especially among the fishermen and peasants, was immemorially old.

Forty years ago, the towns of the Riviera, both French and Italian, still possessed character. Even the railway stations of this coast were inviting, painted in light tones, festooned in the silliest, most light-hearted manner with pink roses and sky-blue convolvulus; guards and railwaymen sang and shouted cheerfully. As for San Remo, it was then a comfortable international settlement of square villas and oblong hotels, in cream and white and pink, set among tufted palms, with gardens of exhibition tangerine-trees, and of flowers like cockcombs, ragged and highly-coloured, resembling mad foliage rather than blossoms; all this being placed in a landscape devoted to growing the pink and mauve carnations, brittle, dry and rather scentless, of the Riviera, so that whole square miles had to be draped with sacking every afternoon to protect them against the coming of night. Above these arid parterres, divided by small trenches filled with water, stood the groves of olive, running up the hills on little loose-stoned terraces, while above the hills rose the mountains, clothed with forests, and crowned with bare rocks or snowy peaks. The various enclaves in the town, Russian, Austrian, Polish and English, possessed their own places of worship, and there was a church with onion-like bulbs, painted blue, in which the Queen of Italy's Montenegrin relations were buried. The shops were luxurious, many of them, and organized for foreigners, but the life of the town, and even of the villas, was Italian, though, as night released or gathered to itself this landscape, for those lingering moments, time and place were lost, and sea and landscape sunk once more into the Homeric world out of which they had come; a world which I comprehended instinctively, though I had read only so far feeble tales for children that had been gathered from the *Odyssey* by some pedagogue.

I took to everything under this sky and by this sea, the food, the fresh sardines, cut open and fried, the sour bread, the acrid black coffee, the flame-coloured persimmons; I admired the umbrageous garden of our villa, with flowers, few but strange, with orchids – can I have imagined it? – growing upon the branches, stout and mossy, of the trees, and the house itself, unluxurious, with a prim Scottish interior, here exotic and suggesting in equal proportions porridge and prayer-books, and with mosquito-nets, a secure but diaphanous shelter, on which in the morning the sun played as it does on clouds; I enjoyed the shopping, the walks, the rides on mules, the drives – and now, as if to complete life's perfection, Edith arrived from Paris to join us for a little. Though it was only six months since I had last seen her, I found my sister a changed person. Tall for her age, she already wore her hair up, the lank, green-gold locks puffed and frizzed now in the mode of the time, and she was encased, too, by my parents' orders, in clothes that, though no doubt designed to suit the young girl of the period, were most inappropriate to her gothic appearance. Still more, though, did I notice an alteration in her way of looking at things, for her absence from home – and, as a result, the discontinuance of the perpetual nagging to which for years she had been obliged to submit – had lifted the whole range of her spirits. She knew, now, that she would be going away again before long, and the result was to make her much more amenable, because hopeful. In the peace that she now obtained for the first time, no longer fearing every moment that she would be found fault with, able to attend concerts and go to galleries with her governess, and come back home without having to face scenes, all her interests had blossomed in the short interval that had elapsed, and music and poetry burned in her blood like fire. She had become the most exhilarating and inspiring as well as understanding of companions. And, in spite of her disfiguring, though expensive, clothes, the brown plumage, physically as well as mentally, of the cygnet had gone, and the swan's green-white ruffling surge of feathers had come to replace it.

Every day was fine, and often we would set out at an early hour in the morning for our expeditions into the hills. The particular person, whoever he might be, to make these decisions – sometimes my mother, sometimes the owner of a neighbouring villa who would invite us to join the children of the house for the day – would suddenly announce the previous evening that tomorrow would be a holiday. We would be ready to start at eight, and soon after that we would begin to climb the steep, cobbled tracks, the mules straining and striking sparks as they went, mounting higher, past cascades where, in damp, spray-blown crevices, grew tufts of maidenhair fern, hitherto only known to me as one of the prides of English florists' shops. The beasts would be continually exhorted by their attendants, smelling strongly of garlic, who walked silently in rope-shoes beside them and told them what to do. After twenty minutes or so, we would reach the level of the olive groves. On we would go, until it seemed as if we had been out whole days instead of hours, the mountain air filling the lungs, inducing a kind of intoxication of well-being. And now we were ascending the sides of the mountains themselves, and could see the flashing tents of the Alps beyond, with clouds floating from them as their pennons. Finally we would reach one or another of the deserted villages that are to be found on the higher slopes here; villages left empty after an earthquake some forty years before. We would unpack luncheon and eat it in the gardens of a roofless house, under the shade of orange-trees. In charge of us, usually, would be my tutor, or occasionally – and with what rapture all the children welcomed the change! – Henry.

As well as these rides, there were other excursions, drives in cabs, drawn by two horses wearing fly-switches and straw hats, *à la bergère*. The hoarse-voiced, extortionate cabmen who drove them, and wore on their heads fantastic short top-hats of patent leather, or bowlers occasionally of the same material, were hired by the hour, and so were determined to proceed at but a snail's pace. Better, more vividly than all else I recall my first visit to Monte Carlo. Motoring there – and that in itself still constituted an adventure – to have luncheon with my Aunt Londesborough, we arrived safely, only to discover that my mother, by nature unpunctual, had on this occasion overlooked the difference in time that existed between France and Italy, and thus had added an hour to our fast. In the unusual predicament, so far as she was concerned, of having an hour to spare, she spent the time in walking us round this citadel of naughty pleasure, as it then was, showing us its elaborate gardens and *tapis-vert*, in which every blade of grass ranked as elsewhere would a flower, and had to be watered separately, whereas each flower was common as a blade of grass, albeit carefully brushed every morning and sheltered every night. Even the leaves of the palm-trees appeared to be clipped like poodles, and numbered, the flower-beds to be creations as artificial as the large hats of the women seated by them, listening to the music of *Sole Mio* being played by a band in a café near by. After this agonizingly hungry interval, we were taken to luncheon at Ciro's, a Pompadour-1890 glasshouse built on a terrace.

After luncheon we walked across to the Casino, and, children not being allowed into the Rooms, we gained admittance instead into the theatre – that enchanting, square, ballroom-like theatre by Garnier – and it was there, while my mother and aunt were gambling near by, that I consciously made acquaintance with the music of Wagner, for the orchestra played the Overture to the *Meistersinger*. But music did not count here – only gambling mattered. And, though we had set foot on the sacred ground, and entered, as it were, into the very narthex, yet the vaulted halls of the Casino, haloed by legend, always retained for me thereafter the fascination of a forbidden place. Ever since that first visit, I have felt a weakness for Monaco, and for Monte Carlo, a place as unusual in its way as Venice, a pleasure-city built of plaster, its houses disposed along rocky ledges, sun-heated, its boulevards lined with oleanders, rose and crimson, and with the primrose hail of mimosas, instead of with plane-trees. As for the Casino, the heart of this principality, and in aspect as representative of its purpose as the most functional of the buildings of the 1930s, the stories I was told about it that day, so long ago, in order to frighten me – tales of wild gamblers who shot themselves, and corpses carried out in pianos – only succeeded in crowning it for me with a special aura of romance.

On the characteristic afternoon, spent in Monte Carlo, that I have been describing, my mother had *won*: almost the only occasion it ever happened. And consequently that same evening, while we dined, the garden of the Villa Teresa resounded with the songs, and trembled at the heavy antics, of two rival troupes of self-styled Neapolitan Singers, for whom she had sent hurriedly on her return, in order to celebrate her triumph over the tables. Through the French windows we could see them, dressed in appropriate costume, the men in red stocking-caps, blue breeches and white shirts, the women in square white head-cloths, wide red skirts, with tightly-waisted white blouses, standing in groups or dashing into action. They filled the night, illumined by lanterns which shone beneath the glazed leaves of the palm-trees, with snapping of fingers, and cries of '*Funiculì, Funiculà!*' with *salterellos* and *tarantellas*. My father was pained and worried, for he wondered how much the whole thing would cost: no such fears oppressed my mother. For once she had been able to obtain some money without asking him for it.

The life at San Remo must have been healthy for I got well very rapidly, though I still suffered from insomnia. On the night I have mentioned, I had been allowed to dine downstairs, but, as a rule, Henry would bring me my dinner to my room, and sometimes, as a treat, Edith would be allowed to share it there with me, and we would talk for hours. But usually by nightfall I was so tired that I would go to bed directly after dinner, and, though I tried to read for a while, would be so sleepy that I had to turn off my light and, the moment I did so, would fall into a deep slumber – only to wake up at two o'clock, with no possibility of getting to sleep again. Once more I would read, but this time with success and for a long period. I read everything I could find, though mostly these books consisted of exciting stories – in the Tauchnitz edition –, of treasure, long buried and mysteriously discovered, or of inventors who by chance had stumbled on a process by which they could turn all things to gold. Often I would still be reading at dawn, and would go to the window to watch the sunrise and look far across the Mediterranean, to where it was said that at this hour, as at sunset, one could distinguish the outline of Corsica, some seventy miles away. A kind of ecstasy kept me awake at the window, because at that age every child is immortal, and I could see in front of me an infinity of days, each one of which held the chance, even if it failed, of being as beautiful, as full of every kind of joy, as that which was dawning. Here I saw suggested, on these vast canvases of earth and air and sea, the sketch of another world that at points fitted into the one before me; a world hitherto hidden from me, and to which I felt I belonged – the world of the Mediterranean. Never again would it be possible to undergo the sort of hopeless misery that I have described. Henceforth one would at least be aware that other things could – and did – exist.

Only once have I been back to San Remo, and I found it then but a trivial and fussy shelter for the sick and elderly. A concrete border edged every former paradise. But in my imagination it still lives with a vividness and beauty which perhaps it never possessed. Moreover, in the course of the intervening years, it had become imbued with the colours and sounds of the other Italian towns which I had been able to see while still very young. And for this great pleasure and stimulus to mind and spirit, my father was responsible. We children accompanied him regularly to Italy or joined him there, even when it may have been inconvenient for him, and though it must have been expensive. Moreover, in spite of his prevailing parsimony, veined as it was with the strangest and most contrary extravagance (albeit this he would never acknowledge even to himself), he continually encouraged us in sightseeing and never grudged the money he gave us for visiting churches, picture galleries or palaces.

First in time came Florence, most austere of Italian cities, teaching the beauties of form more than of colour. Though in these days of my boyhood I would go every day to the Uffizi or Pitti, or to examine the innocent heavens and hells created by Fra Angelico in the Convent of San Marco, it is curious to look back and comprehend how little one absorbed consciously at that age, how much unconsciously. The early Florentine memories that come back to me are less of pictures – except for those of Botticelli, so singular in their apparent easy naturalism and in their actual extreme sophistication, with the naked toes of the figures dancing up from the flowering earth, and necks protruding like those of tortoises from their flower-spangled muslins, that they are not easy to forget – than of casual impressions that have remained: the granite shaft, for example, that once helped to support the roof of the Baths of Caracalla, in shade as far up as its capital, coming then into sunlight, so that the porphyry figure of Justice, with her bronze scales, showed with the colour of a Judas-tree in flower against the Italian sky, or, again, the pillared, delicately vaulted, open-air Flower Market, as it looked of a Thursday, the chief market-day, when it teemed with the accumulated riches of the Florentine spring, flowers simple and flowers rich, thick, rustic double daisies, tulips, with very pointed petals streaked in pink and white, sheaves of tuberoses and lilies, scarlet anemones, roses, dewy, as if the rain had touched them, huge pots of azalea, and wistaria, mauve or white, that seemed, in the way they grew, to carry their native oriental countries with them, and branches of blossoming trees resembling small white clouds that had floated under the arches; or the Lung' Arno in the sun, or finally – and who that has seen this can fail to recollect the first time he saw it? – a pair of milk-white bullocks, their horns garlanded with leaves of vermilion leather, pulling a creaking cart up the long slanting hillside roads, between two lines of thin-spired Tuscan cypresses.

Never, though, did I feel in Florence that same contentment tinged with wonder that always came to me in Venice – because, no doubt, my mind tends to be fleshly, or at any rate, sensuous; I prefer painting to sculpture, velvet to sackcloth, jewels to bones, the canvases of Rubens to the agonized mystics and saints, spread-eagled on dark panels, of Spain. And there exists no city in the world which, even today, though admittedly it can look dingier than Seven Dials or more garish than Blackpool, offers the same allurement and appeal.

My brother fell ill at Danieli's, and was confined to his room for a fortnight. This, though in itself a hard blow for a boy of eleven, was made worse by the prevailing darkness, for my father had taken especial trouble to obtain, both for Sacheverell and myself, rooms that were lit only by the original *bifora*, or small, delicately-arched gothic window, split in half and supported by a marble column. It was a favourite theory of his, and doubtless soundly based in esthetics, that a view looked amazingly different from what it would otherwise look, and infinitely more beautiful, if framed by a window of unusual shape. Certainly the gondolas and sailing-ships of Venice, the mysterious, shadowy canals, or the wide stretch of blue-green water, marbled by its foam, on which floated so lightly the stone raft carrying San Giorgio Maggiore, must be seen through a Venetian-Gothic window. (All the same, he would explain – another theory –, Venetian Gothic was not true Gothic.) It did not matter about Edith, she could have an ordinary bedroom, but he had been determined that Sacheverell and I should, each of us, enjoy this typical experience, which ought, in his favourite phrase, 'to prove splendid training'. But the necessary modern additions of glass and blinds and curtains made the single small aperture insufficient. Poor Sacheverell, thus immured, used to gaze longingly out of the window at the steamers starting for Dalmatia – for already he was familiar with the marvels of that country, since guide-books constituted his favourite reading, and was eager to begin his travels.

A genius – perhaps under-rated today – inhabited often at this time a small palace, painted the colour of bullock's blood, on the Grand Canal: d' Annunzio. But I never saw him here (probably he had gone to France), though he had been pointed out to me one day in Florence, on the steps of the Club in Via Tornabuoni, a small figure, wearing no hat, but very carefully dressed, and with several elaborate rings on his hands. He stood on the top step, partly in shadow, watching the people passing by, and talking nonchalantly to a friend, and as he did so, he fingered continually these rings, so that a stone flashed in one of them.

There were the smaller towns, too: Vicenza, with its vistas, its great mouldering boulders of stucco, through which the brick showed, its clouds of statues above the roof-lines of the palaces, its air of majestic and derelict calm, a theatre set that has achieved immortality, with, as the very heart of it, out of which the whole town grew, Palladio's own Teatro Olimpico, the most perfect theatre ever built. I will not discuss in detail the innumerable wonders of a hundred cities, but there were certain things seen perhaps only for an instant, in these places of such threadbare beauty and elegance, which indelibly impressed a young mind, and to which, when distressed or distracted, my thoughts would revert, finding in them a sort of refuge. Here, in these quiet places, it was possible to find an antidote to the vulgarity and growing brutality of the modern world.

I mention the effect, and lingering influence, of Italy on my brother, my sister and myself, because it provides a clue to the work which later we set ourselves – or which set itself for us – and have since striven, however imperfectly, to accomplish. By this path we came to the classical tradition, through the visual arts, rather than through Greek or Latin. In a sense, as artists, we thus belong to Italy, to the past of Italy, hardly less than to England, to that old and famous combination of Italian influence and English blood. We breathed in, without being wholly conscious of it, the space and proportion of Italy which for centuries gave grace to Western Europe and even to the Marches. We learnt our lessons in a school that teaches by example and feeling rather than by precept; we came to be able to tell good things from bad, to use our own judgement and not believe anything about the arts that we were merely told. So, though it is with what came to be known as the Modern Movement that our names will be associated, it was partly due to this same upbringing that we were able to perceive genius where it existed in unfamiliar guises, to understand at once – to take three things at random – the force and the fire of a Stravinsky, to see the constructive truth of Modigliani's peasants and the new element that had entered into the theatre with Monsieur Diaghilev's Russian Ballet. The several modern manifestations which we have championed in England, when they needed it, thus owe, through us, something to the past of Italy.

These cities and towns, then, and not the dull routine of my second school, nor the listless days at Eton that followed, appear, looked back on, to have represented the *real* part of my life.

CHAPTER SIX

I liked Eton, except in the following respects: for work and games, for boys and masters. Preparation for going there used to be elaborate in the extreme. The school was in mourning for the death of King George III. Yet even grief sincere as that which inspired this obligatory mute's outfit was made to serve the purposes of local trade, because we are a nation of shopkeepers, and schoolboys are for their part as conventional as other savages in their outlook; the correct top-hats, black coats, white ties, and shoes could only be obtained at monopolist establishments in the High Street. Thus I first saw the place, when, accompanied by Henry, I went there from Renishaw, in the golden and hazy days of a first week in September, in order to try on my suits – for which the cloth had been chosen by my parents and the rather amateur measurements sent off to the tailors some weeks before –, to look at my shoes, and fit the top-hat, let it be softened with an iron, or have a wad of paper inserted between the end of the silk lining and the leather flap. I remember the day so well, can almost breathe its air, for I had never been in this part of England before, had never before seen Windsor, the castle floating like a legendary gothic city upon its hill, or like a fragment from the Arthurian Cycle, yet so solid and robust for all its air of fable. Henry and I, I recollect, had luncheon that day in an Italian restaurant opposite the base of the Curfew Tower, and not far from the river – near enough for the aqueous light to throw a Venetian quivering upon the ceiling, and to illumine the enormous jars of lemonade which stood in the dusty window, surrounded by dry, crackling, lemon branches, no doubt supplied to the proprietor by his relatives in Naples or Sicily. Streams of holiday-makers, men with brown faces and without coats – then a very daring innovation –, and with, as part of their equipment, girls leaning on their arms, came from the direction of the river, and stopped to buy fruit at the many barrows, wheeled along by hawkers, who shouted their wares in broadest cockney.

In the summer holidays only a skeleton garrison of gowns and mortarboards held the scholastic citadel, most of the masters being engaged during the month of August in those usual Alpine exploits of theirs which seem so often to culminate in tragedy. It was extraordinary how delightful, easy, cheerful the school looked, without masters, matrons or pupils. Nevertheless, I dreaded going there. The day came nearer – steadily, inexorably nearer. Nothing, except death, could prevent its approach, nothing could cheer one up; so I thought. But my father contrived to delight me with one of the unexpected twists in his character; he provided me with ample pocket-money, and at the same time complaisantly presented me with a small, thin and extremely useful crib to Horace's *Odes*. This little book, a faithful friend to me for several years, had the Latin printed on one side, and a competent literal translation into English on the other side. Moreover, it was of just the right size, and easy to handle in class without fear of detection. In giving it to me, my father explained that he was not satisfied with the way Latin was taught at Eton; it was far better to read the English first, and know the rough meaning of what you were going to translate. In any case, he added, to use a crib only showed a determination to get on. And of his own contemporaries, the one who had shown most skill and persistence in cribbing had since achieved by far the most distinguished career, George Nathaniel Curzon, of Kedleston.

To my amazement, I enjoyed the first month at Eton, because of the comparative liberty the system offered, the novelty of being allowed to buy what you wanted, books, sweets, fruit; in consequence I remember the first few weeks with some distinctness. As gradually I came more and more to dislike the place, I recollect events, such as they were, less easily. There were the feasts, going to breakfast on a Sunday with one of the masters, Stone or Vaughan. 'Toddy' Vaughan, as he was called, had been a housemaster for several decades, and to me the fact that he had been abroad with my father, as his tutor, so many years before I was born made him seem infinitely old. But, though he must have been a good age, he still possessed all the narrow enthusiasm and stunted interest of a schoolboy; the perfect equipment for a master. There were the tea-parties. And I remember one glimpse of another world. My tea, like that of most other boys, used to be sent in from Little Brown's, eggs or sausages, or roast chicken – or something of that sort. The shop was small, old-fashioned and charming; but one day, when I was there, a door opened, and I saw through it a vista of about twenty hags armed with pokers, toasting-forks and long rusty knives, their forms lit by the fires they tended, their draggled, unkempt grey hair and toothless, sweating, scarlet faces, seen dimly through the ascending, fragrant steam. The sound of a universal sizzling supplied music for them. The sight haunted me. No wonder we were not allowed to see through that door, for an utter lack of cleanliness prevailed. Moreover, it seemed wrong that those who ministered so faithfully to our comfort should be exposed to such conditions. Mostly, though, I recall absurd and isolated incidents.

One such episode occurred during the first half-holiday of my first term, about two days after I had arrived. *Absence* is a ceremony which takes place at two o'clock on every afternoon that is not to be devoted to work. A master mounts some steps and calls out from a roll held in his hand the names of all boys who should be present, and they answer him, so that he can be sure that they have not sneaked away. Well, my first *Absence* was in full progress, when, suddenly intoxicated by the possession of a pea-shooter – a weapon that had by some chance never hitherto come my way –, I fired in a friendly manner at a new acquaintance whom I saw at the other side of the crowd of boys, but, missing my aim, instead accidentally hit the officiating master on the neck. The wounded beak, as he was called in the cant term of the school, roared with surprise and anger –, and the boys, some hundreds of them, roared with him. As the noise subsided a little, he suddenly demanded 'Did *you* do that?' and the powerful squint from which the poor man suffered induced me to suppose that he was addressing someone else rather than myself. Had I realized that he was putting the question to me, I might, perhaps, have lied: as it was, I owned up to my crime. Though on this occasion I escaped with a light punishment, the master naturally concluded from my bold behaviour that I was an unusually unruly and obstreperous boy. In consequence he pursued me throughout my career with a special watchfulness, inspired either by a desire for revenge, or, perhaps, by a genuine belief that I was a dangerous malefactor.

In reality of a quiet temperament and a law-abiding disposition, I felt myself quite unfitted for the brief span of fame, and even of esteem, that this startling adventure brought me. Alas, I quickly recovered my unpopularity and retained it until the end of my time at Eton. Indeed, I was astonished and disillusioned only a few days later by an occurrence which brought home to me the fickleness of my school-fellows. Still comparatively fresh from my triumphant exploit with the pea-shooter, I found myself obliged to play football one afternoon. Accordingly, I changed and went down to the field, only to discover that my playmates had already assembled and were 'kicking about' before the game began. As soon as they saw me, however, guided by some instinct of mass animosity, they bore down from every direction, aiming their footballs at me as hard as they could kick. Nevertheless, while remaining, as I say, unpopular, I soon – no doubt owing to physical causes – gained a considerable vitality, which enabled me to take things as they came and to a certain degree to remain cheerful. Moreover, I could on occasion, if I wished, amuse my friends as well as discomfit my enemies.

Again, a most singular episode took place in Lower Chapel during one of my first few terms. The service had been of a tedium unexampled in my experience. The hymn-tunes bumped about, and cringed and whined and followed one like dogs. Finally, towards the end of a hymn there stepped into the pulpit one of those very ancient clergymen who whistle through their teeth in the style of an old-fashioned comedian – Fred Potts, for example –, but, of course, involuntarily. The type, though in this instance admittedly decrepit, was that which at the time the authorities at Eton seemed specially to favour for visiting parsons, the 1906 model, as it were. There had lately been several in succession (they would have found that hard to say, it was the sibilants that trapped the old gentlemen). The sermon proved to be an endless maze of allegory of a rather weak-kneed kind: really, it was hard to bear with equanimity. After about twenty-five minutes of it, the boy who sat next me, a mild and amiable lad in the same duffers' class as myself, took out of his trousers pocket a box of those now extinct matches called fuzees, and flung it down with great force and a gesture of defiance into the middle of the aisle, where it broke and burst into blue-green flames, full of hissing, glowing, incandescent heads, as the fuzees caught fire in batches, and gave off their typical, rather pleasant, incense-like fragrance. Apart from their sizzle utter silence prevailed. Not a boy stirred. The old clergyman himself had stopped whistling – probably surprise produced that perverse effect on him, making him refrain from, as it causes others to indulge in, this music. It was a dramatic, almost dream-like moment. After some minutes, the flaming box was removed by a verger with the aid of a long pair of tongs which, by some means or other, he had procured. He walked out, down the aisle, slowly carrying it at arm's length in front of him. Now the preacher was led from the pulpit, and into it, in his place, strode furiously the Lower Master, splendid in robes. Pointing a trembling finger at the culprit (who was by this time, I think, himself beginning to feel a little alarmed at what he had done), he launched an anathema at him. I remember the very words with which he began: '*You* have disgraced yourself as a Christian, a Gentleman and an Etonian!'

Such ludicrous incidents as I have described are apt to remain in the memory longer than more serious occurrences, for they contain the essence of the public school in England, in its absurdity, its lack of any bias towards learning; and because they could not have happened as one grew older. But, of course, there were other sides to my life at Eton. Though, as I have said, so far from being popular, yet I had succeeded in acquiring various friends. And two principal friendships chiefly enlivened my days here: one with Peter Lycett Green, now the well-known collector of pictures, the other with William King, of the British Museum, and most of the pleasurable hours I spent at Eton were passed in their company. These two, by their attitude of a nonconformity similar to my own, helped to remove the feeling that it was stupid to read at all, or talk, instead of playing games, and we carried on a continual skirmish, and from time to time engaged in pitched battle, with the Philistines.

Peter and William, though both younger than myself, achieved more distinction than ever I did at Eton, and were much higher in the school. But there were, of course, other boys who had come here the same half and were in the same division as myself with whom I liked to talk. And indeed I much appreciated, even then, any evidence of character.

Cranborne, for instance, took the same form as myself when he arrived, and I liked to watch his unruffled and distinctive Cecilian concentration. Nothing that occurred, however startling, disturbed him, even if it made him smile in a charming, rather rueful way. But he was soon wafted into another, higher form more worthy of his ability.

I must also mention the presence in the background of Philip Heseltine, who became better known in later years under the alias of Peter Warlock. I knew him for some twenty to thirty years, and must have met him scores of times in Venice and London and Paris. I even saw him on the day of his death, but though he was my exact contemporary, we were never friends, and I never cared for his songs, which seemed to me, musically speaking, to have come straight out of Wardour Street. He may have had a great knowledge of early music – of that I could not judge –, but certainly his knowledge in other directions in which he was said to be learned was often nugatory. I remember, in Venice, his telling me how painting did not interest him, but only mosaics; it then transpired that he had just come from Sicily, but was unaware of the presence in that island of the great mosaic churches of Monreale, Cefalù and the Capella Palatina.

There were other, older boys, whom one knew only in that peculiar relationship of fag to master. And I enjoyed being fag to Philip Sassoon, very grown-up for his age, at times exuberant, at others melancholy and preoccupied, but always unlike anyone else – as he remained, I am thankful to say, all his life –, and extremely considerate and kind in all his dealings.

Looking back, I find it excessively hard to picture *how* I spent my time; the avoidance of playing games whenever possible, or of watching them being played, is at best – and it could be exciting – but a negative occupation. I took no interest in my work and had lost any ability to concentrate that I had ever possessed. Occasionally, at the end of the term, we would be told to take a story from the Bible and turn it into blank verse. That was the only thing – apart, perhaps, from an occasion when I won the prize for a holiday task without reading the book whereon the examination was based – at which I showed any aptitude. I belonged to no society, debating or literary, and no one ever suggested that I should join such a body – if it existed. I did not, except for my first term, reside in the same house as Peter, but we saw a great deal of each other. In the summer we established ourselves as wet-bobs of a meagre and uncompetitive kind, and spent pleasant spare hours in the afternoons. on the river, or in bathing, or wandering round Windsor, buying books or prints or eating ices or strawberries.

My tutor – Tatham – was consistently kind, noticed that I liked books, and used to discuss with me for a few minutes in the evening what I had read. He was an unusual man: in appearance he resembled a hot-tempered, good-natured walrus, shambling and roughly clad, but he possessed a strong sense of religion and decorum, and was capable of real generosity and fire. Shy, and in consequence rather difficult to know – indeed his nature was obscured by this shyness –, his individuality was marked, and he manifested all kinds of little likes and dislikes, though these were yet less personal than general. Especially – albeit in appearance and opinion so dissimilar to the great Lord Chesterfield, who had nevertheless shared this same prejudice – he hated loud laughter and, if he heard a raucous shout of it at any time, would snap out in his rather thick voice his favourite phrase in this connection, 'I won't have any boy in my house laugh like a cat'.

As for what I read, Peter and I were a little priggish in our tastes in this matter, and each kept a carefully annotated list of the books we read, with the dates of reading them. We were competitive, bidding against each other, as it were, in the highbrow market. We both of us liked works with a reputation. For example, I read nearly all Shakespeare's plays at one draught, in the space of ten days – an exploit about which I was teased by my family, but which, all the same, possessed certain advantages for a boy of my age over other methods of becoming acquainted with these masterpieces. The jumbled impressions intoxicated me, and left behind a sediment, a deposit on the mind. Apart from Webster, I read few other Elizabethan dramatists, and little poetry at that time except Shelley and Pope. I had with me in my room, I recollect, a miniature edition of *The Rape of the Lock*, with illustrations by Beardsley, which already was one of my oldest possessions, for my father had given it to me when I was seven. But for the most part I read novels, Smollett, Fielding, Richardson, Fanny Burney, Jane Austen, the Brontës, Meredith, Hardy, Wells, and plays by Wilde and Shaw – of whom I was a great admirer. I also read Ruskin and Pater, and, oddly, Gissing, and I notice on my list, also, Arthur Morrison's *Mean Streets*.

I read, in fact, without purpose, as cattle browse. But my father, when on occasion asked what books I liked, used to give that little downward, waving flutter of the right hand, descending from almost shoulder-level to elbow, that was one of his favourite gestures, and reply, 'Osbert reads for style; *I* read for information.'

This statement constituted both rebuke and in itself excuse. While protecting me from the charge of absolute frivolity, it at the same time pointed the way to me, by insinuating that I preferred to read novels, instead of grappling, day and night, as I should, with *The Origin of Species* and sprightly primers of Political Economy. It was true that he rated beauty, as he saw it, above all other things – but it was his, and he made it. His sons should improve their minds. Ruskin he commended, but Meredith, who was liable to write in a nasty, sneering way about rich baronets, incurred the full measure of his condemnation. Moreover, the formula I have quoted above was, in addition, another way of regretting that I concerned myself so much with human beings, their behaviour and the things they say, that they interested me more than they did him, and that, in fact, I was dependent on them. In that direction, he had learned, lay unhappiness, if not disaster.

Time was going on. The ninety-nine years of peace had nearly run its term, though no one yet appreciated the fact. The *Entente Cordiale*, that Juggernaut fitted with every modern convenience, and destined to crush the bodies of two generations of Englishmen and one of Frenchmen, and to annihilate for a time the spirit of the most enlightened nation in the world, had started on its career through streets decorated with flags and gaping faces.

King Edward VII, to whom the public assigned much of the credit for the foreign policy recently inaugurated – though, in fact, it belonged to the Kaiser, and to the politicians of the two countries –, was continually moving from Paris to London, from Homburg to Biarritz: and he lived much in public, more than any previous English monarch. Thus it was easy to see the King, and I often saw him as he drove to Windsor, and, too, heard him speak when he came to open the School Library – a memorial for Etonians who had been killed in the Boer War. King Edward's voice possessed a very individual and husky warmth, together with that particular rolling of the *r*'s that distinguished his generation of the Royal Family. There was, as he spoke in public, a geniality in its sound, as of one who found in life the utmost enjoyment, and, in spite of a rather prominent and severely attentive blue eye, and a certain appearance of fatigue, the chief impression was one of good-humour.

In November 1907, the Kaiser paid a state visit to this country, and

King Edward brought his nephew to Eton, where they visited the school buildings. On this occasion the Kaiser obtained for us a week's extra holiday – the only debt, I think, that Etonians of my generation ever owed him. Even on this, the interest charged amounted to usury, for seven years later he took away from us by the sum of his actions at least four years of our lives, and in many instances the whole period that remained. Another royal visitor to Eton at about this time was King Carlos of Portugal, his large figure swathed in a white cloak. King Edward drove through the town of Eton with him, and was alleged subsequently to have sent a message to the school authorities, 'Cheering is forbidden neither in England nor in Portugal . . .' But, though the boys may have been undemonstrative, in any case Eton used on such occasions to present a gay and, indeed, enchanting exterior. Throughout my sojourn there, I always appreciated the unrivalled atmosphere of *festa* and gala that it could develop for such events or for the great local holidays, such as the Fourth of June or St Andrew's Day. The customs of the place certainly lent themselves to the perfect celebration of holidays – more easily, I apprehend, than to habits of work. Every building seemed to blossom. And to me it was a pleasure to find that my birthday coincided with a whole holiday, falling, as it does, on Founder's Day, the day on which King Henry VI was born.

Now the Edwardian Carnival was at its height, but my immediate family took little part in it. Every spring, we would go abroad, and my father and mother now would usually pay a second visit to Italy in the autumn. My father never went elsewhere, neither to Spain, nor Portugal, nor Holland, nor Morocco, nor to any of the other countries that, it might have been supposed, would interest him, except France – that is to say, Paris, as a stopping-place *en route* for Italy –, and Germany. Russia he had visited as a young man, to attend the Coronation of the Tsar Alexander III, but he seldom spoke of his travels there, except to commend the double-gauge railway. It was Italy that appealed to him and he kept to the track he had made for himself.

Apart from a visit about once a year to one of the trivial but popular musical comedies of the day, my father seldom patronized the theatre. Even at that, he preferred the native brand to the Austrian. His real dislike of music helped him, it may be, to enjoy these entertainments, and I think the experience of being able, indeed of finding himself obliged, to laugh at the same jokes as the rest of the audience allowed him to feel to a certain, even agreeable degree, fashioned of the same clay. For the rest he disapproved of the theatre, and especially of the intellectual drama. As a child, therefore, I had seldom been allowed to go to the play; but now, during 'long leave' every half, I would usually accompany my mother or uncle. Often they would take me to see the Follies, a celebrated company of the time, the chief organizer of which was the great Pélissier, an enormous figure of comedy.

In addition, at the end of my holidays, when I was passing through London on my way to Eton, my parents would usually detail Henry to take me to a theatre, and this we would not seldom interpret as meaning a music-hall, a form of entertainment of which we were both very fond. Often he would conduct me to the Alhambra, then still the most typical and, in its own atmospheric way, the most beautiful of London theatres, untouched since the 'sixties, when it had been built. The honeycomb ceilings and stalactites were painted in blue and red, and there was, too, a great deal of dark gilding, though obscured by the clouds of cigar and cigarette smoke that hung under the wide, flat dome. In the background as we entered, I caught a glimpse of the promenade, where women in hats the size of bicycle-wheels, piled up with ostrich feathers, their faces powdered and painted in the various shades of mauve, pink, salmon and cyclamen that had contemporaneously been introduced in the new varieties of sweet-pea – a flower which must remain as typical of the age of *The Merry Widow* as does the camellia of the age of crinolines and muslins, – trailed the trains of their dresses along the carpets in a haze of cheap, strong scent, tobacco smoke and dust. To me, these unknown but formal priestesses of primitive unrecognized rites and urgencies seemed less enticing than portentous, frightening and of an immense age. We quickly gained our seats, and there, from comparative darkness, watched the figures on the stage, consumed by and consuming the light of a world that by the help of a label – a gesture, a mannerism, a lisp, a laugh – they would create. Here, for example, I first saw the minute, irresistibly grotesque figure of Little Tich, surely a dancer of genius, as he stamped magically, with a dynamic power of comedy, upon the boards; his huge boots, half the size of himself, being shaped like skis. His whole stunted body seemed the expression of his dance, rather than the dance an expression of his body: as surely as the lion was created for its leap, so Little Tich had been moulded, the spectator felt, for this purpose alone, for rousing laughter out of a crowd, in the same way that a bellows fans flame out of smouldering logs.

Here, too, I first saw a ballet: in those days still billed as 'The Italian Ballet', *Italian* being used to indicate the identical sort of transcendent excellence that came to be signified later by the use of *Russian* in the same connection. A ballet then always occupied the final forty or fifty minutes of such a formal variety programme as still survived at the Alhambra or Empire, a lingering tradition from an earlier period. Built upon a long, humourless and involved plot, it was executed by surprisingly large women and old men; the representatives of both sexes, indeed, seeming left over from some other era. They used a peculiarly stilted and yet coherent technique of foot, gesture and expression; to these three means, their art, such as it was, had been confined. They aimed at no use of the body, except for heaving, panting, and showing emotion, and at little expression by the limbs. The chief male dancers were heavily moustached, a conventional stroking of these long appendages being a favourite gesture, to show either self-satisfaction or a sudden determination, according to the manner in which it was done. The principal ballerina, if I remember rightly, was titled the Great Leonora but I recall her appearance, a large, dark, flashing woman, who seemed always to be balanced on the knife-like edge of toes surprisingly small for the support of such a frame, or to be indulging in imperious, whirlwind gestures or foot-stamping. The whole thing was staged in a flat and jejune manner, alternating with outbursts of a pantomime-like splendour. One could not fail to be amazed at the lack of reality displayed, and I formed a great distaste for the ballet, little foreseeing the new art at that very moment being shaped in Russia out of the amorphous mass of time by the genius of Diaghilev, or that I, together with those others of my generation interested in the arts, or gifted for them, should find more pleasure in it than in any other form of theatrical entertainment.

The romantic age, it seemed, the romantic gloss, had vanished, both in life itself and in my surroundings. Something had gone wrong, and farce, public and private, was sweeping the boards clear for tragedy – or at any rate for disaster. The shadow was inspissating, becoming homicidal in the world at large, and material and squalid at home. Relations drifted in and out of Renishaw, but it seemed emptier than in the years when I was a very small boy, the guests fewer and fewer (they were to increase again before the coming of the First World War). Partly this was due to my father's fear that they might 'disturb his literary work', partly to his growing dread of any expenses incurred save in building or altering, partly to the fact that he had at last decided that he rather disliked some of my mother's friends, and, looking round, seemed now to have none of his own.

One such occasion, the biggest of its kind, is possibly worth describing. When my sister was nineteen, my father resolved that she ought to have a coming-out party. It was the correct thing to do, and though he disapproved of conventional ways as a rule, for some reason the idea appealed to him. But again, *whom* to ask and what for? Well, my mother could invite one or two of her relations to help her, he decided; and the party must be for the Doncaster Races. Into this last decision certainly entered an element of ancestor-worship, together with his individual brand of extravagance mingled with economy; because he possessed the silver badge which had belonged to his great-grandfather, one of the founders of the meeting, and which, worn in the buttonhole, would still obtain for him a free admission. Hitherto he had never worn it. And in any case he was determined to try the effect of one last sortie from his ivory tower, not yet completed.

Chefs arrived. Enormous parcels were delivered every day from London. New linen was bought. All the silver plate, some of it unused for many years, was got out of the bank. Extra footmen appeared, and Major Viburne was called in to manage the whole thing as if it were an officers' mess. The running of special trains to Doncaster and back was arranged with the railway company, to convey to the Races those who did not want to go by motor. Motors were hired. A Blue Hungarian Band was engaged for ten days. And for a full month beforehand I used to see my father, sitting later than usual at breakfast, with eight or ten small glass jam-pots – Bar-le-Duc – in front of him, labelled in French, red-currant, white-currant, scarlet strawberry, white strawberry, gooseberry and so on. When I enquired what he was doing, he would reply, as one manfully executing a duty, 'Just trying out the jams for the Doncaster party,' for he believed in personal super-vision. Like a soldier, he stuck to it, in spite of the strain on the liver: but after a few weeks, one could see it was beginning to tell on him. Excitement mounted. And when the great day came, and every bedroom was prepared, and the thirty or so people arrived, we were amazed at the total of their combined ages. The whole point of the party had been that it was for my sister. But every single one of the guests, with the exception of my cousin Veronica and one or two others, was well stricken in years, while several had kicked over the matrimonial traces. The only young man present was a nice American, who had been faithfully retrieved for the occasion by a cousin of ours, and who was frankly puzzled at finding himself in this gallery of antiques. Altogether the party was scarcely suitable and revealed the lengthening gap between reality and things as my parents were beginning to see them.

It was a party, I suppose, none the less – but it seemed curiously impersonal in composition and aim. Nobody knew anyone else in the house – unless it were so intimately that to ask them to meet should have been deemed a work of supererogation –, and nobody particularly wanted to know anyone else. In addition, my father detested racing, and Edith loathed it. My mother, alone, enjoyed the pointless stir and activity of it – and, of course, the opportunities it afforded for betting. The meals were long and good. (The Bar-le-Duc jams, then a novelty in England, were consumed with relish.) The Blue Hungarian Hussars, who put up at the Sitwell Arms in the village, may have puzzled and perturbed the habituals of the inn, colliers and agricultural labourers, by their sallow appearance, raven locks and Magyar swagger. But within doors they were in constant demand, whenever racing was not in progress, playing under the gilded Tudor Rose of the Little Parlour, next the Dining-room, during every meal except breakfast, and were in continual discourse after dinner in the ball-room. Every restaurant in Europe must have been ransacked to find the repertory. 'The music makes things go,' said my father, 'and prevents people from feeling they *have* to make conversation.' (Better still, it prevented him from hearing it.) Only 'The Blue Danube', a piece of which the band was fond, was here rather frowned on, being taken by some of the guests, I fear, as a reflection upon their ages. They pretended never to have heard it before. 'What a delightful old-fashioned thing!' they used to exclaim. 'What is it? . . . But let's have something we know. "The Merry Widow", or one of those delightful tunes from the Gaiety!' Trains and motors ran in their ordained grooves; the garden looked its best, swooning under a special weight of flowers. It was usually only visited in the morning when clematis and rose and honeysuckle and hollyhock glowed in the butter-coloured golden haze, born of sun and morning mist – or was it from a ground frost, it was difficult to tell which, for even after hours of hot sun, the grass still remained wet, and the rose-heads full of moisture? –, or in the late afternoon, an hour at which the whole summer seemed to return in epitome, so that it was impossible to believe that we stood on the very brink of autumn in this high country, and the scent of the flowers, out-prest by the warmth, seemed to linger in the air with an unwanted persistence, while the fruit, ripening on the dark red-brick walls, appeared to shine in its own radiance and heat. The house, too, seemed to be in commotion at both ends of the day. In the morning, the housemaids and footmen struggled upstairs with old-fashioned tin baths, resembling Egyptian coffins, and hip-baths like gigantic snail-shells, and enormous cans of steaming-hot water, to the rooms respectively of female and male guests. Then there was a hiatus in activity at midday, when the party had left for Doncaster. Henry would enjoy a siesta: the chef would drink a bottle of wine. The gardener would come round to see to the flowers in the house. Finally, hammering would sound out again from the kitchen. The party would return: baths would be carried up once more. And soon there would be the procession down to dinner, down the oak staircase, across the flagged hall, through the Little Parlour. 'Racing makes one very rheumatic', the guests would say to one another when their knees creaked as they descended the stairs, – for it could have nothing to do with their ages.

Yes, I think the party must have been adjudged a success. If any doubt lay at the back of my parents' minds on this matter, the blame was allotted to Edith. '*Très difficile*,' my father would say, for he reserved his rather restricted knowledge of French for the crystallization of such domestic problems. He complained that she did not play tennis – 'lawn-tennis', as he still called it –, while my mother regretted her addiction to books. She had not 'been out' long, and already she had created a bad impression elsewhere, while staying with relations, as well as having excessively startled the late Lord Chaplin, by inquiring of him, during an evening when she was placed next to him at dinner, whether he preferred Bach to Mozart. She had been hastily withdrawn from circulation and sent home. It would never do.

Sacheverell and I and our tutor were not permitted to attend the meals in the Dining-Room. My brother and I feasted on scraps in our attic. It seemed rather lonely, not being allowed to join in. Never being able to realize when I am not wanted, I decided one evening to bicycle through the park and meet my father – who was that day motoring back from the races – at the gates. I was wearing a best new blue suit, appropriate to the occasion. Freewheeling blithely downhill, through a grove of trees, I paid no attention to where I was going, caught the back of the heel of a cow, which was mouching across the drive, with my front wheel and, flying with an unexpected elegance and agility over the handle-bars just as my father was entering the park, landed, with torn trousers, grazed knees and a black eye, a few yards ahead of him. It was a silly thing to have done. I had let the side down. Further, I had ruined, unnecessarily, a new suit – a fact of which, ever and again, I was reminded during the remaining weeks of the holidays.

Gradually the music faded, the musicians, clothed soberly in black, returned to London, the guests left – many of them were never to see such a party again –, the head chef departed with a large cheque and a scalded hand, the train service relapsed to the normal and the motors stopped breaking down and raced home. My father abandoned the life of the time as he saw it, and sped back to the gothic centuries. In addition to his never-ending studies of medieval life, he was at work on his book *On the Making of Gardens*, and continued entering notes on many and diverse subjects. I find the following jotting under the heading 'Venus', dated September of the same year: 'The author of the book on classical statuary which I have been reading, does not allow for the great interest attaching to ideal types of womanhood. The Venus of Syracuse is really very beautiful. Of course, the proper place for a Venus is in a private or a public bath.'

As for Venus, whether in private or public bath, she was certainly more in evidence in England than she had been for a hundred years. The goddess seemed more openly to be occupying men's thoughts. For the first time for many decades, clothes had become highly stylized again, with an elegance verging on absurdity. At Ascot, and on the lawns of garden-parties, it was to be noticed that women had at last begun to shed once more the multitude of their garments, had left behind the veilings and feather boas and were now clad, skin-deep, in tight silks, were sheathed in satin, or wore slit skirts and silver anklets. For the world took its note from Musical Comedy rather than from the immense tragedies that were being prepared in the wings to replace it, and the production of *Les Merveilleuses* at Daly's in November 1906 had introduced, or at any rate popularized, Directoire dresses. The hats were gigantic now, and covered with ostrich feathers. The colours were those of young grass and leaves, the chequerings of branches against a grey sky, or rose-pink and azure-blue – they had about them a peculiar ephemerality, a butterfly-like character that was the essence of modishness. Paris had again asserted her leadership, and marched behind the smiling mask of the *Entente Cordiale*, to take London captive, yet London was now becoming, in her place, the pleasure centre of the world.

To my delight 'the happiest time of my life' was nearing its end, and when, eventually, my tutor became involved in an Alpine accident, and was killed, I persuaded my father to allow me to leave. As will transpire in *Great Morning*, in doing this I committed a tactical error, but it seemed at the time a great step forward towards liberty. The next half I returned to Eton for the ritual of being given my leaving-book – the inevitable Gray's Poems. In presenting it to me, the headmaster, Dr Lyttleton, mentioned his disappointment and surprise at finding that I was not to take Holy Orders – but his surprise can have been as nothing to mine when I heard him make the remark.

To its credit, one can say, I believe, that the Eton system does little to alter a boy's character; it either develops it, if ordinary, or else, if unusual, drives it in on itself. It exercises in no wise so formative an influence as does a private school. But, albeit that Eton had little effect on my character, I yet believe that my career there – I left in 1909 – and the example of my friends, produced some effect on the life at Eton, by making the average boy more tolerant, so that the intelligent Etonian of ten years later reaped a certain benefit, was given an easier time, and was not so much victimized by games.

There were many problems that puzzled me while I was there. One of them was this: as I regarded some of the bearers of names made famous by statesmen, generals, diplomats and governors, I asked myself how it was possible that these boys could be the sons, grandsons or heirs of generations of men of attainments, often of intellect, at any rate of strong character, possessing in the highest degree powers of decision, qualities singularly lacking in their descendants before me. I wondered if something had gone wrong with the stock and, contemplating them, looked to a future wherein they might be called upon to rule, or at any rate to exercise influence – a position for which they were assuredly not equipped mentally – with (though, it may be, as things have turned out, not with enough) dismay. So much did this question worry me, that on one occasion when my father came down to see me, I asked him whether, in his time at Eton, his contemporaries had seemed equally lacking in interest, capacity and intellect. After, I must say, some considerable reflection, as if he were rather in doubt about the matter himself, he said, yes, but it was, he thought, only an apparent deterioration, in no way actual. Eton taught you, he pronounced, to be a leader, to command. (But was it, I could not help wondering, a good thing to be *taught* to lead, if you had not mental qualities to support such an attitude?) If any increased weakness was really to be remarked, he added, with the curiously practical, almost Chinese application of his ingenious mind, this might be due to a fact he had noticed, that the small children of the rich now had all their food cut up for them, long after they should have been cutting it up for themselves; a process which constituted one of the principal means of self-education for the very young.

How priggish my doubts, and with what cruelty did fate resolve them! For when these boys round me grew up, I was, indeed, to form a different opinion of them, and to come to understand that in part it was only that I opposed my own different but as lively intolerance to that of my fellow Etonians. I possessed a liking for things of the intellect, a passion for the arts, which already I placed above everything. All through my school life, from that first day I have described, the same faces had haunted me. Having gone to two private schools, I had the disadvantage when I arrived at Eton of being greeted by two sets of familiar faces instead of by one alone. They continued to arrive in strictest order of seniority. They accompanied me, at the stated intervals, from class to class, and from game to game. I had observed them as small boys and big boys; I met them now as youths: some of them ordained by the hierarchical system, that then still prevailed, for great positions in the State – positions whereto, notwithstanding, the majority of them never attained, for they were killed in the 1914–1918 conflict, fighting with the vigour and debonair courage of their ancestors. I had seen them in the past as the treacherous and vindictive mob that, collectively, they formed. In consequence it came to me with all the force of a shock to find later, as I shall tell, what brave, generous, loyal and often lovable companions these young boors, dullards and bullies, with whom, on and off, I had been interned for so long, and with whom after that I had lost touch so willingly, but for so brief a while, only for the two years that followed my leaving Eton, had become in that space; a magic interval of metamorphosis wrought by the functioning of minute glands, a wonder of Nature that caused the mob to break up, and then integrate into individuals again (the same process that attends the change from war to peace), a phenomenon comparable at the stage I seek to indicate with that which converts a squirming handful of furry grubs into so many brave butterflies, roaming their whole world of the garden, flitting where they will from flower to flower, in spite of the immense and unpredictable dangers that menace them from all sides.

BOOK THREE

GREAT MORNING

CHAPTER ONE

It was a brief winter's walk, a brisk turn of a special kind, against a background familiar to me, because my sister and I, when we were children, had visited it, and I had never forgotten its wintry vastness, solemnity and gloom. At times the place seemed a toy fort that had become real, and swollen stonily to enormous proportions, its walls and castellations assuming ample material substance, just as the toy soldiers in their scarlet tunics had acquired life; at others, it appeared to be a terrace levelled among stone mountains or, again, a piazza in a small hill town, high up, but under a smoky sky. It was ten minutes to eight in the morning; a fact which, owing to the relative degrees of light, makes a difference to my scene; it was ten minutes to eight, and, swinging our arms smartly, six of us had to walk up and down in twos, at a pace full of winter's zest. The stone mountains that framed this stage gave evidence in their texture, a few of them, of extreme antiquity, but most, on the other hand, displayed a Victorian primness and hard precision, seeming to be the realization in stone of a drill-sergeant's dream. Everything was spick and span, and even the roughest, oldest of these mountains, even the most uncouth in bulk, even Julius Caesar's Tower itself, had been trimmed and clipped, as it were, to provide a fitting background for parades. One or two old trees alone, though they too had been pruned and pared, made for this place some obstinate claim to kinship with Nature and the world outside. And occasionally a very large old raven would croak loudly and walk across the frosty ground in front of us, lifting its claws high, as if the stone burned them. I would have liked to stop and watch this bird, because it had an air of immense age, of being, indeed, although it carried its years so well, as old as anything in this setting; causing one to wonder whether it could be – as no doubt in fact it was – a living representative of the collection of beasts and birds that, in the eighteenth and early nineteenth centuries, had drawn hither, to the side of the now destroyed Lion Tower, all visitors to London.

The raven still stalked slowly and at its will, flapping and croaking, but we had to walk rapidly up and down in a straight line, our swords knocking a little and clanking as we moved. We would glance from time to time at the ranks of men, clad in long grey coats, and now standing at ease. They were drawn up facing the White Tower, and we paced up and down between this massive building and the men. Inside that tower, among much else to be seen, was King Henry VIII's steel suit – feared yet, the custodian once told me, by tourists; these peering crowds of little men still scrupled to touch it, in case some morbid influence from the tomb should communicate to them the maladies of the dead giant.

It was a very clear morning, with a berry-bright frostiness that matched the rooster's music of the bugles sounding their calls, and the stones crackled as we walked over them. But at this season and this hour, more often fog enclosed us and the whole of the vast area of city stretching round us, beyond these towers and bounding walls – for this, the Tower of London, was the very citadel of the fog. Here night could reign for forty-eight hours at a stretch. Then the naked electric-light globes that, as part of the traditional pipe-clayed bareness of barrack-rooms, swung in the draught from open windows of a winter's evening, burnt all day, yet seemed to have no more power than a match would have, if it were lighted in this elephantine and engulfing darkness. For these hours, the barrack-rooms themselves became mysterious.

At any moment of day or night, though, and even when swathed in layers of fog, the Tower of London remained a place of mystery, beautiful and, at the same time, because of its stoniness and crenellation, ugly. The neatness that recent centuries had striven to impose upon these shapes that appeared to have been hacked out of primeval chaos, the accretions, only served to make it more tremendous. After the manner of Maiden Castle or Stonehenge, its origins stretched so far back that no glimpse of them could be obtained. It was a system of life, a city, more than a building; a forgotten palace, from days still dimly to be apprehended in the folds of tapestries, a forgotten church, a forgotten – no, a remembered – prison. Rivalling Windsor Castle as the chief repository of English history and tradition, this formidable fortified mount was not only a world in itself, but the heart, now a little atrophied, of the greatest of English cities, the centre from which it had grown, the centre from which it had been governed. For hundreds of years – ever since, indeed, Gundulph the Weeper, Bishop of Rochester, had, at the command of

William the Conqueror, supervised the building of the White Tower –, this stone mountain had typified its city.

Returning to it at a late hour, after an evening's pleasure, its majesty cooled youthful blood. False and obvious as sounded by daylight the story that at night you could sometimes see in an open space the shadow, thrown by the moon, of the Axe, it was impossible on a moonlit night not to look for it as you passed under vast arches, along the dark green alleys carved by the icy light among these stony ways. All round, the stout and buttressed walls showed their crenellated circuit. And the drive in a taxi-cab through a deserted City, that led up to arrival at the Tower, aided the impression; drives through length upon illumined length of emptiness, where only from time to time a cat howled, and never a human being stirred, past spires and domes and monuments, past Wren churches that are now a memory, through streets and past buildings the names of which men will never allow to die, so that they will rise again, as did the great monuments of Rome, with each succeeding age – and of these names the most famous is the Tower of London.

When we reached it, if the time was past two o'clock in the morning, before we could enter under the portcullis to find ourselves in this castle of the Dark Ages – a place now equally deserted as the streets through which we had just driven –, we had to make an effort to recollect the password, which was changed every night, and though usually typical of the military mind in the simplicity of choice it displayed, yet the later the hour, the greater the mental labour required to recall something that, hours before, had seemed so easy to memorize. I was just twenty years of age, this was January 1913, and London was in carnival throughout the following nineteen months, except for the brief festivals of the banks and churches; then theatres, ballrooms and restaurants shut, and all those who could leave London fled from it with an eagerness and speed they never showed some thirty years later, when it was bombed day and night. Sometimes, therefore, after late hours, one was tired of a morning, and for that reason, of the various kinds of fog I preferred the thick yellow, when, temporarily, all parades had to be cancelled and one could rest.

Today, however, was clear, with the clearness that dwells on hill-tops and the tops of the highest towers – and this was fortunate, for we must show no fatigue. That was not permitted us. So, wearing long, dark-blue coats, with a cascade of tabs flowing down the front under our grey greatcoats, in blue trousers with a broad red stripe, and dark-blue hats peaked with gold thread, we walked sharply up and down, waiting for the clock to strike, and for the Adjutant, a just man and a very splendid figure of an officer, to come on parade. At the last stroke of eight, he would appear, accompanied by the Battalion Sergeant-Major. In his impressive stride, in the bold, severe, critical, yet tolerant, and even amused, ferocity of his glance, he appeared to sum up a tradition, to be the very embodiment of the Brigade of Guards. Meanwhile, we waited for him, and to be told to fall in, at the head of the men. I rather dreaded, however, the lesson to come, for the Adjutant used to complain loudly of my personal version of the ritual voice that regimental tradition obliges the young officer to adopt for words of command – conventional sounds that none but initiates can interpret –, declaring that he could not distinguish it from the croaking of the Tower ravens.

The reader will have noticed that, since last he caught sight of me, I had, in the short space of three years, been translated as completely as any of the characters in *A Midsummer Night's Dream*. But, in the new existence in which I had, with dazed eyes, found myself, I was received with so much kindness, and had discovered so many acquaintances, and even enemies, who, in the same fashion that I had been changed from a schoolboy into an officer, had, in their turn, become transformed by the magic I described at the end of *The Scarlet Tree*, into admirable and zealous friends, displaying the greatest solicitude to help, and to show me how to enjoy the life in which I had been plunged, and, moreover, this world contained such warmth, vitality and extravagance, and, further, was imbued with a quality so much its own, while, above all, the tenets of its faith, and the conceptions that governed it, were so new and strange to me, that I perceived myself, rather to my own surprise, to be happier than at home, happier, in short, than I had ever been hitherto. Almost for the first time in my life, at any rate for the second, I was experiencing the warm human comfort to be derived from friendship with those of one's own age. And the points in my character which must to them, with their outlook, have seemed unusual, even peculiar, were quickly accepted, laughed at with good humour, or even watched with interest.

Looking back, I suppose that the friends I made then – nearly all of them, alas, destined to be killed before two years had passed – were not those, necessarily, who would have chosen me or whom I would have chosen, had the range been unlimited. Our interests were different – theirs, sporting; mine, mainly esthetic – but this did not in the least mar our friendship. Their great qualities, their character and generosity of

mind, completely won me over, and banished the fact from my consciousness, so that I am able to hope that, similarly, my affection for them
prevented them from guessing that I was not the sort of friend, either,
whom they would have selected.

So, on the morning in question, I walked up and down the frosty
square, thinking how fortunate I was to be with my companions. The
curious and enclosed world into which they were inducting me – my first
adult world – was full of luxury, hardship and privilege, and hedged with
shibboleths, traditions and formulae. Nevertheless, within its strict
boundaries of St James's Street – a street that, from its cramped palace of
brown brick, so full of the English genius for understatement, to its clubs
and wine-merchants and hatters, still offers the essence of London, as the
Sierpes, with its sherry-shops and cigar-stalls, presents that of Seville –,
it glowed with a certain warmth of heart. Each young officer off parade,
out of school, was an important unit, and treated as such; a perfect
democracy reigned in the Officers' Mess, Christian names were the rule,
and only the Commanding Officer was addressed as 'Sir'. Much ritual
existed, however, in other directions and at other times. The newly-
joined ensign was instructed not only in the general and accepted code,
but, if he were not already aware of it, was advised on what constituted
for him the right kind of shoes, collars, shirts and suits to wear, being
given pieces of precise information; such as, for example, that when
leave was granted to him, he should never spend a day of it in London,
and that he must, when not in uniform – which he only wore, of course,
on duty –, always, if the King was in London, wear a morning suit and
top-hat.

In those days – and probably until the beginning of the 1939 war the
habit continued –, the Adjutant would attend the first fittings of each
young officer, surveying with a practised eye the whole effect, and
scrutinizing minutely the cut of the tunic of scarlet Melton cloth, the
smoothness of shoulders and waist. Above all, there must be no
wrinkling. And this constituted, withal, an important question, both for
the young man and his parents, since the uniform cost several hundreds
of pounds. The review-belt alone, made of scarlet and gold, cost thirty-
six pounds, I remember, and I only had occasion to wear it once; then
there was the bearskin, as well, to be fitted and tried on, and the perfection
of this proved to be of so esoteric a kind that no-one new to the matter
would be able to tell a good from a bad, and, myself, I never contrived to
master the principles that governed the choice. The bearskin had, of

course, – for it must measure some one and a half foot to one foot and ten inches high – to be sufficiently well-balanced and well-fitting to enable the ensign to carry it on his head, and the Colour in front of him, in a gale, without mishap – and this, even with the best constructed bearskin, was not easy: because the Fore Court of Buckingham Palace gives ample space for the east wind, which the front faces, to play, while the weight of the Colour, although the butt of it is supported most of the time in a pipe-clayed belt, is considerable, and the left arm, to balance, and also for the sake of smart appearance, must swing free.

The fitting of headgear and uniform and belts constituted something of an ordeal. Not only did it without exception occupy a full hour but, while the young officer, prodded from time to time with questing fingers, as if he were a prize bull at a show, stood in the centre of a small closet, full of mirrors, set at different angles, so as to reflect him in his half-finished scarlet tunic, and every detail of his dress, with a kind of dull but yet varied repetition that recalled delirium, during all these minutes, a highly technical conversation was taking place between the Adjutant and the tailor. After they had debated some particularly enthralling point, the tailor would call in the cutter and ask for his view on it: but the cutter, partially blind from his work, would pretend to be deaf also. This, I think, he did as some personal form of subservience combined with defiance, that he had worked out for himself – but at any rate, every question would have to be put at least three times before he would answer. Occasionally, the tailor himself would dart at my shoulder or waist, and rip the seam open, so that the grey padding stood exposed beneath the vermilion stuff. It was true that one felt oneself to be the most important person there – as the prize bull must feel himself; the very centre of the debate. Yet, too, one felt at the same time curiously left out of things: for neither Adjutant, tailor nor cutter seemed to see the man who wore the uniform, only the uniform itself. The tunic glowed, ember-like, in the misty and pocked mirrors, and the cutter peered through spectacles that magnified his eyes to the size of a god's: he jabbed and snipped, but never spoke.

A touch of Ouida, a breath of the Boer War – even though these two influences were in contradiction –, both seemed to linger still about the life I was entering. With its ritual and formality, it was by no means the school of economy that my father seemed to consider it. One had to spend money. To this pursuit I brought the zest and sureness of touch inherited from my ancestors. The only expensive taste I did not share with my brother-officers was that for horses; I abominated them, and the brutes, with that animal instinct of theirs, knew of my loathing and returned it a thousandfold. So I avoided hunting, steeplechasing, racing. The tastes I shared were for nearly all other kinds of pleasure. Worse still, I possessed my own individual lines of extravagance, such as large bills for books, and owing to theatre agencies for visits to ballet and opera – and never did extravagance yield a richer harvest. I could not afford it, and should not have gone – I ought no doubt to have sat in pit or gallery – but I did not. I had received little education, had grown to hate learning – associating it in my mind with authority, father, dons and school-masters –, and here, disguised as pleasure, was my university. The stimulus that the music of Stravinsky, for instance, afforded to my imagination has subsequently been of inestimable benefit to my work.

Hedged though he was with countless shibboleths, in detail so minute as often to be hard to detect, yet it did not prove over difficult for a young officer, albeit his interests were not those of the average young officer, to adapt himself to the life round him. To give examples from my own experience, I was never obliged to conceal my interest in the arts or to pretend to sporting proclivities foreign to my nature. Thus, when the following summer, one day while I was Ensign on King's Guard at St James's Palace, the Captain of it – an awe-inspiring individual, with a heavy, but regular profile, and moustachios left over from the drawing-rooms of George du Maurier – inquired, after an immense effort that resembled the wheezing of an old clock about to strike, but was none the less born of a kindly intention to try to lessen the tedium of long hours spent in the red-papered guard-room, 'Do you like *horses*?', and I replied, 'No, but I like giraffes – they have such a beautiful line,' he took the answer unexpectedly well, and even attempted to smile. Then, on another occasion, it had been my turn to take the Early Parade at 6 a.m. After breakfast, the Adjutant sent for me to the Orderly Room. I obeyed the intimidating summons. I entered, and saluted the great man. He said, looking up,

'Mr Sitwell, it is reported to me that you were late this morning for Early Parade.'

I expressed dissent.

On this, he inquired, 'Were the men on parade when you arrived?'

I replied, 'I didn't notice, sir. I did not look.'

I can see now that my answer, which was quite genuine and unaffected, must have been disconcerting to a mind of such excellent military punctuality and precision. In fact, for the moment it bowled him over, and I was dismissed. Later, though, I was instructed to attend Early Parade every morning for a week – but never did the Adjutant bear me any rancour for my unconventional conduct or retorts. Out of the Orderly Room, he treated me, as ever, in the friendliest possible manner.

Outside this world, stretched for me one other – since as yet I had been granted little time or freedom to make friends of my own choice: that consisting of relations and family friends; though some of these, it is true, had now become estranged from my parents. But I must here explain shortly that my father was modifying at this time one of his own dictums: for he felt more than formerly a certain necessity to see people. He seldom got to know, nor did he wish to know, his peers: those who possessed an ability comparable to his own, or of a similar range and depth of interest. Strange as it may seem in a man of such pronounced character, he needed now a circle of persons willing on every subject to accept as correct his views, some tediously conventional or obsolete, others fantastical and based on chimeras. To obtain applause, which had formerly meant so little to him, he was now willing to leave the shelter of the Gothic tower he had constructed for himself, and so much loved, and to sit in the sun for an hour or two. Those he met during these sorties, however, must never give vent to the slightest doubt of his essential, inevitable infallibility. But the few fringed and barbate antiquaries who survived from his earlier acquaintance showed no inclination to assume this attitude, and in consequence their visits, never very frequent, became more sparse. It was plain to him that the less you knew people, and the shorter the time you had known them, the less likely they were to contradict you. It was, in short, no longer 'such a mistake to have friends', so long as they were not really friends at all.

When, in a flight of fancy, planning some trifle in which even he hardly believed – a set of dessert-plates by Lalique, with a gold medallion of my mother and himself in the centre, or some knives and forks with china handles fashioned in their image, he would now refer to a still mythical host. He would remark defiantly, as though in bravado, or perhaps because he just could not help saying it, or because he wanted to hear what I would say in reply,

'It would be cheaper no doubt to have a quantity made at the same time. Better get twelve friends to join us! . . . They'd be only too delighted!'

'Which of your friends would you suggest?' I would reply cautiously. 'Let us make a list.'

Brought back to reality after this fashion, his eye would go blank, and his fire would be quenched. Even at the best, he must have admitted to himself, they would be acquaintances, and probably not disposed for such luxuries, even if they could afford them. But he would not allow these sentiments to escape him. Instead, he would merely toss his head and make a favourite sound of annoyance and disapproval: 'Chut!', I suppose, it would be rendered in print.

Where was he to find them, this host, willing to hang on his words, to be astounded by his creations at Renishaw, and, in particular, to become in a flutter over his alterations at Scarborough, where he was proceeding with enjoyment, but at considerable cost, to turn the interior of an 1820 house of Italianate inclination into a post-Edwardian dome of pleasure? There were always relations. But one was apt to lose touch. One ought to keep up with them more.

Not only, however, was one apt to lose touch with relations, he must have admitted in his own mind, but the majority of them were inclined to be obstinate, and not easily to fall in with his ideas, or be interested in what he was doing for the family. Had he bought a race-horse, or even a cricket bat, yes, they would have been willing to acclaim his action. But they resolutely ignored his projects.

In the end my father recruited some of the chorus to admire these novelties from among the artistic wives of local clergy, doctors and lawyers; they proved adequate to the task. He need only see them for the meal to which they were asked, and then, after showing them the house, he could go straight upstairs to rest, and spend the remainder of the day in his convenient retreat in the thirteenth century. It was really less trouble than having people to stay: yet visitors here and at Renishaw were more plentiful and frequent than in the years immediately preceding. Among them, though there were few persons of intelligence, was at least one man of genius, – at any rate, of genius within the Edwardian limitations imposed upon him by his epoch: Sir Edwin Lutyens. He often visited us, but these visits were explicable; they were professional, he was paid for them.

One had never seen before, and will never see again, anyone who resembled this singular and delightful man. An expression of mischievous benevolence was his distinguishing mark, as it was that of his work. He would sit, with his bald, dome-like head lowered at a particular angle of reflection, as his very large, blue, reflective eyes contemplated a view, a work of art, or something peculiarly outrageous that he intended shortly to say. Meanwhile he held in his mouth, rather than smoked, a small pipe – he smoked a number of small pipes during the course of the day –, and when he spoke, his speech tumbled from him quickly, like that of an impetuous schoolboy. Though he was so far from staid in demeanour and in the things he said, yet about him there was a quality, perhaps physical, that seemed to survive in him from his Danish ancestors. His sense of irreverence, his spontaneity, his hatred of the pompous, made him a perfect foil to my father, whose admiration for him as an architect allowed a certain licence to the man and to his Jack-in-the-box forms of fun. This, together with his endless, bubbling flow of puns – and the sillier they were, the more their author enjoyed them –, *could* become tiring to those possessed of less vitality than himself. And so, though my father looked forward tremendously to his visits, and would for weeks beforehand make plans for how to entertain him, yet being host did not prevent him from taking to his bed for longer and longer periods of the day when his guest arrived.

Even today his jokes still linger; delayed jokes, comparable to the booby-traps that the German armies were said to leave behind them. Thus, the other afternoon, on sudden impulse as I was passing, I opened a drawer in a cabinet on the stairs at Renishaw. Inside, I noticed an envelope, with something written on it. I took it out, and read: '*A lock of Marie Antoinette's hair, cut from her head ten minutes after execution.*' Carefully unfastening the envelope, I looked in it, and found within some rather coarse grey hair, tied up with a faded ribbon. For a time I was puzzled, thinking how odd it was that so interesting a relic should have been left about, just anywhere, in that manner, wondering why, for example, my father had never told me of it, and how it had come here and who had shorn it – and then, about an hour later, in the way the memory sometimes acts, so that you are able to remember in detail an occurrence which only a little while before was so completely forgotten that it no longer existed, a scene came back to me. It was over thirty years ago, and Ned Lutyens and I were sitting on a sofa in the library at Wood End. My father had just left the room to look for a rough drawing he had made on the back of an envelope, to illustrate a possible alteration of which he had thought whilst out walking, and which he wanted the architect to consider. Suddenly, as we were talking, we heard a rending sound, and found that the cover of the sofa had split, revealing its stuffing. Ned had hurriedly seized a bit of it, pulled it out, and then screwed round it a bit of ribbon he had proceeded to tear off the edge of a curtain. Having done this, he placed the wisp of stuffing in an envelope, on the outside of which he wrote something, sealed it up and threw it into the drawer of a cabinet. He then shut the drawer, and returned to the sofa. All this he had accomplished with remarkable speed, for fear of my father returning to catch him at it. As he sat down, he remarked to me,

'Nobody's likely to find that for a long time, and by then it will have become real.'

When Wood End had been sold ten years ago, much of the furniture had been moved to Renishaw – and this was the cabinet. Had anyone but myself found this piece of horse or sheep hair – and even I had almost forgotten the incident –, it would doubtless, as the author of the joke prophesied, have passed for a genuine relic.

With the exception of the decoration of the ball-room at Renishaw, and of the design of the unfinished Pillared Room next it, even in the earlier years the many alterations that Lutyens planned for my father came to nothing. Nevertheless, year after year, my father would regularly start a new hare to be coursed by the famous architect, but in the end would inevitably employ in his place a local architect, who would more readily fall in with his patron's ideas. In fact, local architects replaced Lutyens for the same reason that new friends replaced the old. My father had discovered a distant range of relatives, too, whom he now invited to stay at Renishaw: the nearer still remained obdurate, blind to the beauties he was projecting, as to those already executed. They seldom saw him; they did not understand him, he said. And yet . . . I wondered. In any case, in whatever direction lay their interests, whether sporting by inclination or no, these never prevented them from welcoming me, a comparative stranger, to their houses now that I was stationed in London: for kindness to young cousins was a tradition that they inherited and thoroughly approved.

Especially did my great-aunt Blanche Sitwell trouble herself about me. At the age of seventy-four, though she no longer rode to hounds, her activity was amazing. She would run up and down stairs like a young woman, and the many contradictory beliefs that inspired her conversation, gave it a special quality, an earnest yet humorous vagueness. In spite of her own carelessness in matters of dress, in spite of her strong and unconventional radical views, she paid great attention to the manners, outward aspect, and even clothes, of her young relatives: and letters

would rain down on me on subjects extending from the way one's hair
had been cut recently, and who was the best contemporary barber in
London, to a discussion of tendencies on the English stage, the disesta-
blishment of the Church, the experiences of her father's old friend and
brother-in-law Sir Frederick Stovin in the Peninsular War, the sweated-
labour conditions in East End tailors' shops, and the abolition of the
House of Lords. All these letters, it was understood, had to be answered
immediately, or a frantic note would arrive demanding the meaning of
my silence. I don't know that my aunt and I shared many interests; but
this in no way spoilt our friendship. At least we shared two: a universal
curiosity about people, and an attitude of rather critical attention to my
father's activities. When in London, and not on duty, I would repair
every Sunday afternoon to her house in Egerton Crescent, off the
Brompton Road, for tea.

Many incidents that occurred in my aunt's drawing-room return to my
mind – one, in particular, which retains its own germ of farcical fun. My
brother, my sister and I were all having tea there on Sunday afternoon.
Edith was sitting in an old-fashioned armchair, the loose cover for which
happened to be lying near by on a chair against the wall. Suddenly we
heard the front-door bell ring, and then the voice, well known to us, of
an old friend of my parents. She was very kind, but such a great bore that
my sister had already pleaded illness as an excuse for not seeing the old
lady that very day at luncheon. Now here she was! And my sister appealed
to my brother and me to rescue her in some way. Telling my sister not
to move, but to sit absolutely still, we seized the loose cover, which
fortunately proved to be very loose, fitted it over her and the chair, and
carried it – and her – out of the room in triumph. Only just in time; for
we passed the new arrival outside the door, and explained to her that we
would be back in a moment, but that one leg of the chair was unsteady,
and that my aunt just asked us to put it away downstairs, in case she
forgot and allowed someone to sit in it. So we smuggled Edith downstairs,
and quietly to the front door, ourselves returning to continue our tea
with a distracted aunt.

A connection of ours, to whom my aunt introduced my sister and me
at this time, was Lady Colvin, the wife of Sir Sidney, for many years
Keeper of the Prints and Drawings at the British Museum. Sir Sidney,
the author and editor of many publications, had been Robert Louis
Stevenson's most faithful and intimate friend.

My sister was a more frequent visitor to the Colvins than was I, but I used also to go to their house, and they were most kind to both of us. Theirs was the first salon in which I set foot, and I recall, rather mistily over the gap of thirty years, the pink glow of the drawing-room in Palace Gardens Terrace; Sir Sidney, sitting with his back to the window, with, outlined against it, his head at the particular downward angle at which he held it, the edges of his beard blurred by the light; Lady Colvin, armed with her fan, reclining on a sofa; and general talk, witty and interesting, and not, as in most houses of the time, about politics – for political controversies were then beginning to rage, – but about pictures and books.

In my new life, talk of books – though I had never experienced it – was what I most felt the need of. So eager for it was I, that I became nervous and tongue-tied when visiting the Colvins. And at the Tower, the point in which my brother-officers and I showed the most divergence was in our reading matter – though, at twenty years of age, we did not realize the gulf that this constituted. Edith, of course, was my chief adviser on what to read, and poetry was then, as now, her most cherished form of literature. In prose, I had already found two authors for myself: one, Strindberg, the other, Samuel Butler – traces of both of whom can be found, I suspect, by the discerning in my literary ancestry. The favourite reading, on the other hand, of my brother-officers was usually the novels of Whyte-Melville – who had himself been an officer in the Brigade of Guards –, and, at this particular moment, or just after, a current popular romance, entitled, if I remember correctly, *Poppy* – at any rate, it concerned the illicit love of a Duchess, over-eager to be cooperative in producing an heir for her husband. My new friends seemed, however, neither to approve nor disapprove of the books I read; so that I had less censorship to fear here than that which overshadowed my reading at home.

Everything that happened at the Tower possessed its own atmosphere. To catch a cold, for example, in the Officers' Quarters – an enormous, unheated Victorian formula for gothic, machicolated with a kind of prim desperation –, and subsequently to be in bed there with bronchitis, proved an unforgettable experience. I have never known a building that seemed to be so much made of stone, as though one were camping in a quarry, and the ailment itself had a special quality, as if the germs that caused it had long been confined to the Tower in the interests of public security. It so happened that I was afflicted with one of these colds at a time when my father chanced to be in London.

His life now very plainly divided itself into two halves: one, fussing about the future – a state of mind much aggravated by the Lloyd George Budget of 1909 and especially the clauses it had contained about the unearned increment in Land Values; the other, fussing about the past. (The present he did not allow to concern him, maintaining that it was a fiction, composed of the immediate past and the immediate future.) Of the first, I find still many evidences, forcibly expressed in his letters. To the second process, of fussing about the past, it was his wont to refer as 'my literary work' – and, indeed, he worked hard at it. Called by Henry at seven, he would present himself at the British Museum Reading Room at its opening at 9 a.m. carrying a circular, deflated air-cushion, slung on his coat-sleeve like a bracelet. He would then slowly inflate the cushion and, first placing it in his accustomed place in Row L, sit down on it. Between the opening hour and twelve, he would spend his time among pedigrees, charts and records. He had a gift for such things, and they would come tumbling at him from their shelves in the same fashion that pictures pursue great experts. Returning to his hotel by taxi-cab soon after midday, he would enjoy a solitary and, because of the hour, rather unpopular luncheon. He could not bear to be kept waiting, and so, since he ate at tremendous speed – a habit which, as I have said, he always justified by alleging it to be a sign of mental energy –, the meal would occupy the smallest possible space of time. He would have Turkish coffee afterwards, chain-smoking three or four strong Turkish cigarettes. Then he would go upstairs for a short siesta in a tightly shuttered room. When he came downstairs, the porter would call a taxi-cab for him, and he would go back to the Reading Room, remaining there until it closed. This routine he followed when in London until the outbreak of the war in 1939. He was then one of the few surviving holders of the 'green ticket', if not the only one, having been admitted before the age of twenty-one – when, in fact, he was eighteen – by special recommendation of Archbishop Tait, his great-uncle and guardian.

On the occasion of which I talk, perhaps attracted by the medieval associations of my domicile to an extent sufficient to banish his fear of infection, he arrived to see me in a taxi. I saw him get out of the cab, and thought how impressive and distinguished he looked, in a silk hat that made him appear taller than his six foot, and in a long coat with a wide collar of Irish beaver. He stood for a moment contemplating the Officers' Mess. I fear, however, that its architecture must have disappointed him, even though its amenities were sufficiently antiquated to allow it to rank with the oldest buildings within the Tower boundaries. It was a strange two-man procession that entered my room: my father first, carrying in his hand a small primer on heredity and eugenics; and then the taxi-driver, staggering under the weight of a dozen or so darkly-bound, foxed and moth-eaten volumes: some consisting of Gregorovius's *History of the City of Rome in the Middle Ages*, others of books by Herbert Spencer and William James. But the strangest feature of the episode was that the taxi-driver appeared also to have read the Gregorovius volumes, for when, pointing to them, I asked if they were not heavy, he replied, with an air of smiling sincerity,

'Well, not to read, sir. They're a treat to read.'

I longed to talk to him, but my father waved him aside.

In return for this small library, I lent my father Samuel Butler's *Way of All Flesh*. He seldom read the books one pressed on him, though he was too polite to refuse to take them. It therefore came as a surprise to find, a week later, that he had read it from cover to cover.

Samuel Butler, my father considered, encouraged self-indulgence; and of all forms of this sin, extravagance was the worst. My bills were mounting, but not so much as my father made out, for he possessed his own methods of calculating, his own mathematical processes. I did not much care; my father had placed me here; it had been no wish of mine, and I had better enjoy myself in the ways in which I saw my companions enjoy themselves. Perhaps the self-indulgence against which my father thundered with the inspired eloquence of a preacher was wrong: but, looking round me, I came to the conclusion that it seemed to make people easy and amiable and kind.

Extravagance has done more for the world than ever has thrift, but a private person is a more likable spendthrift than is the state. (Private persons spend money, at the worst, for their own gratification: states spend it to crush their neighbours. On extravagance the arts have flourished continually, that of building in particular.) The mind of the thrifty is a sad, miserly and miserable mind, without imagination, cutting the coat to the cloth: and it manifests an extraordinary hatred towards the lazy. The rage of the successful little man against the indolent is a moral indignation of the vilest kind, for the gifts of the lazy man to his more industrious brothers have been numberless – and I speak without prejudice, for, as to myself, I cannot bear to be idle for a moment and am, congenitally, a fusser, a plodder, one who takes trouble. All the short-cuts, all the labour-saving devices have been the fruit of ingenuity born of sloth. The lazy man stops to think, and the extravagant is obliged – if he is to survive – to make money. It was this vice which chained me to my desk, and fashioned me into a writer. The urge to spend more than I possessed, to buy pictures and books and works of art, to travel, was the spur to ambition; though always I was vain, and glory is my element. Had I been content, as the prudent advise, to live within my pay and my allowance, I should have learnt to pare and prune and scrape, it may be, but I should never have won renown. I should have remained a mute, inglorious Osbert Sitwell.

If, when I was a young officer, I had been told that one day I would be able to earn my living honestly – for I do not call being so indifferent an officer as I was, earning my living honestly –, or, far more unlikely, to make a name for myself, I would not have believed it. I was singularly incompetent. Though able with ease to understand the most obscure poetry and the most difficult prose, I could never comprehend a single fact or tenet in the Drill Book, a brisk, clever lay-out of the more simple military exercises, simply expressed. I could read it over and over again, as formerly I had been able to read a Latin or Greek Grammar, and nothing of it would stay in my mind, which became a stone, rolling, gathering no moss, a dry, empty stone.

If I have talked little of my ambitions, it is because I entertained none then – except to leave school and to get away from home. That was enough. Indeed, my ideas in general were at this time of rather a negative order. I knew what I did not want to do – most of all I had dreaded entering the army, because I hated discipline and heartily disliked communal life as I had known it at school. Further, I had not enough self-confidence to allow me to cherish ambitions. I was always being told my faults, and it seemed to me that the catalogue of them was just and by no means exaggerated. I agreed with my father in thinking that I was ill-qualified for any profession. And it was precisely this sense of weakness that led me into captivity for a while: since, before being translated into an ensign in the Grenadiers, I had travelled in a strange land, among savage tribes – let us see how it happened.

CHAPTER TWO

The phrase that seemed to sound like a theme through the miserable composition of my school-days, and subsequently through my career in the army, and occurred in every report, public or confidential, was the truncated but haunting sentence,

'MIGHT DO BETTER IF HE CHOSE.'

Such, however, was not my belief, for I was most diffident, though full, as well, of senseless pride.

By disposition I was fond of Nature, but preferred to it, as I prefer today, the study of art and the enjoyment to be obtained therefrom. And in Nature itself I was more interested by those things that approached nearest to art, – flowers and shells and trees and falling water. Outwardly, my character had altered: for when I had gone to school I had been intensely sociable, but now I had grown shy as well: and, by another contradiction born of my schooling, had become both melancholy and gay, being as silent with those I disliked as talkative with those I liked. I loved the solitude as much as I enjoyed, too, the life of cities. Extremely high-spirited, my greatest advantage was that my constitution did not allow me to be depressed, even by the most severe occurrences, for more than forty-eight hours at a stretch. That I must have inherited; its origin was no doubt physical, and connected with my large frame – I am over six foot, and even then was by no means meagre – and with my whole physical set-up; for the fair and florid are perhaps less prone to melancholy than the dark of hair and skin. Perhaps it was this same quality which enabled my ancestors to plunge without fear of consequences into the battles of medieval times, and, later, into their great flights of extravagance: yet this advantage was singular, for many members of my family were given to nervous fussing and fretting, qualities that in the end exercise upon the character an erosive effect. I possessed, further, that disregard for money which I have described, and which brought so formative an influence to bear upon my career. In addition, I suffered to an extraordinary degree – and, looking back, this seems strange in a young man of seventeen or eighteen – from boredom: a fact that deeply shocked my father. People, he said, were never bored in medieval times. It was a modern and degenerate emotion.

This boredom, perhaps, was symptomatic of the artist, constituting a premonition of the feeling he experiences in those terrible moments of repose when he finds himself unable to create. At any rate, works of art, to go to a picture-gallery or concert, or to read great poetry, were the only things that lifted it from me. And here, too, a curious fact emerges, for though I had been conversant since childhood with many of the masterpieces of Italian art and architecture, and though, when my sister was in the house, I lived with music and poetry, yet my overwhelming and, as it were, creative love of the arts came to me through my introduction to modern works, and so in this manner my approach was a little different from the ordinary. Indeed, I had always preferred modern to renaissance, and renaissance to antique art, except in very young days when I had been somewhat of a history-snob: I had consistently appreciated better the works of human genius nearest to my own days: but soon I grew to understand the Primitives, through my love of the Post-Impressionists, and to adore Bach and Mozart through the avenues opened to me by my favourite modern masters, Debussy and Stravinsky. About works of art, as about people, I had always possessed a great and consuming curiosity. I would be happy for hours, talking to someone I had not met before, and reading the strange book of his or her character. There were other qualities, too, that I knew in my heart to be derived from my heredity; among them, the more than ordinary share of pride and vanity that in those days I possessed.

These were humbled every day by my father's continual snubbings and condemnations of all my ways; they were to be further mortified by events. During this whole time, the shadow that moved with us, wherever we went, was growing and darkening; some agency was at work, both in the family and outside it, loosening the fibres, darkening the colours. Something was going wrong in the world, and could surely be felt by the sensitive, through the intense sweetness of being alive at that time; something, too, had gone wrong in the house. The airy vistas and green pleasaunces of the garden were delusive in their grandeur, and behind them lay the mean streets, the pawnshops, the prisons – the prison. But these things could not be seen. As the world looked, in contrast to how one felt it to be, it was at last flowering. This was the moment of Europe's fullest bloom.

Yet for me, the time between leaving Eton and finding – or rather being thrown into – a profession, was only lit by the flame of my animal high spirits, and perhaps by a certain power of imagination. 1910 and '11 were, I think, the peak years, both of my father's irritability and of my own misery. In part, my father's condition was caused by the very width of his range, by the superabundance of his plans and projects; in part, by my mother's utter lack of interest in them, and inability to pretend, by her rages, too, so inexplicably easy to rouse; while, on his side, his perpetual gloomy prognostications about the state to which even the simplest and most natural courses of conduct would reduce one, combined with a lack, as it were, of warmth and spontaneity to render him a very far from ideal companion for her.

My father had thought that it would be easy for him to mould the character of any young girl, and took no account, except in his own case, of the influences of heredity. Throughout his life, it was his ill fortune to misread and misunderstand the character of those around him, and, in consequence, to cast them wrongly for their parts. To them he assigned precisely the merits, no less than the faults, which they did not possess. This was perhaps chief of the qualities that in the end nullified his great strength of character and remarkable gifts, just as his irritability cancelled out his natural kindness.

Often he used to deplore the strange chance by which, having taken so much trouble to get intelligent children, his whole early life having been modelled, apparently, on a sort of Nietzschean-Darwinian uplift scheme towards that goal, we three had been sent down – or up – to him. Just as Dr Arnold had prayed before the procreating of his children, with what beneficial results we all know, so my father, representative of a less pious and seemingly more scientific generation, had entered upon periods of the most rigorous training, both physical and mental – and look what he had received for his trouble! It was really very unfair, most disappointing. And that the Life Force should have shovelled my sister on to him was even more patently unjust than that It should have allocated to him my brother or myself. Birth, no less than marriage, was, plainly, a lottery: but whereas he had gone in for it to obtain for the next generation a straight nose and charm, he had drawn a booby-prize, an aquiline nose and a body inhabited by an alien and fiery spirit. It was difficult to know, really, where to begin the list of just complaints.

The girl was grown-up now, and seemed to have developed a most objectionable sense of pity, which made her an uneasy companion for one. You never knew what she might say or do. Once, though her whole allowance was only fifty pounds a year, he had caught her giving five shillings to a beggar. 'Such a mistake!' And, after all, it was really his money. He should have been consulted. She seemed unable to pass a tramp or a beggar without giving him something, whereas the correct thing to do was not to *see* a person of that kind. She could not play games, and the extent to which she loved music was un-ladylike. She possessed no small talk, and could not, even now, recite Austin Dobson – and was it not even worse: was it not *would* not, rather than *could* not? Because her memory for poetry, he had found out from the governess, was remarkably good. There had also been that unfortunate episode at Bournemouth, which had caused a great deal of pain and worry to older people.

My sister had been paying a lengthy visit to my grandmother Sitwell, to whom she was much attached, at Bournemouth. At first my sister was very happy, for she was away from home, and the tormenting which in her case the word spelt. But the circles of visiting clergy that, wherever my grandmother might be, at once sprang up round the old lady like a circle of plainly inedible fungi, took soon to wrestling daily with my sister over the poems of Algernon Charles Swinburne, with whose works she was at the time intoxicated. They were immoral, the toadstools pronounced, and she should not be permitted to read them. Any reasonable girl should be content, so far as poetry was concerned, with the works of T. E. Brown and Elizabeth Barrett Browning. In the course of time, my sister became so much enraged by the continual attacks made upon her favourite poet that she determined to show her feeling for him in a manner that could not be mistaken.

Very early, then, one lovely September morning, she had flitted, having given no previous notice to my grandmother of her going, and, accompanied by her maid, had boarded the small boat that plied from Bournemouth to Ventnor, Isle of Wight. There, a few hours later, under the bright pennons of the summer weather, with its fleecy white clouds and high-flung seas, a singular spectacle must have greeted the curious eye of any passers-by. A tall, fair, rather thin young lady, paler than usual after her rough journey, yet with colour coming and going from the love and defiance in her heart, disembarked, bearing a large sheaf of red roses: after her, the second figure in this frieze of two, came with faltering steps a woman of about thirty, with all her lady's-maid trimmings dishevelled by the crossing, her face a sour green, and wearing this morning an expression of the plainest condemnation of the whole enterprise in which she found herself engaged, and of dislike (if the spectator could discern that much) both for poetry and the sea; she carried a jug of milk, a honeycomb, a wreath of bay-leaves, and the young lady's coat. After a few moments my sister found an open cab, drawn by a horse so old that Swinburne himself as a boy might have ridden behind it, and drove, with her maid still disapproving, through lanes just tinged with autumn's first fine gold, to Bonchurch: where, alighting, the procession entered the churchyard. After a furious battle with a sexton, who objected to such foreign ways, Edith triumphed and, bending low under an enormous fuchsia, its tasselled flowers of scarlet and purple trailing over a headstone, in the Grecian mode poured the milk, and placed the wreath of bay-leaves, the honeycomb and red roses, upon the grave of Swinburne. This safely accomplished, she drove back with her maid to Ventnor, and returned to Bournemouth and my grandmother. An appalling storm broke and long raged round her head, alternating with calm patches of religious resignation.

My father, when news of this exploit reached him, was most displeased: it was plain that the girl would never make a success of anything. He began to lay his plans. Later on, in a year or two, she had better enter the shop, near Piccadilly, of a once fashionable photographer, whose bankrupt business he had been obliged to take over in cancellation of a bad debt. He could afford to pay her a salary of a pound a week, and she could find out of it her own money for dress and all the pleasures to which in these days the young considered they possessed a perfect right! I was his eldest son – well, that entailed its own place, *ex officio*, in the Universe. For the rest, he would reserve judgement on what it would be best for me to do until it became clearer for what precise profession I showed least aptitude and liking. But for Sacheverell's future he had already arranged: he could either become a lawyer in Sheffield or mineral agent to the Sitwell Estate; which in either case could offer him a considerable amount of work, which he must, of course, for his part, undertake to execute at special rates.

During these years, I could do little that was right. Golf had succeeded puff-ball, as puff-ball ping-pong, for the test of a man's ability as leader. (My father liked the game particularly, for he had been able to lay out two golf-courses, and proposed soon to build club-houses – one was to be planned by Lutyens, with a fan-shaped dining-room, crystal chandeliers and fleur-de-pêche chimney-pieces, so that Sheffield business men could feel at home: whereas you could not really build a ping-pong or puff-ball pavilion.) Everywhere in England and America, statesmen were already preparing their triumphs of 1914 and '39 by spending long days on the golf-course and long nights at the bridge-table. One would be lost in an uncharted world without some understanding of these games. But I showed no capacity for golf – and so, every day in the summer holidays of 1909, of which I am talking, this singular man would send for me, and storm at me about my failures in this respect, as in many others. He made no attempt – and all this genuinely with my welfare taking the first conscious place in his heart – to perceive in what directions my interests lay, to make use of them, or draw more out of me. Instead, he most assiduously and effectively sapped my self-esteem: and when I was just at the age – sixteen and seventeen – to need every grain of it I could summon up.

There seemed no-one to help me. Sacheverell was too young, though he always fought valiantly on my behalf. Edith was still away a good deal, in Paris and Berlin and staying with friends – and, had she been at home, her own state of subjugation would only have been worse than mine, and she could have done nothing to aid me. Nor did my mother, even if she had been about to understand the position, seem now to possess any inclination to come to my rescue. Her own affairs, though she did not in the least comprehend the extent of the catastrophe which was beginning to loom in front of her, were now starting to worry her. She complained, too, of feeling middle-aged. She attended to nothing in the house, chose no wallpaper or cover, undertook no household duties – nor, indeed, would she have been allowed to do so by my father, had she attempted. She contented herself with sitting in her room, among bunches of tuberose and sweet geranium, reading innumerable news-papers. Occasionally, she would give vent to a favourite maxim. One I remember well, because in subsequent years it seemed strange to hear it coming from the lips of the mother of three authors: '*Never put pen to paper*'. In reality, however, this was said in allusion to the growing number of quarrels – mostly on matters of business, for he did not write letters to friends – in which, owing to his habit of letting his pen indulge in comments and strictures that were far more disagreeable than those he was accustomed to pass verbally, my father involved himself.

This tendency was, for its part, the result largely of a growing refusal to see things as they were; a characteristic I must again stress, because of its subsequent most calamitous results. Thus, one day, some years later, he suddenly demanded, 'Where is that cabinet full of beautiful old Leeds china that I arranged in the ball-room last year?' Plainly he believed in it, and thought I had sold it secretly. Yet it had, so far as any of us were

aware, never existed. Never did my father permit anyone to argue with
him, or to state views that were contrary to his own. That there could be
such, he would not allow himself to perceive. Nobody had argued with
him, nobody had contradicted him now for several decades, perhaps for
nearly half a century. If anyone ventured to dispute any opinion he held
– as sometimes we children did – or to combat any particularly extravagant
statement about, for example, some friend one knew much better than he
did, he would omnisciently reply, with an air of final and absolute
authority, and without deeming it necessary to offer proof or divulge the
source of such, no doubt, mystical awareness, *'We happen to know'*. His
natural aloofness had hardened, and encased him. If middle age had
softened him, it was in the wrong places. He began to seek human
sympathy; but unable to see his path in the modern world, he sought this
relief from people who could not supply it, who could only give flattery.
And now, moreover, he was adopting, or trying to adopt – for he was
never really able to succeed in it –, the common ideas of those with
whom, for sake of their sycophancy, he surrounded himself.

The chief and most noticeable point in his private relationships was a
system of fault-finding, as with a divining-rod, that continually grew
and strengthened. This, in its effect, militated against his ever getting
the best out of the people round him: in fact, to sum up in the words my
agent has frequently used to me in the past, 'The worst of Sir George is,
he's so damned discouraging!'

That summer, while at home, I was in such continual disgrace that I
hid myself as often, and for as long, as possible, and, if I heard my name
called by my father, kept out of the way, since I knew it must portend
something of an unpleasant nature, another explanation or rebuke, either
in private, with a formal air of solemnity, or – this in order to satisfy a
sense of power – in front of people for whom I did not care. What my
character needed to regenerate it, my father told me constantly, was for
me to have to do something unpleasant every – and, if possible, all – day:
a doctrine born of the puritanical sense of sin which I have already noticed
as so strange a trait in a man of his origin and outlook in other directions.
What was there? What tasks offered themselves, that were sufficiently
odious and oppressive? Then an idea came to him. I had said that the idea
of the army as a profession did not appeal to me. The very thing! A fine,
healthy time in the open air; and knocking about with a sword provided
excellent exercise, and proved splended training for after-life. What
branch, then, of the service, should it be? Well, I particularly hated horses,

so it had better be the Cavalry. A wonderful life in the open air, which gave one a good appetite – one felt fit for anything. And what an opportunity to use your brains – you could always play polo. He proceeded to recall to my memory what he had told me before; that, some five or ten years previously, when he had been in command of the local Volunteers, a General who had come down to inspect the regiment had said to him, 'When politics took you away from us, the British army lost a Napoleon.' (At this time, he was peculiarly conscious of his all-round universal ability, and used sometimes to say to me, as if to emphasize the gulf that separated me, inheriting, as I did, my mother's blood as well as his own, 'Of course, *I* could have made a success at anything to which I turned my hand'.) Then, again, he would go on to sketch life in the army; of which he knew a good deal, for he had read Froissart and other Chronicles, had been as a young man in the Yeomanry, as well as later the Volunteers, and had talked to Major Viburne about it. One never felt so well as under canvas! And if it was bad weather, one could always go and sleep at home.

Instead, then, of being sent to Oxford, where – who knows? – I might really have learned something at last, I was packed off, very suddenly, to an army crammer's; an institution now defunct, rendered happily obsolete by the reformed system of obtaining commissions.

I suppose all this time I must have been very much attached to my father, or I could not have been so wretched. My self-respect had entirely perished; for of what use was I, if my father so little esteemed me? After all, he was the most intelligent and learned person of his generation who was within my range, the most intellectually developed and nervously equipped. The state of mind to which I was reduced, persuaded me almost to dislike my home, where every tree and vista seemed to re-echo my father's voice. Sometimes I would, nevertheless, hide in the garden with Sacheverell; but he, albeit he invariably took my side, seemed at this period more popular than I was with the family so for the most part I remained in my bedroom. It was high up, and no-one would climb all those stairs to look for me – and, another advantage, I could see for myself through the open window what was happening.

The garden was in gala this year. Over the rounded top of an ancient holly, which grew against one of the angles of the house, where it jutted forward, the lawns lay spread in their richest, fullest beauty. The hedges had grown and were by now substantial, and the whole design, the counterpoint of bright mown grass and deep shade, of water and of trees, had settled down, and looked as if it had existed always. The eye followed the gleam of water from fountain and pool to the lake below, on the surface of which the weed showed here and there in wide, moon-gold patches, the weed supplying a backing to the glint of the water as quicksilver does to a mirror. I heard people talking. Peering out cautiously I observed my father peacocking about on the lawn, among an imported bevy of sycophantic females. He was wearing a grey wide-awake hat, a grey suit, and had, slung round him, a pair of binoculars. He was pointing with a stick towards the horizon, stabbing it, as it were. His voice, very clear and decisive, but rather thin, floated up to the window. 'All that belongs to *me*!' he was saying, in answer to a question, and, with a final stab, 'What we want there is just a cascade between the distant trees. Nothing looks so well or points a view so aptly as falling water! Not everyone can manage it – but it's quite easy for me.' And he added confidentially, with a little smile of self-congratulation, 'Between ourselves, I have over two miles of lead-piping up my sleeve!' The Bevy looked impressed, I thought, by this clever but unexpected piece of legerdemain.

The Bevy had succeeded to, and replaced, the Fun Brigade, and was much more heterogeneous in its composition. All the members of the Fun Brigade had come of the same race, class and creed, and, in a large sense, of the same family. Their interests, if limited in scope, had been identical. No-one belonging to it had been capable of understanding or admiring my father's imaginative creations. Further, though so pliable in other ways, yet the whole body was resolute in that not one member of it was willing to try to find favour with the master of the house by applauding him in this direction. *Esprit de corps* frowned on so great an outlay of money or things one could neither kill, eat, wear nor ride. Thus, when my father with pride showed to these people the lake he had made, the dam which was now being dug out in the Eckington woods, or propounded some new, still more grandiose scheme, they merely smiled wistfully, unconvincingly, while quickly calculating how much it had – or would – cost, and how many pheasants could have been reared, how many foxes torn to pieces, for that sum of money. (Indeed, he seemed to be able to obtain no response from anyone; for when he had lately observed a superannuated collier watching the digging in the woods, and had asked him 'Are you thinking of the fishing there will be?', the old man had replied gloomily, 'No, Sir George – I was thinking what a wunnerful lot o' suicides there'll be in that blinking pool.')

My father needed more than this. Just as I require flattery in order to work at my best, so did he, for the most perfect evocation of vista or torrent. For this reason, for this purpose, the Bevy had supplanted the Fun Brigade, and now reigned at Renishaw in the summer months. There had been, however, an awkward interregnum, when the old guests, piqued by my father's neglect of them, had refused to return, and the new band had not been formed. My mother, bored without visitors in the house, used to send perpetual telegrams to people imploring them to stay. Henry, handing one of the wires to the Postmaster, was heard to ask,

'Mr Wilks, don't YOU know of anyone who would like a fortnight at Renishaw Hall?'

All the same, he was amazed with the former habituals for being refractory, and when someone had inquired of him about a member of the Fun Brigade, a certain Gerald Dancaster, whom Henry considered a mollycoddle, 'Isn't Mr Dancaster coming here again this year?' had replied,

'Well, I rather expected the gale would have blown him in last night.'

The new applausive body, the Bevy, possessed three or four main props, such as Madame Amboise, Miss Camber-Crawshaw and Miss Fingelstone, who could be relied on to lead the whole company in admiration of what he was doing – and for the rest, there were the wives of former supporters in Scarborough, people for whom, for one reason or another, he used to say he felt sorry, adding with a somewhat gracious air, and the particular gesture of his hand, descending in stages and with a slight flutter that always accompanied it, 'We ought to show them a little kindness.' But, immured in his tower, he now felt really a great need for feminine sympathy, as well as for flattery, and he could rely on the Bevy to produce it, so much of it, as it were, for so many days' visit, in the same way that prostitutes provide love by the hour.

Madame Amboise, plump summary of her race and epoch, was in quite a different category from the chorus, whose names, even, she affected never to be able to learn. She was much more cultivated and intelligent, and at the same time much more absurd. An enormous Russian, of middle age, with thick white hair piled up like meringues, and a complexion of palest lilac, in the manner of the many of her fellow-countrymen before the Revolution, she suffered from a dilated soul and was always eager to tell you of its symptoms. But her interests were by no means confined to these, for she was faintly tainted, too, with

European culture of *l'Art Nouveau* period, and further, she seemed to be particularly at home in a world, imperceptible to others, that lay precariously unbalanced midway between politics and the psychic. She carried about with her, moreover, an atmosphere of political scare, bringing with her into this calm, Edwardian scene a premonitory breath of the coming great disasters that were already being prepared on the golf-courses. In consequence, the comfortable did not enjoy talking to her: it was as though a tramp in rags had entered the drawing-room and sat down. They were obliged to ask themselves 'Can there be anything in what she says?' – but only for the moment. Fortunately for their peace of mind, she was so patently ludicrous in other directions – as are so many other prophets once they stray from their precise dominion – that it was soon possible for the inhabitants of the drawing-room to reassure themselves, dismissing doom with a light titter. She was ridiculous, they said: and this was true. But she could not, of course, be expected to recognize it; or that the creaking machinery of her charm, the golden net of her recollections, made her still more absurd. She aimed at creating an effect, and she succeeded. More than on her beauty, she relied on her charm, her voice, and, above all, her sympathy, which she was always ready to dispense, and which was so thick that, as though she were a medium producing ectoplasm, one could almost see it. She liked, too, to darken the background against which she displayed herself with talk of her hard life, and she would insinuate the existence of some great political mystery which had imbued even her childhood with dark tones. When other children had ridden donkeys on the sands, she had sleighed behind a reindeer over the drear Siberian snows – or so she gave one to understand.

Born into intellectual circles in Moscow, she had, in fact, spent her youth in the best tea-merchant and international *milieu* in that city. As soon as she had grown up, her family had taken her to Paris, where she had met and finally married the son of Amboise, the painter, and friend of Ary Scheffer. But the mists of the past had swallowed this rather nebulous figure. Now was the time of *Il Fuoco*, D'Annunzio's famous novel, and I think Madame Amboise, in spite of her northern origin, saw the whole of life through his eyes, rather than through those of a Russian novelist. Be that as it may, in the course of a few decades her life had opened up in the directions natural to her. She had specialized as the confidante and friend of all minor royalties of artistic leanings and unorthodox views, and used to sit in the loggia of the palace at Sinaia listening to Carmen Sylva reading her own poems. She had also drifted into the position of becoming mistress of a rich Englishman, a friend of King Edward's. He was one of those strangely prominent figures, half politician, half journalist, whose semi-inspired and pompous bungling, and easily disavowed statements of policy, marred the diplomacy of the opening years of the century, and whose continual interference in foreign affairs constituted one of the chief factors that promoted the First World War. This great love of hers, though on her side permanent, had after a year or two degenerated into a chronic state of guerrilla warfare: but this in no way caused her to feel any sense of humiliation, and she would talk freely, and as though they were matters of romance, of the various ruses and stratagems she had employed, and of the cunning devices by which she had secreted herself in his house, and the promptness with which his wife had discovered and flung her out of it. These stories combined with her friendships, and her position as the discarded mistress of one of these mysterious beings, lama-like in the diplomatic sphere, and an architect of the recently established but still rickety *Entente Cordiale*, to afford her still an occasional place at a luncheon, though never at a dinner-table, in Paris. She came to us to find peace, as she said – or, perhaps, merely because for the moment she had nowhere else to go. For hours, if she could find one of us to listen to her, she would talk in her smooth, slow, rather deep and evenly accentuated voice. Sometimes she would be very confiding. ' "Madame Amboise, Hélène, may I call you?", D'Annunzio said to me, when last I saw him, "It is not for your beauty that I love you, though that too is unusual, but for the so-velvety bloom of your voice." '

The first time I had seen Madame Amboise was about a year before, when my mother took my sister, my brother and myself – aged respectively twenty, ten and fifteen – to see her in a hotel in London. We waited for her in a room which was called the *Reading Room*. At last a heavy footfall sounded, and Madame Amboise advanced through the open door, clothed like a matador in a trailing cloak of scarlet velvet. She glided towards us as though in a trance, as though not seeing the faces round her, but only ours. From a distance away, still sounded that memorable and mellifluous voice.

'Ah! my friend, my friend, I, Hélène Amboise, have had my love betrayed for a young girl of seventeen! *Écoute!* He has introduced her to his wife and family!'

She would have liked often to talk to my mother about her soul, but on the only occasion she had attempted it my mother had listened most patiently, and at the end had counselled the taking of a strong liver-pill, a remedy that she prescribed for every ill, moral, physical or mental, and this advice had discouraged Madame Amboise. With my father, she had soon realized, too, that it was equally impossible to talk on such matters, because as though he were a character in a Tchekhov play, he would, if the subject were not to his taste, carry on a conversation, apparently in answer to what was said, albeit in reality bearing no relation to it and existing on a totally different subject and level. Thus, while the poor Russian lady would be diagnosing the mysterious symptoms of her soul, he would reply with tender details concerning garden furniture in Byzantine times, or explanations of some pedigree of the twelfth century. Therefore, her feelings pent up in this fashion, Madame Amboise would wait and if she found my sister alone would discuss for hours the state of the interesting invalid prisoned within her large hyperborean body. She would have liked to consult Sacheverell on the matter – he was now twelve –, but he gave her no encouragement. To me she talked not only about her soul, but about her past life, of which I learnt now in much detail. One day, for example, she told me, in slow, low, hollow tones, of her husband and his fate. 'Monsieur Amboise was thirty years older than I, a young girl, and when after two years he retired permanently to the Asylum, his delusion being that everywhere he went he was haunted by the sound of my so-beautiful voice, I mourned him as a father, rather than as a husband.'

Though she was prone to interfere, Madame Amboise was also very kind and friendly, willing to enter into the spirit of anything, and I remember an old friend of my family, Eve Fairfax, and my brother and myself, inducing her to roll down a steep grass slope; it was as though a mountain were descending. Her rendering of English, too, was a great joy, and often supplied a welcome touch of low comedy. Thus, as I write, an effective, if – to make use of a former Bloomsbury colloquialism – 'rather music-hall' sentence of hers comes back to me. After the fashion of many cultivated foreigners, she deliberately made a point of being frightened by domestic animals: and on the occasion to which I refer she had been for a walk in the park at Renishaw, when a frolicsome young heifer had crossed her path. Accordingly, she returned to the house at once, and, looking very large and plainly out of breath, entered the drawing-room where my sister, my brother and I were sitting, and remarked in that velvet voice, the sound of which had earned the famous encomium from D'Annunzio, but which was now punctuated at frequent intervals by a sound like an engine letting off steam,

'My friends, I have met a bull-child in the park – and he has put me into pants. Since then, I am in them always!'

She liked to sit for hours in the garden, holding over her head a parasol with a coloured lining that, under the sun's play, caused hot, Renoir-like tints and tones to pass over her countenance. But she still saw herself as an enchantress, still felt youthful under the mountains of fat which the years had deposited upon her form. She did not, even though she liked to emphasize how graceful and sprightly she had been as a girl, really believe, I think, that she had much altered.

'When I was eighteen,' she used to say, 'and my mother took me to walk in the Tuileries Gardens, people would turn round and stare, and I would hear them say 'Look! See her! What a lark, what a *lark*!'

Though Madame Amboise spent as much of the day as she could sitting out, and talking, or going round the garden with my father, listening to him unrolling his schemes, and was never to be seen writing a letter, yet she invariably received a large post – thick envelopes, heavy, and with several foreign stamps on them.

'It's a rum go,' Henry would remark to me. 'Every day the old Russian grampus gets those letters – and always the same number, seventeen. And it's my belief the handwriting on all of them is the same, though it looks different and the envelopes are different shapes . . . No one could ever *write* on the number of pages that's in 'em. It's too much, altogether. Nobody'd have the time – let alone the wish. It's overdoing it, and them foreigners are a lazy lot, too . . . No, you heed my words, sir: *there's a mystery somewhere*! . . . But she's one of the best of them. I'm sure I don't know where the Great White Chief finds most of the people he asks here now. I've got a good mind to fasten up a notice on the front door *"Rubbish may be deposited here"*!'

I did not pay much attention to what he said. Besides, Madame Amboise would take her letters up to her room when they arrived, and after reading them in seclusion for an hour – which seemed, considering their length, a very reasonable time to take over it –, would descend again, with a visible aura of glory, of international news, round her, and proceed to distribute scraps of information as if feeding the birds.

'Natasha de Roquefort – she was a Keschinsky – writes from her château near Tours; the harvest has been wonderful, and if war comes, will prove a great support.'

'Marguérite de Sedan tells me in her letters that a German spy, wearing a *pickelhaube*, has been found hiding in a *Pavillon d'Amour* at the end of the garden, on their estate in Burgundy. He had a semaphore with him, and had cut off the little fingers of all the children in the neighbourhood.'

'Melincourt writes that war has been postponed until after the winter.'

So the tape unrolled itself upon the news-machine.

It was a year or two before the truth came out and Henry was proved to be right. One summer, when Madame Amboise was leaving us to pay a series of visits to friends in France, she asked a fellow-guest in the house, whom she had known previously, whether she would mind addressing and posting every day seventeen envelopes – already stamped – to the various addresses. It did not matter, Madame Amboise said, what was put inside, so long as it was bulky enough – anything would do, book-catalogues, old newspapers, anything!

'But why seventeen?'

'Because, child, it is my lucky number. Besides, to live in the world, it is necessary, absolutely necessary, to receive every day a large post. Then I can give my hosts the news from England.'

'But surely not addressed in the same handwriting?' her intended accomplice persisted.

'That does not matter in the least,' Madame Amboise replied, 'though there is nothing, my friend, to prevent you from using a different nib for each envelope, if so you wish. It will not be a great charge, and I, Hélène, will, pay.'

Alas, in the end, poor Madame Amboise reached a place where she could neither give nor receive news. The war, which she had so long foreseen, nevertheless caught her unawares. In August 1914, she was taking a cure at an Austrian watering-place, and had been swept off to an internment camp, – the same in which her countryman, Nijinsky, found himself. And in my mind's eye I see her, still intent on her soul and on her love, following the great dancer about, and telling him in her 'so-velvety' voice of her experiences.

These sad days, however, were still in the future, and at the moment, as I looked out of my window, she was bumping and flapping about the lawn with my father. On his right came Miss Camber-Crawshaw, leader of another contingent of the Bevy. One of several sisters, she belonged to the superannuated dairy-maid type, and possessed a voice that, like a mill, ground silence into its component parts. She had joined up in the first place as a friend of my mother's, but half-way through her career had changed sides, and become a Yorkshire intellectual and esthete, eager to support my father's every plan. Beyond Madame Amboise walked, in a flutter or scurry of sweet-pea or pastel-coloured scarves and chiffons, the wife of a doctor from Scarborough, kind, innocent, really nice; while beyond Miss Camber-Crawshaw followed Miss Fingelstone, who made a very different impression.

Little in stature, but plump, Miss Fingelstone belonged plainly, by shape of eye, nose and chin, to the lesser birds of prey; was most like, perhaps, to a small, well-nourished sparrow-hawk. Her brown hands, too, resembled claws, but were hidden by grey suède gloves. Just as such a bird for its own purposes had developed its own ingenious form of camouflage, so this little old lady, when she walked in the garden, always wore a black mantilla, to soften the lines of her musty face, flecked with feather-like markings, the colour of liver. And when, as occurred some years later, I occupied a room next hers, and was obliged to listen all night to her most individual snoring, that seemed to follow its own hideous rules of climax and susurrant diminuendo, I used to lie awake wondering whether this music, too, might not be contrived of her volition and design, calculated solely, like the stertorous breathing of the owl, in order to deceive the mice, on whom she, in reality unsleeping, intended suddenly to pounce. Similarly, she could pour over her watchful eyes, as hard as olives, a film of oil that, as it were, magnified their apparent limpid plausibility, and drew mice toward them, as a lamp attracts mosquitoes. For the same reason, perhaps, she liked to encourage among those acquainted with her the belief that she resembled, physically, Queen Victoria, because this erroneously provided for her the perfect moral background against which to work her schemes, and to carry on her profession: which was to live in Venice on a basis of commissions extorted from any tradesman who sold an article to a foreigner. From the local antiquaries, she reaped a particularly rich harvest: but no object, on a stall, or sold on the pavement, was too small in price to pay her toll. Palaces, flats, statues, furniture, hideous glass figures, provisions, boxes of matches, tortoise-shell combs, shawls, foreign newspapers, picture-postcards of pigeons, all yielded their proper percentage. For this, she was immensely respected, if not liked, by the Italians, and, in addition, she knew every foreigner who resided in the city, and soon became acquainted with all those who came to visit it. In order to accomplish this more easily, she had made herself into an expert – and she was by no means without brains – on various aspects of Venetian life in former times, likely to interest strangers, and wrote books on these subjects – a quantity of small, plump volumes. The books greatly attracted the mice.

It was after these holidays, during my first term at the crammer's, that my father brought the castle – or rather half of it – in which in later years he was to live, thereby substituting for farce, with moments of tragedy, the purest *Commedia dell'Arte*.

He had been motoring with Miss Fingelstone, an Italian, a rival bird of prey, who was called Barone Pavolino, and another friend, an Englishman, all of whom were accompanying him from Florence to Siena, where they were to be his guests. The driver took the wrong road, and the motor then broke down beneath the walls of an immense old castle. On the terrace above, the cellar doors were open, and the peasants could be seen treading the grapes, for it was the season of the vintage. While the driver was trying to mend his machine, my father walked round, outside the walls, through vineyards, to the other side, where stood the garden entrance. Upon the high rusticated piers that rose, one on each side of the seventeenth-century gate of wrought iron, stood, not the usual beautiful Italian garden statues of stone or lead, but two figures rather small for their position, and made, he perceived under the blotches of golden lichen and stains of time – or perhaps of fire –, of white marble. Both represented men in togas; one had a beard, the other figure had lost its head.

My father announced to me his purchase in the letter that follows, written about a month before my seventeenth birthday.

MY DEAREST OSBERT,

You will be interested to hear that I am buying in your name the Castle of Acciaiuoli (pronounced Accheeyawly) between Florence and Siena. The Acciaiuoli were a reigning family in Greece in the thirteenth century, and afterwards great Italian nobles. The castle is split up between many poor families, and has an air of forlorn grandeur. It would probably cost £100,000 to build today. There is a great tower, a picture-gallery with frescoed portraits of the owners, from a very early period, and a chapel full of relics of the Saints. There are the remains of a charming old terraced garden, not very large, with two or three statues, a pebblework grotto and rows of flower-pots with the family arms upon them. The great saloon, now divided into several rooms, opens into an interior court where one can take one's meals in hot weather, and here, over two doorways, are inscriptions giving the history of the house, most of which was rebuilt late in the seventeenth century as a 'house of pleasure'. The owners brought together there some kind of literary academy of writers and artists. All the rooms in the Castle have names, it seems, as the Sala of the *Gonfalonieri*, the Sala of the *Priori* – twelve of the Acciaiuoli were *Gonfalonieri* and twelve, I think, *Priori*, – the Chamber of Donna Beatrice, the Cardinal's Chamber, the library, the Museum. There seem to have been bathrooms, and every luxury. We shall be able to grow our own fruit, wine, oil – even champagne! I have actually bought half the Castle for £2,200; the other half belongs to the village usurer, whom we are endeavouring to get out. The ultimatum expires today, but I do not yet know the result. The purchase, apart from the romantic interest, is a good one, as it returns five per cent. The roof is in splendid order, and the drains can't be wrong, as there aren't any. I shall have to find the money in your name, and I do hope, my dear Osbert, that you will prove worthy of what I am trying to do for you, and will not pursue that miserable career of extravagance and selfishness which has already once ruined the family. – Ever your loving father, GEORGE R. SITWELL.

This letter puzzled me: for I was not conscious of having been extravagant. *I* had not bought a castle big enough for three hundred people – not even half of one. *I* was not proposing to make my own champagne.

CHAPTER THREE

Directly my father had concluded the purchase of the whole of Monte-gufoni, war broke out between Miss Fingelstone and the Baron on the important matter of the commission; to which in its entirety each of them laid claim. This, indeed, was to prove a fight to a finish; but of the bitterness of the ensuing protracted operations, no murmur ever reached my father's ears, nor the faintest breath of their underlying cause. In the end Miss Fingelstone, after many a summer, lost the battle, but then she started at an initial disadvantage, since this was not her own Venetian country, but a Tuscan terrain, over and in which the Baron knew precisely, after a lifetime's experience of similar warfare, how to dispose his troops. Moreover, his mind was bold and in no way limited, and though engaging himself whole-heartedly in the struggle, he prepared, too, grandiose schemes for gaining after-the-war trade.

Before long, he succeeded in persuading my father that an excel-lent trade in wine – for our new property was situated in the Val di Pesa, the best Chianti district in Italy – could be established with South

America. With this delusive aim in view, my father was induced to pay him annually a handsome sum, with which to spend each winter in Rio de Janeiro; where he soon became respected – a good deal more respected than in Florence –, and where he maintained a quite sumptuous second establishment, fitted with every modern convenience, including a flashing-eyed Latin-American wife. The result was that, though the Baron enjoyed himself, the wine business, which in its small way had been a flourishing local concern when bought, now trailed off and disappeared altogether.

It will be recognized, therefore, that, contrasted with such ingenuities, poor Miss Fingelstone's schemes – a penny here on a dozen postcards, a lira there on a china plate, the fraction of a twenty-centesimi piece on a glass of cyprus, or half a lira on a gondola-fare, seemed trivial and without sacred or diabolic fire. Thus, taking into consideration the size of Montegufoni, in which a number of people could live unnoticed, the Baron had prudently decided to provide himself with, and furnish, a flat there, from which he could properly direct his feudal extortions: whereas Miss Fingelstone could only afford to pay, very meagerly, one of the peasants dwelling in the Castle to inform her by telegram when the Baron proposed to be away for a week or two, or planned to leave for South America for the winter. On the receipt of this intelligence, she would, even though it interrupted her in the middle of writing a new work for the mice, entitled *Round the Convents with Casanova*, at once take the night-train for Florence, wheezing and snoring through the blue night of the mountains in a third-class compartment, on arrival catch an omnibus to the nearest village, and thence walk to Montegufoni: where she would wring from the wretched peasants her tribute, and return to Florence, like a Fertility Goddess, loaded with wine, oil, corn and lemons.

Year after year, the Baron and Miss Fingelstone, furiously at battle in all else, united in their efforts to frighten him away from his Italian estate: otherwise they might lose their share of its products. Having previously combined, when the purchase of it was in question, to sing its practical advantages, for they knew he could see its beauty for himself –, having lauded the purity of its water-supply, the ease with which a mountain torrent could be converted into electricity for him, the healthiness of the air, and the sheer joy of living in the Tuscan countryside, they now alarmed him by pointing out continually the difficulties of lighting and heating, the dangers of the night air and the harshness of the mountain climate, and terrified him, both for his own health and that of his family, with stories of some of its present inhabitants having become afflicted with typhoid and phthisis: they even, it was said, borrowed a chlorotic young girl from an institution, and paraded her here for him in a shawl and wheel-chair. These arguments and object-lessons for a time produced a considerable effect, and it took him a decade to acquire immunity from them. As another result of their propaganda and nerve-war, I was not allowed to see Montegufoni until three years later, for he became diffident about his purchase of it.

Pleasures during those years were few. I was not encouraged to join my family in their travels abroad. I had gone up to London in February for an Army Entrance Examination. What do I remember of that visit? The lines of hopeless questions, weakly gelatyped, which as your eyes became more used to the almost invisible ink employed, still further overwhelmed you with their arid impossibility; the faces round, listless and despondent as my own, or brisk and satisfied with a kind of fox-terrier alertness; and *The Dollar Princess*, successor and rival to *The Merry Widow* at Daly's Theatre.

But more strongly than all these things, I recall Madame Amboise; for I had been placed by my parents in the very hotel in South Kensington in which she was staying. There, after the examination was over, I fell ill, developing a high temperature, and she most kindly nursed me, sitting by my bed for many hours, it seemed day and night, and telling me all this while of her soul and of the affairs of her heart. I was feverish, and, in consequence, cannot remember all she said: but I recollect the first time she entered my room, she began, 'You are ill . . . I, too, have suffered.' Then she paused, and brought out very slowly the word '*Hark!*', and after another interval, proceeded, 'You notice? . . . There is a temporary change in my voice. D'Annunzio observed it at once! "What has happened, Hélène," he said to me, "where is the so-velvety texture of your voice, which always reminded me of the odour of red roses?" "My friend," I replied, "it has been destroyed by the whooping-cough: but the doctor says it will return with the summer flowers." ' Through the mists engendered by illness, I can still see, too, her form looming, white, elephantine, romantic, subtle, melancholy and absurd. I recovered quickly; I think a little owing to these stories, which took me to a new land, and thus afforded me a change complete in itself; I lived for many days in a world compounded of Tchekhov and of low comedy, that was yet raised again by the genuine sadness that ran through it. During this time, I grew really to like and know Madame Amboise, though she would talk to me about my own soul, as well as hers, for many hours. And I was grateful to her, too, for recommending my father to send for me to join him and my mother and Edith in Sicily, where they were staying. She liked to see people doing the things that they liked doing.

Accordingly, at the end of March, I went to Naples, where Henry met me and conducted me to Sicily. It was certainly a short journey, a night and a morning: but it was my first sea-crossing, except for the Channel, and Henry's nautical interests, his ability and, indeed, inclination to explain every detail of the voyage, why a rope was lowered here or a sailor shouted there, or some sound of humming issued intermittently from the engine-room, served to make him an ideal companion. In the tender light of the earliest morning, the sky being green at its edges as the sound of an Arcadian pipe, we sailed through plains of unbroken rolling blue, only varying in their translucence. Here, for the first time, between Scylla and Charybdis, I saw a flying fish leap from one sea hedge to another. Soon we approached Messina, which had only recently been destroyed by the great earthquake that seems now – and, indeed, seemed then –, like the sinking of the *Titanic*, to have been a portent to Europe of its coming disasters. We passed near enough to the city to see its painted façades, lime-green, pink and golden, in this light of the Homeric world, and still intact, though through the gaping windows showed the dark-green groves of the mountainous background. In those days, ruins on such a scale, and the result of destruction in modern times, constituted, it is singular to recall, something of a curiosity, a sight which drew travellers to see them; whereas now they encumber the whole world, and the stench of the dead, crushed and torn beneath them, rises up to insult the anthropomorphic god of mankind. But the seas around were smooth as lawns, and even the beggars who lined the quays at Sicilian ports, and collected round the porches of churches and entrances to cloisters, seemed to have none of the sense of ominous horror aroused by Lousy Peter, or by the scarecrow whose voice had first taught me the meaning of words. We landed somewhere near Taormina, then only lately invented as a resort, and we proceeded thither to join my family. With what distinctness I can recollect my first glimpse of the snowy cone of Etna, floating, unimaginably high in its isolation, far above the clouds, as I drove from the coast, up hills cracked by the sun, and out of the fissures of which grew huge bushes of red geranium, as tall, almost, as trees, and the shapes, ragged-edged saws and cylinders, of cactus and agave, strange to my eyes as would be plants from Mars, to the little city above.

On this ledge of rock, baked by the sun, and surrounded by asphodel, iris, and the numberless flowers of the Sicilian spring, every ordinary judgement was reversed, and other standards prevailed. Worries and fears, either personal or national, could not for long exist in such surroundings. Local scandals, local gossip: this was all that mattered, or was serious in a world given up to madness. The streets, with their delicate miniature palaces of tufa, in sepia, gold and black, with the pointed arches of their doorways, through which one obtained a vista of a *cortile* or cloister full of drifts of soft, profuse, light-coloured flowers, translucent-petalled flowers that were new to me, as well as of roses and carnations in March, and their fountains and wells and shrines, and their small shops, displaying for sale objects in wool and silk and olive-wood, the making of which had been imposed upon the inhabitants of the place by kindly but strong-willed English ladies, were crowded with characters native and foreign, noble and the reverse. There was, for example, old Major Frazer, a fine Highland Scot, good and generous, who had resided here for many years and was much respected by the Sicilians. A retired soldier, he had been attracted to the place, perhaps by the cheapness of it, and lived in two rooms, in one of which hung a fine water-colour by Turner, the first I had seen in private possession. He was now a handsome old man, and, when he walked in the streets, always wore, by an adaptation of the local fashion, a rug of the Frazer tartan, thereby imparting a suggestion of Raeburn's portraits to the almost tropical scene.

Of a very different nature was the Baron von Gloeden, the photographer, and forerunner and archetype of many subsequent followers of his profession; at which in some respects he excelled. He specialized in neo-Greek studies and, by a kind of transposition of musical-comedy ideals, he was adept in the recording, for example, of young Sicilian shepherd youths, equipped with a pipe to play, cut from the reeds, a crook and a lamb, and reclining naked and at ease under the dappling shadow of gauze-like clouds of almond-blossom. The Baron himself, a tall, thickly-clad German, with a beard and heavy spectacles, resided in the chief hotel with his sister, but received visitors in a large studio in the town. He did not speak English very well, but possessed a favourite sentence, explanatory of his sister's preference for domestic life, which he proffered to all strangers the first time he met them, and which, since it possessed a fascinating syntax and rhythm of its own, I remember to this day and

here append: 'My sister, the Baroness van Gloeden – or, as you would call her, Miss –, she has not the artistic-spirit, Sicily-loving, got, but in her rooms cakes-and-the-most-delicious-coffee-making, she stays'!

At seventeen, one enjoys every moment of life that circumstances, or more usually parents, permit one to enjoy. My time was limited, my pleasures were circumscribed – chief among them in these years being the visits I paid to Renishaw in October and November, in order to learn to shoot. Sometimes I went there by myself, sometimes accompanied by my father. Then, with so few people in the house, we lived for the most part in the Carolean core of it, and everything as a result looked as strange to us as if we inhabited a different mansion in a different world. But, even though we used only the Little Parlour and the Great Parlour, abandoning the large eighteenth-century apartments, nevertheless you could feel the vastness of the stretch of rooms that lay there beyond, on each side, empty. But were they empty, for at moments during the evenings as we sat by the fire, so many creakings and rustlings made themselves heard, so many of those inexplicable sounds of an ancient dwelling-place, that it appeared as though there were more ghosts than human beings in rooms and corridors? One would say to oneself, it must be the wind: but I still do not believe that it was. Phantoms, when one is young, no more prevent sleep than do the hooting of engines or other modern noise – but those we heard were ancient, issued from some cave in time where they had hidden and to which they returned, or so it seemed to me. After being out all day, however, I usually slept through the night, as one does at that age, and only remember a single occasion when I was woken at about two o'clock. I was occupying a bedroom next my father. A small, sinister chuckle from beyond the wall roused me, and then my straining ears caught the words, spoken in his still, clear tones,
    'They may think I shall – but I shan't',
the first part of this antithesis being spoken slowly, the second, snapped out more briskly, with a crackle, as it were, and followed again by such a laugh as I had heard first. I never found out the subject of this rather ominous consultation with himself, nor did I like to inquire. It had too much alarmed me.

Not only was the house different at this season, the garden, too, offered a different world. Here, because of the smoke in the air, the fall of the leaf comes early, the masts of the elms and the limes in the avenue were already visible, and a Dutch light, clear and crisp, entered through the bare branches, and this in its turn gave a lightness to the house in the mornings which it lacked in more umbrageous months. Moreover, while the approaching winter made the garden naked in some respects, as it did the trees, in others it brought clothing. The yew hedges had not long been clipped, and stood plumb and regular as walls, but the statues – for neither Roman nor Istrian stone will endure the frosts, even of their own country – had been voluminously covered. And, indeed, the shrouding of the statues became here a sort of ritual marking of the change of season, as is the vintage in more fortunate climes. The first to go were Neptune and Diana; they were wrapped thickly in bracken, already damp and brown, and then draped in canvas, so that they lost for the ensuing months the graceful air of epochal allurement which rightly belonged to them, and turned to large, primitive, figures, more fit for winter on these heights; forms that seemed roughly hacked out of chaos, though still compact of it, by neolithic axes. Next, the Warrior and his Amazon, at the entrance to the Wilderness, were padded against the cold, and then it was the turn of the two Giants, holding their clubs. Finally, the fountains of red Verona marble were enclosed in wooden cases, the shape of pyramids and painted a dull green. The very landscape closed in on us, removing Bolsover and other great buildings on the distant hills, by interposing barriers of cloud. But this time, too, had its own beauties, and one early morning in November, when the young light, just born, was green as the first leaves, and exhibited all the delicacy of something that would soon perish, I saw, as I looked from my window, five swans sweep down from above the house towards the lake below, circle it, and then descend upon the waters.

In the October visits, I would start out very early. Coming downstairs, I would find, even at that hour, huge fires of our native coal, age-old product of these very valleys and hills among which I was to spend the day, their actual substance, blazing already in the large grates; vast logs of coal, used in this countryside as wood elsewhere, were flickering and intertwining their blue and green and red flames, and giving life to the sombre, misty rooms. As I opened the door to go out, I could see that on the plateau facing the north front, the great beech trees, which retain their leaves longer than other kinds, were now fully invested in their brief autumn fire, and stood like pillars of flame, freeing themselves in the sunlight from the night's vapours. I got into the dog-cart and was driven down the hill, observing how the sun made the dew on whole stretches of grass glitter as if it moved, and turned peaceful meadows into quivering lawns of fire. When, after some twenty minutes, we reached the beginning of the Eckington woods, there I would find Maynard Hollingworth, Mark Kirkby and Dick Humphries waiting for me. Then for another twenty minutes we would walk through these forest-like hills and valleys, which today exhaled their autumn smell, composed of bracken and fungus and foxes and fallen leaves and the red berries of the rowan which littered the paths after a recent gale. And here and there, too, a birch tree, recently felled, added an aromatic freshness to the air. In the very centre of the woods, the beaters were grouped, talking together and chaffing in their broad tongue.

In this atmosphere I spent an enchanting but eminently unsuccessful day, since my shooting of pheasants was no more competent than my shooting of partridges a month earlier. I think, though, that I felt more shame in missing this larger and more glorious bird. I was a profoundly, almost an inspired, bad shot; I never, I am thankful to say now, approached so near my mark as to wound a bird, or a beater, even.

Rather late in the afternoons, when the autumn sun had already been a little obscured by the net of the mist, night's vanguard, we would go to luncheon with Mark Kirkby, in his cabin, on the spur of a hill in the middle of the woods, a citadel from which, day and night, he could keep watch on the comings and goings of pheasants, foxes and men. We would sit on benches and eat cold pheasant and cheese, and apples and small pears, plucked that very morning from the golden billows of the trees in the stone-walled orchards, trees that from their age gave a special taste to the fruit, to the pears, a certain taste of wood for all their sweetness.

Sitting now in the sunshine that flowed through the door of the cabin, I listened to Mark, 'the Dook o' Ploomley', or watched him, because often he fell asleep directly he sat down, his dog – the Clumber spaniel Plumbley Friar – falling asleep by his side at the same time, for they both lost many hours of the night in guarding the woods. Mark had altered very little except that he looked stockier than of old, his complexion was a little redder, and he seemed to have acquired still more blue protuberances where the shot – as I thought it, though in reality it was the atoms of black powder from an alarm-gun which he had been setting one Sunday morning in the woods and which had exploded full in his face – lay embedded just under the surface of the skin. He had grown stiffer, too, especially about the shoulders: for, since he kept such late hours, he was apt, while actually driving, to fall asleep suddenly, and to wake up in some ditch into which he had pitched on his shoulder. (He had no sons or daughters of his own, but he liked particularly to drive about the country with his builder's cart full of children: usually his wife's nephews, to whom he was devoted.) For the rest, he was, if anything, more sure of himself, more ducal.

In the age in which he existed, and which he just survived, English life still retained its ancient gift of continuity, the threads composing its web had not yet been severed by the gashes inflicted by two wars. Classes were more distinctively separate, while at the same time exercising a greater influence one on another within narrowly defined but acknowledged orbits: certainly among those between whom such a relationship existed, clerk and master, gamekeeper and squire, there was less of social awareness, less watchfulness and incomprehension. And so it is that, though I possessed no liking for sport, only an understanding of its primitive appeal, Mark Kirkby became a friend.

It is difficult for someone not acquainted with such a mode of life to imagine how busy Mark was throughout the year, how much there was for him to organize, besides the actual shooting-parties and the strategic disposition of shots and beaters. Each month brought its own activities. The game in the woods was wild, without hand-rearing or importation, so the year began for him at nesting-time. Then there were footpaths to watch, and trespassers to follow: while, to discourage other kinds of raiders, dogs or foxes who might disturb sitting birds, he would, in order to kill the scent, daub a wide ring of gas-tar round the nests. Soon summer would be drawing on, with the ceaseless fight it entailed against vermin; there were stoats and weasels to be trapped, and magpies' nests to locate and destroy. With August came the time for bushing: that is to say, thorns must be cut down and placed in the open pastures between the woods, so as to prevent the netting of partridges. Then, after the harvest had been reaped, there were the rakings to be gathered and their transport to the various feeds to be arranged. Mark excelled, too, in the fashioning of sham pheasants, birds made of sticks and bracken fastened together with wire, that had then to be tied on the branches of trees as a lure for poachers. Even the veterans were sometimes taken in, and Mark was always a proud and glad man when he heard of some antagonist of many years' standing having fired at one of these dummies. As October drew near, the hedgerows that divided the park-like land of the meadows adjoining the woods had to be searched in the golden-veined mornings for what he termed 'snickles', the local word for snares (so that the wags of the countryside say of a young man going to marry a woman older than himself, ' 'e's been fair snickled'). Usually a few of these wire circles would be discovered towards the climax of the pheasant season. There was night-watching to be done, especially during the moonlit nights before Christmas, when every sound in the valley seemed to lie on the air of this white silence for an instant longer than at other times, and every crepitation and murmur could be noted. The alarm guns had to be set and moved at frequent intervals, and some time during the winter the rakings would give out, and then Mark would insist on the birds being fed with threshed corn, and, in consequence, boxes were installed, and he would have a shack at each feed, so that he could count the birds and sum up the stock. In snowy weather was the time to read the hieroglyphs that only snow provides for those cunning enough to decipher them, and thus to learn the paths and ways of the vermin, and the entrance to their homes, or whether there has been any unusual visitor or disturbance. At this time, too, if young trees had been planted, there were rabbits to be kept down. And, all through the year, there were dogs to be trained. His day dogs, – Clumber spaniels, as a rule –, must, above all, be hard-working and possess powers of endurance, and unite the qualities of setter and retriever, while for night work he chose dogs of the bull-mastiff breed. For the use of these, a dummy was placed on a hillock behind his cottage. Training began at dusk, when only the outline of the figure was visible, and the first step was to teach the dog to land with front paws straight on the dummy's shoulders. Later, a real man, protected by leather clothing, mask and gloves, would be substituted – though not seldom it was difficult to find a man willing to take on the job –, and he would adopt the local poacher's many tricks of dodging, sparring and running away. All this was necessary: for poachers, it must be remembered, in such an isolated and lonely tract of country, set in a very thickly populated industrial district, constituted a real and constant menace; moreover, they were a dangerous set of men, and Mark's life had several times been threatened. On one occasion, three of them, who owed him a grudge, launched an attack on Plumbley Cottage. Mark at once got up, and fired his gun, before dressing, through the open window. And he and Mrs Kirkby – an ideal companion for him and a woman of great courage – put the culprits to flight, collared one and followed for a considerable distance the other two, who were by then crawling on hands and knees to avoid identification.

Usually, though, the happenings were of a more rustic and peaceable order. There would be, perhaps, unaccountable sounds in the night, voices coming from far off, or the cries of unseen water-birds, coot or geese, that fly at so great a height as to be invisible. For this sound there was in the locality a special name, which must go far back into medieval times. 'What's that noise?' someone would ask, to receive the answer, 'It's the Gabriel-hounds overhead!': for the packs that the Archangel lets loose at night are held to carry a burden of omen for those who hear them. And Mark, indeed, was superstitious himself and he would relate how, one night in his cottage, a grandfather clock which had not worked for years struck suddenly the hour, and a little later a messenger arrived from a village near by to say that his wife's aunt had died at precisely the instant it had struck. On one occasion he had fallen into the dam in the valley; an enterprise of my father's, newly constructed. How he got out he never knew, for he was a feeble swimmer. It only emphasized his distrust of my father's activities in the architectural field; especially he disapproved of dams and pools and lakes and fountains, and the cost they entailed, remarking in his builder's lingo, 'I dorn't horld with all this lading and teeming.'

So, of a late afternoon in the cabin in the woods, we listened to Mark giving his version of such high acts, and the days passed, both elongated and telescoped by the pleasure I found in them. As, previously, in the month of September, I had mooned about, with my eye on everything except a possible covey, to the dismay of all those who had my true interests at heart, while the partridges glided past my very nose and shirred their wings in my ear, so now, similarly careless, I trudged through the damp and fragrant woods, where sometimes the bracken grew as high as my shoulder. A sort of intoxication of happiness, that had no connection with shooting, but a great deal with poetry, and with that first childish experience of rapture upon the cliffs at Scarborough which I have described in *The Cruel Month*, enveloped my whole being.

These, then, were among the interludes, brief and few, from the crammer's; at which establishment I passed two years that saw the death of King Edward VII and the Coronation of King George V. I was given by Peter Lycett Green a seat outside the Abbey from which to view the procession. It was a wet June day in England, but the arrival of the Abyssinian envoys lit with an African splendour even this darkness. Their lion-skins and cloaks of gilded feathers impressed me more than anything I saw that morning. And it was almost the first time that, thus watching its living representatives drive by and dismount, I realized the continued existence of Ethiopia into the modern world; but before King George's reign was over, we were, even the laziest-minded of us, obliged to take it into account.

In the autumn of the Coronation Year, my grandmother Sitwell died. She had been growing weaker for the past twelve months, and it was sad for those who loved her to see one on whom so many had depended, now dependent on others. Her firm will and able brain had not failed her, but an immense fatigue assailed her. Though her hair was white now, she did not look older, but the passage of the last few years had made her finer, had given a sense of transparency and had deepened her expression of resignation and sweetness. At her death, with the breaking of so many links – for most of her household had been in her service for a lifetime –, Ernest de Taeye and his wife came to live at Renishaw, and, in consequence, the garden began to show a floral splendour and ingenuity it had never before known.

No doubt Ernest missed my grandmother, for though she had not the artist's sense of levels and proportion that my father always exhibited in the continual plans he would put forward for a lay-out, she possessed a much greater love and knowledge of flowers, and was thus able to appreciate immensely all Ernest's cleverness and care. Moreover, she could express her feelings, and tell him of the pleasure she found in the results of his work: whereas this my father could not do. Nevertheless, my father, also, cherished a great regard for Ernest, and showed it in his own way, by erecting three new hot-houses, a practical tribute, and by building for him in an unused kitchen-garden – that had in the eighteenth century been a paddock for the Sitwell race-horses – a mansion. Assuredly one could not call it, as my father did, a 'Gardener's Cottage'. It was too substantial, too stately, for that, and in order to build it the old quarry in the park, from which the stone for Renishaw had been cut, was reopened.

During the next twenty years, he came, I think, to love Renishaw more than he had loved Hay Brow. He was an artist and, after the manner of artists, was always at work. When himself not planting or overseeing, yet things growing, or the prospect of their growing, were always in his mind, in the same way that situations, characters and psychologies abide with a novelist. All fruits and flowers were to him obviously the symbols of a divine order and providence, a fresh source of marvel to him every day; and of this trait there were many outward signs. Thus, I loved to watch him, slightly stooping now, with a forward tilt of his large body, and crowned with his Flemish straw-hat with its enormous brim sloping downward all round, crossing from behind the stables to the back of the house, carrying a basket with a bunch of grapes in it, or some peaches plainly almost too delicate to be touched. Somehow, as he almost stumbled along, thrown forward by his weight and height, he conveyed, by the very manner in which he handled the basket, an idea of the beauty and precious inviolability of the fruit. And the way he pointed out to one, too, the monstrous ingenuity of some recently acclimatized arrival from Africa or China, saying, with his slight Flemish accent, in his serious, solemn voice, 'Them's a lovely new thing!', this emphasized the same quality. He worked without ceasing. Only on Sunday afternoons would he nominally take a little time off, and even then I would see his huge figure, standing still, absolutely motionless, at a distance in the park, and, as I approached nearer and could see his face, would perceive that he was contemplating some tree with an indescribable expression of loving regard, as though in mute praise of all creation.

CHAPTER FOUR

By the middle of December 1911, it was recognized that I was a failure, too, at the Establishment for Young Gentlemen in which I had spent a little over two years. Indeed, I had contrived that autumn not to pass the Entrance Examination into Sandhurst – in those days no easy matter, especially for one who, like myself, suffers from a race-horse-like eagerness to win, even if engaged against his will in the contest: a nervous craving that shows itself, too, by a curious physical as well as mental intentness, causing pains to run along the arms, the hands, to the extremities of the fingers. After the result of this examination had been announced, a pause of a month or more ensued; during which period I seemed to be in a No-Man's-Land, a vacuum, a spiritual Coventry in Pont Street, London, where my parents had taken a large, hideous and rather haunted house. Every person living in it seemed to be affected by the prevailing atmosphere. Even Henry had lost his tumultuous humour; for he was engaged at this period in the smouldering dispute with his employer which ended, a year later, in his most prolonged temporary disappearance from the scene. The pantry was desolate, void of personality. Even his foil, Pare, appeared unable to rouse him, accustomed though he was by a judicious course of questioning to draw him out. But perhaps this was merely due to Pare's own growing depression; he was suffering more. The light he could see was dwindling; with increasing difficulty he groped his way, and his wife, who during the last twenty years had suffered from long periods of insanity, had grown worse again, so that the restraint put upon her had become more stringent, and he was hardly allowed to visit her. His face was developing a tragic, staring seriousness of its own, broken ever more seldom by the smiles that formerly Henry's tales had brought to it. But Henry's and Pare's new melancholy was scarcely greater in degree – even though they possessed more obvious reason for it – than Sacheverell's and mine. Many matters were going wrong in the household.

No leaf moved. One waited for the storm, and wondered what manoeuvres, if any, were taking place behind the screen of silence. Sacheverell was on holiday, and we spent much time together. I was now just turned nineteen, and was promoted to have a shilling a day as pocket-money; it did not go very far. However, we would contrive somehow or other to visit the current exhibitions, or to go roller-skating at Olympia, where the idle of all ages bumped and rolled and clanked and danced along the vast wooden floor to music: for it was the moment of one of the periodic crazes for this form of exercise. Of the exhibitions, the most notable was that of Futurist paintings, organized, at the Sackville Gallery, by Marinetti and his English followers. Prefacing the catalogue to it was a fiery manifesto by the Futurist Boss, calling on the Italians to destroy their ancient monuments; an ideal since realized in another way. There was, however, about both preface and the work shown, combined with a certain lack of sensitiveness, a genuine, if somewhat literary, dynamism, and a breath of prophecy pervaded the whole gallery. The twentieth century, with its unparalleled disasters and catastrophes, had at last smashed and bungled its way into the realms of art. The very titles of the paintings – such as *The Street Entering a House* – exercised, nevertheless, an invigorating effect upon the imagination. But the canvas I best recall from the show is the *Café Pan-Pan* by Gino Severini – the first time I had heard the name of this artist, who was destined to become a great friend of both my brother and myself, and to do much work for us. The picture to which I allude presented, in an admirable convention, the movements of people dancing at a café.

At Olympia, the noise and rhythm lulled the heart-aching sense of expectancy that living with my father and mother in these years promoted. Thus, always waiting for some volcanic disturbance to be sprung on one, it was yet impossible beforehand to tell from which direction the storm would come. Nevertheless, as we clanked round the rink at tremendous speed, to the popular tunes that were now for the first time becoming tinged with ragtime, Sacheverell and I could not help wondering why the next few months, and my place in them, were never discussed. It was difficult, with my inexperience, to foresee in what manner I could be lassooed. The sinister hush continued to prevail, and I was still involved in no plans for my future; which now, suddenly, was never mentioned. I was not even found fault with: nor did my father any longer even invite me to join him in his simple Sunday expeditions, to see the furniture, china and silver on view at the Victoria and Albert, round the marble halls of which he would walk with an air of irritable concentration.

He seldom now visited a picture-gallery, for he sought only for decorative themes, and would say, after contemplating, for example, some great picture by Botticelli or Titian, or a carving by Michelangelo, 'I am afraid it gives *me* nothing', as if to help *him* design a spoon, or the leg of a chair, had been the whole aim of the particular genius at whose work he was looking. But these halls, though he disapproved of their architecture, 'far too fussy and unquiet', constituted a foretaste of his heaven. For hours he could roam, examining the details of cabinet or table, fountain or fork, as it pleased him: (but what a pity, he reflected, he had not been there at the time these objects were made, to offer his advice!). Sometimes he was accompanied on these tours of inspection by his only friend – though even at that, the friendship was all on one side –, a quivering shadow, with a wide mouth and palsied jaw, and a top-hat quaking on his head, known among us as the Silver Bore. This naïf, middle-aged bachelor, the personification of burgess respectability, had been animated in infancy with a false equivocal energy by some cousin to St Vitus, so that he often intimidated other equally innocent people by the winks he gave them and the faces he made. He had been at Eton with my father, and had remained attached to him. My father asked him to stay with us for a week every seven years, but when my family were in London, this loyal friend would call and talk to us about Queen Anne

Silver – nothing later than Queen Anne was to be regarded, and foreign silver was, to say the best of it, un-English. My father never listened to what he said, and seldom seemed to see him, so that sometimes, as children, we wondered if the lively wobble with which his old friend faced life had not been designed in the first place to catch my father's attention.

Then a portent occurred: a General Sitwell, a cousin of whom I had never heard previously, or who had only been glimpsed hazily through the mazes of Indian jungles or African scrub that had imperially concealed him, now sprang, fully accoutred, from the pavement of Pont Street. He and my father were much closeted together; the silence that surrounded me became greater. Something, at last, was in the air: what could it be? Even Henry, who usually appeared to possess a special insight into the workings of my father's mind, could not help me. Then, one morning, I found out: for I read, suddenly turning a page of the newspaper that had just arrived, that a 2nd Lieut. F.O.S. Sitwell had been granted a commission in the Yeomanry, and was, from the Yeomanry, attached to a famous regiment of Hussars. For a moment, I wondered who this stranger, bearing my name and the initials that I associated with school-life and had grown to hate so bitterly, could be. Then I understood. I was now under Military Law. For me to refuse to fall in with these plans, which would culminate in my transference, after a few months, from Yeomanry to Hussars, would have rendered me guilty of mutiny. It seemed better to go quietly.

In Aldershot, a polar cold prevailed, and the air was thick with fog of the texture of a polar bear's pelt. Out of these unfathomable, and therefore vast, spaces of frozen fur, of white and yellow, there showed occasionally a horse's teeth or glaring eyes, or a frostbitten or port-nipped military face, conjured up out of the gloom and darkness, like a materialization at a séance. It was a reiteration, I realized at once, in starker and more uncompromising, less interesting terms, of the Blankney theme: horses in a fog that has no end. I arrived at last at the enormous barracks, an exotic edifice of iron pillars and verandahs facing north, that had been designed, it was said, for some swamp or jungle in Jamaica, and by a typically imaginative, if erratic gesture of the nineteenth-century War Office, had been erected here instead. At present it could scarcely be seen, and remained a darker, sadder, denser, bulk in the fog, but at the same time one's ears detected signs of a dreary, ant-like routine of bustle and fuss. Men shouted, sergeants commanded: bugles every now and then indulged in a brazen, idiot bray; a band gave bursts of practice, too, from time to time and, judged from the hollow melancholy of its hooting and thumping, must be lost for ever in the fog, and yet, by the same test, must be playing somewhere under the tinny resonance of corrugated iron; in a shed, which, colouring the music, imparted to it the particular suggestion – except that the sound was of much greater volume – of a rusty, superannuated gramophone needle, grinding out a cracked record. Horses, too, could be heard snorting derisively and stamping within their iron temples. The fog, the enveloping, all-pervading, barrack-coloured fog, here, at this point, produced a sort of amnesia, so that I remember no single activity. I must, I suppose, have reported my presence to the officer in charge, but I can recall nothing more until I was in my room, changing for dinner. To the thought of that meal I clung as to some fact of accustomed life in uncharted seas or desert. Everything else was unfamiliar; but dinner, one knew what that was – or thought one did.

It was the leave season, and only two officers were present: one a taciturn, somnolent, mutely disagreeable Scottish cousin of mine, whom I had never hitherto met, the other a spry, pin-headed younger man, with a long, silky moustache, and a cavalry lisp. I never discovered if my cousin had a lisp or not, for I never heard him utter sufficient words to make it possible for me to judge: since a routine of port and a fall on his head once a week from horseback kept him in that state of chronic, numb confusion which was then the aim of every cavalry officer. Yet he must, I realized from the first, be able in some way to receive and communicate ideas, for he had played a riding-on part, plainly enough, in the successful plan for my lassooing that had been engineered by my father and the General. As neither of my companions spoke, either before the meal or at it, except to say, 'How d'e do?', but ate on through many courses, not so much in gloomy silence – for gloom entails a prior process of feeling, or even of thought or reflection –, but in what is best termed a silence of bestial chaos, such as may have preceded the coming of the Word, and since I was of a sociable disposition and hated, too, to see people so plainly frustrated and unhappy, I determined to 'make things go'. I talked on all kinds of interesting subjects and invented a number – on this I must insist – of first-rate jokes for their entertainment. But the surrounding and enveloping silence, an active silence, as it were, and not a mere negation of sound, made it seem gradually as if I were talking to myself in an enormous illuminated cavern, filled with sparkling silver objects. Gowk, my cousin, and Fribble-Sadler said nothing, but slowly drank their claret, and gave each, from time to time, the sort of glance that the Gorgon Sisters must every now and then have exchanged among themselves when a stranger was present and as yet unpetrified. I talked on. For if complete silence came again, it would be worse, would signify defeat, and so I persisted, now giving my companions a lively and enthusiastic account of the Futurist Exhibition. Still I went on; I felt that I must somehow lift the atmosphere, which was becoming more and more like that of a dramatic monologue by Strindberg I had lately read, entitled *The Stronger*. Port, even port, brought no loosening of tongues, though it flushed the masks – or was that effect, could it have been, caused by anger? It was not for a week that I fully comprehended how unfortunate an impression I had unwittingly created: because this listlessness and coma constituted a source of pride, a regimental tradition. For a period of two years at least, no young officer must speak, except to his horse – and even then it would be more correct to pat the animal than to say a word to it. When, after the conventional interval had elapsed, he was allowed, once or twice a week, to open his mouth – but only, of course, to an exact contemporary –, it must be to talk of horses, or, perhaps, for such a flight was sometimes, on festivals, allowed, of dogs. Tribal Taboo, that was the meaning of the silence.

The next morning – it must have been morning, in spite of its night-darkness – the bugles, which seemed only just to have stopped, began to bray again, and set off barking, as invariably they did, the miscellaneous packs of dogs in the Officers' Quarters; a whole rasping chorus of bull-terriers, Irish setters, and half-wit, bandy-legged Sealyhams and Aberdeens. Each morning, each day, precisely resembled the last. That year, fog and snow and ice continued for ten weeks, far into the spring, dimming buttons, and tattooing faces with red and blue marks, till they resembled, when you could see them, the masks of the native warriors of Australia or the furthest Pacific isles. Waited on, muzzle and hoof, the horses did not seem to mind the cold. Riding School, the first duty of the day's whole enjoyable round, took place at an hour still lost in the winter darkness – can it have been six o'clock or five? At any rate, so dark was it still that one could only *feel* the snow, not see it. In the centre, under the arc-lamps, shining like moons through their circles of peat-dust, that gave them aureoles, stood the riding-master, red-nosed, but silent, large-featured and stiff as an Easter Island figure. Though his chief criticized us little, the sergeant was voluble enough, his language vivid, as he shouted at the rolling, flustered recruits cantering round in a circle without saddles, 'Stop bumping about on your bloody backsides there like a set of Piccadilly 'ores'.

At about 7.30, after, as it seemed, many hours, guided as to direction by instinct, I shuffled, as quickly as bruises and stiffness would allow, through the fog, across the darkness, to breakfast; always a less talkative meal than dinner. Again, bugles were braying, and already the band practice had started somewhere in the iron torture-chamber across the way. It continued all through every day; bassoons, trombones, trumpets, droning on, drums thumping, steering an unpredictable course, until abruptly stopped by the enraged Bandmaster, but only to start again, through the intricacies of selections from *Véronique* and *Our Miss Gibbs*, or of a march by Sousa, equally complicated and subtle. Directly after breakfast, there followed pointless but elaborate manoeuvres that continued for hours in the Long Valley, as it is called, which was at this season a white steppe. I could never get through these exercises without incurring public humiliation, since my horse, though odious, was well trained. Thus, when the Commanding Officer used to send for me, as he often did – and, I may add, with no view to congratulating me on my efforts –, this agile and vindictive beast would often set off towards him at the fastest gallop, meanwhile, by one of his tricks, causing me to measure my length somewhere in the intervening wastes of snow and sand, and there abandoning me, would arrive, the cynosure of all eyes, the solitary half-centaur moving through this vast expanse, panting and foaming, in front of the great man.

When we returned to barracks, where the braying and droning still sounded, louder than ever, from under the tin roof, the officers, including myself, had to preside over *Stables*; a function which, comparable to the morning and evening services in church, took place twice a day. When Matins were finished, came luncheon, and the munching of good food in silence; after which ensued two hours' drill on the Barrack Square, when the snow had melted, or, before that season at last arrived, in the shelter of one of the tropical verandahs that had been built originally, as I have said, to snare that rare bird, the North Wind. With blue noses, chattering teeth and frozen feet, we stuck it. Then came Evensong in the stables, followed, if we were fortunate, by a lecture on *The Care of the Horse Through the Ages*, *The Place of the Horse in the Twentieth Century*, *How the Horse will Replace Mechanical Means of Transport*, or some kindred subject.

In the course of these lectures, we did not hear much of the war that was being prepared for us, except that on occasion a lecturer would give us a discourse on *Cavalry Charges in the Coming War*. He would tell us that he hoped it would constitute no breach of trust if he informed us in strictest confidence that the authorities knew that a war was drawing near on the Continent, that we should become involved in it, and that it would be a Cavalry War. At last the Horse would, thank God, come into its own.

At half-past seven a bugle-call announced that dinner was on its way, and at ten to eight another, that it was time to go across to the Mess-Room. At moments I wondered if these braying tongues had only been instituted, out of a kind of vanity, to call attention to the silence that prevailed among the officers. Certainly music fulfilled for them some function of this order. When, for instance, guests from other cavalry regiments were fortunate enough to be invited to sample our particular brand of speechlessness, a small string orchestra would set the prevailing silence, as if it were a jewel, by playing selections from one of the musical comedies of the day. It was at these times that one felt loneliest. And so it came about that one night, unable any longer to bear the insufferable boredom, I called for a bottle of champagne and discovered how the darkness could be artificially lightened. This was the first time I had drunk wine since the occasion described elsewhere, when, as a boy, recovering from a long illness, I had been so heartrendingly implored by the doctors to take to drink. Then I had not liked wine, but now it seemed to alter the whole of life, banishing worries about the following day, enclosing one in the golden circle of the present. I began at last to understand the chapter on port in *The Egoist*, a novel I had always much admired, except for these two pages, which had hitherto conveyed nothing to me. The Riding School at five the next morning receded into the distant and pleasant glow of the future; even the thought of the boxing contest in which, for the amusement of the mum and swollen faces round me, I had after dinner to take part, ceased to distress me. And when the moment came I hit out with a will. Only physical force could impress these people, interest them, or lift them from the torpor whereto regimental tradition and years of training had brought them, up to a height where once more they smiled, and almost framed a syllable.

When the snows melted and the fogs dissipated, it was only then that the whole horror of Aldershot, and the arid fantasy of the life round me, grew visible. For the first time I could see clearly, after ten weeks, the full uniform of the Regiment, when occasion arose for the officers to wear it, a pseudo-Hungarian caprice of frogs and flaps and feathers designed by the Prince Consort in exotic mood, or perhaps merely in an attempt to escape humdrum: for the first time I perceived the endless array of yellow brick buildings and iron huts painted a port-flushed purple, squatting among the trees in a perpetual khaki mist of dust. Little Prussia in its very essence, all round lay sand-dunes and fir trees, and indeed the only fit purpose of such country seemed to be as a combined Reserve and No-Man's-Land in which to collect obsolete types, and set up rifle-ranges and targets. And with what precision has the unrivalled genius of the English tongue found a name for the place. Yet to everyone the word does not evoke the same images, for when, some years later, during the season of Russian Ballet, which opened in October 1918 at the Coliseum, my brother continually had to leave the theatre early, explaining, as he got up, to Diaghilev, by whose side we sometimes sat in the stalls, that he had 'to return to Aldershot by midnight', the great impresario eventually asked, 'Qu'est-ce que c'est, cette Aldershot – c'est une femme?'

To me, certainly, Aldershot was a hard mistress. The climate, too, matched the name miraculously. And the Barracks, witheringly cold throughout the winter, red-hot in summer, completed the effect, so that scarlet, as for clowns' noses, was supplied by one extreme for half the year, and by the other for the rest of it. Moreover, once or twice the two combined in the same day, with the result that I contracted what I took to be frost-bite – but I suppose was merely an Aldershot super-chilblain – in the early morning, drilling on the Square, and, in the same place, a genuine sunstroke in the afternoon.

During this time, I was receiving almost daily letters from my father. My heart would start to bump, for I was already learning to dread these letters, and the instructions they gave me as to how to spend my allowance: most of which was apparently to be dedicated to the cult of the horse. Moreover, the financial details contained in them muddled me. The annual amount I was to receive had been calculated on an ingenious basis, the method employed being to strike an unhappy medium between the value – translated into terms of modern money, on a system also devised by my father – of the allowance customarily made to eldest sons by Lords of the Manor at the time of the Black Death (it worked out, I recollect, down to a groat) and that recommended to him by Major Gowk as a fitting sum for an officer of the present day.

The first brief letter I received at Aldershot from my father contained orders for me to show him my cheque-book: commands repeated at frequent intervals during the ensuing years. But the second to which I have referred, and which follows, plainly affords clues to the life I was obliged to lead. Dated Feb. 12, 1912, it runs:

. . . With regard to the clothes, they will be paid for by you out of the allowance. I will talk to you about the mackintosh. Archie Gowk's calculation was that the total amount of £530, which tallies near enough to yours and my own, should be made up as follows:

		£
(1)	Mess bills (including all subscriptions, sporting and otherwise)	170
(2)	First servant and laundry	30
(3)	Stable expenses	150
(4)	Clothes and Uniform upkeep	50
(5)	All other expenses	130
		530

I have therefore arranged to pay you £530, but if you receive pay, you must pay back to me what you receive.

Coutts and Co. may take as long as ten days from the date of the order, before you receive the cheque-book from them, but as you have plenty of time in which to pay your Mess bill, and as the ten days are nearly over, I think you can afford to wait.

The dreary round of Aldershot continued. Hating every moment of it consumedly, in my turn I was much disliked. There could be no doubt that I was by a long head the most unpopular of the officers; though several others among them were regarded, for one reason or another, with suspicion by their comrades. Usually, the unpopular emerged from this state after the passage of a few years. Even the Adjutant of the time – he had been away the night I arrived – had still the lingering cobwebs of unpopularity clinging to him: in his case, the reasons for it being that he was an unusually intelligent man, liked conversation and, worse yet, talked French as easily as he spoke English.

What little leisure I gained occasionally, through some error in the official calculation of the time-table of duties, I spent in my room, reading. These were my most pleasant moments in the week, and even today I can remember what I read, particularly – for I had so few half-hours in which to read that one book lasted me for weeks – the *Clayhanger* series, in three volumes, by Arnold Bennett. I sat in an armchair by the fire, and got up out of it every two or three minutes to put a record on the large hornless gramophone, which had already made a twenty-pound hole in my allowance and hopelessly upset my father's calculations as to

the ideal way of spending it. For many years subsequently he would refer
to its purchase, as to some boundary-mark of iniquity: 'It was at the time
you bought that gramophone'. Meanwhile, it effectively protected me
against the clamour of the Barracks. And so it is, to this day, that the
inappropriate rhythm of Viennese waltzes is mingled in my head with the
grocer's or mercer's world of Arnold Bennett's novels. They seemed
wonderful to me then, with their lists of facts and their painstaking
analysis of materials. But, looking back, truth compels me to admit that,
with one exception, the prophets of my young days seem from this
distance to be an uninspiring band. There was Wells, a man of genius,
with his naïf social paradise, served up many times, but unvaried in its
ingredients: the scientific hero, who had discovered how to blow up old
worlds in a new way, and his emancipated mistress, togged up in essential
tweeds. Their appearance in the divorce court assumed in these novels the
place of honour held, let us say, in the books of Charles Dickens, by a
wedding in church: his earlier romances, such as *The Island of Dr Moreau*,
or *The Time Machine*, were drenched in nightmare, and contained, as do
dreams, many twinges of future truth. There was Arnold Bennett, giving
us detail after detail about life in the Siege of Paris, or about the way in
which to run hotels; there was Galsworthy, never a hero of mine, with
his neat pictures of middle-class life, where the parlour-maid always knew
her place, and with his sense of social injustice, which a little resembled
the repulsion felt by a well-brought-up young girl on learning the facts
of life. Only Shaw, with his genius and his laughter, towered then above
his contemporaries and juniors, as he still does today, a lifetime later, a
Prince and Cardinal of Literature, the greatest European figure and writer
since Voltaire.

In the Ante-Room, it was of course, impossible to read anything except
the *Morning Post* or the *Pink 'Un*, and no one spoke, except to mumble
grumpily to himself. But one day, when I was sitting there, I watched a
Major reading the newspaper, and noticed his face begin suddenly to
swell, twitch and turn plum-purple. At last – I had not dared to break the
silence and ask if I could be of any help – he threw down the rustling
pages, and appeared to be making a struggle to frame words. Seeing this,
a brother-officer came immediately to his aid, patting him on the back,
and saying, 'What's the matter, Snorter, old boy?' – or Piggy, or Pongo,
or whatever may have been his regimental, taboo nickname. I listened
carefully, and gathered the gist of what he was trying to tell us. He had
been reading, it appeared, the report of an incident on board a ship going

to South Africa, when someone had insulted Paderewski. 'I wish to God the feller'd killed him,' the tongue-tied Major bellowed, that organ at last freed by emotion from its years of atrophy. 'I don't believe he could play a choon if he wanted to! He ought to be shot, that – Padderoosky!'

From time to time I still tried to reach London. Though only thirty-six miles away, the capital seemed infinitely distant. There were many things there this spring and summer that I wanted to see; among them, the second Post-Impressionist Exhibition and a small show of drawings and paintings by Augustus John; there were operas to hear, and concerts. I wanted, also, to keep in touch with the few friends I possessed, and from whom my incarceration at Aldershot cut me off no less effectually than a decree of banishment to Siberia. In June, therefore, I asked for the two or three days to which I had become entitled. But when the Commanding Officer inquired where I wished to spend it, and received the reply '*London*', I could see the look of genuine consternation and amazement that passed over his face. 'London!' he plainly said to himself. 'Imagine wishing to leave Aldershot, earthly paradise that it is, for so mean a city!'

'But what can you do there; what can you want to do? There's nothing to do,' he reiterated in a tortured voice, and with a soldier's simple vocabulary. When he had recovered sufficiently from the shock, he refused permission. But I think his story of 'the Young Officer who wanted to go to *London*!' went the rounds: for Generals, when they visited us, surveyed me carefully, as if I were a dangerous wild beast, and the senior regimental officers seemed to regard me with increased distaste. 'What can be the state of mind', their eyes clearly goggled the message, 'of a young man who wishes to leave Aldershot to spend a few days in London!' *London!* Why, you could not even kill anything there! (It was tantalizing, too, to see all those living creatures behind their bars, walking, pacing, climbing, swinging about in the Zoological Gardens, and not be able to get at them, not to be able to fire a single shot!) No huntin': no shootin': no polo, even. Of course, there was always Tattersall's, that they admitted, but it need not occupy more than a single afternoon. You could be back in the dear old Mess in time for dinner.

I persisted in my efforts, however, and in the end, in late June, succeeded in reaching London one evening, with a day or two to spare. I had beforehand booked a seat for Covent Garden, where there was a season of Russian Ballet, as it was termed. Detained at Aldershot, I did not reach the theatre until the moment when the curtain was going up, for the first time in London, on *L'Oiseau de Feu*. I had been so tired by the

day's riding that I had nearly decided not to go – but directly the overture
began to be played, I came to life. Never until that evening had I heard
Stravinsky's name; but as the ballet developed, it was impossible to
mistake the genius of the composer, or of the artist who had designed the
setting; a genius plainly shared, too, by the chief dancers and the
choreographer. Genius ran through the whole of this ballet. Nevertheless,
Stravinsky towered above the others, a master. It may be that today the
music of this particular piece sounds almost traditional when compared
with his later work, such as *Le Sacre du Printemps* or *Les Noces*, but as I
heard it and watched the accompanying dances, I was aware that for the
first time I had been given the opportunity of seeing presented upon the
stage a work of art, imbued with originality and with the spirit of its own
day; not a tawdry glut of colour and rushing movement (like Reinhardt's
spectacles, that had somehow burst right out of the theatre into enormous
barns like Olympia – with them I was already acquainted), but a
performance in which every gesture, every line, every tone, meant
something; a work of art that could not have existed before, and would
cease to be given in its perfection, within the brief season of the dancers'
finest span. Because, for the first time, I was able to watch, in addition,
the dancing of great artists, Karsavina, and Adolf Bolm, who was superb
in his part. Karsavina was then at the height of beauty and of her career,
the greatest female dancer that Europe had seen for a century. The long,
plangent ripple of the harpstrings as the Firebird entered appeared to offer
to one some hidden meaning, just as the gathering of ogres and sinister
satellites round the crouching, wasp-like figure of their baleful master,
Koscheii (played that night by the great Cecchetti), seemed to bear some
relation to life as I knew it. The gates of life could be opened, if one
possessed the key, and the powers of evil, chaotic and uncreated, ill-
proportioned and anomalous, could be put to flight by one feather plucked
from that rare bird. The raging of the old tyrant, and his sycophantic
cronies and dependants, *could* be faced. Now I knew where I stood. I
would be, for so long as I lived, on the side of the arts. (They needed
champions as well as exponents; at least my life in Barracks had taught
me that.) I would support the artist in every controversy, on every
occasion.

CHAPTER FIVE

Towards the end of August, a stir in the atmosphere of the militarist capital could be perceived, and the reason for it soon became evident. The army was shortly proceeding on manoeuvres, and with it the cavalry regiment to which I was attached. I dreaded the prospect, because I was to accompany my tormentors. Fortunately, second thoughts in the Orderly Room eventually reached the sound, and indeed ineluctable, conclusion that, under the eyes of countless Generals, I should add no lustre to the reputations of those who had instructed me in the military art, and therefore, that since some officers had to be left behind in charge of barracks, I had better form one of this small group. Of what followed I cannot be sure: for the kindly censorship which governs memory has expunged it from my records. I remember a few days, summer days free from Gowk and Fribble-Sadler; quiet days, for trumpet and drum no longer echoed under hot roofs, while beyond, in other barracks, in the more distant perspectives of low gables of corrugated iron, the bagpipes, too, had ceased their sinister whinings, so unsuited to these particular wastes. No batmen whistled. No horses whinnied. Then, I went!

In effect, I ran away to Italy, to have a talk with my father, in order to try to persuade him to modify his plans for my future. But it seems plain that before leaving I must have obtained some sort of official sanction to go; otherwise I could neither have left the country nor later have entered a regiment. Whatever may have happened, at any rate I left, bearing with me the sense of being held in dislike, and even in contempt; a feeling from which my brother-officers of the Grenadiers three months later rescued me at the Tower.

Even before this interval had elapsed, almost in a week, my spirits had renewed themselves, so strong at the age of nineteen is the natural recoil. The few days I spent in London completed the effect of contrast between England and Italy. It was only the middle of September, but this year the fog had already coffined the city for the winter, and the ragged, fiery manes of the gas-fires barely showed beyond the radius of a few yards. Through slow miles of murk I drove one night with some friends to a masked ball at Covent Garden Theatre. These public dances were then a feature of the London night in the autumn and winter months, and were singular in the general air of gaiety that prevailed; an air unusual in our capital at any time, and never to be observed perhaps, except in the carefree years immediately preceding the First World War, when the great, soft, headless, amorphous mob of rich people of indeterminate origin produced by the business activities of the previous century was bent on pleasure, though having, it seemed, little knowledge of how to obtain it or how to spend the accumulated millions. That night, the lightness of spirit appeared to gain from the wall after wall of darkness that the dancers knew to be enclosing them outside. Parties of masked figures watched from the tiers of boxes the glittering, shifting pattern made by the couples on the floor, spread above stalls, orchestra and stage. This – 1912 – was the year when syncopated dance-music first conquered England; soon the music-halls were to ring with moaning nostalgic prattle about Alabama and the Mason-Dixon Line, and already in a few advanced night-clubs a small negro band would hoot itself hoarse with whip-poor-will chuckles; but here nineteenth-century waltzing still prevailed. The dancers crowded the space, slowly revolving, singing, and blowing paper trumpets. The company was recruited chiefly from the professional pleasure-lovers, the idle and dissolute, the stage-door hangers-on and bar-proppers, and I remember this was the first time I had seen men of education drunk. There were several of them, each dancing by himself in the lobby in a rapt and sullen *pas seul* that resembled in its solemn elaboration a tragic figure out of some ritual antique dance. (The sadness of the intoxicated is a theme never sufficiently emphasized.) The very next day I escaped into Italy, then the garden of the world, full of a beauty and happiness that seemed to be an emanation from the soil itself, just as our fogs and damp pleasures appear to rise from the square miles of poisoned clay clamped under London pavements; I passed, moreover, straight from an English autumn into an Italian, then a season new to me, and perhaps the most beautiful and characteristic that any country offers, with its skies so clear, and of such a depth of blue transparency, showing between the great white clouds, flat-bottomed, that are evoked by the heat; the Italian autumn, with its pyramids of figs and peaches, its dust, its roses and oleanders, and brown, baked hills, spiky here and there with dark cypresses, and its terraces hung with opalescent, smoky bunches of white grapes, or the bloomy, jewelled clusters of the darker kinds.

In Florence, I found my mother and father were staying in a hotel, long established for foreigners, in the Piazza Santa Trinità. My father had greatly perturbed himself about an outbreak of cholera in Naples during the late summer. He suspected the Italian Government of suppressing news about the gravity of the epidemic, and had, in consequence, arranged with friends who lived in the afflicted city a private code, whereby he could read from day to day the progress or recession of the plague: thus, morning and evening, telegrams arrived for him. *Aunt Maria better* signalled an improvement clearly enough, *Calling in another doctor* was to be interpreted with equal ease to token a grave deterioration; whereas, perversely, the apparently comforting words *Aunt Maria had seven hours' sleep yesterday* meant, in reality, *seven hundred more deaths yesterday*. Unfortunately, the excitement these messages aroused in their receiver often caused him temporarily to forget the key to what they conveyed, or to read them in contrary, or even in both, senses. This aggravated his distress, and almost equally he tormented himself about one of the Balkan wars that were always current in those years, and in which he took a personal interest, recalling the lessons he had learnt – and taught – in the Volunteers. Nobody else in Florence appeared to be troubled in mind. Day after day, week after week, the weather offered the same tropical noons and fresh evenings, most plainly uncontaminated. It was impossible to remain there without beginning to enjoy life.

Even my dread of the little talks which I knew must ensue with my father, cast no shadow before them; though already long experience had taught me that in any matter touching money, or wherein money was indirectly concerned, or that appeared to infringe plans he had made – and these were so numerous, and himself changed them with such rapidity, that it was almost impossible not to transgress in this respect –, he would render any proposed discussion most awkward by countering at once with the familiar 'No!', repeated thrice with great speed, like the firing of a machine-gun, or with the still more absolute 'Certainly *Not!*' In addition, he magnified in his own mind the difficulties which, when he so desired, he was able to detect at every point in the compass. Molehills reared their haunted summits and fantastic peaks in all directions: but the real mountains he failed ever to perceive. Thus, the following year, when, while recovering from mumps, I wrote to tell him that the doctor ordered me to go to the seaside for a fortnight, he at once replied that unfortunately he could not afford to put me up in his house at Scarborough, much as he would have liked to do so, unless I agreed to pay him 4s. 9d. a day for board and lodging and a weekly sum for laundry. I could not resist saying in reply that I preferred to go somewhere cheaper and more amusing.

I dreaded the talks with him: and even more than the financial discussions I knew they must include, trembled at the thought of having not only to try to persuade him to alter his mind, but, first, to confess my proved failure in life, of which he had long been so sure. It was a great mortification to be obliged to admit that I was unhappy in the life he had chosen for me: while, since he so firmly held the doctrine that weak points must be strengthened, rather than the strong be emphasized, the fact of my failure itself would perhaps only confirm him in the idea that, infallibly right in his choice, he had selected the one career which I ought to pursue. Notwithstanding, I realized that I must make a start to tell him. I dared not delay.

My news was by no means well received. Nearly every day, he would send for me to his room, and while he rested on the bed, festooned with a mosquito-net, so that, like the Deity, he remained only partially revealed, he would, from his cloudy cover, harangue me on my defects and delinquencies. As a rule, on my entry, he would rise from the bed, disengage himself for a moment from his floating gauze and, after creeping stealthily on tiptoe to the door, would open it suddenly, with a snap as it were, for he habitually suspected Henry of eavesdropping. This was part of the unusual relationship existing between them, of the way each studied the other, while never allowing it to distract him, or prevent him from playing his own hand to perfection. Each gave a most accomplished performance and when, in fact, from time to time the great man *was* found outside the door, he would make it signally clear that he was only there in pursuit of his calling, and occasionally, while my father and I were talking, we would be disturbed, after a brief period of utter, almost unnatural quiet, by clothes being brushed just outside, with so ostentatious a loudness that the sound seemed almost to frame its own meaning, 'Here I am, Sir George, still at work in your interest, never a moment for my own pleasures, never an instant's rest! Here I am, and don't pretend you can't hear me and don't know I'm outside!' In any case, Henry was far too heavy to listen for long with comfort. No eavesdropper should weigh over eleven stone (as my father told him later, which Henry listed as one of the reasons for giving his notice the following winter) and at his sixteen the boards would creak and moan as though in pain. Having found or not found Henry there, as the case might be, and having in either case shut the door again with a loud decisive slam, my father would then lock it, to prevent anyone, and especially my mother, from rescuing me. This action had about it something symbolic: it was the sure portent of storm: after that, there could be no hope. One day, the usual summons arrived. 'You're in for it again, sir, I'm afraid,' Henry announced. '*He* wants you at once. And he's humming to 'imself something terrible!' (Humming – or what might be mistaken for it, an angry buzz-like sound, similar to that to be heard during the irascible dartings of a wasp hither and thither – was acknowledged to be the harbinger of the worst scenes.) I hastened to my father's room. He was in so great a hurry to begin what he had to say that he did not get up from the bed, but called out, 'Come here immediately and lock the door! I've an important matter I'm afraid I must discuss with you.' My heart sank, and my mind ran swiftly, though heavily, over the list of my recent misdeeds; a bill for eight pounds for theatre tickets, a suit still unpaid for, a letter which I had been writing and had lost, in which I had revealed my feelings – no, it must be something worse. Foreboding settled in every finger-tip. After a momentous but poignant silence, he observed, in the even, carefully lowered tones which he reserved for family secrets and for accusations, but at great speed,

'Sit down! . . . Between ourselves, in *my* opinion, the Greeks have definitely beaten the Bulgarians!'

The relief of finding that only a major international complication was to be the subject of this confidential talk proved overwhelming. I could never have imagined so sweet a war.

Nothing, no amount of worry, could make one unhappy for long in Italy, at the age of nineteen. The country was too heartening, and the people, with their vital natures, too welcoming, to allow of more than a passing depression. From one window, in a passage outside my bedroom, I could see the thin spire of a Tuscan cypress and part of a tiled dome, set in a perspective that, in the Florentine light, and of an evening especially, though so bare except in its essentials, seemed, while you looked at it, to offer the whole of Italy, together with the secret of its beauty. I would spend hours there, gazing at this view, in a kind of ecstasy, akin, perhaps, to what saints may feel when they contemplate the source of all virtue. Hardly less matter for wonder and excitement did I find in Montegufoni, which I saw for the first time during this visit to Florence, three years after it had been bought in my name.

Twice or more every week, we would set out, rather early in the morning – since it takes an hour to drive there, through mountainous country, from Florence – to spend the day, returning to our hotel in time for my father to receive his evening telegram to the effect that Maria was better or worse. In the days spent at Montegufoni, however, he seemed to be at his happiest. While we wandered through the high, cool rooms of the great house or, if it were not too hot, along the three sun-baked decks of the garden, Henry would be unpacking an ample luncheon of cold chicken, and Angelo Masti, the peasant in charge, would hurry in with a large, flat, cylindrical cheese, the *pecorino* of the neighbourhood, with a basket of figs and late peaches, tinged with green, and grapes, all still warm from the sun – some of these being of the kind called *fragole*, the small, plump, blue grapes, so different from others in their internal texture, and in their taste, which recalls that of the wood strawberry, that they might be fruit from the planet Mars or Venus – or a huge flask, covered in dry, dusty rushes, of the excellent red wine of the Castle itself. Presently, too, a very strong, pungent scent approaching us indicated that Angelo had just bought a large clothful of white truffles from a boy outside, who had been collecting them in the woods. (The white variety is only found, I believe, in Italy, and most commonly in Piedmont and Tuscany, and round Parma: it is coarser than the black, and, in its capacity to impregnate a dish, more resembles garlic, a fine grating of it on the top of any substance being sufficient.) His wife would cook for us, and send in a dish of rice or macaroni sprinkled with them. And these things to eat and drink would be placed on a table covered with the coarse white linen used by the *contadini*, under a ceiling painted with clouds and flying cupids, holding up in roseate air a coat of arms, a crown and a Cardinal's hat.

My mother seldom accompanied us on these expeditions, for she preferred to remain in Florence, reading the English papers, the arrival of which, though two days old, at an uncertain hour about midday, constituted her greatest excitement here –, then, a week or two after I had joined my parents, she returned to England. So, for the most part, my father and I were alone, and on these occasions, though still a little depressed by the Baron's stories of the impracticability of the place as a residence, he would seem to be in his least unaccommodating mood, full always of information, and often of pungent comments. I must emphasize here that, once he had emerged from his tower, he could be, when he wished – or when, perhaps, he forgot to be otherwise – a most interesting companion. The comments are more difficult to recall, since naturally they were rooted in topical and personal matters. But the occasional superstitions of a man who prided himself on a total absence of them always amused me, and, therefore, I can recollect a prophecy of his at this time, which, alas, came true. He had been reading in the papers, I suppose, about the particularly top-heavy chariot of bronze which had lately been presented to the nation by its sculptor, Captain Adrian Jones, and erected on the top of the Arch on Constitution Hill, to celebrate the completion of a hundred years' peace between England and the United States; or perhaps he had seen a photograph of it. At any rate, he remarked seriously, 'Such a mistake to challenge the Fates! It means that both countries will be involved in a war within five years!' However, such an idea was happily unthinkable.

In describing to me some of his travels in Italy, which for the last decade had been the mainspring of his life, he related an incident illustrative of the – until lately – seemingly almost inexhaustible artistic riches of Italy. Visiting Siena the previous year, to look for furniture and objects, he had several times been to see a jeweller from whom, finally, he purchased a Primitive, rather cheaply, for some hundreds of pounds. The old man – he was over eighty – had not brought it out until my father had already been to the shop on several occasions. It had been forgotten, he explained, being the last of eight hundred triptychs and altar-pieces he had bought half a century before. He had given five pennies each for them to a rag-and-bone man, who used to go round the churches, collecting them, and then pile them in the piazza and burn them for the sake of the gold he could extract from their frames and backgrounds by this method. The jeweller had sold them all – except this one, which he had mislaid – many years previously for 5 lire 60 centesimi each, and had congratulated himself then on a remarkably profitable transaction.

A second story, of a very different kind, concerned my father's friend of Oxford days, Carl von Buch, who in 1880 had helped him to expose Sir William Crookes's favourite medium on the premises of the British National Association of Spiritualists. Well, it appeared that this collaborator in the showing-up of human credulity had at last seen a ghost himself!

This story, since he knew von Buch to have possessed a stalwart lack of belief, similar to his own, came as a blow to my father. Perhaps, after all, one had better not be so certain; there might be something in it! And, in fact, from now onwards, his attitude began to crumble. But the process took many years, and he was at the moment busily employed in inventing explanations, equally improbable as the event. Nevertheless, to listen to these, and to the stories, interested me more than to hear the mock-Gothic details to which I was so often treated. He could see that I liked it, and, in consequence, these long afternoons spent with him thus were cordial, and perhaps helped me in my task of persuading him to relinquish his schemes for me as a cavalry officer. At any rate, we reached a compromise, by which I was to enter the Grenadiers. Persuasion at first was not easy; for, since life in the Brigade of Guards was known not to be cheap, he had to agree to an increase of allowance. Happily, he had been told that the discipline was very strict, and he warned me, formally, that I should not enjoy the life any better. He noticed in me very strongly, he added, the tendency visible in all my mother's family, to shirk disagreeable things! They seemed to perceive nothing wrong in enjoyment (*he enjoyed beauty*: but that was different), and, so long as people amused them, asked nothing better of them, never wondered whether the influence of such persons was frivolous or the reverse. On the whole, however, he was in excellent humour, and, if sometimes he turned irritable, a mere glimpse at one of the numerous stone cannon-balls which encumbered the courtyards, or of some opening which might prove to be an oubliette, by exciting his passion for Gothic life – or, rather, death –, soon restored his mood. The happiest moment of all, perhaps, came with the discovery of a woman's skeleton at the bottom of the Castle well, said to be as deep as the tower is high.

The hours soon passed. Now moving on heavier, more uncertain feet, Henry would be packing up the empty dishes in the hamper. (Throughout the afternoon, shouts of laughter had swept up the stone stairs from the vaulted room where he had been drinking red wine and entertaining the peasants with his talk.) At six we would return along the slanting Tuscan roads that, before many weeks had passed, I came to know so well as to be able to recognize what point in the journey had been reached by the particular smell of pine or heath or olive-oil, or whatever it might be, appropriate to it. At last the city lay before us, every church, of golden stone, or zebra-striped in black and white marble, every bridge, every dome of dusty terracotta tiles, every cypress tree and pine seemed long-settled in peace, fine and secure as did, similarly, the future before us: that two wars would sweep over Europe, and that this very city, among the two or three proudest flowers of European civilization, the property of the world, would suffer damage from bombardment, within the brief boundaries of three decades, that was barred beyond the flight of the most evil imagination, and was no more within the realms of possibility, of things that happen, than the family disasters which were, too, so surely preparing themselves. Alone, one voice of earliest youth had pronounced the coming of doom upon the world, had cried it with a singular, whining persistency, in the sombre darkness of the earliest northern morning, 'Rags and Bones, Rags and Bones!' or 'Youth must die and Great Babylon will fall!'

One of the friends I had made at my crammer's, a gay if perhaps vapid young man who spent his days in an endless fatigued fog of cigarette-smoke, had come, a year or so previously, to stay with us for a few days. He was amiable, and so I liked him, and he most certainly harboured no evil intention towards us, but while in the house, my mother mentioned to him how worried she was about money affairs, and he gave her the name and address of a financial adviser he had found, who had helped him out of all sorts of trouble; a benefactor, who seemed to be able to arrange almost anything for one. Soon after, my mother went to consult this invaluable adviser at his office, and from that moment she was unable to escape from the web he spun. Of the consequences of this meeting, the young man – he must have been just twenty-one – who had given her the name and address of the money-lender was the first victim. It was after this fashion that she fell into the toils of a notorious miscreant.

His very appearance constituted a danger-signal, and should have been sufficient warning – and then, had any inquiries been made about him, his antecedents would have been made plain. His stunted, stooping, paunchy body, with over-delicate hands and feet, carried a heavy head, as though he was wearing a mask, with a beak like that of an octopus, which spiritually he so much resembled, and a small imperial and moustache that were dyed, as was his hair, a total and unnatural black. This gave him a slightly foreign mien; there was just a suggestion of Napoleon III, or perhaps, too, there may have been a touch of oriental or of creole in his blood. Certainly there was about him an emanation of evil. As a rule – and I saw him several times – he wore striped trousers, a frock-coat, and a grey top-hat that, like his face, had acquired a tinge of yellow in it from wear, or as if in some way tainted. In the street, as he walked, at a rather slow, self-important pace, he would glance shiftily from side to side, nervous no doubt of meeting some of the hundreds of victims he had blackmailed and squeezed in his time, and who might, in the desperate straits to which he had reduced them, use physical force upon him.

Julian Osgood Field was born in New York in 1849, went to Harrow in September '67, and left in December '68. He matriculated at the age of nineteen at Merton College, Oxford. He became acquainted with Swinburne, who stayed with him on several occasions between 1869 and

'71, just at the time when the poet was at the height of his fame. And I have seen it stated that Jowett thought highly of him. After '71, we hear no more of him until the nineties. Almost exactly twenty years after he left Oxford, he published the first of his three books – of which I have seen two –, assuming as an author the signature 'X.L.' This volume, consisting of short stories, several of which had already been printed in magazines of literary repute such as *Macmillan's* and *Blackwood's*, was entitled, appropriately enough, *Aut Diabolus, Aut Nihil*, and at the time of its appearance enjoyed a certain vogue, and for several years was in demand at the libraries. In fact it is almost unreadable, dull as sin. But the second is duller, and no less evil. Named *The Limb*, and inscribed to Charles Gounod, as *souvenir affectueux*, it is concerned chiefly with scenes of Russian life. In the Harrow School Register, the entry under Field's name, and obviously revised by him, states him to have been the author of numerous plays, and to be the only foreigner who ever had a play accepted by the Comédie-Française. The rest of his life, more clearly documented, can be read in old numbers of *Truth*, and in *Truth's Cautionary List*: that of a swindler who ruined numberless people.

At first, it seemed merely as though my mother had got herself into a scrape of the kind in which any unthinking woman, not versed in business, might find herself involved.

One might have expected my father, whose lack of faith could so easily convert molehills into mountains, not to have been unaware of what was going on. He could not, you would have thought, have remained in ignorance of how distracted with worry she was, or of the reason for it. But so it proved – and in fairness to him, it must be remembered that his letters were tampered with, so that no warning should reach him, and that, further, at no stage until the very end was the full extent and depth of the pit which Field had dug to swallow her up, and her family with her, visible. Out of each small lawsuit sprouted another, more grave; beyond each vista lay one further, and more calamitous. With each new revelation the seriousness of the whole affair became emphasized. She told us nothing. Even if she had wished to remember the various promises by which she had been led on, the various traps into which she had been so easily lured, she could not have done so. Once a thing had happened, it died for her. Besides, she did not wish to remember: she wished to forget.

The few benevolent people who knew what had been happening, did not venture to interfere or to enlighten my father; for, as the reader will have understood, he was not an easy man to approach. One morning, after my mother had returned to England, I received a letter from my friend who had been at the same crammer's, and whom I have mentioned as having introduced her to Field. He had now been for some months gazetted as an officer to a well-known regiment, and wrote to inform me that he had backed certain bills for my mother at Field's instigation, that they had fallen due and had not been met, and the solicitors had written to warn him that unless they were paid immediately, the Colonel would be told, and he would have to leave the regiment. I at once decided that the only thing to do was to inform my father – as I write, the scene rises up before me. I persuaded him to come for a walk with me, saying that I particularly wished to talk with him. We started out, and after an uneasy silence of a moment or two, I said, 'I'm afraid I must tell you that Mother has got into the hands of a moneylender': to which he replied, 'I never heard such nonsense: if she were, *I* should have known about it!' – which was, in fact, the very reverse of the truth. However, I persisted and, in the end, my words, together with the unfortunate course of events, which could not be made to vanish by a pure process of contradiction, persuaded him of the truth.

My mother, the daughter of an enormously rich man, had been married from the schoolroom. Money held no meaning for her. Even the simplest sums were beyond her computation. Further, she had reached an age when reason is apt to lose its sway. Her debts amounted to some two thousand pounds. She signed papers that made her responsible in all for thirty thousand. By these processes she received a total amount of six hundred. Field and his accomplices swallowed the rest, and he aimed, beyond her, at her relations with their great wealth. His plans were in essence those of a blackmailer more than of a moneylender. And in his calculations he showed the typical conventionality of the cramped criminal mind. His schemes were all based on the assumption that the husband would pay without demur the money to be extorted from him, rather than allow his wife to face the case to be instituted against her, and in which the moneylender had arranged so that it would appear as if she were the culpable person. It had never struck him that my father would refuse to settle – and up till the last moment he could not believe it. My father, however, was a more unconventional and combative type than he had met so far in his professional life. He steadfastly refused to pay: all the more resolutely because he now found that Field had a year or two before entangled a young cousin of ours – a boy of nineteen or twenty –

in his toils. Had the moneylender then been shown up, my father maintained, had the young man's parents declined to pay the sums levied on them, and instead, allowed the case to come into court, Field would have been exposed, and, consequently, my mother would never have fallen into his clutches. The only way, therefore, to render Field harmless for the future and unable to ruin thoughtless people, he argued, was to allow the cases against my mother to proceed. It was a duty. No doubt, other reasons helped him, some consciously, others unconsciously, to this decision. And he never, I think, understood how black the cases against her would appear to those who did not know her. As it was, every familiar turn of speech in her letters, everything that could count against her, told remorselessly. Even a phrase quoted from a letter to myself, in which she said, 'Can you get hold of So-and-so?' – words she habitually used if she wanted to send for anybody, as 'Can you get hold of your Father?' – were taken to mean that she had wished me to lay a trap for him.

The main and subsidiary lawsuits often came one after another, with a deadly iteration though conflicting in tendency and results. Thus I find that Sir George Lewis – of Messrs Lewis & Lewis, who acted for my mother – in writing to thank me for a letter of congratulation I had sent him on having won an action for her, says how great a comfort it must be to me to think of the entire matter being ended: while a month later, just as I was going to the Front, my father writes to tell me that the whole thing has started again. And I have a letter written from Eton by my young brother, in great misery of spirit, at the age of seventeen, reminding me that at least one of these sordid lawsuits had taken place every single half since he had arrived there; and it was true, the series lasted from the spring of 1913 – and already the worry of it had taken root at the time of which I write, in 1912 – until the appalling culmination in March 1915. So henceforth, for years, life carried this terrible duality for us, a development and continuation of the double thread of life that had in earlier days taken so heavy a toll of childish nerves: the apparently prosperous, traditional life stretched over and disguising the frenetic disputes, the rages and the cold hardness. Now, however, this duality had assumed a more objective, purposeful and evil embodiment. It coloured every day for each of us, and made us fear the next, and the new revelations it might bring. Everything had to it this sad and horrible aroma. And, as usual, my sister, who was most at home, bore the greatest share of the suffering. In my own case, youthful spirits proved irrepressible: it was not conceivable, even now, that family affairs should take so grievous and desolating a turn as in fact they took. For though my mother was of so unpractical a nature, so undeveloped in certain respects, my father was an undeniably clever and capable man, of considerable experience. With some degree of ease, therefore, I was able to support possible misfortunes in which I could not quite bring myself to believe. Nevertheless, when this has been allowed for, and though, as I have said, my physical and nervous make-up did not permit me to remain depressed for more than forty-eight hours at a stretch, yet in the account of my life that follows, this undertone of sorrow and apprehension must be borne in mind. I shall say little more of this squalid business, the materialization of the dark shadow that the reader has seen at times clouding the sunnier early years. I shall mention the climax in its place, without comment: here I shall only ask the reader to imagine the contaminating sense of insecurity, that occasionally retreated, but only, always, to come back with greater force, a feeling that underlay all these years, and their beauty and laughter, and to picture for himself the difficulty sometimes experienced in meeting old friends again, because of the chasm caused by explanations or the lack of them.

Ten days or so after I had told my father of Field's existence, he returned to London. At present these affairs still looked as if they would easily be put right: this was the first time I had been left abroad by myself – and it seemed as if the whole world were opening to me. That Florence and Aldershot could be situated in the same globe was scarcely to be believed. Never had people looked so beautiful or appeared so interesting as in this city. Ambitions were not mine. I had no wish to be a General, an Ambassador, a Prime Minister, least of all a captain of industry or finance. If only, if *only*, people would leave me alone, would cease to tell me what to do and how to do it, what a wonderful, exciting place the world would be! In any case, I found I could be happy all day, visiting galleries, or walking round the streets of Florence. Even better than a day spent in wandering about the city, were the long, sunny hours at Montegufoni: which, during the ensuing weeks, I really grew to know and love.

Now, in mid-October, the gardens resembled those of an English June; not only were they filled with roses and carnations, not only with an exaggeration and profusion of plants already known to one in England, so that the little green bushes of lemon-scented verbena, that in favoured positions, and draped with sackcloth, may survive our winter, were here grown almost to trees, showing tawny, flaking trunks, covered with spikes of grey-blue blossom, as well as with their aromatic green leaves, but there were other and more unfamiliar flowers. Further, since I had never previously been in Italy in September and October, there were fruits, as well as flowers, new to my eyes in the guise of growing, living things: lemons, no longer wrapped in their twists of tissue paper as in a shop in London, but here displayed at each step in their redolent and simultaneous developing, as if the old, glossy-leafed and fragrant trees – still standing in huge seventeenth-century jars of dusty terracotta that yet bore a shield of the arms of the Acciaiuoli Cardinal, surmounted by the wide, tasselled hat of his office: treasures of which such care was taken that they were carried out from the vast old lemon-house at the end of the second terrace in the spring, and back there in the late autumn, when they were further protected by scaffolds hung with screens of straw; as if, then, these trees, spangled with ivory-white buds and rosettes of gold-flecked, perfumed blossom, as well as bearing fruit at every stage, from small, dark shapes, no bigger than a hazel-nut, to fruit of green bronze, and then gradually coloured and shaped by the sun, to the finely-drawn elliptical ripe lemon, painted with so gay a brush, were engaged in giving an all-the-year-round exhibition of their powers.

The garden offered reptilian and entomological, as well as floral, wonders. To comprehend the character of the place, the reader must be reminded that these great stone terraces, into which the sixteenth- and seventeenth-century owners of the Castle had converted the ramparts and bastions of a medieval fortress, carried their own systems of minute life. There were colonies of ants, marking the worn and tawny tiles with an invariable streak of moving sepia; there were two kinds of lizards, blue-green and emerald-green, living in warm crevices, behind south walls. There were cicadas, playing selections, day and night, from their voluptuous repertory of music; butterflies, large and small, and huge moths; and there were the flickering illuminations of fire-flies. Then, in the afternoon sun, when everything was at its fullest and largest, the roses wide open, the heliotrope scintillating with its particular glitter in the light, there would sound the comforting buzz amd bump of beetles, not the dragging kitchen-beetles of England, with their obsequious insolence, but bold scarabs, armoured warriors or priests in their robes of blue and green and purple. And, too, one would obtain occasionally a glimpse of sidling, poisonous creatures, sad, bad and dangerous to know; tarantulas, or elongated, parchment-coloured scorpions that were said to have waxed thin upon the bones of the Saints who reposed in the Chapel.

Over a hundred people – men, women and children – were still living in the house, yet every day new features came to light in rooms that had recently been quitted and were beginning to be restored. For the next twenty-eight years, except at the very climax of the two wars, the noise of hammering, scratching and scraping was to rise up from dawn to dusk at my father's command. Already many of the rooms echoed with it, and a cloud of dust hung over the Court of the Dukes of Athens; the existence of which, for it had been filled up with a warren of rooms, had only lately been revealed. This court was just behind the tower, which rose from one corner of the Great Court, and had been built, so the tradition of the neighbourhood alleged, in imitation of that of the Palazzo Vecchio. The story was that an owner of the Castle in the thirteenth century had publicly sworn that if a certain prayer were granted by St Anthony, he would never live out of sight of the Palazzo Vecchio tower. Not long afterwards, he obtained his desire, but since he was greatly devoted to his country estate, had meanly sought to avoid the payment of his oath by constructing at Montegufoni this counterfeit.

The Muses, then, had often brushed this romantic residence with their wings. Its fault, in so far as it had one, was that apart from the Grotto, with the surmounting balustraded outside staircase, apart from the tower and the baroque eastern façade, it possessed no features of supreme architectural interest. The statues were not by the great sculptors, nor the frescoed ceilings by the great decorative painters of the period – albeit as yet we were not sure what might not be revealed, for in some instances the large halls had been divided into four, by the insertion of an extra floor and partition walls, and the frescoed ceilings had been covered over and were only just beginning to show above my father's dust-storms. Montegufoni atoned for its deficiencies, however, in other ways. The vistas of painted rooms were splendid and pleasant: the terraces an enchantment: but above all, the general atmosphere was overwhelmingly touched with poetry. As plainly as the grapes of the valley belonged to the vats in the vast old cellars, the Castle – a construction, rather than a house – belonged to the landscape, dulcet but poignant, in which it stood, crowning a little hill in a wide valley that rose on all sides again toward the horizon. Below, in the trough of the valley, a small, clear stream ran through a wood of cypress, clothed, in its perpetual sweetness, so easily in-breathed, and here, too, one could listen to the music of the few Italian singing-birds that, being small enough to have escaped the Italian sportsman's shot, if not his aim, survive to sing; while the country, as if to compensate for so much delicacy by adding strength, offered a romantic and rugged landscape to the north, so that, across the Great Court, from the windows of the state dining-room – a very long, narrow room with a pretty Tiepolesque ceiling, a painting of cupids carrying away the Crown of Athens – could be seen a cool, blue vista of distant mountains, crowned, as a rule, with snow. But it was the number of small pointillist touches – so hard to reproduce – that in their sum gave the house its character. For instance, in the space under the Cardinal's Garden, which sailed so high in the air, was a little vaulted room with a balcony. This chamber had been used in the late seventeenth and eighteenth centuries for distilling scents, and in it I found stored in a dark corner large sacks of shells, rose-pink, lilac, pearly, fresh as if the sea had just receded from them, that must have been placed here two hundred and fifty years before, when the Grotto was made, in case it should ever be necessary to patch or repair the mosaics of the interior walls.

The cellars, replacing medieval dungeons – though some of these still existed –, reached to a great depth beneath the structure. Each contained two or more vats: and one of the dark, vaulted rooms, lit by a grating and the light from an open door, offered music as well as wine. The very first letter I had received addressed to me at the Castle came from *La Società Filarmonica di Montegufoni* – in other words, the village band: for the inhabitants were still sufficiently numerous to support an institution of this kind, just as, similarly, they had their own tailor's, cobbler's and carpenter's shops. The letter contained a warmly-phrased request to me to become patron and president, and I was delighted with it, though my father, who noticed me reading it, and at once inquired, 'How are they?' (a ruse he had lately worked out, and now always adopted to find from whom a letter came, by the pretence that he recognized the handwriting, and also by the distraction he caused you, in the middle of reading, because in order to obtain silence you were inclined to blurt things out), when I told him about the invitation, rather skimmed the joy from it by remarking, 'Such a mistake! They only want twenty-five lire from you!' Howbeit, I accepted the proffered honour, and, now that my father had returned to England, I would sometimes, of an afternoon or evening, attend a rehearsal, and it must be admitted that those hours offered some of the strongest and strangest physical sensations of a lifetime.

From above, from the courtyard, or the room adjoining it, only a little muffled rhythm, a bumping and squeaking, could be distinguished, but once you entered the inmost and deepest stone chamber in which the band was playing, the sound conquered and prevailed over every other feeling. The effect, I think, owed its resonance to the fact that the cellar was surrounded, at each side and above and below, by similar echoing apartments, and that there were several storeys or depths of them. Be the cause what it may, the volume of droning and buzzing and clattering was so tremendous as to seem to add an element to Nature herself, as you breathed the sound, inhaled it, drew it in through the very pores of the skin, lived in it, as fish in water. The music might not be good, but you were plunged and immersed in it. The sound vibrated through every cell in the body, so that you felt a part of it and that it was a part of you. The tunes, exclamatory, dramatic, old-fashioned, possessed a rusticity, both in their kind and in the playing of them, that I have nowhere else encountered, yet it cannot be denied that they were powerful, and rendered with power.

The sunset hour was at hand, and it was time to return to Florence. As with the particular speed, or sense of it, that comes before dusk, we rushed along the ridge road and then descended into the nearest valley, the cool air rising from the narrow stream that ran through a wide, stony bed greeted us already with a breath of evening freshness. By a bridge – about two miles from Montegufoni – stood the remains of a chapel that had once been frescoed by Giotto. A shaggy white dog, belonging to the special breed that so noisily guard the broad farm-buildings of the Val di Pesa, barked at us ferociously from the middle of the road: even the approach of the motor would scarcely persuade him to move. In the adjoining village, the pallid surfaces of the walls, in light greys and parchment and ash colour, caught a glow from the scarlet pennons that streamed across the sky. A child threw a stone, which rattled on the side of the machine: yet, though so poor, the place was peaceful, and the inhabitants friendly.

Soon the famous monastery of the Certosa, disposed upon its cypress-pointed hill, lay below us, seeming by its size an ancient town rather than a single building. And then came Florence itself. When we reached it, the dark streets were sprinkled with lights and the hard golden palaces and dazzling, striped marble churches of the city held within them a certain mystery and sadness, as well as their usual hubbub and confusion. We crossed the Arno by the Ponte Santa Trinità. There was no cloud, no threat, except men's folly, which often can be an agreeable thing. And even when I got out at the hotel and went upstairs, I had no unpleasantness to fear. For the first time in my life I was enjoying a period which ran counter to my father's dictum that you should do at least one distasteful thing a day.

CHAPTER SIX

Having returned to England at the end of November 1912, I joined the Grenadier Guards and, a week later, was posted to the battalion stationed at the Tower of London.

The effective head, 'the Lieutenant-Colonel', as he was known, of each of the four regiments of the Brigade as then constituted – Grenadiers, Coldstream, Scots Guards, Irish Guards –, possessed as his headquarters or appropriate shrine a kind of small Greek temple in stucco, with fluted pillars and capitals of the Doric order, placed, as if for the sake of inviolability, behind the stout, spear-like iron railings of Birdcage Walk. Besides being so important a military mandarin, the Lieutenant-Colonel was, as well, an institution comparable to that of an Elder in the monasteries of the Russian Orthodox Church, healing, and bestowing advice or reprimands. In other respects, he more nearly, perhaps, resembled an idol. Summoned hither, to the temple of the particular cult to whose worship he had been dedicated, the neophyte, not yet fledged or newly-joined ensign – or as for that, any officer who had conducted himself in a manner contrary to, or perhaps, even, only exaggerating, regimental tradition –, would find himself first involved in a flurry of stamping sentries and saluting orderlies (a process which, singularly enough, only served, by the apparent aura of respect it with such irony produced for him, to make his own feeling of inner instability the worse).

Then, ushered almost at once into the august presence, he would be obliged to salute, in his turn and as smartly as he could, the idol seated at a desk, behind the cloud of incense composed of his own cigarette smoke. Directly the ensign beheld the old image, who would be puffing at a substantial but delicately aromatic Turkish or Egyptian cigarette, he would realize that here, before him, was the improbable realization of an ideal; an ideal cherished by a considerable number of contemporaries, including most officers and all the best tailors and haberdashers, hosiers, shoemakers and barbers in London, indeed in England. The English always put substance first, rather than its treatment; and just as roast beef is – or, alas, was – their principal dish, so everything here, also, was of prime material: and thus, though too restrained to suggest dandyism, yet everything about him was immaculate, of the finest quality and cut: cloth, linen, and the man encased in them. Every pore of the skin, every hair of his grey moustache and eyebrows, was unemphatically – for emphasis would smack of ostentation – in its right place, and showed in miniature the same kind of order and beautiful military precision that the regimental parades exhibited on the grand scale. His manners, too, imbued though they were by their quality of rather impersonal affability – and though it was quite evident, as well, that the idol realized that affability was not his whole practice and that at times it was his duty to instil awe –, were memorable in their perfection. At a single glance it might be deemed possible by the inexperienced, such was the apparent sincerity and straightforwardness of his self-presentation, to know all about him, even to write a testimonial, *strong sense of duty, hard-playing (golf, cricket, polo), generous, brave, fine shot, adequate rider, man of the world, C. of E.* These same attributes, too, seemed to belong to the objects on his desk, the photographs, in simple silver frames or leather – the best photographs of the best people, in the best frames –, the silver cigarette-lighter, made in the shape of a grenade, the silver pen-tray and rack, the pens and pencils, the regimental trophies and presentations, even the blotting-paper which lay spread out under his hand without a stain.

When I compared this polished, kindly and agreeable individual, of unfailing courtesy, with Major Gowk of the cavalry regiment from which I had just made my escape, I understood my good fortune. The realization of an ideal always, no doubt, carries with it its weak points, but of one thing you could rest assured: the idol before you would never treat any man, especially one younger than himself, with unfairness: nor, you could be equally certain, would his predecessor have done it in the past, or his successor do it in the future. For the type was fast. When the time came for this elderly man to retire, another, almost identical in appearance, would reign with the same elegant ease in his stead, behind the same cloud of cigarette smoke, at the same table, covered, it might seem, with the same photographs, the same objects.

To show the quality of delicate understanding that a machine of such military efficiency could on occasion, and most unexpectedly, reveal, I jump ahead five years, towards the end of the First World War. By that time, I was twenty-four, and a Captain. A very strict rule existed that no officer should be seen, except on duty, in the company of a private soldier. One day an officer who had joined the regiment since the war started, and was fighting it out in the corridors of the War Office, reported to the Regimental Orderly Room that he had seen me having a drink with a private soldier in the Café Royal. When summoned to the presence, I explained that the private soldier in question was Jacob Epstein, and that I refused to cut a distinguished sculptor who was a friend of mine, just because he happened to have enlisted. To my surprise the Lieutenant-Colonel, purely out of a sense of decency – for it can be imagined that Epstein's sculpture was not numbered among the Regimental Orderly Room's ideals –, took my part. He saw the point perfectly, and called to order the officer who had reported me.

Throughout the months that ensued between December 1912 and the outbreak of war, my background varied constantly: the Tower, Aldershot once more – but after the town I had known, how strangely different and comparatively pleasant an Aldershot this seemed! –, several months of leave, Pirbright, Purfleet and Wellington Barracks. It was eight o'clock in the morning. School was finished with. Though finding myself a member of a profession for which I showed no aptitude, and though aware of my deficiency in this respect, yet now the lines would begin to be engraved on my right hand, differently from my left. December 1912 was the month in which my life, my own life, began. As I looked at my home, I could see how quickly things were altering. In April 1913, while I was still at the Tower, Henry quitted my father's service for ten years. That, in itself, marked the end of an epoch. Robins now took his place, and had, in his turn, to get to know all the points of *The System*: that plan for the better ordering of his life which my father had devised. At their first interview, my father had looked at him and said,

'I know *some people* make out I'm difficult to get on with, but *I* don't agree with them!'

It was not difficult to perceive the trend and accent of things or to notice how the various shadows had come out into the open, and were now parading themselves, their blackness touching the dawn and dusk of each day, of each day in each week. Life, however, in spite of it, seemed so welcoming, so enchanting, that these patches of moving dark would surely disappear: though my instincts never allowed me to accept the burgess view, so often proffered, that 'the worst never happens', and so, for moments that in their horror stretched to hours, and for so long as my physical cheerfulness would allow me, I would wonder whether the shadows, now in part materialized, might not take on full substance. As I looked back at the view sweeping to so great a distance behind me, I could see nothing of the sort, nothing to offer a warning by parallel. Shadows, of course, must have existed when one had been down there, but how swiftly they had vanished. Similarly, life lay spread before me, stretching on all sides toward a horizon, peaceful, golden and illimitable. But what kind of life? I asked myself. That for which I must look, and which heredity itself had taught me to seek, was a continuation of that of my father – and still more of that of his father, less exceptional; in the same houses, in the same county, in the same country; the same kind of existence, domestic and official, the same professions, the same posts.

All this was inscribed in my left hand, but what there was in my right, I could not tell. It was easier to deduce from frame, appearance and trend of mind what characteristics I had inherited and from what direction. It was plain at this age, I think, that I embodied two chief strains, Sitwell and Somerset: from them comes what, in combination, gives me any particular quality I may possess as a writer; a way of seeing things, a mind that loves and comprehends modern art, a faculty for enjoyment, and a natural demand for it, or gusto, qualities that are allied with or rise out of the physical constitution; to them, of all my relatives, I am chiefly drawn by inclination, though our tastes are so different, and it seems to me that in my reflection in the looking-glass I could – and can – observe the traits that I know from portraits, just as, very clearly, I can identify in my sister the traces of Plantagenet blood, so that she might by her cast of face, in the mould of body and in the shape of her wrists and hands, have sat for the portrait of Lady Elizabeth or Katherine Somerset, or their cousin Queen Elizabeth, or for the golden effigy in the Abbey of their ancestress, Queen Eleanor. Looking at myself, as I was then, I recognized the height, and breadth of shoulder, the straight, fair hair, the long, bridged nose, with winged nostrils, the rather florid, fair colouring; these I had seen in portraits at Renishaw and elsewhere. But there were other things, besides, and to take wit, if I may claim it, that is always a personal possession, an accident of birth or upbringing, a power never fully under control, in essence explosive and anarchic, composed of diverse and unresolved elements. My mind, I believe, was modern, in accord in many respects with the age in which I live, but it may be remembered that I have also in me the blood of a family which today yet bears, as it should, the old Royal Arms of England, quartering still the lilies of France – which George III surrendered – with the leopards, and carrying under the shield the words *I disdain to change or fear*; blood which in its very pulsing ever showed steadfastness and a peculiar loyalty to tradition.

I went to Wellington Barracks in September 1913 – at the end of Army Manoeuvres, on which I had proceeded with the 1st Battalion from Aldershot. Each day, we marched some twenty to thirty miles, and by dark I was usually too exhausted to know or care where I might be. My incapacity as a soldier must, indeed, have been conspicuous; if sent out, as sometimes one was, with a map, to find the way for the battalion, expeditions inevitably had to be sent out before long, in their turn, to find me. And I still remember the shock of recognition with which, the sun and breeze suddenly lifting a light fog, I discovered myself to be by the side of the formal canal, among the herds of deer and piebald flocks of Jacob's sheep, in Sir Alfred Dryden's famous but secluded estate of Canons Ashby, about two miles from Weston, my grandmother's old home. I had possessed no conception that I was within a hundred miles of it! In these Manoeuvres, though, some friends of mine distinguished themselves as much as I disgraced myself: but it all came to the same thing; for in those days to spring a surprise on the Staff by doing too well was equivalent to doing badly. To be over-zealous and super-successful was a fault! Thus I well remember the consternation caused when, the Intelligence Officer falling ill, my friend Geoffrey Moss temporarily took over his work, and since he possesses an acute and untrammelled mind, nearly put an end to Manoeuvres by capturing two motor-cars full of 'enemy' Generals. They had hurriedly to be released, for they had envisaged no such move on the part of a junior officer, and their faces flamed red as the tabs they wore, with anger.

Another feature of that ten days I recall with more appreciation. One Saturday night to Monday, the Brigade of Guards camped in the park of Mr Alfred de Rothschild, at Halton in Buckinghamshire, and officers and men were given many treats by the generous owner, who most sumptuously entertained the officers. This fragile, beautifully neat old gentleman with an anxious expression, who seemed to sum up in his own person a century of luxurious living and sly financial domination, inhabited a large yellow stone house, with lofty French slate roofs and towers and turrets, that stood at the top of a hill, well screened under the higher Chilterns, among acres and sweeping acres of carefully mown grass. The first afternoon, he gave us a performance of his private circus. It was a somewhat grotesque occasion. The little old man, dressed in a blue suit and wearing a blue bowler hat above the minute white screw-curl on each temple, acted as circus-master himself, and stood holding a whip in the middle of a miniature ring at the top of one of his poodle-smooth lawns. Tiring of this circus, I walked away, I remember, to examine the rustic details of a summer-house near by, attracted to it by the curious rattling sound it emitted in the golden breeze of mid-September: but the mystery was quickly solved, for the ivy that covered this retreat proved to be made of painted metal, and so clanked faintly against the walls with each breath. But no doubt it always remained neat. Inside, stood on a table a telephone of ivory and gold. The interior of Halton, spacious and ugly, contained many superb objects, mostly of French derivation. I climbed a few steps up one side of the double staircase, to examine more closely a Watteau, hanging on the wall above. But soon I felt someone was following – and sure enough, at a few paces behind, a hefty stranger, of what is known as 'respectable appearance', was watching me intently. This proved to be Mr Alfred de Rothschild's private detective. And in the house at the same time, I was told, there resided as well a doctor and a lawyer, in case the old gentleman fell ill or wished to add a codicil to his last testmament. To such lengths, such heights or depths, can great wealth lead a being endowed with a highly strung nervous system and some imagination. In addition to his own lawyer, doctor and detective, Mr Alfred de Rothschild possessed a private orchestra of string instruments, which played during and after dinner. And if the programme of music it discoursed was on this occasion rather banal, it may have been chosen to suit the military taste. The dinner itself was a masterpiece of French art, and the accompanying wines were memorable.

Alas! the life we led, in bivouacs, with noses blue from cold at night, and with sausages or herrings as the pinnacle of every meal, was not so luxurious, and it was with joy that I found myself in London again, at Wellington Barracks, where I remained until shortly before the outbreak of the war in 1914. I occupied a room on the second floor, overlooking the Parade Ground – from this height almost hidden – and, beyond it, the trees and water of St James's Park. On the left, one could not, during those years, see Buckingham Palace, because the front was entirely screened by a criss-cross of scaffolding and canvas, behind which the new, hard, Portland-stone façade, a soulless model, was growing, stiffly as a cactus, to replace the rather charming but dingy confusion of that by Blore. This temporary, many-storeyed maze of poles and planks and platforms and screens was impressive and interesting in the manner of a drawing by Piranesi. But, at night, the view in general from my windows became transformed, for then the thousands of lights across the St James's and the Green Park, and as far as you could see, dyed the ragged edges of the clouds, suffusing the whole vast vault with a flush of rose and orange, and made anyone who looked beyond the dark surrounding banks and mounds of the leaves become conscious that he was, indeed, in the quiet heart of the greatest and most famous of cities, the light of which could thus enflame a whole sky to its apex. Here you did not, it is true, have the feeling of the continuous traditions of a thousand years of fierce life, or of the desultory and savage outbreaks of history, that assailed you at the Tower, but merely of having access to every pleasure, every mystery, every whisper, of the town. Moreover, unlike the Tower again, there was no Officers' Mess, and so no official regimental feasts occurred: *Belshaz-zars*, as they were called, which, because of their habitual length and dullness, as well as for their occasional horseplay, young officers rather dreaded. Here private rather than regimental life prevailed, and every evening could be spent where or with whom you chose, except when the duties of Picquet Officer confined you to barracks for a day and night, or for the twenty-four hours spent on King's Guard, or the fifteen on guard at the Bank of England.

So far as I know, though it has been for so long one of the spectacles most familiar to inhabitants of London, and most loved by visitors, little has been written about the Changing of the Guard: to the crowd, the performers in the ceremony cease to exist when they have marched away: and so I propose to give for a page or two an account of the very individual life led by the officers on this duty, who, after the manner of monks, albeit for twenty-four hours only, are immured in the seclusion of a brick building from which, though situated in the very centre of the capital, you can scarcely hear the passing of traffic. First, the new Guard marches to the ceremony, just as later the old Guard returns to barracks, to the military music of the drums and fifes of the battalion from which it is drawn. If the King is in London, the ceremony takes place, as all Londoners know, at about ten minutes to eleven, in the Fore Court of Buckingham Palace, or, in the monarch's absence from London, on the Colour Court at St James's: but, as a spectacle, Buckingham Palace is to be preferred as a background, because of the greater space it affords. The drill exhibited has many of the merits of a work of art, such as only the most accomplished forms of dancing or skating display. But of all the difficult tasks, the Ensign – the youngest officer present – has the most awkward allotted to him: marching just behind the Captain and Lieutenant of King's Guard and in front of the detachment of men composing it, the whole body progressing in slow time – an exercise which itself requires the greatest skill – at right angles to the Palace, he must lower the Colour in salute to the Colour of the King's Guard relieving or being relieved, and hold it stretched out in that position for some twenty paces. Many weeks of practice on the barrack square are required before perfection is attained – if ever it is – in this stately ceremonial crawl to the solemn and inspiring strains of the March from Handel's *Scipio*, which the Grenadiers have adopted as their own, in the same way that the Coldstream use the March from *Figaro*. After this part of the performance has been concluded and the new Guard has taken over, and while the sentries are being posted and the detachments placed in position, the officers of the King's Guard mounting and dismounting walk up and down together in twos, according to the military rank they hold, while whichever regimental band may be playing gives selections from its repertory.

The oncoming Guard was on duty until relieved twenty-four hours later. During this space of time, the officers had to remain in the part of St James's Palace allotted to them – an inner section, built of stout, dark brick, more nearly recalling, save that there were no trees, part of some college or close than the centre of a palace: this haven they were not allowed to leave, except for tours of duty and inspection, when they visited the sentries at Buckingham Palace and Marlborough House, and except for a few minutes in the afternoon when they were permitted, if they wished, to walk across to the Guards' Club or the Marlborough Club, then both situated within a stone's-throw, in Pall Mall. (All officers serving in the Brigade joined automatically the Guards' Club, though not the Marlborough.) As the Ensign had to go out on a tour of inspection at 2 a.m. it made a long day for him, and life in the guard-room with its view of lead flats and dingy crenellations, though it possessed an air, and seemed the very core of St James's, became a little monotonous and might, indeed, have grown insupportably to resemble a prison, had it not been for the munificence of King George IV, who had directed that, after his death, an annual sum should be paid to the officers on guard. It was not enough to defray the whole of the expense, but it certainly enabled them to entertain their friends to dinner in a handsome manner, and, in consequence, the long room, in the evening, with its table arranged with silver trophies, and its food, celebrated for its excellence, as no doubt that gourmet, King George IV, would have wished, became a place where many distinguished – and undistinguished – people could pass a most pleasant evening. The quality of the company depended chiefly on the Captain of King's Guard and his range of friends: certainly I passed many delightful hours in congenial company there: and among my own friends who dined with me in later years, when from time to time I was Captain, were Sir Edmund Gosse, Sickert and Robert Ross.

Whether the guests were amusing or whether they were dull, it was always with regret that the younger officers saw them leave – they were obliged by custom to be out by ten minutes to eleven. Soon the Ensign would be left alone, with nothing to read except the evening papers – of which, then, there were six or seven, in their various shades of pink and green, as well as white – until his final tour of inspection, when he marched through the garden, very large and dark and full of shadows, of Buckingham Palace – or 'Buck House' as shibboleth decreed it should be called: an abbreviation, no doubt, remaining from before 1825 when the former Buckingham House first became known as Buckingham Palace.

The days spent on King's Guard were of so special a nature as perhaps to resemble a little those spent by Catholics during a Retreat, though, of course, devoted to more material pursuits and duties. The resemblance consisted of the way in which the days added up and each fresh period joined on to the preceding, to make, as one looks back, a separate small lifetime of a month or two months in all, but in their quality completely unlike any other kind of existence the same individual has led. The things which afforded a sense of continuity with the life of the world outside could, moreover, be counted on the fingers of the hand. But, in addition to the few I have mentioned, one other link existed: it was permissible to have your hair cut; and, all the more because there was less reason on those occasions for my native impatience to frustrate entirely the hairdresser's art, as it so often did, and because, on the contrary, it constituted a most pleasant diversion, I always arranged for an appointment. Accordingly at about 5.30 in the evening and carrying a black bag of instruments, Mr G. F. Trumper, hairdresser to King George V, would come to attend me.

Though the hours spent on King's Guard had been long, and the night was to be short, yet the routine afforded a complete break which removed, as it were, this space of time far from the run of London days, and made it seem both longer and shorter than it was. The Guard at the Bank of England, on the other hand, provided a very different existence. The Ensign was the only officer on duty, and he had to start from Wellington or Chelsea Barracks, without drums or fifes to support the faltering rhythm of his footsteps and those of his small detachment of men, on a long march through the hard, endless streets of the city, at about five or six o'clock in the evening, and to remain at the Bank till 9.30 or 10 the next morning. The Brigade of Guards had first been called in in the year 1780, at the time of the Gordon riots, to protect the original building – before Sir John Soane's edifice was in being – when the Government had thought it to be in danger from the drunken mob. And though cries of 'No Popery!' no longer rent the air of Threadneedle Street, day by day the Guard was still posted there. For, just as tricks of speech lingered, relating to past times, so did many obsolete customs survive. And in this connection I must record that a year or two subsequently, when the shortage of man-power first evinced itself after the great slaughter of 1914 and '15, and forced the authorities to examine the placing of sentries, with a view to abolishing all those not strictly necessary, I was told how it was discovered that two guardsmen were always on duty at a certain spot in Whitehall where the reason for their presence was not immediately obvious. On inquiries being made, and the records inspected, it became plain that when Sir Robert Walpole had been Prime Minister, he had formed a habit of walking from Downing Street, near by, and of sitting on a garden-bench there for a while to rest and take the air, and that, because his life had been threatened, sentries had eventually been posted on each side, at the suggestion of Queen Caroline, to ensure his safety. Walpole had resigned in 1742, the bench had crumbled to dust over a century ago, but the duties of the men, and their successors, had continued.

Similarly, the Bank and its Guard remained singularly unaltered. In 1913, it had not yet been added to, and remained almost unmodified since the time of Soane. After the business of the day had been finished, at the hour at which we arrived, this one-storey building, emptied altogether of life, and with its garden-courts and cloisters, resembled a monastery or a deserted temple rather than the most famous financial institution in the world. By one of the passionate paradoxes of its creator – surely the most original of all English architects –, it seemed to offer a quiet, leafy, well-kept retreat from the world. And, to one on guard, the most striking feature of it was the absolute silence, even deeper than that of St James's, that prevailed during the hours of duty. Officers and men received a special fee for duty here, and the Ensign was allowed to have two guests to dine with him. The serving of dinner, the silver and linen, were just what they should have been; grilled sole, and fillet of beef to eat, and rat's-tail spoons and eighteenth-century forks with curving ends, to eat them with; all sound, unadventurous, irreproachable – safe, in fact, as the Bank of England.

How different in their quietness and, indeed, solemnity, were these evenings from others spent with the friends I had made lately! Hitherto I had scarcely been aware that such people existed as those whose houses I was now for choice to frequent, who lived for amusement and for things of the mind, eye, ear; a world of drawing-rooms, it is true, but drawing-rooms where it was at least possible to catch sight of such figures as Debussy and Richard Strauss, Chaliapin and Nijinsky, Delius and Sargent and Diaghilev. (It will, however, be noticed that even now the majority of artists whom I met belonged to entertainment, rather than offering a purely creative type.) This, my second world, offered me a wide choice of friends. My locale varied from Wellington Barracks or the Tower of London to Downing Street, from the cab-shelter, where sometimes I had supper after a dance, to Lambeth Palace – in a technical, L.C.C. sense, by no means a place of entertainment –, from my Aunt Londesborough's house to the Cabaret Club, where the lesser artistes of the theatre, as well as the greater, mixed with painters, writers, and their opposite, officers in the Brigade of Guards. This low-ceilinged night-club, appropriately sunk below the pavement of Beak Street, and hideously but relevantly frescoed by the painter, Percy Wyndham Lewis, appeared in the small hours to be a super-heated Vorticist garden of gesticulating figures, dancing and talking, while the rhythm of the primitive forms of ragtime throbbed through the wide room. Over it presided Madame Strindberg, the third and not least exceptional of the great writer's wives.

Dancing more than conversation was the art which occupied the young men of the time in the Cabaret Club: (I had taken with ease and delight to modern ballroom dancing). Indeed, I only remember one fragment of conversation. Late at night, I was introduced to the mother – or, as some said, merely the duenna – of a girl who, though still young, had for some years been confidently expecting to make her début on the stage; a purpose that had been furthered by several notable friendships. In appearance the daughter – if such she was – recalled the convivial female intimates of Hogarth and Captain Laroon; she belonged to a type almost extinct today, rotund and highly-coloured, having about her a kind of full-blown, rustic but frowzy freshness, like that of a dewy, but lolling and drooping rose, of an early morning, and an air at the same time sullen and good-natured, quick to smile and equally to take offence. On this occasion, however, her long course of professional disappointment had, perhaps, overcome her, and she could not speak a word. Her mother, in more expansive, if sentimental, mood, looked at her fondly and remarked to me – 'Poor child . . . she's thinking of her dad who was killed . . . He was an Admiral, in the Army!'

For talk, however, I found other resorts more interesting, and I have always preferred private houses to restaurants, and talking to shouting. Mrs Asquith, by nature no less than by habit ever hospitable, used to invite me to Downing Street, then a centre of such an abundance and intensity of life as it had not seen for a hundred years and is never likely to see again: for at that time it contained a social dynamo as hostess. Alas, her example, and the influence it exercised on politics, was sufficient to enjoin, for the future, carefulness, and to exalt a contrary model, of primness, smugness, sealed lips and *Punch* humour. Mrs Asquith's audacious comments, those called forth from a witty and original mind, were governed, in spite of their apparent sharpness, by invariable standards – though standards not of taste, but of truth. In the first place it must be borne in mind that she was an extremely religious woman. It has been related, for example, that at the time of the Armistice in November 1918, she went down on her knees in a crowded omnibus, to say a prayer. If this be true, it will have been a genuine demonstration of feeling, for she lacked all self-consciousness or pretence. She got on well with the simple: the silly and the flighty, the greedy and the mean were her quarry; but even the barbs she directed verbally against these, though outspoken, were ruled by the strictest Scottish moral sense. In art and life, she was always on the right side; just as her politics, too – though not every reader may agree with them – were generous and inspired by Christian charity.

Her conversation was inspiring: in the common phrase, she spoke her mind: or, at any rate, with the utmost rapidity she thought of things she would like to say, and said them. For example, when she came to stay with me in Scarborough a few years later, meeting my father for the first time, she glanced at him critically, and, pressing my arm, remarked in a sympathetic, hissing and over-audible whisper, 'Oh, Osbert, what a look in the eye! *Cold* as *ice*! But if you want help, let me know, and I'll talk to him!'

My Aunt Londesborough, too, was now established in a marble-lined mansion in Green Street, having not long returned from the Durbar, laden with large presentation portraits of jewelled and dusky potentates, which, in spite of their colour, resembled white elephants in size and usefulness, and were discreetly hung in the country. She had also brought back with her an Indian boy, Bimbi, and when she gave a dance, he would stand, in his native robes and high pink turban, on one of the landings of the marble staircase, directing the guests in the manner of an eighteenth-century page. Here, too, as at Mrs Asquith's, you met many foreigners, albeit of a different kind – not foreign diplomats, politicians, artists or musicians, but Hungarians and Austrians of the hunting sort. In addition, there was always a solid mass of relatives. Among them my cousin, the Duchess of Beaufort, and her two daughters, Blanche and Diana Somerset: gay and delightful girls, full of zest, with an ability to instil amusement and liveliness into their surroundings, into all they touched – into the hunting-field itself, I suppose: for I believe they were always eager, even when in London, to return to Badminton, and to resume a life spent largely in the saddle, anxious, however much they might be enjoying themselves, for the autumn to bring back cubbing, and for the winter to allow them whole months pursuing the fox. With a tolerance that, as I had learnt when attached to the cavalry regiment at Aldershot, not all those who seem to have been born on horseback can show, they teased me, in their warm, luxuriant voices, so typical of their family, and laughed at me, but did not in the least mind my being interested in other things. So I could talk to my Uncle Londesborough about various modern composers of whom few of the guests in the house had heard, for the majority of them were kept too busy toeing the monotonous gilded line that led from Ascot to Goodwood and to Cowes, to have time to hear any composers but Puccini and Verdi. They were not believers in experiment. But with him I could discuss Chabrier – still then unknown in England, though many years dead –, Stravinsky, Schönberg, Debussy and Ravel.

Another house at which I was a frequent visitor during these and ensuing years was Mrs George Keppel's, in Grosvenor Street, surely one of the most remarkable houses in London. Its high façade, dignified and unpretentious as only that of a London Georgian mansion can be, very effectively disguised its immense size. Within existed an unusual air of spaciousness and light, an atmosphere of luxury, for Mrs Keppel possessed an instinct for splendour, and not only were the rooms beautiful, with their grey walls, red lacquer cabinets, English eighteenth-century portraits of people in red coats, huge porcelain pagodas, and thick, magnificent carpets, but the hostess conducted the running of her house as a work of art in itself. I liked greatly to listen to her talking; if it were possible to lure her away from the bridge-table, she would remove from her mouth for a moment the cigarette which she would be smoking with an air of determination, through a long holder, and turn upon the person to whom she was speaking her large, humorous, kindly, peculiarly discerning eyes. Her conversation was lit by humour, insight and the utmost good-nature: a rare and valuable attribute in one who had never had – or, at any rate, never felt – much patience with fools. Moreover, a vein of fantasy, a power of enhancement would often lift what she was saying, and served to emphasize the exactness of most of her opinions, and her frankness. Her talk had about it a boldness, an absence of all pettiness, that helped to make her a memorable figure in the fashionable world. The company of her two daughters added to the pleasures of frequenting her house: Violet, cosmopolitan and exotic from her earliest years, with a vivid intelligence, a quick eye for character, which had bestowed on her an irresistible gift of mimicry and the ability to gather unexpected pieces of information about people and things, which she was wont to impart in a voice, eager but pitched in so low a tone as sometimes to be inaudible; Sonia, though still in the schoolroom, with a very strong personality, too. She was tall for her age, and down her back swept a mane of golden hair, like that to be seen in some of Renoir's paintings: while her manners were exquisite, her views were still definite as only those of a child can be, and she expressed them in a voice full of the most caressing charm.

With the sumptuousness of the entertainments at my Aunt Londesborough's and at Mrs Keppel's I could contrast the archiepiscopal
austerities of Lambeth, with its cohorts of curates devouring the modern
equivalent of locusts and wild honey. But even the wild honey would
have proved, I apprehend, to be tame. After dinner, at 10.15 or 10.30 in
the evening, many guests repaired to the Chapel, which had been so
hideously frescoed in the time of my Tait relative. I remember with what
relief – for the company of the clergy sometimes intimidates me, who am
frightened by no other men – I used to ask for a taxi, and tell the driver
to take me to the Alhambra, where I arrived just in time to hear the last
half-hour of a revue, entitled, if I remember rightly, *Swat That Fly!* And
there I would meet all my friends from the Brigade, admiring the serried
ranks of beauties on the stage, the curls and legs and eyes in line. Or else
I would hurry away from Lambeth in order to see the performance of
Gaby Deslys at the Palace Theatre or elsewhere – a star, in her kind, of
European celebrity.

Among relatives whom I often went to see, there was my cousin Mrs
George Swinton. Her house was full of painters and musicians, and the
most intelligent of their audience. Though I had known her for many
years, this was a friendship I had chosen, as well as inherited, belonging
to the right hand as well as the left. Her glorious voice was at its height,
and she was unchallenged as a singer in her own line; and I would often
go with her to concerts where she was performing. Of more recent
friends, and with a very different personality, there was Lady Sackville,
certainly one of the remarkable characters of the period. She lived in a
world almost entirely imaginary. She never told one the same story twice;
for, to her, truth was relative and depended on how she felt when she was
talking: and while the tales often retained the same features, in each new
version these would be rearranged, albeit with a surprising ease, grasp
and power of conviction. But there was nothing petty about her: she was
capable of acts of imaginative kindness and of cruelty, she was clever and
cunning and silly and brave and timid and avaricious, extravagant and
most generous, possessed the best taste and the worst, and was, in all,
one of the most vivid personalities I have ever met. And I am sure that she
never afforded her friends, still less those nearest to her, a dull moment;
the opposition in her character of aristocrat and Spanish dancer, gypsy
and woman of taste, was too pronounced to allow of it.

Occasionally, I would be taken to supper, too, at All Souls' Place – that
piazza consisting of one house behind All Souls' Church in Langham

Place – by Felicity Tree and by her sister Iris, who was then very young, but possessed a honey-coloured beauty of hair and skin that I have never observed in anyone else. Viola Tree, and her husband, Alan Parsons, would often be there as well, Viola contributing her own particular vein of warm-hearted vagueness and humour, and her spontaneous and inexhaustible gift of mimicry; while, singly or together, Sir Herbert and Lady Tree could be depended upon to supply an entertainment of the most delicious personal fantasy, based on the flimsiest and most delicate foundation of sense. Though I, with the rest of the world, have seen quoted and heard repeated so many of Sir Herbert's remarks and exploits – as, when, for example, he went to a post-office and asked for a penny stamp, and on being given one, demanded, 'Have you no others?', and, after a sheet of them had been produced, considered it exhaustively, head by head, and then, selecting a stamp in the very middle, pointed at it, and remarked with decision, 'I will take that one'; and though, equally, I have read, heard, or been told of many of Lady Tree's epigrams, such as when, being offered two kinds of fish at a dinner-party, she remarked, 'Ye cannot serve both Cod and Salmon', or when – another ichthyophagous bon-mot – on a similar occasion haddock was handed to her, and she exclaimed joyously 'Cry "Haddock!", and let slip the dogs of war', yet nothing can do justice to the captivating absurdity with which they both invested everyday life.

The world seemed enchanting to me. Albeit, perhaps, all the persons I saw in these years had attaching to them the freshness of my own youth, and of a moment when I was consciously enjoying myself for the first time, yet surely life in the decade preceding the First World War offered something that no other periods had given – a quality pleasantly grotesque (it was to grow even more, but less pleasantly, grotesque after 1918): a richness, above all a variety, lacking in previous epochs. The belles of the Edwardian summer survived in a kind September splendour, like the ephemerids that haunt the roses and rich autumn daisies until the first blast of winter is to be felt in the air. Their spirits were higher than – or as high as – those of the young, their appetite for amusement quenchless. I can boast that at the age of twenty, I was taught the tango by Mrs Hwfa Williams, a woman already for three generations famous for her chic. And she danced with spirit, with a sense of fun and joy! It is not easy for someone afflicted with deafness to be amusing, it calls for unceasing alertness which must be a great tax on energy, and it will be understood that she was no longer a young woman: nor was she rich, so she could not entertain: but the sense of the pleasure she found in every moment of the company she was in, and her amusing comments, gave her a unique position. At every dance to which she went, she was surrounded by a crowd of young men, waiting for her arrival, and they always addressed her as Madam. This reception must surely, in itself, have constituted some sort of reward for the trouble she took. The chief disadvantage she suffered from her deafness was that, until she caught a chance word or two, she had to adapt her expression in sympathy with the reputation of the person speaking – a smile for the whimsical, a laugh for the witty, a striking look of interest for the dealer in the dramatic, a tear for those who wore their hearts on their sleeves. Sometimes this method, imposed upon her by her disability, misled her for a while as to the trend of the conversation, but once she grasped a word, she would right herself in an instant, so quick was she.

The social world, I was saying, was more miscellaneously composed than ever it had been: it offered the most singular contrasts, while the ready friendliness found in so many places provided for me a lively intoxication. Indeed, the London of which I talk possessed such warmth and life, and existed, comparatively, so short a time ago, that I am continually surprised at its complete disappearance and extinction. Equally, the sight of a survivor from it astonishes me.

CHAPTER SEVEN

Never had Europe been so prosperous and gay. Never had the world gone so well for all classes of the community: especially in England, where an ambitious programme of Social Reform had just been carried through, and Old Age Pensions and Insurance schemes had removed from the poor the most bitter of the spectres that haunted them. In Western Europe there had been no war of any sort for nearly two generations, and for a thousand years, if an outbreak had occurred, standards of chivalry prevailed. And I remember from my own childhood, what must have been a common experience with members of my generation, reading the Bible, and books of Greek, Roman, and English history, and reflecting how wonderful it was to think that, with the growth of commerce and civilization, mass captivities and executions were things of the rabid past, and that never again would man be liable to persecution for his political or religious opinions. This belief, inculcated in the majority, led to an infinite sweetness in the air we breathed. Even if war came one day – and it was unthinkable, the point of greatest danger having passed in 1911 –, it would be played according to the rules: the loss of life would be on the Boer War scale (in no war had there existed the incidence of mortality to which the two great conflicts have inured us, and of which the first was in this respect the more dreadful). There was, as yet, no hint to be detected of the sorrows and terrors that lay in front of the most highly cultured races of the world. In England, the political warfare that existed, and then only at the level of drawing-rooms, merely added to them a breath of excitement. If Lady Londonderry cut, let us say, Mrs Asquith, on account of the Home Rule Bill, the world in general yet sped towards its ultimate re-creation or perfection. All classes still believed in absolute progress – and the loss of this certainty has whittled down, more than anything else, the feeling of life's joy. Then it existed, and appeared on all sides to be justified. There was no disillusionment. Happier, wealthier, wiser – and younger, too, for our age – every day, we were being conducted by the benevolent popes of science into a Paradise, but of the most comfortably material kind: a Paradise where each man and woman, even if no longer born with an immortal soul, could by means of such devices as false teeth and monkey glands have conferred upon them a sort of animal and mechanic immortality of this world, and where, even if not destined for angelic honours, they could at least aspire to the monetary eminence of Rockefeller or Rothschild. Not only did the future, which to every age appears golden, seem without measure enticing: but, if a moment's doubt ever intervened, we could examine too, the solid merits and achievements of the present, in themselves a sure gauge of the years to come. Look at Sir Thomas Lipton; look at turbine engines! How could you doubt?

Hitherto, in London there had been little for the pleasure-lover to do, little for him to see. The wealth of the great city, unbelievable to those in the street, had always hidden itself behind doors: but now they were thrown wide open. Young men from the prosperous classes, such as my brother-officers and myself, would find themselves invited to as many as five or six entertainments a night. An air of gaiety, unusual in northern climates, prevailed. Music flowed with the lightness and flash of water under the striped awnings and from the balconies; while beyond the open, illuminated windows, in the rooms, the young men, about to be slaughtered, still feasted, unconscious of all but the moment. For a hundred years the social scene had not been so attractive to the eye. Further, as a result of the influence of the Russian Ballet, the art of spectacle was again beginning to be understood, and hostesses took pride once more in the beauty, no less than the costliness of their entertainments: while, in addition, in a few houses, the discovery had been made that life could be more enjoyable if you surrounded yourself with intelligent people, or at least admitted one or two to panic the assembled herds. Night by night, during the summers of 1913 and '14, the entertainments grew in number and magnificence. One band in a house was no longer enough, there must be two, three even. Electric fans whirled on the top of enormous blocks of ice, buried in banks of hydrangeas, like the shores from which the barque departs for Cythera. Never had there been such displays of flowers; not of the dehydrated weeds, dry poppy-heads and old-man's-beard that characterized the interbellum years, when a floral desiccation that matched the current beige walls and self-toned textiles and carpets was in evidence; but a profusion of full-blooded blossoms, of lolling roses and malmaisons, of gilded, musical-comedy baskets of carnations and sweet-peas, while huge bunches of orchids, bowls of gardenias and flat trays of stephanotis lent to some houses an air of exoticism. Never had Europe seen such mounds of peaches, figs, nectarines and strawberries at all seasons, brought from their steamy tents of glass.

As guests, only the poor of every race were barred. Even foreigners could enter, if they were rich. The English governing classes, – though still struck dumb with horror if a foreigner entered the room, and albeit, when obliged to talk to him, they still often shouted at him in English baby-language, a result of the Public School System –, had grown used to the idea that foreigners existed and were – well, foreigners. Xenophobia had temporarily disappeared, and we were toppling to the other extreme. If foreigners did not hate us, and were not hateful, they must all love us and be lovable. The eternal innocence of an island race asserted itself again, in a contrary direction. Was it likely that the Kaiser would visit England so often, and so many Germans come to London, and so plainly love it, if they were planning a war against us? And the Russians, under

the guidance of the Tsar, they, too, would prove a progressive, parliamentary people, like ourselves. Our system was the envy of the world, a
millionaire's cheque-book lay hidden in every errand-boy's basket. Every
foreigner loved and respected England. Occasionally, a brother-officer
would mention to me that he believed there was going to be war with
Germany, and that it should spell quicker regimental promotion, but the
rest of us dismissed it as a phantom called up by professional keenness.

Who could wonder that foreigners loved London? Though as different
from Vienna or Paris as Peking, it was no less essentially a capital, with
all the attractions of the centre of an Empire. It remained unique in being
a masculine city, as it had been throughout its history, created to the
same degree for men as Paris for women. The luxury shops were
unrivalled in their appeal to male tastes, were full of cigarettes, and
objects made in leather, glass or silver, better than those to be seen
anywhere in foreign capitals; solid, plain, unimaginative, but showing
the English feeling for material, the English sobriety. As for suits, shirts,
shoes, ties, hats, London was acknowledged, throughout the world, by
all races, of all colours, to set the fashion for men. And these years, 1913
and '14, were the last when there was a successor to the long line of fops,
macaronis, dandies, beaux, dudes, bucks, blades, bloods, swells and
mashers, who for so many centuries had given life to the London world
of pleasure. To these was now added the *nut*, or, more jocularly, the k-
nut, as personified by a young actor, Mr Basil Hallam, who in this respect
both summed up and set the tone, in a song entitled 'Gilbert the Filbert,
the Colonel of the Nuts!': the refrain ran –

> I'm Gilbert the Filbert, the Nut with a K,
> The pride of Piccadilly, the blasé roué.
> Oh, Hades, the ladies all leave their wooden huts
> For Gilbert the Filbert, the Colonel of the Nuts.

Dressed in a grey tall-hat and a morning-coat, Hallam gave a rather
languid rendering of this song at the Palace Theatre every night in *The
Passing Show*, a revue which was running throughout the summer of 1914
and until after the outbreak of war. It was no unusual greeting for a
young man, wearing a new suit, to be told, 'What a k-nut you look!' The
nut must be thin, clean-shaven except for a small, cut moustache, and
have an air of concave and fatigued elegance, in this taking after his
Dundreary grandfather rather than his father the swell. On the other
hand, he had to dance with vigour and ease, in the new style. The nut

died fighting in the trenches of 1914, and Mr Basil Hallam, his amiable exemplifier, was killed two years later, in August 1916. He was in a captive balloon with a rather inexperienced observer, and when the balloon was shot down this man had difficulty in fixing his parachute harness. Hallam stayed to help him and was too late to save himself.

In London, in the streets, you still saw a few carriages, but they diminished day by day, and seemed to be part of life's decoration. And decoration was in the air: many busied themselves with it. The currents that showed were mostly foreign, and reached life through the theatre – a new development. Every chair-cover, every lamp-shade, every cushion reflected the Russian Ballet, the Grecian or Oriental visions of Bakst and Benois, or else the vulgar and colossal coloured fantasies of Reinhardt and his aides or of the rebels against his rule – but both dreams equally in the German taste. The galleries in Bond Street and elsewhere, though they could not, in so far as modern pictures were concerned, vie with those of Paris, showed for the most part eighteenth-century English pictures, Italian old masters, and modern English as well as French paintings: for the dealers had struck the Pre-Raphaelite camp, in which they had dwelt for so long, and had moved on. England possessed its own painters again, and a ferment such as I have since never felt in this country prevailed in the world of art. It seemed as if at last we were on the verge of a great movement. It must have been in the winter of 1912, I think, that I visited the Chenil Galleries, then situated in a little room near the Post Office in King's Road, Chelsea, and saw a collection of small paintings by Augustus John: young women in wide orange or green skirts, without hats or crowned with large straw hats, lounging wistfully on small hills in undulating and monumental landscapes, with the feel of sea and mountain in the air round them. By these I was so greatly impressed that I tried to persuade my father to purchase the whole contents of the room; they cost twenty pounds apiece. Alas, I did not possess the authority necessary to convince him. But this was only one out of many exhibitions: for there were many English artists then with a future, who today have no past.

My sister, whenever, too rarely, she was able to escape from her captivity with my family, would come round the exhibitions with me. Fortunately for my enjoyment of art, from the first my approach to a picture was the foreign attitude of 'What pleasure is to be obtained from it?', rather than the more usual national attitude of 'What would Ruskin say; what addition of moral worth can I refine by mental labour from the picture in front of me?' But I had no desire to obtain virtue by wrestling with angels: I was content to admire them. And if there was anything I did not understand, my sister would help to make it clear for me. No conquest of fresh esthetic territory was ever hidden from her by fog: and her perceptions had an enthusiasm about them I have seldom known equalled. But, alas, under what she thought, as, tall, fair and rather thin, with the lines of her face developing every day into the classic mould of the poet's, she walked round examining the pictures with me, must have been always the feeling, 'What sort of row shall I find when I get home?' For she had not yet left my parents; that was to be next year, by which time she had realized that if ever she was to become such a poet as she hoped – she had already begun to write poems – she must free herself from her state of absolute bondage. It was impossible to do any work at home, in the atmosphere of hysterical violence that prevailed. She would stay with Helen Rootham, and go with her as often as possible to the gallery of the Queen's Hall, where they always occupied the same seats. Sacheverell, too, on his short periods of leave from Eton would come round the exhibitions with me: and he was, even thus early, at the age of sixteen, in correspondence with the leaders of the Vorticist and Futurist movements. He was now a boy very tall for his years, well over six feet, and having, with the curls at his temples, his rather tawny skin, and straight nose – with the pinched-in nostrils that are so typical of my mother's family – something of the air of a farouche young shepherd, but a shepherd of lions rather than of lambs. He was already immersed in his lifelong search for knowledge, infused by a passionate love for, and divination of, beauty. His range and depth of learning put me to shame then, as they do now. When he was able to get away from Eton, we would spend the whole time together, and I used to take him with me to the opera and ballet, and in my company, I am glad to say, he saw Chaliapin at the very height of his powers, in *Khovanshchina*.

In the theatre, similarly, there was much to see: new plays by Shaw and by Granville-Barker and by Arnold Bennett in collaboration with Edward Knoblock. There were the unforgettable Shakespearian productions of Granville-Barker, interpreted and mounted with learning and imagination, and with the most consummate skill and tact, the parts played to perfection. Perhaps the most memorable was *A Midsummer Night's Dream*. In the scene in which Titania and Oberon and their court are visible, the stage presented the semblance of a grassy knoll, and the fairies, to separate their race from that of ordinary human beings, were painted with gold.

The whole stage picture possessed its own illusion and leafy perspective, and succeeded in making the magic element of the play singularly credible. For this, the late Norman Wilkinson, an artist of original ability in the theatre, was responsible. Very full, too, of character was Albert Rothenstein's mounting of *The Winter's Tale*; for he succeeded admirably in transferring the quality of his drawing on to the stage. In the winter of 1911 and spring of 1912, the elephantine production of *The Miracle* had filled Olympia (still echoing with the clatter of the expelled roller-skates) with the incense and tenebrous colour of a medieval cathedral as seen by a Jewish impresario: and the years that followed also saw Reinhardt's heavy-footed oriental phantasies of harem life, played with a plethora of turbans, gongs, kohl and henna. But, above all, there was the opera and the ballet. The Russian operas, never before performed in London until these years, relieved one suddenly from the Viking world of bearded warriors drinking blood out of skulls that had been for so long imposed by Germany. They pleased the eye, at last, as well as the ear.

Though, perhaps, those who belonged to my generation never had the chance of seeing pure acting at its best – for Irving was dead, and Sarah Bernhardt was an old woman –, nevertheless, what a privilege we enjoyed in going to hear and see Chaliapin, that rarest of salamanders, a great artist with a great voice!

One evening, in after years, when I had grown to know Chaliapin fairly well, Lady Aberconway and I went to congratulate him, in his dressing-room, after he had taken the part of Salieri in Rimsky-Korsakov's *Mozart and Salieri*. Mozart had been played by a young Italian tenor, of whom Chaliapin was a warm supporter, having proposed him for the part, and to a certain degree coached him at the rehearsals. The Italian was small – or perhaps not, for one of Chaliapin's attributes was that, though a giant, he never looked over life-size, but merely reduced the scale of others, even tall men. At any rate, on this the first night, this protégé had enraged Chaliapin by the lightness of his singing, and by the airy way he played the harpsichord on the stage, lifting his hand up and down in a fashion against which he had been warned by the great singer. When, therefore, we arrived and opened the door, we found the enormous Russian shaking the young Italian as a mastiff might shake a *griffon*. After we entered the room, he desisted, saying in explanation, 'And the plot of this opera is that *I* have to be jealous of *him*!' And, as an instance of his lack of self-consciousness, I remember, not long before his death, his telling me that in order for a man to keep well, his skin must be used to fresh air, and it was therefore absolutely necessary to go naked for part of the day. For this reason, he made a practice of having luncheon alone in his sitting-room in a condition of Nature, at any hotel where he might be staying. At the time it presented to my mind a strange picture that amused me, but I have often wondered since whether his death from pneumonia may not have been connected with his adoption of this health-habit.

In the same theatre in which Chaliapin appeared, on other nights or at other hours, another art, besides opera, was to be seen in its perfection: the ballet that blooms for a year, it seems, every century, was enjoying one of its culminations. It becomes inevitable, when writing of it at this time, that the word *genius* should recur with frequency, almost with monotony, in these few pages, for no other word can describe the quality of the chief dancers or the influences at work: Stravinsky, Diaghilev, Karsavina, Fokine and Nijinsky. Of all the productions of these years, *Petrouchka* must be mentioned at the head of the list; the music the first work of a composer of genius grown to his full stature (*L'Oiseau de Feu*, wonderful though its music is, was the more derivative work of a very young man); as moving and symbolic a creation of its time as Mozart's *Don Giovanni*. I have seen other great dancers, but never one inspired as was Nijinsky; I have seen other great dancers play Petrouchka, but never one who, with his rendering of a figure stuffed with straw, struggling from the thraldom of the puppet world towards human freedom, but always with the terrible leaden frustration of the dummy latent in his limbs, the movement of them containing the suggestion of the thawing of ice at winter's edge, evoked a comparable feeling of pathos. This ballet was, in its scope as a work of art, universal; it presented the European contemporary generation with a prophetic and dramatized version of the fate reserved for it, in the same way that the legend of the Minotaur had once summed up, though after the event and not before it, the fate of several generations of Greek youths and maidens. The music, traditional yet original, full of fire and genius, complication and essential simplicity, held up a mirror in which man could see, not only himself, but the angel and ape equally prisoned within his skin. The part of Petrouchka showed Nijinsky to be a master of mime, gesture, drama, just as, in pure dancing, his rendering of the Spirit of the Rose, in *Le Spectre de la Rose*, was the climax of romantic ballet.

His profoundly original ballet, *L'Après-Midi d'un Faune*, to the music of Debussy, produced at Covent Garden on 17th February 1913, and his amazing feat *Le Sacre du Printemps*, a ballet that will always stand alone, the most magnificent and living of dead ends, proved his genius as a choreographer, no less than as a dancer. But let us turn for an instant to his less revolutionary creations; to, for example, *Le Spectre de la Rose*. In Nijinsky's *Diary* he relates how, when he was six or seven years of age, his father threw him into the water to teach him to swim, and how he felt himself to be drowning, but perceiving the light through the water above him, became conscious of a sudden accession of physical strength, jumped and was saved. That striving to escape, to live, may account for his miraculous leap across the window into the room in the ballet I have named; something that no-one who saw it will ever forget. This great dancer seemed to hold all physical laws in abeyance and for an instant of time to remain, at the height of his leap, poised and stationary; when asked how he achieved this defiance of the law of gravity, he replied, 'It's very simple: you jump and just stop in the air for a moment.' Even as I followed Nijinsky's movements on the stage, I realized that I was watching a legend in process of being born: for he was by nature fabulous, a prodigy. Now the legend is complete, even to the affliction that has fallen on him; reducing him for a time to the status almost of the puppet he so often portrayed, but with occasional chinks of light filtering through into his tragic mind. No less true, though happier, is the legend of his partner in triumphs, his complement, the great Karsavina; in *Le Spectre de la Rose*, as graceful and romantic a spiritual realization of the flesh as Nijinsky, a being of a new creation, born of the rose, was an epitome in flesh of the spirit.

On 23rd June, I was present at the initial appearance of a great new dancer, a man the coming decade was to reveal as no less individual and significant an interpreter of rôles in satirical, grotesque and baroque ballets, and no less remarkable a choreographer of them, than Nijinsky had shown himself to be in the range of classical, romantic and revolutionary; Massine – or Miassine, as his name was then spelt –, in after years a valued friend of my brother and myself. *La Légende de Joseph*, in which he first danced, had been designed as a spectacle, rather than a ballet, to the music of Richard Strauss. In it, figures costumed by Léon Bakst, and such as might have been portrayed by the brush of Paolo Veronese, feasted in an enormous scene, pitched, at a hazard, half-way between Babylon and Venice, and extravagantly furnished with huge twisted columns of bronze and gold, the creation of the fashionable Spanish decorative painter, J. M. Sert. This ballet, the last pre-1914-war production by Diaghilev, was typical of that phase of the Russian Ballet. Lavish, profuse, full of sombre colours, blues and greens, and dripping with gold, like the music, it helped to overwhelm the dancers, even Karsavina, with her great allurement and experience, who played Potiphar's wife. As for Massine, I think only the most expert could have foretold from the timid movements of the young man – timid, perhaps, because it was his first appearance, no less than because the sentiment he expressed fitted the rôle – how fiery and idiosyncratic a dancer, though ever in the great tradition, he was destined to be.

We belonged to a doomed generation, and the enlightened Liberal statesmen then in power, men of the highest principles and attainments, and of great forensic ability, presented to it – and it included some of their own sons – the 1914 war as a coming-of-age gift. Even today you see references to the immense achievements of the Liberal administration of 1906–14 – and admittedly its leaders were men of intellect, and sometimes of imperial vision – but can any Government whose policy entails such a lack of preparation for war as to make that seeming solution of difficulties a gamble apparently worth while for an enemy, and thus leads to the death or disablement of two million fellow-countrymen: in fact, practically the whole male youth of the country; can any Government which introduces old-age pensions, so as 'to help the old people', and then allows half the manhood of the country to be slaughtered or disabled before it reaches thirty years of age, be considered to have been either benevolent or efficient?

That the military element to which I – not of my own choice, it is true – belonged, might be wiped out, was, perhaps, less hard to predict. But even among Edward Horner, Denis Anson, Duff Cooper, and their friends, men such as Raymond Asquith and Patrick Shaw-Stewart – men sure of themselves, young, full of vigour, with a wit all their own which I take, in essence and origin, to have been a legacy from the old Whig Society – war and accident were to reap a full harvest. Only my friend Duff Cooper survived the next five years, and when one considers the extreme courage and defiance of consequences he continually showed during his career as a soldier, this is, indeed, a matter for wonder. I always immensely enjoy his witty, cultivated, irascible, and yet genial company. During the 1914 war, he left the Foreign Office to enter the Grenadiers, and while we were both young officers at Chelsea Barracks, we used sometimes to sit for a moment in the corner of the Ante-Room and grumble together about the rather rigid minds of the higher military authorities. When, twenty years later, I was able to write and congratulate him on his appointment as Minister for War, in his reply he alluded indirectly to this, with the words, 'It is rather a comfort to have all the generals under me at last'.

As for those friends of mine who were already soldiers, brother-officers, or those contemporaries with me at the crammer's who had succeeded in obtaining commissions, and were in other regiments, they stood, even at that moment, in the shadows. I attended in 1913 and 1914 many coming-of-age parties, when we toasted a future which was to have no substance. All these anniversaries were celebrated in much the same manner – including my own, though that had been preceded by a twenty-one years' discussion of plans. As late as 21st June 1913, I find my father writing to me about it; though perhaps, where this occasion, the subject of so much fantasy, was concerned, in a – for him – rather subdued and matter-of-fact tone. 'I have been talking this morning to Hollingworth and Ernest about your coming-of-age. We think about the sixteenth of June the best time, as the foliage then still looks so fresh and well, and the evenings are almost at their longest. We shall turf the lawn beds, so as to have the long tea-tables against the yew hedges, plant the garden for June, sow half an acre of sweet-peas and iris for cutting, force grapes and peaches earlier, and plant early strawberries and vegetables. Have you any other suggestions? . . .' In fact, no blue-stencilled white cows, no dragons, no reproduction in fire-works of the Sargent group, none of the intended fanfaronade, separated the dinner-party I gave to some thirty brother-officers and friends, on the night of 6th December 1913, from the run of similar occasions that I attended that year. One thing alone removed it into a different category: the fact that the host was alive two years later. I cannot think of a single other host at such a party who outlasted the winter following.

As the nights of 1914 wore on, their splendour increased. Day and night mingled in a general glow, and sometimes the regimental duty seemed exhausting of a morning: but one must not show fatigue. There was as yet no disturbance in the air round us, no ruffle of wind across the century-old calm. The continuing differences between the Government and Opposition about the Irish Home Rule Bill remained the only subject of political gossip and excitement. And then, in the evening papers of 28th June came the news that an Austrian Archduke had been shot, while performing a tour of inspection, in a town in some rather outlandish portion of the Austrian Empire. Few people, especially among my brother-officers, knew anything, either of him or of his place of assassination: though some there were who had visited this part of the world in order to shoot moufflons. I was total in my ignorance; except that I was aware that the famous Villa D'Este, perhaps the most beautiful Italian garden in the world, belonged to him, for the Archduke Franz-Ferdinand was heir of the House of Este. A few people I saw seemed oddly perturbed at the murder. It was difficult to understand why. The place, wherever it was, remained a long way off; and throughout the lives of my generation foreign royalties and heads of states had been murdered with regularity: Grand Dukes without number, King Umberto of Italy, President McKinley, the Empress of Austria, the King and Queen of Serbia, the King and Crown Prince of Portugal, to take at random a few examples in which the attempts had been successful. There was nothing else unusual; no warning – only one or two signs so slight, so vague, or so tinged with superstitious feeling, that no-one except a person long trained by continual trouble at home to be of an apprehensive turn of mind would have noticed them.

I had observed, for example, a sudden, almost unbearable restlessness, in about the middle of June, filling the hearts and minds of many of my contemporary brother-officers; young men, nearly all of whom had, a week or two before, been content with their lot, but were now experiencing an anguished desire for change, like the sudden wave of restlessness that is said to seize on birds and animals before a volcanic disturbance. One planned to join a polar expedition, another to be transferred to an African regiment, a third to start a ranch in South America, a fourth to go to China. It was as though some wind possessed the air and was scattering them, or as if their souls were growing impatient, still anchored within their bodies. Their plans, however, were not destined to be realized. By the late autumn, they were dead.

Something else that might have been an indication, I recall. Nearly all the brother-officers of my own age had been, two or three months earlier in the year, to see a celebrated palmist of the period – whom, I remember, it was said, with what justification I am not aware, that Mr Winston Churchill used sometimes to consult. My friends, of course, used to visit her in the hope of being told that their love affairs would prosper, when they would marry, or the direction in which their later careers would develop. In each instance, it appeared the cheiromant had just begun to read their fortunes, when, in sudden bewilderment, she had thrown the outstretched hand from her, crying, 'I don't understand it! It's the same thing again! After two or three months, the line of life stops short, and I can read nothing.' To each individual to whom it was said, this seemed merely an excuse she had improvised for her failure: but when I was told by four or five persons of the same experience, I wondered what it could portend. But nothing could happen, nothing.

I spent Whitsun, 1914, in Somerset, with one of my new friends. Most of the guests I had grown to know well in the antecedent months, with the exception of the Baron and Baroness von Kühlmann – he was Counsellor at the German Embassy – and Captain Schubert, the military attaché. On Sunday morning, the two German men suggested that I should go for a walk with them. As we climbed a hill that ran abruptly towards the sky, the talk of my two new acquaintances – and I noticed that for Germans their manners were unusually ingratiating – veered towards English politics, and then settled, like a bird alighting, on the Home Rule controversy. Suddenly Kühlmann asked me,

'How would your Regiment act if ordered by the Government to oppose the Ulster Volunteers?'

Though by nature as yet politically unsuspicious, since I believed that nations were governed by wise men, actuated by common sense, and that, therefore, there could be no likelihood of a war – yet this question rather startled me. In any case it was one that plainly should not have been put by a foreigner, more especially a foreign diplomat, to an Englishman, above all not to an English officer, however young and unimportant. Fortunately, I answered, almost before I had had time to think,

'Naturally, we shall obey orders; that is what we are there for.'

But all the same, I reflected, how odd this is: because if I shared the prejudices of some of my fellow-countrymen, I should think the Germans were planning something, and were, in pursuance of it, neglecting no source of information, however slight. But that was impossible! The talk, nevertheless, had grated on my nerves, imparting to the whole day an unpleasant flavour, and leaving me with a permanent wish to avoid their company.

This incident had taken place, of course, late in the month of May; some weeks before the shooting in Sarajevo. Another occurred about ten days after the assassination. Though but a tenuous indication of the trend of events, indeed so volatile in essence as scarcely to bear the strain of transcription, yet this, too, was somehow tinged for me with the darkness of the future. I was having luncheon at a table alone, when an acquaintance asked me if he might sit at it, as the room was full. Our talk was dull, neutral, with no life in it, but towards the end of the meal he turned to me and said quietly,

'Do you see the man over there, by the window, with a beaky nose, and a white moustache and imperial? Wearing a pink carnation? Well, he's a very remarkable man. Look at him carefully, and I'll tell you about him.' Glancing in the direction indicated, I saw a rather tall, broadly built man, with a strange yellow face, strongly marked features, and pale, sunken eyes. He was dressed in a well-cut English suit, and had taken trouble, it could be seen, about his clothes generally. It was difficult racially to place him. He did not seem to be a Jew, he was too tall and sturdily built; but apart from his frame, there was about him an oriental air. He might have been a Turk or a Cypriot – I have since seen money-changers in Cyprus who a little resemble him.

'There must be something up,' my informant continued, 'or he wouldn't be here! His arrival is always a sign of trouble, and every European Chancellery makes a point of knowing where he is. His name is Basil Zaharoff.'

Certainly there was something both evil and imposing about his figure: and as he grew older, the shell hardened and became more typical. His personal appearance should have put all with whom he came into contact on their guard – it is, indeed, singular that western man, while refusing to place credence in anything that he cannot see, while rejecting absolutely omens, prophecies and visions, should at the same time, as he so often does, deny the evidence of his own eyes. This armament-monger most exactly resembled a vulture, and it is no good pretending, in order to avoid the obvious parallel, that he did not. To some it may cause surprise that a man who traded in weapons of death and the prospects of war, and grew fat-bodied on the result of them, should have resembled the scaly-necked bird; but whether or no it seems strange, depends on one's view of the world, and of the immense and startling range of analogy, simile and image that it offers. There, in any case, the likeness was, for all to behold: the beaky face, the hooded eye, the wrinkled neck, the full body, the impression of physical power and of the capacity to wait, the sombre alertness. In later years, I met Zaharoff several times, and came to the conclusion that though the results of his deeds might be evil, his interests were, in fact, of too material a nature to allow him very high flights of imaginative wickedness. He was in outlook merely a super-croupier. And once, in later years, when he was living in Monte Carlo – where he was said to have acquired a large interest in the Casino –, I heard him introduce himself to a millionaire friend of mine with the startling phrase, 'I am Basil Zaharoff . . . I have sixteen millions!' – or it may have been sixty! I felt an interloper in a magic circle, but surely such a man, I reflected, could not be a very subtle wrongdoer. He only wanted power in order to amass more money; not money in order to obtain power – but then, again, the vulture does not want to kill you, only to eat your corpse. Already in every capital, the birds of prey were assembling, hovering, watching: the politicians would supply the carrion, though not in their own persons.

CHAPTER EIGHT

With a sense of amazement tinged with consternation my father observed that my attitude to life was yea-saying; that I enjoyed myself, that I had made myself at home in my new surroundings. Soon his feelings became stronger and deeper, and he grew alarmed, as he drew from my attitude the conclusion that I could not be doing all those disagreeable things every day which he held to exercise so formative an effect on the character. As a result, his former anxiety to see me follow a military career was not equalled by his determination to compel me to relinquish it. The thing to do, he reflected, was to get me out of it – right out of it into some other profession that he could be sure I would dislike. But could one be *sure*, he asked himself, after my recent conduct?: for if I liked being in the Brigade of Guards, I might like anything. In his mind, he turned over the various careers open to me. They all seemed to offer a regrettably pleasant life. However, one could think about that later. The great thing was to make me leave now. How could he winkle me out? It was far from easy. What levers were there to his hand? Chief of them was my extravagance.

In other generations of families circumstanced as mine, when a young man lived prodigally for a year or two, the father would murmur to himself with an air of indulgence *'Boys will be boys'*, and then, after making an armed demonstration, would pay up. But my father's genuine sense of the necessity of thrift for others, mingled with atheistic uplift and a horror of pleasure, made him resolute in his refusal to contemplate taking up an attitude of this kind: it would only encourage the extravagant strain that I must inherit from my mother's family – and so he fell back on the favourite adage of rich people (how often have I not heard them use it – and the richer the more frequently, and with the greater force!): 'The kindest thing to do is not to give them more money, but to teach them how to live within their income.' It was no good to help me in any way except by advice and oppression: and the first included indirect, as well as direct, methods.

I suppose I was extravagant, by inheritance, disposition, outlook, and by the kind of company I was obliged to keep. But, on the other hand, my father had told me continually that he wished me to behave in the same way in which others of my age conducted themselves: what he meant by this was that he would not mind my squandering several hundreds of pounds on hunting and polo, for he was certain in his own mind that I should be profoundly bored by these sports, and resent having to spend the money on them: but expenditure on going to the opera was another thing! I *liked* it!

The reader must once more leap forward with me, this time to an autumn in the middle 'twenties, when my father and mother were installed at Montegufoni, and Henry had come into his own again. By that time, his hair was turning grey, his face was less red, more sunburnt, but he had put on still more weight. Every day, for a fortnight past, Henry's ankle had been growing more swollen, the pain in it more acute. At first his master attributed this to old age – Henry must have been about fifty-six or seven – and I recall one day, while my father sat with me at breakfast – himself breakfasted some hours earlier, at six, – he adopted an almost lachrymose tone of voice, as he said to me,

'Poor old Henry; he's getting an old man! I hope, dear boy, you'll try not to ring your bell too often, as he finds the stairs difficult.'

It soon became obvious that old age was not Henry's trouble. Plainly, it was gout: but with his combination of will-power and great bodily strength, he refused to give in, despite the endless, unevenly tiled corridors down which he was constantly obliged to hurry, the stone-paved spiral staircases, hardly wide enough for his bulk, which he was perpetually forced to climb up and clamber down. And – what made the torture worse – he knew that my father was watching him, had guessed what ailed him, and was, indeed, only waiting until Henry was compelled by his agony to surrender, to order him upstairs and confine him for several weeks to a diet of bread and water. My father was, of course, eagerly looking forward to the vicarious puritan pleasure he would derive from Henry's prescribed abstinence: whereas to Henry the two bright spots in the long Montegufoni day were the heavy but excellent meals he had taught Adaouina, the Italian cook, to serve him; with plenty of macaroni, red meat, followed by pudding, and grapes and figs, and accompanied by a whole *fiasco* of very strong Castle wine. Day after day, the duel went on: still my father, though it cost him an effort, would not mention to Henry his lameness: he knew it would be more effective to refrain from saying anything about it until in the end his servant could bear the pain no more and should be constrained to avow it.

At last the moment which my father had been for so long awaiting, albeit with impatience, arrived. Just as he was leaving in the motor, to spend the afternoon in Florence, and while Henry was in the act of putting a rug over his master's knees, this movement of leaning forward, by throwing an extra weight upon his feet, made the poor sufferer give a loud roar.

'It's no good, Sir George,' he confessed, 'I can't go on. My ankle hurts me terrible. It's torture! I'm afraid I shan't be able to wait at dinner tonight.'

My father, though this was the first time Henry's pain had been admitted by the victim, did not betray by the tremor of an eyelash either pleasure or surprise. There was, perhaps, only a faint glint in his eye, as he answered lightly,

'Dear, dear! It sounds to *me* like *gout!* . . . Fortunately, it's quite simple to treat! You just give up all meat and red wine for at least six months, indeed, you'll probably have to give it up altogether for the rest of your life. But one soon gets used to it. Better go to bed for the remainder of the day.'

My father pounded on, along the road to Florence, in his motor, well known in Florence as 'The Ark': a secondhand lorry engine, of the 1914 war, which he had bought at enormous cost – it was worth about £70, and he had been persuaded to pay £1,800 for it –, and for which he had then ordered a new but still more expensive body. The front of it had been specially built so that he could lie by the side of the driver at full length, and thus 'rest' his back, while the remaining space, being by that degree reduced, was made proportionately more uncomfortable for those who travelled behind. (As a consequence of this deal, he always maintained that he knew as a matter of certainty that it was impossible to buy a motor for under £4,000.) He was well pleased with the way things were shaping. I went out by myself for an hour's walk in the cypress wood. When I returned, I was amazed to meet in the Armoury an old hag I had never seen before, of a curious grey dishevelment, who, with protruding lower lip, gabbled to herself. I said *Buona sera, Signora*: she seemed not to notice me, but went on her way; for at this very moment the cook appeared, and treating her with noticeable respect, conducted her upstairs. The explanation was that this was the sorceress of the Val di Pesa. Henry had been in such pain that Adaouina, who had helped him to climb the stone steps, had been really concerned for him: what could be done? She thought for some minutes. Then she had remembered that the witch, as well as possessing the touch that withered, could, contrarily and in addition, heal. Henry was in favour of the experiment of sending for her: many sailor superstitions lingered in his blood. An hour later she had arrived, not by broomstick, but by bullock-cart. Having reached his room, she looked at his ankle, and then, with a ritual flourish of the wrist, touched it. In that instant, the patient had experienced – but for an instant only, since if it had been longer the pain could not have been borne – an intense agony, so unendurable as scarcely to seem real: and so apparently had the witch, for both she and Henry had bellowed and shrieked during that moment without restraint. (I shall never forget the yell, even as it sounded from the other end of the Castle.) Then his pain had vanished altogether, and did not return for eighteen months.

When my father returned from Florence, about six, and drove up in the motor to the outside staircase, with an unwontedly happy expression on his face, which plainly showed how much he was looking forward to going upstairs to give the invalid advice, there, instead, he found Henry, smiling, waiting to open the door of the car. My father mastered his natural indignation, and remarked,

'Better, Henry, I see!'

'Yes, quite well now, Sir George, thank you! It must be due to my giving up all those things you told me to, this afternoon.'

My father was not going to take this lying down, so he said,

'The danger is still there! You'll have to be very careful. Probably it's due to high blood-pressure – and you're not as young as you were, you must remember. I think you said your father died of a stroke . . .'

'Yes, Sir George.'

'How old was he at the time of his death?'

'Ninety-six, Sir George.'

My father, seemingly stunned by his answer, said nothing more: nor did Henry inform him of how his own cure had been effected. Perhaps it was as well. His master had had as much disappointment as he could stomach in a day, and with his horror of all forms of superstition, he might have grown really angry, had he come into possession of the truth.

The same state of mind which has formed the theme of the above digression was in evidence now, in 1914. He was looking forward immensely to cutting me off from the things I liked, since, besides being extravagant, they must be bad for me. Theatre tickets were a work of Satan – if he had believed in Satan: while what he termed 'Hot-House Fruit' was a symbol to him, comparable with the *Whore of Babylon* to the Calvinists. He manifested, in a very fully developed state, the anti-Skimpole complex of Victorian times. A bill of mine he had opened, for £3 3s. 3d., with Solomon's, the famous fruiterer in Piccadilly, was in his view something with which I should have to reckon on the Atheists' Judgement Day. Yet, for him, peaches, if grown and not bought, constituted a reasonable luxury – though not for others, so that when, later, he left Renishaw, having handed it over to me, he proposed to blow up the hot-houses he had built not so many years before. And, again, in the same connection, when towards the end of the 1914–18 war he read in the papers an appeal issued to the public by the Government of the day, urging that peach-stones should be collected, either for making gas or gas-masks – I forget which –, he threw himself whole-heartedly into this novel form of war work, remarking to us, with pride, and with a certain sense as of one dedicated to a task of abnegation, 'I've managed to get it up to fourteen today!'

Financial arguments were, as will be imagined, frequent and bitter. In the same way that, in the manner I have just related, he assumed that every motor-car cost £4,000, so now he leapt to other similar conclusions, from which he could never subsequently be dislodged. It was impossible to argue with him, once he had made up his mind. For example, he captured a bill of mine from an old-fashioned firm of hosiers and haberdashers, which had continued to set out the items of its bills in an elaborate style. Among the details he read,

To one pair Laced Pyjamas £2 8s. 4d.

These garments, of a type then almost universal, were frogged across the chest, instead of buttoning in the usual way; and this was what the word *laced* signified technically. My father, however – and nothing would ever subsequently rid him of the idea –, read *laced* as *lace*, and henceforth tenaciously clung to the belief that, arraying myself after the fashion of some of Aubrey Beardsley's figures, I habitually wore pyjamas of *Point de Venise* or *Bruxelles*. Very draughty wearing they would have made in the winter climate of the Tower of London, as I told him: but he would not listen, nothing would shake him in his conviction, and for the rest of his life I used to hear him, from time to time, confiding in acquaintances, 'As my son *insists* on wearing *lace* pyjamas, Lady Ida and myself are obliged to economize. It's hard, but young people today seem to think they have a perfect right to everything. I should never have dreamt of wearing lace pyjamas myself at that age!' – as if it constituted one of the comforts of the old.

Of course the tendencies in the family, and my mother's extravagance, coloured his vision to a deeper hue in these respects: but this, in its turn, also tinged the whole of life for his children, as if viewed through the faulty, discoloured lens he supplied, the perspective of which they could see to be untrue, and yet had to accept, if they were to keep up any relationship with him; although they were obliged equally to fight against it, in order to make sense of the outside world. One had constantly to keep in mind his generosities, his kindness and the quality of his thought. He ends a letter in which he prophesies my total ruin with a most moving comparison. 'What horrifies me is the self-indulgence shown in the accounts, large sums for hosiery, hairdressers, theatre-tickets. While you have been doing this, I have had to exercise the strictest denial, giving up almost every pleasure in order to keep out of debt.' And yet during these very same years, he had been spending tens of thousands of pounds on 'improvements', thousands, as we have seen, at Scarborough, and eight or ten thousand at Eckington, on making a fantastic garden, with enormous stone piers, and monoliths – one, with a flaw in it – for the entrance: all this, within the grounds of a little house that had been built as a school for the village by an ancestor of ours in 1720, but for the past hundred years had been a farm. (When he took me to see this, and had asked me what I thought of it, I had replied, without thinking, 'The garden seems to me too large for the house': I should have known better than to say it. Even as I spoke, I noticed an expression of delight, and of some sort of calculation, pass across his face; but I did not realize what this portended until, when I returned home about eighteen months later, I walked down with my father to The Folly, as the rest of the family called it, and found that the house had now doubled in size. As my father watched my face register the surprise and annoyance I felt, he remarked, with an air almost too affable, 'You told me you thought the house too small for the garden, so you see, I took your advice and built on!') He had been spending a good deal on making a dam in the woods, and several thousands on renovations to an old house that belonged to us in Warwickshire, where he proposed, too, to construct in cement a garden cloister of large size – happily, this feature never materialized. The two golf-courses and their pavilions, and the over-sumptuous furnishing of one of them – he had lately designed for it a type of walnut table, with legs like the parts of a jig-saw puzzle, so that one longed to fit them together – and other anomalies of taste, had cost tens of thousands. He was preparing for habitation a vast *castello* in Italy, and buying for it furniture appropriate to the opportunities for spending that the many periods of its architecture offered him. Unfortunately, here his desire for bargains overcame his extravagance, and since he would never pay enough for objects, he would, with a few exceptions, obtain only the second-rate in great numbers, but each worth a little less than he had paid for it. In addition, he lived in two houses, waited on by plenty of servants, and with excellent food. I am sure, though, that, absurd as, when these things are considered, the peroration to his letter that I have quoted may appear, yet when he wrote it he believed every word it contained. And this genuine sense of abnegation in all he did throws light on an incident that occurred later, in 1919, just after the end of the First World War. It was a sparkling, bitter winter early afternoon. My father was walking through Leicester Square, with my brother on one side of him, and with me on the other. We were both in the uniform of the Grenadiers, with large grey great-coats, and my father was wearing a top-hat and a blue heavy coat with a wide fur collar. Suddenly a bonneted Salvation Army Lassie came up, and holding out a wooden money-box towards my father, jingled it, and said to him, very gently and sweetly,

'Give something for Self-Denial Week, sir!'

My father stopped walking, as if overcome by the shock he had received, and then, after fixing on her for some instants a look of the utmost severity and moral disapprobation, pronounced, in patient saint-like tones, these words,

'With *Some* People, Self-Denial Week is *Every* Week.'

Then he proceeded on his way.

The one thing my parents never denied themselves or others was a row. They could not exist in a peaceful atmosphere. Consequently, after many months of freedom, it was with a feeling of the most profound depression that I accepted an ultimatum from my father, and left London for Renishaw about the 20th of July 1914, to take up civilian life. He had made up his mind by now. I must enter the Town Clerk's Office at Scarborough. No profession could afford one a more perfect training for after-life. Start at the bottom, and climb right to the top – the top consisting, I inferred, in being Town Clerk at Scarborough. No more was heard now of Governor-Generalships and Embassies. No, the Town Hall at Scarborough was to be my life: and he repeated with enthusiasm, 'right from the bottom'; for, by one of the innumerable contradictions in his character, a success story was that which he had come to require. Previously the newspapers he read had produced no effect on him, but now that his character had softened, their little propaganda tales of Sir Thomas Lipton as an errand-boy bringing his share of tea – or someone else's, I forget which – to his old mother, and of the eye-moistening exploits of Barney Barnato as a curly-haired child (for in those days the rich were as much and unjustly revered as now they are reviled) had begun to influence him. In addition, his Gothic interest still continued, indeed grew more painful, and since he was really very loosely tethered to the modern world, I believe the Town Clerk's Office at the same time summed up a civilization so strange to his way of thinking as to fascinate him. Roll-top desks, files, efficiency, tea-shops, red-tape: all these exercised over him the same potent attraction that a top-hat holds for a savage, or the primitive art of the Congo and the Pacific Islands for the sophisticated esthete. Better still, before I entered the Office, I must go right back to the beginning, and learn a good commercial copperplate. As it was, my handwriting – by which, he assured me, people judged character almost exclusively nowadays – would gravely prejudice my career. I should get nowhere. Accordingly, before my apprenticeship at Scarborough began, I was to reside at Renishaw for a month or two, and under his restrictive eye learn from starting-point the whole art of calligraphy, as well as how to read double-entry accounts. Into these mysteries I was to be inducted by an instructor from Clark's Commercial College. I hated these plans, but, though even now I did not realize that war was so near, I fell in with them with a definite and curious sense of fatalism. I knew, with utmost inner conviction, that they were futile, and held no solidity. They remained flat on the paper, like a drawing. I was very tired when I left London, tired from pleasure and not from work.

At Renishaw there were few alterations, with the exception of one important change in the scene: my father had grown a red beard which joined him in appearance all the more strongly to medieval Italy, of the time when Norman blood still ran in the veins of its nobles. Men with beards are liable nowadays to grow slovenly – the tramp, and not, as in the Victorian Era, the dandy, being the type of the bearded man of our epoch –, but he became, if anything, more scrupulous: the beard was just a red flag that he waved perpetually at the bull modernity, when he was not adoring it. (Meanwhile, this new development rescued Robins from the daily dangers attendant on having to shave him; since my father was wont suddenly to say 'No!', in a loud, angry voice and to dismiss the whole operation, leaving it half done. In London, on the first occasion that this happened, Robins marched straight out of the room and, without offering an explanation, went down to Brighton for the day. Nothing was said, except that the next morning, when Robins came to call him, my father remarked, 'You should pay no attention another time.')

In spite of the troubles I expected, I have never known a greater calm to prevail. Silence was once again enclosing me. But this time I was not afraid, and I was not unhappy. I was no longer eighteen, and I had made friends. I had found people who believed in my ability, and told me so – it astonished me, for in what direction could it lie? – who liked me and let me see it. Every day now brought me letters from them, telling me that they missed my company, and letting me have the news. Obviously, *they* did not think I was never going to appear again: so I shed that fear, just as, in the same way, the sense that I was going to be shut up in my shell for ever had vanished. I knew now that life could be beautiful, even if it was not good, and at last felt entirely in tune with my epoch. Nor did the absolutely blank future which extended in front of me, beyond this sudden break, persuade me that I should ever see the inside of the Town Clerk's Office at Scarborough. The stars were not casting in that direction.

The old gentleman from Clark's College had already arrived. He probably was not really old, but he seemed so to me. He was unassertive and kind, in a tactful but soulless way. I worked in the open air, and so, all day long, while I was learning from him or walking with Sacheverell, he sat in a deck-chair, his head crowned by a billycock, always so inappropriate in the country. It seemed to suggest somehow that its wearer had been implicated in a crime – though the only crime with which in reality he had ever been connected was the conspiracy against my liberty: and his genial if serious Scottish intonation when he spoke acquitted him of any personal share in this. He had just somehow got himself involved in it. A kitchen-table had been placed on the grass, near the marble paving outside the garden door, so that my father could see that I was really working. Almost as if I were captive to a Roman General, or a criminal in the stocks, I was thus made to parade publicly my humiliation as I sat there at the age of twenty-one, practising how to make pothooks.

l l l l l l l l

Bitterly I resented every moment of it, as people passed and inquired what I was doing.

'Unfortunately, his handwriting is so unformed and childish that he is having to learn to write,' my father would explain, with the familiar condescending, downward flourish of his hand.

As well as feeling incapable of effort, I was restless, and gradually developed an uneasy sense that things outside were going wrong. The news – we were in the last week of July now – was openly becoming serious. For some time there had been talk in the papers of 'ultimatums', a word then new to me, having only lately been re-issued from the diplomatic mint as a reliable method of producing war. I sat at the table, and gazed up at the skies, trying, because the thought of war was so new and tremendous, therein to read the trend of the future, as many thousands of men have done before me through countless ages in times of crisis, for savages and the most civilized all share, at the deepest level, the same superstitions; only ours reach us by more devious routes. The vast arch above, dwarfing the earth, was as full of clouds as, on a map, the oceans are full of continents: drifting masses of gold and grey that at moments approximated to the familiar shapes of countries in the atlas, defining themselves in the wind that blew there, so high up, in the lofty azure, gold-flecked spaces, though here, on the ground, everything was calm, and no leaf moved. I became so mazed by staring that at times I almost distinguished that marching host – which has so frequently been seen before in times of trouble – armed with spears and lances, carrying banners, woven of cloud and sun, and wending its way endlessly into the infinite, to storm citadels and ramparts all the more difficult to attack because the whole time able to change their shape and nature.

The weather was very hot: the lilies, which grew so easily in the light, leafy soil of Renishaw, were larger and more fragrant than I had ever known them, and Ernest had produced a specimen with a hundred heads. From the open window over the low wooden door to the garden, to which as a child of three or four I used to run the moment I arrived in the house, the same air I always associated with the place came at me; the wafted, commingled scent of stocks and clove-carnations and tobacco plant and box hedges, with the faint acrid harshness of coal-smoke lying under it. It blew in, warmly, steadily, scenting the house. Everything seemed the same, but with a strange, uneasy difference. Except that Henry had gone, and Robins was here in his place, there were the same people: my father, my mother – she was upstairs, ill from the strain of her worries –, Edith, Sacheverell, my Aunt Florence, who, now that my grandmother was dead, came to stay with us more often, Helen Rootham – who had arrived for a visit to us – Hollingworth, Stubb and Pare. Major Viburne was in charge of the household-books, Miss Lloyd had once more come to stay. And I found Mark Kirkby in the stables, getting stiffly out of his cart with his dog. The two of them, and the old grizzled pony, looked three of one kind, I reflected.

Two nights before I met him, at the end of the last week of July, he had fallen asleep for a few minutes, sitting on a bench in his cabin. He woke up with a start, thinking he heard some sound, and moved cautiously to the open door. In the breathlessly hot night, as he stood there, everything seemed deserted and silent, except for an owl's thick hootings and snorings down below, and for the scamperings of nameless night creatures under the bracken. It was rather dark, but clusters of bright stars showed the banks of trees stretching for miles each side of the stream. Suddenly, a flash appeared in the sky, on the right, at the high end of the hill, and, large as a moon and brighter, a fire-ball – in the folk-mind of man so sure a portent of disaster – swept just above the line of the tree-tops, and sailed majestically down the valley to the distant horizon. As it passed beneath him, he heard a faint, crackling sizzle break the strange silence. Here was something he had never seen before, and it had filled his mind, as it now filled mine when he told me of it, with a certain disquiet. Superstitions, as I have said, lurk in all of us. And the fact remained that the guardian of the woods, himself so securely tied to the material world, rooted in the very soil, had seen what I had looked in vain for, in the skies: a portent – the most ancient omen of war. And who are men, he said to me – though in other words –, to dismiss a sign from heaven because of the titterings of science or the hissing voice of Common Sense?

This, however, was a solitary occurrence: otherwise, the existence familiar to us from childhood continued, inside the house and out. Helen was playing Debussy in the ballroom; Edith was in her bedroom copying into her notebook a passage from Baudelaire, and trying in general to avoid the trivialities of the day; Sacheverell was talking to Major Viburne, and then went to see my mother, who was still in bed, the windows wide open, and the air laden with the sweetness of geranium leaf and lemon-scented verbena from the broad window-boxes, painted green. My father was immersed in the usual multifarious tasks to which he set himself. Whatever else had altered in him, there was no sign of any slowing-down of his mental activity, nor any lessening of his desire to create beauty as he saw it. Recent experiences had in no wise deterred him from making his plans for changes in the house and landscape. But this did not induce in him an easy mood. Especially was he worried now over the subject of a new dam. Half a mile long, this narrow sheet of ornamental water, placed between high, wooded slopes, had not long been completed, and was to carry either a colossal statue of Neptune, rising from the middle of the water, or a leaden ship, he had not been able to make up his mind which. Meanwhile, something had gone wrong with the bed, and, since this building experiment had been paid for out of trust funds, I redoubled my expostulations about it. Eighteen months before this, I find the sub-agent writing to Turnbull, 'The new dam in the woods is somewhat of a nightmare to me. It does not fill as it ought, and I am afraid we shall soon hear that the water is finding its way into the colliery workings, though there are none just under it.' Sure enough, the water vanished, and the coal company, alleging that it had flooded the mine, refused to pay the rents due for it. When I learnt of this, I could not refrain from saying 'I told you so' to my father. But, though concerned, he proceeded to bring an action against the coal company. This lawsuit was pending at the time of which I write, and hung fire for many years, since much evidence had to be collected and sifted. The legal expenses therefore mounted to vast heights, but in the end the warnings I had issued proved unnecessary, for, after a whole decade had passed, the two parties reached a compromise out of court, my father obtaining costs and a large sum in settlement of his claims. Henceforth, I apprehend, he looked on the making of a dam, or, indeed, the creation of any decorative scheme that appealed to his imagination, as a possible source of riches. There was no holding him.

At present, then, neither stone statue nor leaden ship could be proceeded with, but he was in no way dismayed, and he allowed other ideas to occupy his mind. He was planning a new garden terrace, to run the entire length of the hill-top, and was again surveying the site for the Island Pavilion, and spending many hours aloft on a complicated wooden platform erected in and above the lake, at the correct altitude, as if he were on the second storey of his imaginary edifice on the imaginary island – for that, too, had to be constructed, the existing island not being situated in the perfect position for it – so that he could decide how to obtain the finest views, and note how best to make use of them. The Island Pavilion, he would explain to me in the intervals of my pothook exercises, was to be built entirely for my sake. It was a great sacrifice – and he hoped I would bear it in mind – but it should prove a most valuable asset in entertaining one's friends. But though in any case it spelt severe self-denial for him, the building need not really cost more than a few thousand: just run up an island – while it was being done, we ought to drain the twenty-two acres of lake, and grow early mushrooms under flower-pots in the bed, the soil would be just the thing, and thus defray part of the cost. Then, becoming enthusiastic over his new plan, he added that you could manure the ground with the fish that would be stranded, – roach, perch, pike and gudgeon. Nothing was so good, he'd been told, for cultivation as fish-manure. The crop would be splendid. You could easily make several thousands by this means and might, indeed, more than pay for the whole expense. It would be an interesting little experiment. Just buy your own fleet of lorries, grow early mushrooms and cucumbers, and send them into Sheffield. You might start your own shop there and make a fortune. What had we been talking about? Yes, it was a great sacrifice on his part, but he was willing to make it. Just run up an island, build on it in the local stone. (It would be delightful opening up the old quarry – one never knew what one might not find in it, and if the trees were cleared, it might make a charmin' place for picnics. You could cut out a Rock Chamber, like the one he'd seen in Sicily.) Local stone always looked best: a building of three storeys, diminishing in size from the top at each stage, so that you could have a terrace or broad balcony all round, the whole thing surmounted by a graceful tower, in tiers. To the south, the ground floor would look out on a swimming-pool, with a stone balustrade round it, enclosed within a pillared colonnade – Ionic pillars and capitals were the most suitable for a purpose of this sort, Corinthian were over-ornate – and there would be a dining-room and kitchen. (You might line the kitchen with tiles, such as he had seen in South Italy, showing a contemporary picture of how a banquet was prepared in the sixteenth century.) It would be considerate, perhaps, to build a special boudoir for the cook, where she could rest, put her feet up, let her hair down, and feel at home. Just imagine the difference it would make to the life of the servants, nothing they'd love so much as setting out on a fine morning, just before or after sunrise – really the most picturesque part of the day –, and spending the whole day in the delicious fresh air. It would be as good as a holiday. In fact, he should tell them tomorrow, holidays would not be necessary in future. He never took one himself. It was a pity that architects always raised unnecessary points against their own interest, and Lutyens, he was sorry to say, had been in one of his silly moods the other day, and when my father had remarked how much the servants, and especially the cook, would enjoy it all, he had blurted out that he wondered if the cook would enjoy sculling half a mile before breakfast. A great pity to say things like that; which reminded him, he said, of something he'd been meaning to say to me for a long while: I must still be careful about my sense of humour. That joke of mine the other night had been most unfortunate, and might give friends quite the wrong impression.

My father was not getting up so early that summer. First, about nine o'clock every morning, he would walk through the gardens and down the steep hill. Today – it was the 2nd of August 1914 – I watched him as he went. He was dressed in a smart grey suit, and wore the rather pointed brown shoes which he bought ready-made for eighteen shillings and sixpence, and a wide-brimmed grey hat, a little resembling a cowboy's, and was carrying a grey umbrella lined with green against the sun. Hollingworth would meet him at the boathouse – where, too, there would be waiting a man, bearing an ulster and various other parapher-nalia –, and would row or sail him to the foot of the scaffolding. There my father would alight and first girding himself with a leather strap to which was attached a pair of binoculars, and clutching, in addition to his umbrella, an air-cushion, shaped like a life-buoy, and carrying, under one arm, a copy of *The Times*, the *Architectural Journal*, the *Lancet*, the *Athenaeum*, and the *Financial News* of the day before, he would carefully, very carefully, mount the wooden ladder to the platform, furnished with a single chair, and a rug to put over the knees. Depositing the cushion, and putting down the papers, which gave ever and anon a flapping sound in the faint breeze, as of a dying vulture, he would advance to the wooden rail, and, hooking the handle of his umbrella on to it, easily within his reach, glance, first, downward at the lake that lay like a looking-glass, and showed banks of wood running deeply to an inverted sky. Hollingworth crossed it in a boat – and that recalled to my father's mind: he really must build those two wings on to the house – a storey taller than the rest, shaped like square towers! It would be so much more convenient for Hollingworth; he could have a delightful modern office in one of them. It was true that he said he did not want one and would much rather remain where he was – but that had nothing to do with it. He'd love it, when it was finished.

Up at the house, or rather, just outside it, I was back again, with my bowler-hatted mentor, learning to make pothooks. It was a week or two since I had started, and I realized that no progress had been made: it depressed me. Perhaps my father was right, and I never should be able to do anything.

Sacheverell's face appeared at an open window on the third storey, and he called me. In a moment he ran down from the top of the house, three steps at a time, in a rush of young feet, a tall figure, broad-shouldered, thin, with an unusual grace, resembling a little Saint by Cosimo de Tura or Crivelli. He was worried by the news in the papers. What did it matter if my father *was* angry at my stopping work? We must hurry up and have a talk, before my mother appeared. We hastened to the long walk in the Wilderness, entering between the stone Warrior and Amazon, and walked up and down, out of sight, between the dark banks of holly, where the nettles grow so tall, they sting your hands as you go. Sacheverell urged me to telephone to London. It was an agony of suspense, he said, waiting for news: and, indeed within a day, the feeling of tension – I realized it now he said it – had inexplicably and intolerably increased. Yesterday had been an ordinary day, with a threat of worry: whereas today was two days – or a day or three days – before the Great War. But it was not easy. We had to telephone without being seen, for no trunk-calls were allowed by my father. But in the evening I managed it. I had thought of just the person of whom to inquire: a very shrewd and politically-minded brother-officer, older than myself, who was with a Battalion which had been moved to the Tower, so as to be in London in case of developments. I knew I could trust his acute intelligence and balanced judgement. I got through to him. 'The scare is off,' he said; 'the news is much better: there is no chance of war.'

The nervous tension continued to mount, in spite of what he had said. The next afternoon I left Renishaw, abandoning, as I knew, for ever the prospect of the Town Clerk's Office.

I arrived in London at six in the morning, and reported to the Reserve Battalion, already in course of formation. In the afternoon I went to say good-bye to many friends, who, as it happened, were never to return to England. Two or three of the most confident I heard instructing their servants to pack their evening-clothes, since they would need them in a week or two in Berlin. Later, I called on my Grandmother Londesborough, now grown a very old lady. She was a great-niece of Wellington's, and perhaps some lingering anti-Napoleonic tradition inspired her parting remark to me, 'It's not the Germans but the French I'm frightened of.' Still, even then, it was not certain that war was coming. But in the evening, I went to the Mall, and waited. If the Lord Mayor's Coach arrived, it meant war, and presently, after dusk, sure enough it came trundling along through the Admiralty arch toward the Palace. As it entered the gates I heard the great crowd roar for its own death. It cheered and cried and howled. How many of those voices could have been heard in two years' time?

War hysteria quickly asserted itself. Haldane, the most efficient War Minister of the age, was chivied out of the War Office, and Lord Kitchener, god of the hour, but a deity who had grown stiff in the joints, sat in his chair, turning a stern face to the world. Recruiting songs vied with genuine patriotic appeals. In the music-halls, Miss Phyllis Dare was singing, 'Oh, we don't want to lose you, but we think you ought to go'. Soon whole mattresses of white feathers were coming out, and being given away; for in 1914 the reactions were simpler, quicker and more direct than in 1939. Fortune-tellers reaped a rich harvest, and *Old Moore's Almanack* reached a new sales-level.

Several times before I left England, I met Sir Edward Grey, the Foreign Minister, and heard him, to my relief, explain most interestingly that the war could not last more than three months. The Germans could not stand the strain, and must inevitably collapse financially. Under his Roman mask, he was a very humane man and could not face the consequences of his policy. I also consulted a fortune-teller: the only time I had ever visited one. It was not certain when I was to start for the Front: but this was to be expected every day. I lived perpetually on the edge of departure; and some friends, anxious, I suppose, to know what was going to happen to me, made an appointment for me with a celebrated mistress of the psychic art, an unconvincing little person with an over-eager eye. Her lair, with its screened lights, oriental draperies, its divans and incense, was disconcerting and pitifully counterfeit. Crystal-gazing and hand-reading were her specialities. I plumped for palmistry. She told me many things that meant nothing. At the end, she said,

'You will come back and go on with your career.'

'What is it?' I asked, for I had no wish to be a soldier indefinitely.

She looked surprised, and then replied with conviction, 'That is very clearly marked on your hand. Look, there's the star of fame! You're a writer, aren't you?'

I thought of the pothooks and laughed.

BOOK FOUR

LAUGHTER IN THE NEXT ROOM

CHAPTER ONE

In 1918, though we who had fought were even more disillusioned than our successors of the next conflict about a struggle in which it was plain that no great military leaders had been found, we were yet illusioned about the peace. During the passage of more than four years, the worse the present had shown itself, the more golden the future, unreal as the conventional heaven, had become to our eyes: an outlook common, perhaps, to those of all ages of war and revolution. And today – the 11th of November 1918 – that long present had suddenly become changed to past, clearly to be seen as such. Hence both the joy and the earnestness of dancers in street and square tonight: hence, too, the difficulty of finding a way in which to describe to the reader the movements that so precisely interpreted conflicting emotions: the long drawn-out misery and monastic stultification of the trenches, and then the joy of a victory that in the end had rushed on us with the speed and impact of a comet – for it *was* difficult, I realized that fully, as, with my companions, Diaghilev and Massine, I stopped to watch for a moment the shifting general pattern of the mass of people.

With something of the importance of a public monument attaching to his scale and build, the great impresario, bear-like in his fur-coat, gazed with an air of melancholy exhaustion at the crowds. I do not know what thoughts were passing through his head. The dancer, on the other hand, so practical an artist, and in spite of the weighty tradition of his art, so vital in the manner in which he seizes his material from the life round him, was watching intently the steps and gestures of the couples, no doubt to see if any gifts to Terpsichore could be wrung from them. As for myself, when I looked at the couples – and a few who were dancing by themselves! – I felt lonely, as always in a throng. My thoughts turned inwards, and to other occasions.

It was curious that now that the battle was over and the Captains and the Kings had become dead leaves overnight, rattling down from their trees, whirling head over heels in the air, my mind, which had so perpetually during the course of it avoided thoughts of war, and even when compelled thereto by professional necessity could never for more than a few seconds at a time fix itself on such matters as maps, or even instructions for an offensive (which I could understand no better than formerly I had comprehended the drill-manual), did not busy itself with the future, enticing as that seemed to all of us, but reverted ever to two scenes. First to the landscape of an early September morning, where the pale golden grasses held just the colour of a harvest moon, as they shone under the strong, misty sun of autumn in northern France; a wide flatness of gentle, tawny land, where dead bodies in khaki and field-grey lay stiff and glittering in the heavy dew, among the blue clouds of the chicory flowers, which reflected the sky and, as it were, pinned it down. (Though khaki differed from field-grey, and the helmets were dissimilar, the attitudes were the same; so, too, were the greenish-grey skin and the incurious eyes.) These flowers that seemed cut rosettes of azure paper I had always loved as a child at Renishaw: but now they came to hold a terror for me, to be haunted by the thought of dolls lying spangled with them; dolls whose knees *should* move, but never did, whose eyes *should* shut. Though tainted subtly by tear-gas and by the smell of earth freshly flung up from the craters, and by the odours of decomposition, it was a superb morning; such a morning, I would have hazarded, as that on which men, crowned with the vast hemicycles of their golden helmets, clashed swords at Mycenae, or outside the towers of Troy, only to be carried from the field to lie entombed in air and silence for millenniums under their stiff masks of thin virgin gold: (how far had we descended, crawling now, earth-coloured as grubs, among the broken stumps of trees, and the barbed wire, until we were still, among the maggoty confusion, and our faces took on the tints of the autumn earth and the rusty discoloration of dry blood!). Then the alternate scene switched before me: No-Man's-Land, that narrow strip of territory peculiar to the First World War; the very dominion of King Death; where his palace was concealed, labyrinthine in its dark corridors, mysterious in its distances, so that sometimes those who sought him spent hours, whole days, a week even, in the ante-chambers that led to his presence, and lay lost in the alleys and mazes of barbed wire. Throughout the length of time that the sun takes, you could hear their groans and sighs, and could not reach them. All that was over, for everyone. No wonder that the world rejoiced at a cessation that seemed more splendid than many a thing won!

So that night it was impossible to drive through Trafalgar Square: because the crowd danced under lights turned up for the first time for four years – danced so thickly that the heads, the faces, were like a field of golden corn moving in a dark wind. The last occasion I had seen the London crowd was when it had cheered for its own death outside Buckingham Palace on the evening of the 4th of August 1914; most of the men who had composed it were now dead. Their heirs were dancing because life had been given back to them. They revolved and whirled their partners round with rapture, almost with abandon, yet, too, with solemnity, with a kind of religious fervour, as if it were a duty. It was that moment which sometimes only occurs once in a hundred years, when strangers become the oldest friends, and the dread God of Herds takes charge. As a child I had first beheld his countenance, sweaty and alight with rage slaked and with pleasure, on Mafeking Night: but this evening he was in more benignant mood, chastened and by no means vainglorious. A long nightmare was over: and there were many soldiers, sailors and airmen in the crowd which, sometimes joining up, linking hands, dashed like the waves of the sea against the sides of the Square, against the railings of the National Gallery, sweeping up so far even as beyond the shallow stone steps of St Martin-in-the-Fields. The succeeding waves flowed back, gathered impetus and broke again. The vision which rose before the eyes of the soldiers was very different from that which has lately opened for their sons: it was a deliverance from mud – and mud as one of the great engulfing terrors of mankind can easily be under-rated – from mud and poison-gas, from night patrols and No-Man's-Land, and going over the top, from tetanus, tanks and shell-fire, from frost and snow and sudden death. To their dung-coloured world of khaki in sodden trenches, it seemed until today as if the politicians had clamped them for ever.

No-one, then, who had not been a soldier, alive on the morning of the 11th of November 1918, can imagine the joy, the unexpected, startling joy of it; for in 1945 victory came with deliberate step, in 1918 at a gallop. It had flung itself on us. The news had been – or at any rate had seemed – beyond what could be believed: the only way of persuading oneself of its truth was by doing something one had never done before, such as dancing in Trafalgar Square. It was with this feeling, I think, that the units composing the crowd danced. When the news had first come with a ringing of bells and sounding of maroons, men and women who had never seen one another before, spoke, to ask if it were true. All day long the news pelted in, as the first of the two tidal waves that were to destroy Europe swept over it to the furthest end. Russia had already been submerged for a year: now the Kaiser was in flight, the routed German armies were returning home, as is their habit after laying a world waste, and were kicking their officers in front of them. In Bavaria, the Communists had seized power, and were torturing in a ten days' coven, and in Hungary, too, under their leader the infamous Bela Kun, persecution and death were rife, and anyone with a clean shirt had to hide. The Emperor Karl had been deposed in Austria, which was now little more than a derelict great city lost in the mountains. In remote turreted castles all over Germany and Austria, the princes cowered, had not even the heart to go hunting. The dark wind of destruction tore like a falling angel across the European sky. In short, the popular reign of piracy, exalted to a creed, had begun. Whole classes were eradicated so that the world should in time be made safe, on the one hand, for a beer-logged trades-unionism in the victorious countries, and, on the other, for Hitler and Bolshevism. Hitler belonged to the people: like Stalin, he was no gentleman – and when I say *gentleman*, I mean what I say, and say what I mean, without fear of ridicule, since the world still contains the truth of its evident meaning. Boasting, roaring, tears, dervish-like howling, fist-shaking, lying over never-ending toasts in vodka and champagne were, by general consent, substituted for the traditional decorous voices and considerate behaviour of the old diplomacy. That day, we entered a world of wolf-and-buffalo politics, where to howl over your prey is to be realistic, where to bellow is to prove strength, and to whine is to show grace: the world in which we still – but only just – survive: the world in which the sabre-toothed tiger and the ant are our paragons, and the butterfly is condemned for its wings, which are uneconomic.

In London, however, the capital of the burgess order, the citizens were dancing, oblivious of the creaking of the scaffolding under them. To them – and to me – it appeared that they danced not without reason. Only six weeks before, the Allies had been so plainly losing the war. Though eyes were tired, they saw open up before them long vistas of quiet, renewed activity, displacing the former almost universal prospect of a stretch of noise and misery, followed by death. Even furnaces and factories looked attractive to those coming back from mud and darkness. Slum or castle, town or a cottage in an isolated region, each seemed equally welcoming to those who returned. During four long years, furthermore, the sole internationalism – if it existed – had been that of deserters from all the warring nations, French, Italian, German, Austrian, Australian, English, Canadian. Outlawed, these men lived – at least, they *lived*! – in caves and grottoes under certain parts of the front line. Cowardly but desperate as the *lazzaroni* of the old Kingdom of Naples or the bands of beggars and coney-catchers of Tudor times, recognizing no right, and no rules save of their own making, they would issue forth, it was said, from their secret lairs after each of the interminable check-mate battles, to rob the dying of their few possessions – treasures such as boots or iron-rations – and leave them dead. Were these bearded figures, shambling in rags and patched uniforms, and pale with a cellar dampness that at first put men off their guard, so that they were unprepared for their ferocity; were they a myth created by suffering among the wounded, as a result of pain, privation and exposure, or did they exist? At any rate, the story was widely believed among the troops; who maintained that the General Staff could find no way of dealing with these bandits until the war was over, and that in the end they had to be gassed.

Now, however, the barriers which war had created were down, and the singular conditions it had produced were finished. Life was thawing, would soon flow with an amazing rush and profusion, bringing friends, travel, experiences of every sort. We were on the verge. The world lay open again. The old instinct for travel of the British peoples, as much a part of their insular composition as is their poetry, revived. This was the greatest renewal of life that had come for a century – so it seemed, and for this reason the crowd danced. Not only was it the places they had lived in before the war had wrenched them away, that now rose up before men's senses, but they saw once more a future, now again so much longer than the past. Those of my generation had hardly been given time before the war to discover in what direction they were going; now, at least, we knew what we wanted: though some, no doubt, wanted too much, and some too little. A kind of light revolutionary fervour inspired us. What I wanted at that time I wrote in *How Shall We Rise to Greet the Dawn?* This appeared a week after Armistice Day in the *Nation*, then edited by H. W. Massingham, and the chief organ to publish my satires. I here reproduce lines from it because of the insight they afford into the mind of a young man of the epoch.

How Shall We Rise to Greet the Dawn?

How shall we rise to greet the dawn,
Not timidly,
With a hand before our eyes?

    .   .   .

We must create and fashion a new God –
A God of power, of beauty, and of strength –
Created painfully, cruelly,
Labouring from the revulsion of men's minds.

It is not only that the money-changers
Ply their trade
Within the sacred places;
But that the old God
Has made the Stock Exchange his Temple.
We must drive him from it.
Why should we tinker with clay feet?
We will fashion
A perfect unity
Of precious metals.

Let us tear the paper moon
From its empty dome.
Let us see the world with young eyes.
Let us harness the waves to make power,
And in so doing,
Seek not to spoil their rolling freedom,
But to endow
The soiled and straining cities
With the same splendour of strength.
We will not be afraid,
Though the golden geese cackle in the Capitol,
In fear
Lest their eggs may be placed
In an incubator.

Continually they cackle thus,
These venerable birds,
Crying, 'Those whom the Gods love
Die young'
Or something of that sort.
But we will see that they live
And prosper.

Let us prune the tree of language
Of its dead fruit.
Let us melt up the clichés
Into molten metal,
Fashion weapons that will scald and flay;
Let us curb this eternal humour
And become witty.
Let us dig up the dragon's teeth
From this fertile soil
Swiftly,
Before they fructify;
Let us give them as medicine
To the writing monster itself.

We must create and fashion a new God –
A God of power, of beauty, and of strength;
Created painfully, cruelly,
Labouring from the revulsion of men's minds.
Cast down the idols of a thousand years,
Crush them to dust
Beneath the dancing rhythm of our feet.
Oh! let us dance upon the weak and cruel:
We must create and fashion a new God.

To some, wiser than I, the future appeared in other colours; though these, too, proved delusive. Thus, on the night in question, among the guests at Swan Walk, in addition to Miss Ethel Sands and those I have mentioned, was my friend Madame Vandervelde, the English wife of the Belgian statesman. She was very well informed about matters political, and she possessed an energy which inevitably heightened the spirits of others in her company, while at the same time it left her with neither leisure nor inclination to be depressed. Yet tonight the prospect before us a little quelled her spirits. She foresaw an era of political assassination (two German Governors had recently been killed in western Russia, she remarked), and that the whole of Europe would go Bolshevik. After that, it would only be a question of how long the new doctrine would take to cross the English Channel, which usually delays the arrival of every idea, whether political or esthetic, for at least twenty years. Albeit this picture appalled me, both my brother and I admired the Bolsheviks for putting a stop so quickly to a war that had become for the Russian troops, left without arms, increasingly a shambles, and for defeating Germany in so novel a manner, by first themselves pretending to be vanquished, and then by inoculating the German armies with the virus of defeat and revolution, which had, in fact, worked on them so swiftly. The war had made us impatient of politicians who relied on oratory rather than arms, and of generals who had never a new idea, but insisted on their forces being sacrificed in the old, inefficient way. Besides, we were ignorant of the sort of horror that was taking place in Russia even while we talked. But I said little, for Diaghilev and Massine were Russians, and were present. And Diaghilev, indeed, dwelt on the low cunning of the Bolshevik leaders, and remarked how strange it was to have been born and to have lived in a great country, to think that you knew by sight, or at least by name, every prominent leader of opinion, and then to wake up suddenly one day and find your country ruled by men of whose very names, both real and assumed, you and the large majority of your fellow-countrymen were totally ignorant.

Yes, the barriers were down, there was no doubt about that, and it was difficult to see the future, though most of us regarded it with varying degrees of hope. Democratic Europe, expressing itself through the League promised by President Wilson, the noble-minded man of the coming era, would never allow another war to break out, (or that was what we held with our heads – because it was only common sense for every nation to avoid war – as opposed to what we feared in our hearts). War was to us the evil – and that was over. So we fell, soon, to talking of other things.

Though this dinner at Swan Walk had been arranged a week before, when no-one had been able to foresee so rapid an end to the destruction, it seemed to me most happy that Diaghilev and the new great dancer – for such Léonide Massine had become in the four years that had passed since his début in *La Légende de Joseph* at Drury Lane in 1914 –, should dine at my house on the night of the Armistice: most fitting, for several reasons: chief among them – and with that I will deal in a moment –, that the return of the Russian Ballet to London had constituted a private and sole omen of peace. That one would ever see the Ballet again had seemed a hope beyond ambition: nor afterwards, when I had come back to England, was there any sign that the Company would ever reappear in London. For years little news of it had reached England, and none of its most faithful followers could say where it was. Therefore its return in September 1918 possessed for my brother and myself all the force of a portent. The projected season was first announced in an advertisement in the press on 29th July of that year, but little more was heard of it until the very week, the very afternoon that, with a singular lack of the publicity which usually attended Diaghilev's ventures, the Ballet Company made its bow on the stage, and proved itself as remarkable as ever, though different now, re-created; as it continued to be re-created throughout the years until the great impresario's death. This time its productions manifested a new accent, a new emphasis, more modern and with a Spanish tang often occurring in them as a result of the long sojourn of the *Ballet Russe* in the Peninsula under the special patronage of the King of Spain, but for whom it would probably have had to be disbanded. It was through the royal kindness that the Company had been able to be transported to England: but it was all the more of a marvel that Diaghilev had arrived with it, for he was a very bad sailor, and entertained, in addition, a great superstitious horror of the sea, since it had been foretold many years before that he would die on the water, while on this occasion he had been obliged to face, not only the usual horrors of a rough passage on the Channel, but also the lurking, omnipresent menace of the U-boats. It must be remembered, moreover, that even in normal times, when urgent business should have taken him and, let us say, Stravinsky from London to Paris, he would often travel only so far as Dover, when, after having luncheon, and regarding disconsolately from the window the movement of the sea outside, he and his companion would return by the afternoon train to the safety of the Savoy Hotel. And it was said that once on board, if the sea proved to be stormy, and though he was a man without religious belief, he would order his faithful Tartar servant, Vassili, who had been in Diaghilev's service since he was nineteen years of age, to kneel down in the cabin and pray for his master's safety. (Certainly this had occurred on an Atlantic crossing.) It was, then, under these circumstances little less than miraculous that the Ballet had actually reached England.

Now, for two whole months it had again been delighting a London audience. The most popular of its productions – and in consequence that given most often – was a ballet based on Goldoni's comedy of the same name, *The Good-Humoured Ladies*, danced to music arranged by Vincente Tommasini from some of the five hundred sonatas of Domenico Scarlatti's, and given a simple Guardi-like setting by Léon Bakst. In this work it was the grace, pathos, entrancing cleverness, the true comic genius and liveliness of a dancer new to this country, Lydia Lopokova, which made the chief impression and won for the Company in general fresh devotees in every part of the house. Her face, too, was appealing, inquisitive, bird-like, that of a mask of comedy, while, being an artist in everything, she comprehended exactly the span and the limits of her capacities: the personification of gaiety, of spontaneity, and of that particular pathos which is its complement, she had developed the movements of her hands and arms in a way that hitherto no dancer had attempted, thereby achieving a new step forward in technique. Her wit entered into every gesture, into everything she did. Moreover this great ballerina, fair, with the plump, greenish pallor of arctic flowers, formed the perfect foil to the dark, grotesque quality which Massine instilled into his masterpieces of satiric dancing and choreography. These two famous artistes led the Ballet into its second Golden Age, with such superb creations of grotesque genius as *La Boutique Fantasque* and *Le Tricorne*, though *Parade*, with Karsavina and Massine in the leading rôles, was, in essence, the most tragic and the most original of the newer spectacles. *Parade* had already been given in Paris, but not in England; while the two new productions were to be ready in the near future, and to be presented in London the following spring, when the Company was to provide a whole evening's entertainment at that beautiful theatre the Alhambra, to my mind always the best house in the capital in which to show ballet.

At present, the Company only filled a part of the bill at the Coliseum, with a single item from its repertory at the two performances. One result of this was that the true lover of ballet was now to be found sitting next to those who worshipped at the shrine of the Red-Nosed Comedian. Fortunately for myself, I was happy with both arts, though I cared more passionately for the first. Moreover, the amateur of the Ballet had himself at last changed, for now the leaders of the intellectuals and their followers flocked to it, replacing the old kid-glove-and-tiara audience of Covent Garden and Drury Lane. Many of the newcomers seemed more mazed by the music-hall turns than would have been the wearers of the stiffest shirt-fronts and most scintillant diamonds from the Royal Opera House, while, for their part, the members of the general audience gazed in wonder and anger at the bearded, angular balletomaniacs, who talked with confidence of things of which they themselves had never heard, in voices clear or squeaky, but that could not be shaken off their tone.

In the audience at this time was very frequently to be seen Lady Ottoline Morrell. With a mass of chestnut hair falling on each side of her face, with her emphatic features, and wearing a yellow gown with a very wide skirt, she resembled a rather over-life-size Infanta of Spain, and there was something, too, in her appearance that recalled the portraits of her remarkable ancestress, Margaret, Duchess of Newcastle, the poet. I recall being amused when one night, oblivious, plainly, even of the name of the kind of theatre in which she now found herself, she gazed with an air of considerable disapprobation at one of the turns, and then sighed in her very individual voice, muffled but distinct for all that, 'Rather Music-Hall, I'm afraid!' Though Lady Ottoline had been one of the earliest supporters of the Ballet, when first it came to London, her personal distinction, her individual style, her way of looking, talking, thinking, her magnificent manner of dressing, her brocades and silks, as natural to her as tweeds to the owner of a fox-terrier, made her seem as much out of place at Covent Garden as at the Coliseum. Notwithstanding, Diaghilev, one of whose failings was an inclination to find repose in the bosom of the fashionable world, which Lady Ottoline despised for its complacent stupidity, yet came to depend on her for advice. And she knew precisely how to manage him. With certain other geniuses – for it is by no means a fault confined to the foolish, and is perhaps in the present dustman-democracy age over-condemned – he shared often a snobbish attitude: (it may have been necessary to him in his profession). At any rate, on one occasion, when he had motored down to luncheon at Garsington, Lady Ottoline's country-house, and was plainly chafing at the company he found there – for on the day in question there were writers and painters of an unfashionable kind, but without the genius which would have rendered them supportable to him –, and remained glumly regarding the shaggy figures round him, Lady Ottoline roused him from his sullen lethargy by pointing at Miss Dorothy Brett, the painter (who had a studio in the house), and by insinuating into his ear the healing phrase, 'That woman is sister to a Queen'. It is true that the Queen in question was Queen of Sarawak, but the words nevertheless produced a tonic effect.

This, however, occurred later than the time of which I write, and when social life had already begun to blossom again a little. At present, almost the only entertainment London afforded for Diaghilev was tea at Garland's Hotel in Suffolk Street with Lady Ottoline. There, too, in her old-fashioned sitting-room, furnished with plush, and a marble clock on the chimney-piece, the ballerinas would be found after the first house, eating strawberry or raspberry jam in silver spoons, dipped previously, after the Russian mode, in tea without milk. We talked, as many did in her lifetime, of Lady Ottoline as we sat in the drawing-room in Swan Walk, a room that glittered with colour like a parrot's tail. But soon we set out for Monty Shearman's rooms in the Adelphi, for he had invited us all some days before to come to a party he was giving.

It was not until we reached the far corner of the Mall that the full degree of the general rejoicing became evident. We had found a taxicab – by no means an easy feat at the end of the 1914–18 war – but we were obliged to crawl, so thick was the crowd, and so numerous were the revellers who clambered round, and rode on, the roof. Eventually we reached the Adelphi. The spacious Adam room, covered with decoration as fine as a cobweb, was hung inappropriately with a few large pictures by the Paris School – by Matisse, for example, – and by several of the Bloomsbury Group, its satellite and English Correspondent. There were a number of paintings, for instance, by Mark Gertler – at that moment an artist much patronized by the *cognoscenti* (heavy designs of Mile-End-Road figures, very stiff but oily, of trees, fleshy in their aspect, under the solid shade of which trod ape-like beings, or still-lives, apples and pears of an incomparable rosy rotundity falling sideways off cardboard cloths – yet these possessed some kind of quality). Here, in these rooms, was gathered the élite of the intellectual and artistic world, the dark flower of Bloomsbury. And since this name has occurred twice already in this paragraph – as it surely must if one is to attempt to describe the achievements or environment of the early post-war generation –, a word or two is necessary to indicate what it stood for before its so rapid decline.

The great figures were Roger Fry, Virginia Woolf, Clive Bell, Vanessa Bell, Lytton Strachey and Duncan Grant. After them followed a sub-rout of high-mathematicians and low-psychologists, a tangle of lesser painters and writers. The outlook, natural in the grand exemplars, and acquired by their followers, was one of great tolerance: surprise was never shown at any human idiosyncrasy, though an amused wonder might be expressed at the ordinary activities of mankind. The chief, most usual phrases one heard were 'ex-quisitely civilized', and 'How *simply too* extraordinary!', the first applying to some unusual human concatenation, the second to some quite common incident of burgess life, such as a man going to a railway station to meet his wife returning after a long absence from home. But, no less than by the sentiments themselves, the true citizens of Bloomsbury could be recognized by the voice in which they were expressed. The tones would convey with supreme efficacy the requisite degree of paradoxical interest, surprise, incredulity: in actual sound, analysed, they were unemphatic, save when emphasis was not to be expected; then there would be a sudden sticky stress, high where you would have presumed low, and the whole spoken sentence would run, as it were, at different speeds and on different gears, and contain a deal of expert but apparently meaningless syncopation. The Bloomsbury voice, too – that characteristic regional way of speaking, as rare and ritualistic outside the bounds of West Central London as the state voice of the Emperor of China beyond his pleasances and palaces – originated, I believe, more in a family than in a flock. Experts maintain that it originated as an apanage of the Strachey family – of Lytton Strachey, that is to say, and of his brothers and sisters, in whom it was natural and delightful –, and that from them it spread and took captive many, acclimatizing itself first in the *haute vie intellectuelle* of King's College, Cambridge: thence it had marched on London, prospering particularly in Gordon and Mecklenburgh Squares and in the neighbouring sooty piazzas, and possessing affiliations, too, in certain country districts – Firle in Sussex, for example, and Garsington in Oxfordshire. The adoption by an individual of the correct tones was equivalent, I apprehended, to an outward sign of conversion, a public declaration of faith, like giving the Hitler salute or wearing a green turban. Once, indeed, I was privileged to be present when one of the Lesser – but now Greater – Bloomsburys took the plunge. I had known him well before he joined up, and then, gently-spoken reader, he talked as you or I do – and so judge of my surprise when, in the middle of a dinner-party, I heard his tongue suddenly slide off sense, making for a few moments meaningless but emphatic sounds that somehow resembled words, and then, as quickly, creak into the Bloomsbury groove, like a tram proudly regaining its rails!

Tonight, at Monty Shearman's, the Bloomsbury Junta was in full session. In later years, towards the moment of its disintegration, Bloomsbury, under the genial viceroyalty of my friend Clive Bell, took a trend, hitherto unexpected, towards pleasure and fashionable life: but in these days it was still austere, with a degree of Quaker earnestness latent in it. (But then Roger Fry, its leading and most engaging esthetic apostle, came of Quaker stock.) The women were of a type different from that to be seen elsewhere. Something of the Victorian past clung to them still, though they were so much more advanced than their sisters, both in views and intelligence. Virginia Woolf, for instance, notably beautiful with a beauty of bone and form and line that belonged to the stars rather than the sun, manifested in her appearance, in spite of the modernity that was also clearly hers, a Victorian distinction. She made little effort to bring out the quality of her looks, but she could not destroy it. It has often occurred to me, when I have seen Roman patrician busts of the fourth century, how greatly she resembled them, with her high forehead, fine, aquiline nose and deep-set, sculptural eye-sockets. Her beauty was certainly impersonal, but it was in no way cold, and her talk was full of ineffable fun and lightness of play and warmth. She possessed, too, a beautiful, clear, gentle speaking voice. Though sometimes, when many people were present, she could be seen swaying a little, preparing herself with nervous effort to say the words, to break through the reserve that lay over her, yet I have heard her dare to make a speech. It was at a dinner for the London Group of painters about a year later than the party. Roger Fry, who was president or chairman, had asked me to be present and to speak. When I arrived, I found to my great pleasure that I was sitting next to Virginia. But she was pitiably nervous that night because of the prospect of having to make a speech; her distress was obvious. I felt miserable on her behalf and tried, indeed, to comfort her: for after having just fought an election, oratory held temporarily few terrors for me. I concluded – and it may have been the case – that she was unused to the strain of these occasions, and had only consented to speak because Roger was one of her oldest friends. If so, what happened was the more astonishing. I spoke first, and adequately, I hope, in a matter-of-fact sort of way. The audience laughed at the jokes I made. Then I sat down, and the moment I had dreaded for Virginia arrived. She stood up. The next quarter of an hour was a superb display of art and, more remarkable, of feeling, reaching heights of fantasy and beauty in the description of the Marriage of Music to Poetry in the time of the Lutanists, and how, in the coming age, Painting must be similarly united to the other arts. It was a speech beautifully prepared, yet seemingly spontaneous, excellently delivered, and as natural in its flow of poetic eloquence as is a peacock spreading its tail and drumming. Somehow I had not foreseen this *bravura*; it was a performance that none present will ever forget, and, as she sat down, I almost regretted the sympathy I had wasted on her.

There were few women of a distinction equal to Virginia's in the room tonight: but all, pretty or *fade* or plain, wore their own clothes, either more fashionable than elsewhere, without fashion, or smacking of Roger's Omega Workshop, wholesome and home-made. Some of the men were in uniform, but a proportion – equally courageous in their way – had been conscientious objectors and so were able to appear in ordinary clothes – if *ordinary* is not, perhaps, a misnomer for so much shagginess (the suits, many of them, looked as if they had been woven from the manes of Shetland ponies and the fringes of Highland cattle in conjunction), and for such flaming ties as one saw. It was a singular dispensation – though welcome to me, because I admired their moral bravery, sympathized with the standard they upheld with a singular toughness, and liked them personally – that in the next few years several of the chief artistic and literary lions of the fashionable world, itself in every country then invariably chauvinistic, had been conscientious objectors: but the war, thank heaven, was over, and a moratorium on patriotism set in for about fifteen years. Those present tonight included several, I recall, who had worked at farming in the Arcadian colony presided over by Lady Ottoline Morrell. At Garsington during the war some of the best brains of the country were obliged to apply themselves to digging and dunging, to the potato patch or the pigsty. Lady Ottoline had thrown herself into the rôle of farmer only in order to help her friends – to her credit, ever to be found in the minority – in a time of affliction to them, when intellectuals discovered that mind was more than usually contemned by the majority of the nation. Among the ribald, however, it was rumoured that some employed by her came in the course of time to regard themselves as very able and competent farm-hands, shockingly underpaid, and that they were perpetually threatening to strike. Indeed it was alleged that some cantankerous if cultivated hinds had broken into the Manor House, shouting 'Down with capitalist exploitation'. If this be true, it must have been disturbing for Lady Ottoline, as she sat, quietly eating bull's-eye peppermints out of a paper bag, in her room of small, sixteenth-century panelling, painted green like that of her ancestral Bolsover, discussing sympathetically and seldom with more than one person – it might be D. H. Lawrence, the present Lord Russell, Aldous Huxley or Mark Gertler – the sufferings and foibles of mankind, thus to be reminded, too, of their perversity and ingratitude.

Some of the donnish farm-labourers who were supposed to have invaded her sanctum with their harsh cries for 'More' had gathered here tonight. All equally, soldiers, Bloomsbury beauties, and conscientious objectors – all except Diaghilev – danced. I remember the tall, flagging figure of my friend Lytton Strachey, with his rather narrow, angular beard, long, inquisitive nose, and air of someone pleasantly awaking from a trance, jigging about with an amiable debility. He was, I think, unused to dancing. Certainly he was both one of the most typical and one of the rarest persons in this assembly. His individual combination of kindness, selfishness, cleverness, shyness and sociability made him peculiarly unlike anyone else. As I watched him, I remember comparing him in my mind to a benevolent but rather irritable pelican. A man now of about forty, he had achieved no renown (though he had possessed a high reputation for wit, learning and personality among his own friends from Cambridge), nor had sought any until the publication of *Eminent Victorians* raised him to the zenith of fame and popularity with a generation no longer tolerant of either the pretensions or the achievements of the Victorian great. Some chapters of this book I had, in the autumn of 1917, been given the pleasure of hearing him read aloud – rather faintly, for he was recovering from an attack of shingles, and sat in an armchair in front of a large fire, with a Shetland shawl draped round his shoulders. I remember that our hostess, a cousin of Lytton's, pressed her lively young daughter of seven to allow him to see her imitation of him. While the precocious mimic showed off, Lytton watched the child with a look of the utmost distaste, and when asked by the mother what he thought of the performance – one of real virtuosity –, remarked in a high, clear, decisive voice, 'I expect it's amusing, but it isn't at all *like!*' As I say, he was at this moment enjoying great celebrity: my father, however, as was his way, had never heard of his name (it could not, I suppose, penetrate the loopholes of an ivory tower of medieval construction). Thus one day, a few years later, when Lytton had come over to have luncheon with us at Montegufoni, and when the issuing of his *Queen Victoria* had carried his work to an even wider public, his host demanded angrily, after the visitor had left, 'Who is he?', and further initiated what remains a haunting mystery, by adding, 'I do wish you'd ask some really interesting people here. I don't know why you never invite the great novelist.'

'Who do you mean?'

'Mitchell, of course. You know quite well!'

But though my father, after this, often mentioned the Master, and held him up frequently to us as a pattern of style and content, neither Sacheverell nor I was ever able, though the problem fascinated us and we tried perseveringly to solve it, to gain any clue to his identity. Sometimes we thought that he was, perhaps, an idealized composite figure formed from the various celebrated novelists of the day, Hardy, Conrad, Wells, Bennett, including all their various excellencies in his books, and with this workmanlike name thrown in to give reality to a dummy. All that we could get from my father, when we pressed him for the name of one of Mitchell's masterpieces, was, 'You know quite well. I saw you reading one of his books only the other day! He's much the finest of them – a real genius, they say!' Certainly the elusive Mitchell was absent, again, tonight: but among those I recall as being there were, in addition to Diaghilev and Lytton Strachey, Clive Bell, Roger Fry, Mark Gertler, Lady Ottoline, D. H. Lawrence and his wife, Maynard Keynes, Duncan Grant, Lydia Lopokova and David Garnett.

To everyone here, as to those outside, the evening brought unbelievable solace. The soldiers could return home, the members of the rustic community at Garsington could come back to London, and to work that was their own and would make them famous: the writers could write the sort of book in which they were interested, the young men and women could see the people they wanted to see, without immediately being ordered to Baghdad or York. No one, I am sure, was more happy than myself at the end of so long, so horrible, and so more than usually fatuous a war. When the party began to draw to a close, I left the Adelphi alone, on foot. In street and square the tumult born of joy still continued. Smilingly, the people danced; or intently, with a promise to the future – or to the past, which weighed down the scales with its dead. Strange things occurred. Late that night, a young man who had been at Monty Shearman's party almost succeeded in setting fire to the plinth of the Nelson column, as if in inauguration of an epoch that was to dismiss the lessons of our history, and emphasize that henceforth one man, whether great hero or criminal, genius or cretin, was as good as another. The next afternoon the rejoicings were still in full swing. My brother – now also an officer in the Grenadiers – came up to London from Aldershot, and on his return that night, so he told me later, saw at Waterloo Station drunken women being rolled along the platform like milk-cans, and piled into the guard's van – but this was an aspect both of war and of the coming of peace that the public resolutely ignored. Only virtue and heroism exist to war-eyes.

The sight of the scenes in the streets left me in two moods, unhappy and furious at the waste of lives and years, and frantically glad, on the other hand, that the struggle was over: full of improbable hopes and equally of probable fears. The first found expression in the poem already quoted, the second in that which is appended below. This poem, published shortly afterwards, was dedicated to my brother and seemed to me, as I wrote it, to have a vein of prophecy in it: a sense which unfortunately the intervening years have justified. In addition, a singular story attaches to it. It was included in the first book of poems by my hand alone (I had already appeared jointly with my sister): but many months before the volume was published in England or America, Witter Bynner was kind enough to send me some cuttings relating to this poem (he had later found out it was by myself) from Californian newspapers. It is a long time ago, but one such extract is before me now, and explains itself, though the title of the journal is lacking. It is dated Berkeley, Dec. 28th, and runs:

UNKNOWN POET SCORNS WAR
STANZAS FOUND ON MENU
GOOD VERSE, SAYS BYNNER

A poem scribbled on a grease-spotted menu in a San Francisco café bears so obviously the marks of genius that prominent authors and critics are today looking for the author of the unsigned verses. The owner of the copy received it from a French waiter on the night of the peace celebrations . . . Bynner says that in the technique and word selection, the unknown writer shows himself to be a master of his art. The only mark of identification is the letter M. The title is THE NEXT WAR.

The Next War

        The long war had ended.
        Its miseries had grown faded.
        Deaf men became difficult to talk to,
        Heroes became bores.
        Those alchemists
        Who had converted blood into gold
        Had grown elderly.
        But they held a meeting,
        Saying,
            'We think perhaps we ought
            To put up tombs
            Or erect altars
            To those brave lads
            Who were so willingly burnt,
            Or blinded,
            Or maimed,
            Who lost all likeness to a living thing,
            Or were blown to bleeding patches of flesh
            For our sakes.
            It would look well.
            Or we might even educate the children.'

But the richest of these wizards
Coughed gently;
And he said:
   'I have always been to the front
   – In private enterprise –
   I yield in public spirit
   To no man.
   I think yours is a very good idea
   – A capital idea –
   And not too costly . . .
   But it seems to me
   That the cause for which we fought
   Is again endangered.
   What more fitting memorial for the fallen
   Than that their children
   Should fall for the same cause?'
Rushing eagerly into the street,
The kindly old gentlemen cried
To the young:
   'Will you sacrifice
   Through your lethargy
   What your fathers died to gain?
   The world must be made safe for the young!'

         ·   ·   ·

And the children
Went . . .

The poem was correctly quoted. As for the initial *M.* it may have been a shortening of *Miles*, under which name my satires were invariably printed in the *Nation*, during and after the war, until I was quit of the Army. Even then, however, the odd destiny of this poem was not fully accomplished. Some twenty years later, when it had become plain that we were on the verge of the war its lines had predicted, it was published in the columns of the *Nation's* successor and descendant, the *New Statesman and Nation*.

   Nevertheless, at the moment the Next War was still twenty years ahead in time and it seemed clear that men were not such fools as ever to let it occur again. The crowd had reason to be glad. For drunk and sober, for living and dead, for the bodies torn and twisted, and eked out with the flesh of others, the war was over, the first great democratic war, and we were entering the period for which we had fought. Now the years had arrived in which we could prove our worth. For me, as for many others, a period of the most intense activity set in: all the energy repressed for years, or let loose into unsuitable channels, was freed at last. I attempted to make up for the years of which I had been cheated. Within two years I had stood for Parliament, produced a long book of poems, become an editor of a quarterly devoted to modern art and literature, interviewed D'Annunzio at Fiume, contributed innumerable articles on many subjects to the newspapers, and in conjunction with my brother had organized the first large exhibition of modern French pictures held in London since 1914. We had also contrived to arrange – no mean feat of diplomacy where my father was concerned – for Severini to fresco a room at Montegufoni. I had formed, also with my brother's help and advice, a collection of modern pictures, defective in some respects though it was because of our lack of money; I had written art-criticism, and had become a regular contributor of *vers-libres* satires which appeared as leading articles (the only ones of their kind in any paper) to the *Daily Herald*, then edited by George Lansbury, with Siegfried Sassoon as the literary editor. From these I selected two satires, and adding to them a third which had appeared in the *Nation*, made of them a sixpenny book, entitled *The Winstonburg Line*, devoted for the most part to an attack on a great historic personage. This assault was directed against a policy that, by supporting ineffective armed resistance to the new regime in Russia, made of it an enemy, for ever suspicious, and at the same time sealed the fate of those poor weak creatures it had deposed, and who were now held in its clutches. This pamphlet was published by the late Mr Henderson of 'The Bomb Shop' in the Charing Cross Road, an elderly Scottish Socialist in a brown tweed suit, with a flaming red tie, spectacles, and a Trotskyite beard. He was very kind and genial, in spite of a certain cynicism of appearance, as well as enterprising, and under his auspices the volume sold at Albert Hall 'Hands-off-Russia!' meetings and elsewhere in such great numbers – though without profit to myself, for I had neglected to ask for a contract – that for many years it remained my best-known work.

It will be seen from the foregoing passage with what fury I applied myself to life; equally it will appear from what follows that it did not impress everyone, any more than did the similar multiform energies unloosed by my brother. Thus Miss Burton, Robert Ross's faithful housekeeper, who now let rooms in Half Moon Street, confided to her tenant and my friend, Lord Berners, that 'Them two Sitwells 'ave got into a grove'. On another occasion, again, I heard myself described as lazy. Arnold Bennett was present when this judgement was passed, and began to roar with his laughter, with which he was obliged to struggle as with his words, until his whole face grew red, rather as the body of an octopus changes colour, and the upstanding hair of his head, and his moustache, always so bristly, seemed to bristle still more. When he had mastered his attack, and could again get his breath, he remarked, 'That's good! The trouble with Osbert is that he has seven professions, not one, and a life devoted to each.'

Of some of the activities to which he referred, I shall have something to say in their place, or at any rate in that which, for the greater convenience of the writer, I assign to them: but I will refer now to the quarterly, because it was a matter which greatly occupied my mind in November 1918. Elsewhere I have written of how a first meeting with Arnold Bennett had led eventually to my becoming one of the three editors of *Art and Letters*. Arnold had most generously offered to finance my editorship of it: but this in the end had not proved necessary, for Frank Rutter, the owner of the paper, wished to reconstitute it, and of his own accord offered to Herbert Read and myself the joint-editorship of the literary side, while allowing us, moreover, to influence him in the pictorial. It was in connection with the revival of *Art and Letters*, at the old Café Royal, with its smoky acres of painted goddesses and cupids and tarnished gilding, its golden caryatids and garlands, and its filtered, submarine illumination, composed of tobacco smoke, of the flames from chafing dishes and the fumes from food, of the London fog outside and the dim electric light within, that the three prospective editors had luncheon. This was the first time I had met Herbert Read, at the time a very young officer, beginning his career as a poet. I had seldom known then anyone of a finer, more unselfish, personal quality, possessed of so little self-conceit, or with a more true and whole-hearted devotion to those paintings and writings which, though others may think sometimes wrongly, he esteems. Perhaps I liked him so greatly because of the difference in temperament between us; like a Roundhead, he is extravagant only in the lengths to which art-austerity carries him: whereas I am extravagant in all else. He bears a plain distrust towards the sumptuous and the easily pleasing; whether owing to the early struggles which he has so vividly, and often touchingly, described in his autobiography, to his experiences in the war, which had earned him the D.S.O. and the Military Cross, or to his very nature itself, he had already developed a look of premature seriousness. His rather rueful smile was not easy to

command; but when it suddenly broke up the gravity of his face, it
certainly lightened his whole appearance. Making an acquaintance, which
grew into friendship, with him was a source of great pleasure to me at this
time, and subsequently to my brother and sister.

Most of the contributors to *Art and Letters* were friends of mine already:
and the majority of them were young, of my own age, though among
them, too, were numbered men older than myself, such as Matisse
(whom I have never met) or the veteran soldier and writer-painter, Percy
Wyndham Lewis, who had returned lately to civilian – I nearly wrote
civil – life. For many years now, he had been simultaneously at the centre
and on the outskirts of the circus dirt-storm his presence invariably
provoked. In fact, his geniality had long been proverbial. He had been the
leader of the Vorticists, the editor of *Blast*, a celebrated publication of pre-
war days; he had been, in earlier times, a student at the Slade School,
though I do not know quite when.

In those days whereof I write, a Norwegian fishing-cap made apparently
on a pudding-basin model, and I suppose of some kind of cloth (though
the material more suggested brawn) – with a short, fat all-round rim, the
front of which just afforded shade to his eyes – had long ousted his black
sombrero, in the same way that a robust and rather jocose Dutch
convexity had replaced the former melancholy and lean Spanish elegance
of his appearance. A carefully produced sense of mystery, a feeling of
genuine suspiciousness, emanated from him and pervaded all he did,
hovered, even, over the most meagre facts of his daily life in the large,
rather empty studio. But he was covered, too, with bohemian bonhomie,
worn like an ill-fitting suit, and he could be, and often was, a diverting
companion and a brilliant talker.

Every Thursday evening when we were in London, my brother and I
would dine at a restaurant on the first floor of a building in Piccadilly
Circus, in company with certain friends, who as a rule comprised T. S.
Eliot, Herbert Read and Ezra Pound as well as Lewis. Each of us sat, back
to the wall, at a separate table, and this distance helped to make
conversation self-conscious or desultory. Ezra Pound was inclined to
mumble into his red beard, a habit perhaps brought on by his defensive-
ness, the result, in turn, of attacks delivered on him during the years of
his domicile in England. He was particularly a type the English do not
understand or appreciate. As a consequence of his attitude and conduct in
the 1939 war, little good is heard of him today: and it is perhaps as well

to recall that among the considerable number of poems he has written, some of which are apt to seem pretentious – for his scholarship is not sure and he often relies on it overmuch –, there are some very beautiful and original works. His kindness was very great to many young authors and artists, but he seldom allowed it to be suspected by its recipients. And I remember almost the last time I met Yeats, I mentioned that I had seen Pound in Italy, and he remarked, 'Anyone *must* like Ezra, who has seen him feeding the stray cats at Rapallo.' More important than all else, it must be remembered that he discovered Gaudier-Brzeska, and did much to make known the genius of T. S. Eliot; whose work was a source of so much pleasure and excitement to my sister, my brother and myself, both at the time of which I write and through all the years that have passed since. I had already enjoyed the privilege of counting Eliot as a friend for some twelve months. In the autumn of 1917, he and my brother and sister and I were among the poets chosen to read their verse for charity one afternoon at Mrs Colefax's house. The night before, a dinner-party was given for the chairman, Sir Edmund Gosse, the organizers, Madame Vandervelde and Robert Ross, and for those reading. It was then that we saw Eliot for the first time: a most striking being, having peculiarly luminous, light yellow, more than tawny, eyes. His face possessed the width of bony structure of a tigrine face, albeit the nose was prominent, similar, I used to think, to that of a figure on an Aztec carving or bas-relief. Though he was reserved, and had armoured himself behind the fine manners, and the fastidiously courteous manner, that are so particularly his own; though, too, the range and tragic depths of his great poetry were to be read in the very lines of his face; and though, in addition, he must have been exhausted by long hours of uncongenial work, his air, to the contrary, was always lively, gay, even jaunty. His clothes, too, – in London he usually wore check or 'sponge-bag' trousers, and a short black coat – were elegant, and he walked with a cheerful, easy movement.

My work, no less than my inclination, had brought me, in the last two years before the end of the 1914 war, into touch with many of the creative intelligences then at work in England. The Poetry Bookshop constituted, under the most considerate and, indeed, inspired of hosts, Harold Monro, a great meeting-place: for not only was he a friend of all the poets of his own generation, but new work always attracted, though it may sometimes have irritated, him. He was indulgent to all poets. He liked new ideas even when they did not match his own, and in the large, comfortable, panelled rooms above the shop, he would often of an evening bring together whole schools of poets of the most diverse faith, opinions and temperament.

Whatever outbreaks had taken place, one left Harold Monro's parties enlivened, and grateful to him: for he was an excellent host. But though I formed several friendships at the Poetry Bookshop, the chief were with my host and his beautiful wife Alida. When I felt worried I would often go in and interrupt the business of selling books, in order to consult them and gain the benefit of their valuable advice, or sometimes myself to amuse them by describing some ridiculous incident of literary life, until occasionally customers would grow resentful and Harold would be recalled with a jolt to inquiries and prices.

Harold Monro's establishment was, of course, in its scope and personnel, in the volumes of verse and the occasional or regular periodicals it published, as different from other bookshops as it was removed from them in space, for it occupied a medium-sized house of Rowlandsonian aspect – with a pediment bearing in its centre, within an elliptical frame, an appropriate date – in Devonshire Street: a narrow street, running out of Theobald's Road, rather dark, but given over to screaming children, lusty small boys armed with catapults, and to leaping flights of eighteenth-century cats. Nevertheless, albeit the Poetry Bookshop was so unlike in character to the ordinary run, yet there were others in their various ways no less distinctive, and this is perhaps the place to emphasize how large a part bookshops played in the lives of my brother and myself – as, no doubt, of all authors, who, even those most widely apart, share perhaps this one trait in common. Thus the broad length of the Charing Cross Road, sloping downwards from the Palace Theatre to the Hippodrome, especially constituted a favourite saunter in a free hour. Walking down the road, and zigzagging continually across it, you came first to Jaschke's, now Zwemmer's, the spot of all others in which to find new editions of foreign books and the latest quarterlies or monthly magazines devoted to modern art and literature from Paris, Rome, Berlin, Munich, Vienna and the other capitals of intellectual life. A little further along, you reached 'The Bomb Shop', which I have already mentioned, where the proprietor waited, standing near a table at the back, ready to discuss politics sympathetically with any of the eager Fabians, Socialists, Anarchists or Bolshevists who peered myopically through their thick lenses at the books stacked on shelves painted scarlet, or who read the newspaper-cuttings relative to capitalist atrocities that hung pinned up on the wall.

He showed himself equally ready, too, to slang, in his sharp Scottish voice, any intruding Tory who ventured to make a remark of any sort. Books, the political theories and implication of which prevented their being in demand elsewhere, could always be obtained here, for this was the rather combustible political centre of the district. Almost opposite, a little higher up, you could visit one of the esthetic centres of the quarter, as devoid of all political tendencies, except a love of personal freedom, as it was full of ideas: a shop presided over by C. W. Beaumont, now the eminent writer on choreography and dancers, the historian of the ballet in Western Europe and the leading English balletomane. Even in those early days, he was already a friend of my brother's and mine, for we had first met him in 1913.

The scene of so much action was small, consisting of a front room of no great size, a winding iron staircase at the back of it and, behind the shop, the proprietor's diminutive sanctum, lined with books, lit always by electric light, and containing many relics of great dancers, past and present. On a shelf on one wall could be examined a speciality of the shop, a line of flat figures cut out of wood, and painted to represent dancers in such works as *Carnaval*, *Petrouchka*, *L'Oiseau de Feu*. Sitting by the door – and, as for that, so minute was this closet, by everything else, by wall and books and window – Cyril Beaumont, with his closely-cropped, suave, orange head of hair which revealed the shape of the cranium, was always to be found smoking a cigarette and occasionally glancing at the desk before him, a Babel's Tower of books and papers. He would be thinking out new schemes – such as the printing-press below, now celebrated, which he was already then planning – with so much intentness that the entry of a customer would often give him a start. Notwithstanding, once he had grown used to the idea, he was, plainly, pleased to see us, and would tell us of many things, of incidents, for example, that had occurred during the day, and of strange customers, for life in the Charing Cross Road is always full of surprises. Mrs Beaumont would enter, too, to talk or sometimes give us tea.

I was a habitual, too, of bookshops in other parts of London. Mr Shepherd and Mr Gilbey of Hatchard's had been numbered among my friends from the time I was still a boy, for I had dealt there almost as a child, and certainly owed to it disgracefully large bills when I was fifteen or sixteen; but my family had bought caricatures and books from this famous institution ever since it acquired its present name, and if I am not mistaken, before that, in the latter years of the eighteenth century. Other booksellers I grew to know well through other causes: because, when I was joint-editor of *Art and Letters*, I went round personally to canvass the bookshops for orders, and I have always remembered my pride when, after a talk with me, my friend Mr J. G. Wilson, of the august house of Messrs John and Edward Bumpus, doubled the dozen he had asked for; because already, though he was then a stranger to me, and not the friend and guide he became, I knew him to bear the reputation of being one of the shrewdest judges, no less of literature than of the book-market, whom London – or should I write Scotland? – possessed.

As will be seen from the foregoing pages, I had found then very numerous friendships among an unusually large range, I believe, of persons: but I acknowledged no claim except that of the artist. I had shed, too, many inherited friendships, and tried to free myself from the shackles of class: (but voluntarily to unclass oneself is no easy matter!). With the same eagerness with which I sought new intellectual contacts, so I fled from my elderly relatives, near or distant. When I saw them, I tried to elude them, for the war had drained my patience, and they seemed to enclose me in the atmosphere in which I had grown up. I loved to be with my brother and sister: I sought, too, the society of various cousins of my own age: but the rest, the Golden Horde, now stiff-jointed, and unable to hunt more than four days a week, the Fun Brigade, its laughter stifled or wheezy, the Bevy, all of these I endeavoured to shun.

By the end of the following month, December 1918, I had already fought and lost an election, and by the middle of April had succeeded in leaving the Army – ever a difficult thing to effect when troops are no longer wanted in great numbers. After a long period – or at least it seemed long – in a Military Hospital in London, I was given a medical board, and told I could go on leave pending my release from the Service. I suppose I was in the ward for about a month or six weeks. The hospitals everywhere were crowded with the victims of the great plague, Spanish Influenza as it was called. Placed on arrival in the Influenza Ward, I contracted the illness three times, and it affected my heart. But the nurses seemed impervious to mortal ills, chatting brightly through the groans of the dying under the naked electric-light bulbs swaying in an icy draught. Tea was the great uplifter of souls – Indian tea, of course. Even the corpses were called at four in the morning.

Into this artificial paradise created by germ and tea-leaf immersion, visitors were admitted on certain afternoons – it may have been on every afternoon –, and the silent elongated forms of Aldous Huxley and Lytton

Strachey could occasionally be seen drooping round the end of my bed like the allegorical statues of Melancholy and of a rather satyr-like Father Time that mourn sometimes over a departed nobleman on an eighteenth-century tombstone. Lytton's debility prevented him from saying much, but what he did say he uttered in high, personal accents that floated to considerable distances, and the queer reasonableness, the unusual logic of what he said carried conviction.

As for Aldous, Nonchalance, perhaps, more than Melancholy, should have been the image we took him to represent. He was then very young, I think twenty-three. Though often silent for long periods, he would talk for an equal length of time with the utmost fascination. Versed in every modern theory of science, politics, painting, literature and psychology, he was qualified by his disposition to deal in ideas and play with them. Nor would gossip or any matter of the day be beneath his notice: though even these lesser things would be treated as by a philosopher, with detachment and an utter want of prejudice. But he preferred to discourse of more erudite and impersonal scandals, such as the incestuous mating of melons, the elaborate love-making of lepidoptera, or the curious amorous habits of cuttlefish. He would speak with obvious enjoyment, in a voice of great charm, unhurried, clear without being loud, and utterly indifferent to any sensation he was making. Thus the most surprising statement would hover languidly in air heavy with hospital disinfectants. 'From his usual conduct', I remember his announcing on one occasion, 'one must presume that Every Octopus has read Ovid on Love.' Unconscious of the public interest, Aldous would proceed on his conversational way in a genial effort to amuse me. And to the invalids, as they lay there with nothing to do except read an old, torn, tea-stained copy of the *Tatler* or *Punch*, a whole new world was revealed. Many of them understood for the first time what was being said round them, for they were in that passive state where they were bound to listen, so that truth could enter. How greatly I enjoyed this conversation! But soon Aldous would fall to silence again, drooping into a trance-like state of meditation.

These and other distinguished visitors, then, created a stir among the inmates of the ward, for they little resembled the friends of other patients, either in appearance or in their conversation. It was plain that every one was enjoying himself: and this suited nobody. So it was soon rumoured with confidence among nurses and doctors, I was told, that if I remained there much longer, such was the force of my subversive example, 'the whole ward would go Bolo' – then regimental and hospital cant for Bolshevist. In the course of time, however, I got better – or at any rate well enough to be allowed out for walks. My sojourn in the Military Hospital had in no way helped me, and I still felt very ill. Indeed it must have shown in my looks, because when I met Roger Fry one day in the street, he was so much struck by my pallor and thinness that, with his invariable kindness, he said that, plainly, I needed feeding up, and must come and have luncheon with him the next day in his studio in Fitzroy Street. I arrived there accordingly, and found luncheon set out for two amid the confusion, the rags, paints, turpentine, pile of drawings, books, shoes, dead flowers, cracked looking-glasses and shaving-brushes and all the other litter of a painter's room. My generous host, who would certainly never have troubled to provide such delicacies for himself, had ordered oysters: but as I tasted the first, a horrible doubt assailed me. Waveringly, I began:

'What *unusual* oysters these are, Roger! Where did you get them?'

'I'm glad you like them,' he replied, with the spirit and intonation of the quarter. 'They come from a charming, dirty little shop round the corner!'

After that, I somehow curbed my hunger, and hid the oysters under their shells. As he cleared away the plates, he took a tin out of some steaming water, and said,

'And now we will have some *Tripes à la Mode de Caen.*'

Setting my jaw, I ate on.

My illness continued for some weeks after I left hospital: but, all the same, life was returning, flowing into its old channels.

I had not seen Monte Carlo since the visit I had paid it for the day when I was eleven, and it was so long since I had been in a Mediterranean country – for four years at twenty is a long time. Now, in March 1919, the little pleasure-city was balanced between two worlds, past and present. The Russian influence was already dead or dying: but its symptoms remained, the great villas, to be pulled down later or split up. People still talked of the luxury in which the Grand Dukes had lived here, of how, when they went back to Russia, they would send their linen from St Petersburg right across Europe, to be washed at Charvet's, the famous shirt-maker in the Place Vendôme in Paris, and of how, when they could not come to Monte Carlo in the winter, special trains from the Principality and its neighbourhood would bring them carnations and roses for their Muscovite banquets. But today the members of the Imperial family who had frequented Monte Carlo were scattered, many of them in prison or murdered. Only the Grand Duchess Anastasia, whose behaviour had not long ago shaken whole countries – notably Germany, where her daughter had married the Crown Prince – was still to be seen, wearing a flaxen wig, sitting on a stool at the bar of the Hôtel de Paris or in the old Sporting Club. The Grand Duke Dmitri, on the other hand, subsequently for many years to be met in these surroundings, was still near to the horror of Rasputin's death, which he had helped to plot and carry out, and had not yet arrived here. Harry Melville, that stylized cosmopolitan, the singular product of the genteel eighties and epigrammatic nineties, was staying at the Hôtel de Paris, and in the intervals of telling those interminable stories that won him a certain social renown, was working excessively hard at introducing his many acquaintances to one another, especially, I thought – he being perhaps actuated in this by the genuine spice of wit and grain of malice in his nature – those least equipped by disposition and circumstances to make friends. But, if this were so, the great conversationalist, as many had for long deemed him, defeated his own purpose, for, when present, he prevented all others from making their views heard, stifling them under the lightweight *longueurs* of his tortuous and trivial monologues: nevertheless, he was by habit gay, and by conviction he wanted others to enjoy themselves. Among the persons to whom he ceremoniously presented me were the mistresses of several Grand Dukes now lost, captive or massacred in the country which for so long had cherished them. These placid French-women, of middle age, so well conducted, so quietly if fashionably dressed, who still liked to dance a little, had been pastured for almost a generation on meadows of malachite, where the field flowers to be plucked were composed of diamonds, rubies and sapphires: yet now they could hear nothing of the fate of their masters. One must make the best of things, they would sigh to themselves: they were not badly provided for, with enough to leave to their relatives, to give their nephews and nieces a start in life.

Among the few persons to whom Harry Melville introduced me that I wanted to meet – though, even then, not fanatically, for I had never seen her dance, and knew little of her – was Isadora Duncan. She was dividing her time between Nice and the Hôtel de Paris at Monte Carlo. We spoke for a moment one evening. The next morning, early – early, that is to say, for Monte Carlo, about half-past nine, I went out for a walk.

Suddenly, in front of me, down a steep street which seemed crushed between the grey, bulky backs of elephantine hotels, and yet, for all its featurelessness, to bear a resemblance to a complicated stage background, I saw a figure advancing with a peculiar grace of carriage and spring of step, in her hands a bunch of violets and narcissi. It was Isadora Duncan. The beauty of the apparition – she was no longer young – was entirely unpremeditated. Though she had known tragedies, there was an irresistible air of life in her approach, and as she advanced she appeared to bring with her some of the care-free sweetness and innocence of the antique world, of Greece and the heroes in their world of sea and sky and trees. So, she walked down this street, where, under the light, even the dull plaster façades seemed burgeoning with the spring, until she came to the young avenue of pepper trees, the plumy leaves of which made a trembling shadow on the pavement. Now, however, she recognized me, and we walked together. In the next few weeks, I saw a certain amount of her, and came greatly to like her. And I had reason, withal, to be grateful to her, for I had developed a rather severe infection of the eyes from the Riviera dust of those days, and the foreigners' doctor whom I had called in told me that it would be a long business and that he must come to see me twice a day (at a charge of two guineas a visit). But when Isadora Duncan heard this, she said, 'Nonsense. I'll take you to an eye-doctor I know in Nice: only you mustn't mind having to wait for half an hour in a queue.' She motored me over there in the afternoon, to a house in a back street. After I had waited in the queue, I was summoned into the dingy consulting-room, where a fat, bearded little figure peered up at my eyes. After a careful examination, he mixed me some drops, grunted, squeezed two drops into each eye, charged me ten francs, and sent me away. By the next morning, to the other doctor's great consternation, I was cured!

A few weeks later, I accompanied Mrs Greville, a close friend of mine, to Biarritz, and Sacheverell joined us there. He had been in Paris, and for the first time in his life had seen streets lined with galleries full of modern pictures, of an unmistakable style and audacity, full of a beauty that is the reward of adventurousness. I recall his excitement as he told me of the shop windows, showing paintings that could belong to no other age. He had been especially impressed by the work of Picasso and of Modigliani, and had made arrangements for an exhibition in London the following summer by the various modern masters of Paris. He had also purchased a fine drawing by Modigliani, and brought this with him, together with the remains of a very exquisite silver-point drawing of Modigliani and Jeanne Hébuterne in the nude by Herbin.

It was at Biarritz that the news reached me that I was at last a free man, released by the military authorities. Immediately packing my uniform, my gold-braided hat and great grey coat with brass buttons, in a hamper, I launched it on the turbulent waters of the Bay of Biscay. At first the waves kept on bringing it back to me, as if to indicate that a new war was coming, but eventually I could see a speck floating away under the wheeling sea-gulls towards the Spanish coast, where doubtless it was washed up, and its contents taken to be connected with some spy mystery of international ramification – or is it still locked, perhaps, in the frozen Antarctic, or caught and mouldering in the Sargasso Sea? My splendid peace-time scarlet tunic, the fitting for which I have described in *Great Morning*, had been lost – and never to this day has it been found, unless by moths, satiated with their favourite feasts of camphor, naphtha and D.D.T., and now winging their way, as if hunting, through forgotten lofts. The bearskin I still retained in London, and later gave to Mrs Powell – my brother's and my own dear friend, cook and housekeeper from 1917 until her death in 1930 – so that she could have it made into a muff.

Mrs Powell had an ample, beautiful presence, like that of some Venetian with braided hair in a portrait by Titian or by Palma Vecchio, and she resembled, too, one of the mysterious women who sit, always in the background, in the intense shade cast by the fat-leafed trees in a picture by Dosso Dossi. Since she had been given but little education save that which the spectacle of nature afforded her, I often wondered at her generosity of spirit, no less than at her usually fine taste in objects and literature, and her true and subtle understanding of people. In the course of time she became a leading authority on my father's psychological foibles and cunning plans for my improvement, as well as expert in foiling them on my behalf.

Just as, herself an artist in her own profession, she had esthetic feelings, so that in later years she was the only person who warned me not to sell a magnificent picture by Modigliani which hung in my London house, and she could understand also the full scope of the masterpiece Arthur Waley had created in his great translation of Lady Murasaki's novel, *The Tale of Genji*, so, too, she found a pleasure, comparable to the gratification that can be provided by pictures or books, in the material of food, and when she came in would greet one with such words as, 'I saw the loveliest piece of turbot in the King's Road: a really *lovely* thing', or 'They've a *beautiful* saddle of lamb at Bowen's, sir, I wish you'd go and see it'. And the phrases she used, after this style, were perfectly sincere, the meaning to be accepted literally. She loved her art and was expert at it.

It is a singular instance of poetic injustice that the only direct mention of a dinner cooked by her, in the journal of a well-known writer, records a curious culinary solecism, which I remember, and of which it was always impossible to find any explanation. This entry occurs in Arnold Bennett's Journal for 15th June 1919, and I reproduce it here, since it a little gives the impression of life at Swan Walk at that time.

Dined at Osbert Sitwell's. Good dinner. Fish before soup. Present W. H. Davies, Lytton Strachey, Woolf, Nichols, S. Sassoon, Aldous Huxley, Atkin (a very young caricaturist), W. J. Turner and Herbert Read (a very young poet). The faces of Woolf, Atkin and Read were particularly charming in their ingenuousness. Davies, I liked. He had walked all the way from Tottenham Court Road to Swan Walk. A house with much better pictures and bric-à-brac than furniture. In fact there was scarcely any what I call furniture. But lots of very modern pictures of which I liked a number. Bright walls and bright cloths and bright glass everywhere. A fine Rowlandson drawing. Osbert is young. He is already a very good host. I enjoyed this evening . . .

Though fish before soup was an unique abberration, sometimes Mrs Powell's enthusiasm, no less than the inherent profusion so evident in all she did or said, carried with it consequences equally unusual, and always to herself unexpected. Thus when, for example, she purchased cran-berries, in order to make a sauce to accompany a turkey, there might arrive – admittedly because calculation was not her strongest point, but also, no doubt, because this lavishness fitted in with her entire temperament – a whole scarlet mountain of these bitter berries. After the fashion of goats on the hills we would be obliged to feed on them for weeks on end, and even then many would ultimately have to be given away. But her esthetic perception seldom led her astray, she never bought any food that was not perfect in its own fashion, nor did she ever purchase an ugly object for use in the house. Once, however, it is true, I returned from abroad to find that in my absence she had made for me a cushion of black satin, and had embroidered upon it an ice-cream-pink rose, with a few leaves of an arsenical green, and had placed it in the drawing-room: but she quickly saw her mistake, and before I had been home two days, and though I had thanked her most gratefully for her present, and I believe had shown no signs of my real feelings, it was withdrawn. It just disappeared, and was never seen or mentioned again. But to pictures she brought an eye unafraid, observant, receptive, and unaffected by the current trends of respectability and condemnation. Almost the only time I saw traces of her having been annoyed was when a contemporary chat-spinner had contributed the following item to an evening journal: 'The Sitwell brothers have achieved the impossible, and persuaded their cook to work in a kitchen hung with pictures of the modern school.' I came in late the night that this had appeared, and found on the table a piece of paper addressed to myself. On it, scrawled in Mrs Powell's straggling hand, was written:

SIR,
 Please tell the young gentleman who wrote about the kitchen that servants are individuals like other people, and not a separate race. I happen to like modern pictures. – Your obedient servant, E. POWELL.

But she liked old masters too, and, shortly before her death, spent a holiday in Spain, with a friend, Mercedes, a niece of the Grand Penitentiary of Seville. She stayed for a happy day or two in Madrid, to see the El Grecos there, and at Toledo, and then moved to Seville for Holy Week. She appreciated and understood the people and the works of art and the dances and music, even Flamenco, and her power of enjoyment, her generosity, which a little resembled that of a Spanish woman, and the lovely amplitude of her flesh, won her many friends among the Spaniards. I like to think of her, in an embroidered shawl, and wearing a mantilla and high comb, sitting in the garden or the *patio*, full of orange blossom and of violets, so much finer and more scented at Seville than in any other region, taking the air, so delicately fragrant, full of light as a crystal, even in the shade, but when I write of her it is in London again that I see her, going out, finding a pleasure in the frosty morning (for frost seems to carry you back to the country and its life), having to be careful not to slip on the pavement, and so moving at a leisurely, stately pace, with the muff on her arm. At her side would accompany her my enormous tawny mastiff, Semiramis, lifting her paws and prancing with the joy of the morning, and having some of the same steadfast and beautiful attributes.

A most handsome muff, indeed, the bearskin had made, and its adaptation was less wasteful than the way in which I had disposed of the other portions of my uniform. But this casting of it upon the waters had been symbolic and necessary to me. By means of it, I vainly sought to be rid of my own past. Yet, though perhaps less diffident than formerly, I was still doubtful of my own capacities, dissatisfied with them as every young artist should be: (otherwise what causes would impel him towards new experiments?). In particular, therefore, I remember one long walk with Sacheverell by the lion-voiced waves of the Atlantic. Here, though the air was soft in spite of its strength, the ocean had the force of a winter's gale in Scarborough, thundering upon the rocks, beyond the dry, powdery sands into which the feet sank so that walking was difficult: but we went on and on, while Sacheverell rallied my spirits – for I was still ill, weak, and angry after the cruelty and folly of a long war, and distressed, too, by new and more grave difficulties with my father, many of them arising from my own fault, as well as harassed by the slowness with which I worked – and adumbrated a sketch of the future, telling me in what direction I should evolve, and what would be my standing in twenty-five years' time, if my writing developed as he hoped it would. Even then he already exercised the curious power – which, contrary to the usual process, has grown with the passing years – of being able to inspire other artists, whether older or younger than himself, with a new creative force. But the diffidence I have mentioned was not, I believe, the attitude that I adopted in the world: it was a part, only, of my character, and not to be viewed by the public – least of all by that section which had read of, but had not read, my work. I possessed my share of vanity and conceit as well, a quick mind, a quick tongue – which often spoke before I was ready – and I hope a sharp pen. To many, therefore, who were led to adopt this view of me by angry critics, I seemed – for the great public of the newspapers has no sense of background or of category – an arrogant *arriviste*, who indulged in what could, at the most kindly, be considered as automatic writing; who had no sense of the past, no care for tradition or for the future. And in the course of the next ten years, many caricatures of me appeared, and showed me as an elderly dwarf, obviously of middle-eastern origin. This was of considerable help to me, for my unknown enemies were surprised and baffled when they saw me, large, fair and, I suppose, of a very English style.

In the space since the reader parted from me at the end of *Great Morning*, I had, by means of another of those transformations to which my biography has accustomed him, though still an officer in the Brigade of Guards – a Captain now –, become a writer; a poet, more precisely, for up to this point I had attempted nothing else but verse. (Indeed, it was only because a friend of mine, a respected contemporary novelist, stole my stories, and because I resented the manner in which he twisted and spoilt them, and because I felt I could write them better myself, that I took to prose.) It is difficult to assess how high or low I stood then in public estimation, for I have never been aware of it, any more than I have been class-conscious. Moreover, it is still more hard from this distance to appraise exactly the joint position at that time occupied by my brother, my sister and myself: but it is necessary to try and form some idea of the measure of them, in order to set the stage for this act, so that the eye of the reader can properly gauge the scale and perspective. I find it, however, no more easy to focus myself in the mirror of the past than I do now to recognize my likeness presented, and thus, as it were, guaranteed, by the numerous reflections in the looking-glasses that line a tailor's fitting-closet. There sometimes, left alone for a few minutes while the cutter goes to fetch more pins or find a new chalk, I try to turn myself into a stranger, examining intently my personal appearance, to see how I must look to others, and what could at first sight be deduced from my physiognomy, build and characteristics. But this effort to bisect myself, to split my consciousness in two, into looker and looked-at, induces after a few seconds the sensation that a great flood of time has passed by, accompanied by the same degree of physical nausea which afflicted me as a child when I tried to capture and define for myself the idea of eternity. And, moreover, how little knowledge is to be derived from it! Only, perhaps, the consciousness that the middle-aged stranger sitting opposite, facing you, must be related to your family, for his features and general air constitute a variation on a theme well known from earliest years. It is impossible to guess even his profession. In the past two decades I have been mistaken, several times in each of the capacities, for an actor – an actor by trade, I mean, and not for any particular star – and for a Russian Grand Duke. Thus, in instance of the first, I remember, when travelling up by train from Folkestone to London, a lady suddenly leant forward and earnestly asked, 'Excuse me, but *oughtn't* I to *know* your face? . . . Are you on the boards?' As for the second, one incident was rather strange: I was sitting in a cubicle at Trumper's, having my hair cut, when a stranger approached me, bowed, and began to talk very rapidly in Russian. When, having listened for a moment, I said, 'I don't understand Russian, I'm afraid', he regarded me with a look of mingled anger and amusement, and after saying in broken English, 'It may suit you at present, sir, to pretend that', bowed again and walked away. Never once,

I think, has my trade – in spite of a permanent stain of blue or purple ink on the left inner side of the middle finger of my right hand, surely an occupational symptom, if one were needed – been correctly divined. But then, when even I regard my own image, I can see for myself how difficult must be the problem.

Similarly, it is hard to see oneself as one *was*, to see oneself from outside, looking back through the dust of a lifetime. Yet we must, my brother, sister and myself, although we were young, have been already well-known enough for people to turn round and look at us in the street. Indeed, it was hardly a year later, when I first met Ada Leverson, that she had looked up the entry devoted to my family in *Burke's Peerage*, and, upon reading at the end of it the technical description of the Sitwell coat of arms, '*Barry of eight, or and vert, three lions rampant . . . crest, a demi-lion rampant, erased . . .*', had been struck, she told me afterwards, by its prophetic nature, because, she averred, Edith, Sacheverell and myself were clearly the three lions rampant, and my father must be the demi-lion, erased. And yet, if one is to conclude that we were already famous, one of the lions was a boy of only twenty-one at the time. Certainly he – Sacheverell – was the most precocious of us three, for the poems in his first book were written when he was eighteen, and published when he was twenty. And *Southern Baroque Art*, which revealed a whole new world in a new way, and is, in prose as in esthetic criticism, a work of the first order, appeared when he was twenty-five. Incidentally, it was written when he was twenty-two, and I may add, for the comfort of young writers, that I hawked about in person this magnificent and now celebrated book, and saw it refused by several eminent publishers, although when finally published it obtained an immediate and immense success, and set a whole generation chattering of the Baroque and the Rococo. My sister had already published two remarkable books of verse, and a third volume in conjunction with me. She was also editing an annual collection of modern verse, *Wheels*. This yearly anthology, which ran for six years, attracted considerable attention from the critics. One notice, I recall, described the first series as 'conceived in morbid eccentricity, and executed in fierce factitious gloom'; a sentence I have always liked.

As for myself, though, as will emerge, my father was determined to prevent it, as far as lay within his power, I was resolved to devote my future, my whole life, to writing: that was the urging of my left hand – and of my right: for the years stretching ahead now that the war was over seemed so infinite a time, albeit I always greatly worried in a neurasthenic way about my health – an unpleasant trait which in part I may have inherited –, that it seemed there would be time to accomplish everything one could wish. Besides, at that age, one felt oneself to possess enough energy to furnish the whole of the seven careers that Arnold Bennett later declared were mine. And so I allowed my left hand to encourage me to attempt to effect a compromise with politics and with my father: the claims of political careers in so many directions in the past asserted themselves, and gave me enthusiasm: while, in addition, the brutality and stupidity of a long war, and the muzzle that, during its course, it always clamps on the mouth, had left me and many of my contemporaries as eager now to speak our minds as those older than ourselves were determined not to heed us. In consequence, I fought an election at Scarborough, where my father had contested seven elections in the Conservative interest: but I stood in the service of the most unpopular of political faiths at that time – and ever since: as a Liberal, of the old kind, and without being furnished with the approval of Mr Lloyd George. At first I had obtained the promise of Labour support, but later a strong Labour candidate of local origin – a member of the influential Quaker clan, the Rowntrees – came out against me. H. W. Massingham, with his usual courageous directness, urged him in a telegram – though Rowntree was a member of the family that owned the *Nation* – to stand down: for Rowntree was then a man of about seventy, I suppose; I was twenty-five, and Massingham considered that younger men were needed in Parliament, and had a belief in my ability. Indeed, in his telegram, he went so far as to say that he would regard my return for the constituency as a guarantee of peace. The Conservative candidate was Sir Gervase Beckett, the sitting member for the division, and brother to my godfather. The old borough of Scarborough had now been merged in an electoral district which included Whitby, Pickering and the country between.

The Orderly Room, instructed by the War Office, allowed me three weeks' leave in which to conduct my campaign: (but it was difficult to avoid a feeling that Liberals were not popular in high regimental circles; were, indeed, classed with dangerous revolutionaries). Accordingly, I went to live at Wood End, taking with me Richmond Temple, a dynamic and resourceful friend of most modern outlook who had just left the Air Force, and who was capable of acting with great speed and decision, as well as being by nature endowed with the gift of infusing energy into those round him. Immensely I enjoyed being brought into personal contact with the remarkable variety of types to be met with in this area:

solicitors and trawler-owners, Wesleyans and Methodists, Quakers and Catholics, tradesmen and fishermen, dry schoolmasters and sly insurance-agents. Some of the farmers, living in isolated communities on the moors, spoke so broad a tongue that only occasionally one recognized a word such as 'bloody' (pronounced 'bludy') and clung to it as a raft of sense in an unchartable sea of sounds. The ancient houses of Robin Hood's Bay, again, were manned by whole crews of sea-captains, retired. These old men, at the time, owing to the war-boom in shipping, each worth some twenty to fifty thousand pounds, were bulky, bearded, and still spent the day up ladders, which they dwarfed, painting their own houses and making them shipshape. In Scarborough, in the old town, there were the colonies of fishermen and their wives whom I already knew, and on the South Cliff a memorable population of curates. The life that opened for me, though it lasted in this intense form only for so few weeks, forced me to be adaptable; to be at home at high-tea with members of the Low Church and the Sects, at supper with the fishermen, or when reading a play by Bernard Shaw in the inappropriate setting of a circle organized in a drawing-room by a curate (I have always remembered the little cough he gave, when, while he was reading, he came suddenly in one scene upon the word '*damn!*' and substituted for it, in such a jolly voice, the more innocuous '*drat!*'). Accompanying me everywhere, on all occasions, was my mastiff, a huge animal, like a lioness of palest gold, and I have always thought that her appearance, steadfastness and devotion on the platform won me more votes than any speeches that were delivered: for if the English love – or loved – a lord, how much more do they love a dog! The meetings varied in interest; but there would always be present, at the back of the hall, wherever it might be, a thin old gentleman with a bald head, secured by a few thick strands of hair as though it were a runaway football or a melon caught in a fine net. Directly I had finished speaking, he would rise to ask whether I agreed with him in his view that the Pope had been solely and in person responsible for the outbreak of war in 1914, and of the Bolshevik Revolution in 1917. Then, also, there would be sitting in the third or fourth row a lady with white hair, and an expression of sickening kindness, who thought it was cruel to clip or cut trees, and wanted me to promise, if I were returned, to protest to the French Government concerning the gardens, with their pleached alleys, at Versailles, and the pollarded avenues that enclose many French roads. And at every meeting, wherever it might be, I was asked to make sure that the Kaiser was hanged.

During the progress of the campaign, indeed after only the first two days of it had gone, my father decided to come over from Renishaw and stay at Wood End, so as to give me the benefit of his experience and advice. It was the same with everything. If he saw a poem of mine, he would rewrite it, or, if he had found out that I was working on one, he would rush in to 'help' me, always saying in explanation and in the most affable manner possible, 'Two brains, dear boy, are better than one!' As for the election, if only I would listen to him! It was quite simple to get in, he said (though himself had been rejected five times out of seven), if only one knew the *right way* to set about it! When I was preparing a speech, he came continually spinning into my room like a tornado with a few new hints. Last time, he said, I had made a mistake, to his mind, a great mistake! I had been quite wrong to talk about what I believed in. Never on any account mention the War or the League of Nations. People weren't interested. The voters did *not want* to be troubled with problems: they liked facts. Give them tables of interesting figures, and a little comparison between costs of living in the reign of Edward III – or Edward the Confessor, only that might be rather too early for them; as a rule he'd found they weren't very much 'up' in anything before the Conquest – and those of today. A few more figures after that, and then, just as they weren't expecting it, swing sonorously into a peroration, culminating in a passage, if possible, from Byron. For instance, that quatrain from his 'Ode to Napoleon Bonaparte'. It would apply to the Kaiser, and the audience would love it.

> 'Tis done – but yesterday a King!
> And arm'd with Kings to strive –
> And now thou art a nameless thing:
> So abject – yet alive!

Nobody, I could be sure, would vote for a candidate whose speech did not end with a quotation, and the longer the better. He was afraid the one he had given me was a bit short. Horace, however, was out of date. My father would, too, waylay supporters, or possible supporters, and point out where I went wrong, and, worse, would instruct the agent in his business, and the Committee and Chairman in their duties. In short, it soon became impossible to get anything done at all while he was in the house. My mother swept to my rescue. 'Leave it to me, darling!' she said lightly, 'I'll see to it.' She watched the situation closely and when, about ten days before the election, he discovered – as he was often wont to do – a new pain, this time in his back, just at the waist, she allowed it to be seen that, although as a rule she declined to take his illnesses seriously, she regarded this as of the utmost gravity. She advised him to go to bed at once. He allowed himself without much difficulty to be persuaded, for he was frightened by her alarmed expression, and as soon as he was safely ensconced, she sent the footman out to buy a strong mustard plaster, and had it applied to the place. The plaster naturally produced a feeling of heat and a discoloration of the skin. My mother came in, just after, looked at it, and asked:

'Does it burn, George?'

When he admitted that it did, she said:

'Then it can only be shingles! It's a dangerous complaint. You ought to be very careful.'

She told him, further, that it was very lucky for him that she had found it out and that it was better not to call in doctors, for they never understood that kind of thing; the only cure was prolonged rest and to keep warm, and never leave his room. It would be madness to get up. He seemed much flattered at her concern, and followed her advice. Thus though there was absolutely nothing the matter with him, he was kept in bed until the very day of the election, when she hired a Bath-chair for him and sent him to the booth to vote for me. He had by now really begun to look pale and worn, and his air of pathos, together with his vehicle, and his obvious bravery in coming out, straight from his bed, to record a vote for his son, made a most favourable impression and must have gained many waverers to my cause. However, I did not win. When the result of the poll was declared, Sir Gervase Beckett had obtained some twelve thousand votes to my eight thousand, while the Labour Candidate had won a few hundred and had forfeited his deposit.

I nursed the constituency for two or three years afterwards. At first, I had not wanted to do so, because I longed to devote myself entirely to my proper work. Realizing in what direction my inclinations lay, my father at once wrote to me in an opposite sense. (Never be good at *one* thing. Learn to make up your weak points.) On 17th July, 1919, he sent me a letter which included the sentence, 'Whether you do or do not intend to take up political life, you should fight the next election'. Four days later, he was writing more emphatically:

I think you ought to make good your position as a poet, and am all for your having leisure to bring out a volume. But I don't think your life should be sacrificed in this. You have mentioned to me that an ordinary balance sheet is Greek to you, and it is obvious that at present you have no capacity for dealing with business matters. You would do well to try and fit yourself for that and for public-life.

On 5th September he repeated some of the various pieces of advice he had given me at the election. 'As to politics, remember that at the moment people are not interested in them, and (if you are) avoid speaking on directly political subjects. Give them good facts. Be careful of your humour, which is dangerous.' When, however, it became clear that, fortune favouring me, I might win the seat for the Liberals at the next election, he at once became gravely concerned, and advised me to give up politics and turn to farming. I had grown to like the life I had been obliged to lead, and to love the district, and I relinquished my candidature with a sore heart, forced thereto by an attack of poverty from which my father suddenly perceived himself to be suffering. I had made one discovery, however, which helped to ease the wrench: that though it might have been possible for me to win the friendship and confidence of the electors, and though they possessed their full share of northern idealism, yet nobody else in the neighbourhood or elsewhere was in the least curious about the particular new world that I wanted to help build, and had thought to be a chief and abiding interest for English people. In general, the voters contented themselves with repeating either that no new war would come, or else that the inclination to war was so firmly planted in human nature that it would be wrong to try to uproot it: though they were eager, too, that each child should have a better start in life than his father, and thus, through education, be able more easily to assimilate the moral and ethical truths contained in those Sunday papers they patronized. ('At his age, *I* couldn't read the *News of the World*!' a father remarked proudly to me, as he pointed at his son of thirteen.) For the rest, the Germans must pay; the Kaiser must be hanged, and we mustn't be soft with the French, or truckle to the Americans either. Get rid of the Junkers and you would lay the road open for real democrats, people uneducated, and therefore qualified to govern – house-painters, for example! Only those who were of my generation understood the nature of the recent war, or what it meant. It took me a full lustrum to recover from the state of spiritual and mental fury, misery and despair, into which experience of the war in France and observation of the civilians in England had thrown me. I was still thinking about the last war – and the next, which would come inevitably within a generation unless men made a real effort for earth-wide peace –, at a time when most people had entirely forgotten it, except for a compulsory two minutes on recurrent November days.

As I had walked home to Swan Walk, however, on that night of 11th November 1918, though my life, as I then saw it, was to be divided between the creation of beauty and the giving shape to ideas, and an effort to improve conditions of life for the workers and to prevent the recurrence of slaughter which, though it temporarily raised the wages of the fathers, massacred half their sons, it was, nevertheless, and though the election was so imminent, not politics that occupied my mind, but writing; how one was to crystallize, refine, condense to the ultimate point, and yet retain nimbleness, wit, above all, energy. It was impossible, it seemed to me: for very often I doubted with a haunting, mingled rage and despair: though it never occurred to me, oddly, to doubt my political abilities.

Now I must trace my steps back further than the opening of this chapter, and try to explain the course of my personal life, the things that had happened to me and those round me – or, if not explain, at least record them: what had happened, and why, quite apart from the impact of the war, in itself violent as an earthquake, the world to which I was now returning as a civilian was so greatly altered; why the people reassembled round me, by the force of my left hand, were, though in some respects so much intensified in their character as previously outlined, in others so greatly changed; why those I collected about me, by the force of my right hand, were so different in kind, and how, too, in the space of four brief years, during which – quite apart again from family disasters that rent the fabric of private life, as the war of public – I had been obliged to surrender so much time to duties distasteful to me, the claims of my right hand had asserted themselves, and I had been able to substitute new friends, chosen by myself, for many inherited and tedious associations.

CHAPTER TWO

Even when my father and I were on the worst of terms, he would favour me with his views on the war in talk or by letter. Though, if it were in conversation, the discourse must not be allowed to go on for too long, since he possessed in the highest degree the art of squeezing the life out of an hour and of making it drag its weary length along, nevertheless a short ten minutes on a subject impersonal, and not entirely confined to the errors of his children, was always a delight. The nonconformity of the opinions he aired was exhilarating, albeit, of course, he was so far carried away by the consciousness of frustration and futility that must haunt all individuals, as opposed to units, caught in an age of democratic wars, that often plainly he trespassed across the borders of common sense in an opposite direction. Moreover, he was a little prejudiced, by his love of German medieval art, and because the Kaiser, on account of his family pride, his similar interests, and perhaps because, too, he claimed to be an authority on nearly every subject, had always been a hero to him. Indeed, the two men bore some resemblance to each other, physically as well as in mind (they had been born on the same day of the same month, though a year divided them in age, the Kaiser having been born on the 27th of January 1859, my father on the 27th of January 1860), and as they grew older and adopted beards, this likeness emphasized itself: but I do not know if my father was aware of it. Ever since the war broke out, then, he had pursued his own line about its origin and conduct, and had remained firm in his attitude until the end, often becoming the dupe, as he was wont to do, of his own propaganda: (a habit which finally made him liable to the propaganda of others, too; so that after the war he changed, and adopted a new bellicose, contemporary-newspaper attitude towards Germany). Thus, as early as the day after war was declared, he wrote, from Renishaw, to me in London:

I don't blame the Germans. I think the Czar's want of judgement has brought this upon Europe – unless, indeed, it was Russian statecraft to force Germany into war . . . I fancy the Kaiser spoke truly when he said the sword was being forced into his hand . . . However, this reading of the situation will be very unpopular at the present moment.

And, as late as 8th August 1918, before the sudden swelling of the Allied fortunes, he was writing:

. . . We are told we are fighting for the triumph of democracy, which has so managed the affair that we could hardly expect to get at this moment the *status quo ante* terms we could have obtained after the first battle of the Marne. But what we have really been fighting for, of course, during these last three years is the triumph of Bolshevik principles in England – bound to come if war continues much longer. Everyone of sound military judgement knew at the beginning of the war that we could not hope to break completely the military strength of Germany: we could, however, without ruining civilization, as we have already done, have made Germany accept peace without spoils, which would have meant popular reforms in Germany, and have kept Russia alive as a counterpoise. Now we have got to the gambler's last stake, and must go on for a time on the chance that Germany may go Bolshevik first.

'Everyone of sound military judgement' meant, of course, himself, the former Adjutant of the Volunteer Regiment he had commanded, and the omniscient Major Viburne, who had been staying at Renishaw when the war broke out. At any rate, from the first moment my father had begun resolutely, and almost with unction, to prepare for the worst. He threw his gothic imagination into this, as formerly into the more decorative aspects of life, with real abandon: but his frame of mind varied. In some moods he would make notes on the various projects he had not yet had time to undertake – life, he noticed, was beginning to sweep him past at a great pace, though I doubt if he or any victim really could estimate fully the speed of his transit – and meant, directly the war was over, to embark upon: in other moods he would allow his forebodings equally full play. Personal, no less than national, ruin loomed: (that was true, but he did not comprehend the kind or direction). By the 10th of August 1914, not a week after war had broken out, he had already made certain plans for preserving his family and belongings; he wrote from Renishaw:

If the Germans come over, I think of sending your mother and Sachie to the Peak, and shall stay to dismantle Renishaw of tapestry, pictures and china . . . If the Germans don't come over, we may let Wood End for several months, and go into lodgings at Scarborough.

The pattern, however, did not work out quite as he designed it. And the family – that is to say my father and mother, for family and household were both much dispersed – settled itself once more at Wood End in November 1914. Edith had now established herself in a small top-floor flat in Bayswater (in spite of its size, for many years it became a centre in London for painters, musicians, writers, and especially for young poets), Sacheverell was at Eton. Henry Moat had left my father's service in April

1913, this constituting the longest of his absences. On leaving he had applied at the agencies for a job, stating, as one of his qualifications, that he spoke 'five languages including Yorkshire'. Eventually he had found a very well-paid situation, which he thought would suit him, as butler to a rich, retired fur-merchant in Hampstead. He did not, in truth, ever grow used to the ways of the house, and in consequence, as soon as the war broke out, joined the Army Service Corps.

In the house then, Pare alone remained, of all my former friends; Pare to whom day and night were the same and brought nothing but work and sadness. He still was not allowed to visit his mad wife, whose condition had seemed to worsen every year. The servants who had replaced those who had left were foreign: a Swiss footman, a French maid. But Scarborough itself, the town and the people, were unchanged in most respects, though the town was full, and busy with a military activity new to it. I had a good many letters from my mother and father, Miss Lloyd and Major Viburne, and could, as a result, piece together what was happening there. Miss Lloyd, now growing into a very old lady, had taken upon herself – as might have been expected – innumerable labours on behalf of the local young men who had volunteered for service. In addition to these tasks occupying most of the day – cooking, knitting, sending parcels –, she had fallen a little under the spell of the then epidemic spy-mania, which always intoxicates and renders its victims happy by allowing them to exaggerate their own importance in the contemporary scene. And this, in turn, threw upon her more work, for it necessitated her remaining, for at least half an hour at a time, in the bow-window of her drawing-room, with the brass and shagreen telescope she had inherited from her uncle clapped to her eye, searching the wide seascape for the periscopes of German submarines, and the convergence of streets below her house for disguised 'Huns'. And she would, indeed, make amazing discoveries, since half-coconuts and bits of fat were still suspended in the window-box for hungry beaks to peck at, and in consequence she would sometimes, with the aid of the lens, misinterpret the distance of the scurry of wings immediately below, and read instead of it a distant naval engagement, which would leave her in a temporary vain agony of disquiet. Nor did her duties terminate with the day, for often at two or three in the morning she would creep to the window to look for Germans signalling out to sea, giving their chiefs news of the latest Rectory Sale of Work or Scout Jamboree.

To Major Viburne, too, now well over eighty years of age, the war had brought new interests, new life. While it was true that he had, together with all the other old gentlemen in clubs, long foreseen the struggle coming, it was equally not to be denied that his own military experience had been limited. Long ago, I had been present in the pantry at Renishaw when a footman who had been startled during dinner by Major Viburne's tales of his own martial prowess had asked Henry:

'Excuse me, Mr Moat, sir, but in what war did the Major see service?'

Henry had replied, to the young man's complete satisfaction:

'My lad, the old boy served right through the Canteen Campaign, from start to finish!'

And so it was that now ancient memories stirred in him, memories of other wars – of which he had read in other newspapers. It can be imagined how frequent and how free were the advice and exhortations he lavished upon the somnolent forms of fellow-elders in the Gentlemen's Club; sometimes, again, one of them would rouse himself and similarly address the Major, when he, too, was asleep in his armchair, dreaming of the days when he had been Captain Commandant of Scarborough Castle. When awake, or not talking, he was reading *Caesar's Commentaries* again, which somehow made the present war seem so much more vivid.

My mother's troubles appeared at this moment to have taken a turn for the better, even to have dispersed. First of all my cousin, Irene Denison, had on her own initiative and without the advice of her parents or mine made a most gallant effort, at a sacrifice of part of her own fortune, to save my mother before it should prove too late. Next, in November my mother went up to London for a few days, for a lawsuit that Messrs Lewis & Lewis were conducting on her behalf against Julian Field. She won it, was triumphantly vindicated and the action exposed his dealings. Yet she was still unhappy and agitated – though perhaps agitated is not the correct word, for in the day-time she averted her mind from her troubles, which returned to haunt her only at night.

My father was immersed in his usual interests, and on 8th December wrote to me from Scarborough:

I don't think I told you I am turning the Ladies Room at the Renishaw Park Golf Club into a locker-room. It will be so much better for them to have as a sitting-room the cottage beyond – which will open into the passage. This will make a splendid room, two storeys of windows, a coved plaster roof and a south aspect. I think I shall put up in it the 16th century Italian marble chimney-piece, as it may as well be there till it is wanted elsewhere, as lying about . . . I have been busy getting copies of wills for the family history. Mary Revell, who was a

Sitwell, in 1670, John Milward, who was Francis Sitwell's brother-in-law, in 1679, Hercules Clay, who was Ann Sitwell's grandfather, in 1685; and Mrs Kent, who was her stepmother, in 1687 . . . Mrs Revell had a table-carpet in her bedroom, but no floor-carpet. John Milward leaves his hawks and spaniels to one friend, except his setter-dog, Lusty, whom he leaves to another . . . I have been working, too, at old costume. The modern coat was only invented about 1670–75: before that it was doublet, waistcoat and breeches. In this way, I think I have been able to date the picture of old Derby . . .

So things were going, until the morning of my last day in England before I left for the Front – the same morning that Germans came over the North Sea and chose to bombard Scarborough!

The noise of the great naval guns thumping and crashing through the mist, which magnified the sound, was enormous. It was about 8.15 a.m., my father was just dressing, and lost no time in finishing the process and getting downstairs. A piece of shell went through the front door, pierced a wooden pillar (part of the elaborate Edwardian decoration he had installed) and then buried itself in the smaller hall, while many fragments penetrated into the house. The Swiss footman went upstairs and watched the attack from the roof. My mother, who was in bed when the bombardment took place, refused to move: but half an hour later, after it had just stopped, she rose, dressed, and, in order to see me before I left England the next morning, caught a train, unusually crowded, to London. Her maid supervised the luggage, but my mother personally took charge of a rather heavy piece of shell, which she was anxious to give me as a mascot. She entered my sister's flat, where I was having tea, and pressed her offering into my hands, saying:

'Here you are, darling! I've brought it with me specially, for you to take to France. I'm sure it'll bring you luck!'

My father had taken refuge, with the rest of the household, except my mother and the footman, in the cellar; though, as will appear in a moment, he had found a more dignified name for it. In those days he still possessed no motor, and so when, as soon as the German ships had sheered back into the grey vapour that separated our two countries, he emerged into daylight again – but cautiously, since he feared that the retreat might be a ruse; the object of a new raid, if it occurred, being in his opinion the determination of the enemy fleet to secure himself as a hostage –, he sent immediately for his medical attendant of many years' standing. When the doctor entered the room, my father said to him, without preface:

'Dr Mallard, if the Germans come back, I shall need your motor to drive me to York.'

'But what will happen if Mrs Mallard wants it, Sir George?' the poor man asked despairingly.

'I'm afraid I really can't help that!' my father snapped at him, and allowed a look to show plainly his disgust at other people's selfishness.

Meanwhile his power of fantasy had set itself to work on another plan for the moment when the emergency he foresaw should arise: an alternative of which he often told me in later years in example of the heroic lengths to which he would have gone and could go. A little way beneath the western, tall, brown-brick wall of our garden, in the depths of the Valley, as it was called, a wooded public pleasance, with a road running through it, lay a small but rather elongated shallow pool, carrying in its centre a diminutive island where elegiac trees drooped over the water. In the middle of this rose a rustic thatched hut of the sixties, fashioned of wood that still retained in places its bark as a shelter for earwigs, while the outside – and inside – of the cabin was much discoloured by bird-droppings: for it was the home and haunt of many water birds. Hither my father proposed to wade or swim, or, who knows, perhaps proceed by some private method of funambulation, should he be surprised in Scarborough by the returning Germans and unable to make a get-away in Dr Mallard's motor. In this idyllic retreat, he had determined to hide during the Captivity, residing there, a Wild Man of the Weeping Willows, living among – and I suppose upon – the ducks and other decorative fowl to which in more peaceful times it was abandoned.

'I should have been quite happy, too,' he would comment at the end of a disclosure of his plans in after years, 'with a few books down from time to time from the London Library.' And then he would add the familiar reproof, '*I* never *allow* myself to feel bored!'

Of this Red Indian's dream of his, he did not inform me at once by letter. (It might be dangerous to me as well; the Germans were sure to steam open his letters, and by that means would find out that I had gone abroad): but he told Sacheverell of it during the Christmas holidays. Nor did he allow his fears to prevent him from writing to me of other things: for when I reported to the Adjutant in the front-line trenches, only two days after the bombardment of Scarborough, I was at once handed a letter from my father! I read it later, by myself, and was startled out of the dull melancholy that had settled on me when I arrived – at the first sight of the flying fountains of dead earth, the broken trees and mud, and at the first sounds, growing ever more ominous as one drew nearer to the bumping and metallic roaring which resembled a clash of comets – by the sheer fun of its contents.

WOOD END, SCARBOROUGH
16th December 1914

MY DEAREST OSBERT,

As I fear a line sent to Chelsea Barracks may not reach you before you leave tomorrow, I write to you, care of your regiment, B.E.F. so that you may find a letter from me waiting for you when you arrive in the trenches. But I had wanted if possible to give you a word of advice before you left. Though you will not, of course, have to encounter anywhere abroad the same weight of gunfire that your mother and I had to face here – it has been my contention for many years that there were no guns in the world to compare for weight and range with the great German naval guns, and that our own do not come anywhere near them – yet my experience may be useful to you. Directly you hear the first shell, retire, as I did, to the Undercroft, and remain there quietly until all firing has ceased. Even then, a bombardment, especially as one grows older, is a strain upon the nervous system – but the best remedy for that, as always, is to keep warm and have plenty of plain, nourishing food at frequent but regular intervals. And, of course, plenty of rest. I find a nap in the afternoon most helpful, if not unduly prolonged, and I advise you to try it whenever possible.

— Ever your loving father, GEORGE R. SITWELL

Undercroft was a word new to me, and it was some time before I discovered with what trisyllabic majesty the simple word cellar had clothed itself.

So bored was I with life in France and Flanders and, as I have before had reason to stress, so incompetent in many ways as an officer, that I seldom or never knew where I was, in relation, not to the precise locality, but to the whole map. One or two places, like Ypres, possessed their own fame and history whether in war or peace; the rest was 'the Front', a monochromatic geographical entity of its own, floating, cloudlike, across a continent. I felt utterly lost in a world in which all my old friends, with whom I associated regimental life, were dead, and already remembered here by but a few: while my new friends, of a few months' standing, had not yet been passed out from Chelsea Barracks. The very excess of bleak boredom and grey discomfort – albeit that seems an inadequate description for so entire and black a universe of physical sensation, of wet and cold and stench and mud – afforded me a sort of careless courage. Yet it was ever with dismay that I would hear, as alas I often did, a brother-officer remark, no doubt with a kindred sentiment in his heart,

'The Boches won't get me now! I've been out here too long!'

Whether with them it was that many dangers survived had induced a feeling of false security, I do not know, or what the chief cause responsible for it may have been, yet always I noticed that the man who said it would be dead within the space of a few days, or more often of hours. The chance, when one reasoned, of continued existence in this world after the war, seemed as remote as that of life after death to an unbeliever. (My father, however, wrote to me on this matter, and treated it on a basis of computation or assessment. It would be a serious matter, losing an elder son, even if he were not altogether the success he ought to be; and so, it appeared, he had been making inquiries. '*According to the Insurance Companies it is eleven to one against an officer being killed in a* YEAR'*s fighting with the Germans, so I hope we may get you back safe and sound.*'

Even in the depths of spirit, however, to which the monotony of the life reduced me, I did not hate the routine here as I had hated it in my private school. I had known worse. At least there were no masters, matrons, or compulsory games. The discomfort was, at times, perhaps a little greater, the food, though tinned, perhaps a little more palatable.

Though my friends were dead, and the sadness of this lay over me – albeit the abruptness of it still rendered it difficult to grasp –, yet, since I was young, new relationships established themselves. And in the Regiment, I found that the old tolerance, which had always so greatly surprised me, still flourished oddly in this harsh soil. I must again emphasize – for it cannot be exaggerated – the degree to which, voluntarily and involuntarily, I continually showed myself to be of an unmilitary and even anti-militarist disposition. Not only, as I have said, did I hardly know *where*, precisely, I was, but so deeply bored was I at this period that, although in some directions my memory is very retentive, an inner censor – perhaps the same who censors nightmares after waking – stepped in to delete certain facts from the record. Thus I am now quite unable to recall with what battalions I saw service in France and Flanders, though I can still, on the other hand, quite well recall with what battalions I served in England a year or two earlier. Again, at moments driven desperate by the placid acceptances of conventional minds, I quite often said, in my own way, what I thought. I remember, for example, one very wet day, when out for a route-march during a week's break from the routine of trenches and billets in farms, covering my uniform with copies of *The Times*. These were soon turned by the weather into a very sodden, dirty grey mess, and in consequence I arrived at the end of the day looking very disreputable. When the Commanding Officer inquired what it meant, I replied,

'You seem to forget, sir, that it's very wet and I've had a long walk.'

This unmilitary reply would have infuriated many commanders, less sure of themselves and of the discipline of their officers and men: here it raised no flicker of rage. So that, in the sense of companionship, I was happy enough, and it was only when – this occurred once or twice the following year – all the officers of the Battalion or Battalions were gathered together for a dinner that I found myself ill at ease, disliking then, as now, and as always, the manner in which the coalescent group-soul released from a herd manifests itself. At some of these occasions, I would see the very young, slight figure of the Prince of Wales, then an officer in the Grenadiers, with his extreme charm, his melancholy smile and angry eyes, trying like myself, I suspect, to pretend he was enjoying himself.

For the rest, in the trenches one day was sad, cold and hopeless as the next. Sleep was the greatest prop and happiness known to any of us, I believe. To me assuredly, whether dreamless or the reverse, it was, during this period, peculiarly happy. Though often in ordinary life of a melancholy or terrifying nature, my dreams were now peaceful and even radiant in feeling, imbued with the happiest imagining, and this certainly affords an inner psychical strength. Sometimes I have thought my subconscious mind to be lazy in the background it presents. Seldom, indeed, does it carry me to interesting places, such as when once it transported me for the night to the immense halls and galleries of the palace of King Nebuchadnezzar, and allowed me to look at the flat domes and colonnades, and towers stepped like Aztec pyramids, to examine at my leisure the detail of the great bas-reliefs in porphyry and basalt which adorned its walls, so sheer and lofty, and to watch the procession of men with blue-black beards, hook noses, and yellow skins hurrying through corridors to attend their royal but graminivorous master. For that hour's entertainment, a whole system of architecture had been improvised, a lost civilization revived. But this was very rare: as a rule I am rationed in this other life, and usually am merely given distorted variations of the scenes most familiar to me, three in number like the crows'-foot alleys in perspective of the Renaissance and seventeenth-century stage: Renishaw awry in a vast, flawless summer day or night, with its enormous rooms in the wrong order, or on occasion a new wing, suddenly revealed to me by my father – something he had been keeping secret –, but always beautiful, though with an atmosphere of curious suspense; or the rolling winter seas of Scarborough, dashing gigantic wings to batter falling cliffs, under the pounce and glitter of bitter-beaked seagulls materializing out of a misty nothingness of white foam and yellow sky, while a voice cries slyly in the hollows under the lull, '*Rags and Bones! Rags and Bones!*'; or London, with a prim brown-brick street, very neat and orderly, with its shops and railings. But now, in the trenches, I was granted compensatory dreams, being allowed in them to see the people I wanted to see, and with whom I wanted – or thought I wanted – to spend my life. The background was of no importance: and though one of the chief deprivations I felt in these years was my enforced absence from Renishaw – which I hardly saw during the years of war, never in the summer, and only for more than a day or two when ill or at a moment of very severe personal distress – I seldom dreamt of it, or of Italy, which again would have saddened me when I awoke by the comparison the present would have offered with the past. The dreams of which I tell left, on the contrary, no after-taste. They were, as I have said, concerned with people more than places, and the degree of psychological observation latent, I suppose, in every novelist, whether practising or still in chrysalis, gave a peculiar sharpness to their doings and sayings: they behaved in this sharp, swift world reflected from their own behaviour, in a fashion that was more essentially typical of themselves than themselves were in everyday life! Or, very often, sleep was dreamless, came on with the force and suddenness of a knock-out, and in one instance, after a particularly long and trying period in the trenches, though by nature a reluctant and nervous sleeper, I slumbered for eighteen hours, only waking at six in the evening.

Next to sleep, but certainly inferior to it as a pleasure, came reading. As a pessimist, and in an effort to make this existence seem more tolerable, in general I avoided works of a cheerful tendency, and once more abandoned myself to the genius of Dostoievsky. To have been Raskolnikov or Mitya Karamazov would constitute a worse destiny than to lead this life until you were killed – lead this life, so dull in spite of its risk, and with the prospect of the humiliation and sadness that threatened us at home continually under the mind. In this way, heroic tragedy proved a comfort. When after reading *The Brothers Karamazov*, *Crime and Punishment* and *The Idiot*, *King Lear* or *Othello*, I needed a change of feeling, I turned to the novels of Dickens again: for they were connected with the life of a great city, and I felt a craving for metropolitan interests. For so long as I read, the white winter vapours of Flanders and of France – mists so dull and lifeless, except to our eyes when we were on duty, for then every shape stirred stealthily, and the whole static world assumed movement at a sound – were exchanged for the glorious golden fogs (or such they now seemed to me) of my native city, and I exulted accordingly in the creative force of this great novelist, so dear to me and so familiar from boyhood. With what certainty he would have comprehended and rendered a night of duty: rats and mud, and the particular horror they hold for human beings, he already understood (think of the opening of *Our Mutual Friend* on the waters of the Pool of London!), and he would at once have captured the feeling of these coffin-like ditches, where death brooded in the air after the same manner that some fatal disease, such as malaria, hangs suspended, but ever-present, over the deserted marshlands of Italy and Greece. I had always, in so far as I had considered the question, regarded myself as being of both an imaginative and an apprehensive turn of mind: but here the suddenness of death and its sadness, the sense, above all, of waste, transcended any preconceived idea.

The second night after my arrival, I was sent out on duty just behind the line, lightly held at this point, though the enemy was within a hundred yards. Before me in the white, misty evening, pervaded by vague moonlight, could be seen just across our trenches the narrow territory of No-Man's-Land; to which the futures of all of us were restricted. Among plantations of barbed wire – whole copses, waiting to be felled one day, to be twisted into crowns of thorns – lay mounds of rags, broken trees, rusty helmets and the skeletons of animals. This must be, I thought, under my mind, the promised land – promised by that figure with bearded face and battered top-hat from whose discoloured lips I had in earliest infancy learnt my first words, 'Rags and Bones! Rags and Bones!', as he slunk along beneath the nursery window. Suddenly the fabric of the whole wide night was ripped by a shot, and I had time to see, before he fell, a black flower or star expand upon the temple of a boy of twenty, who was within touching distance of me. There was a gush of blood, black in the greyness, from his mouth; he groaned, stirred, shuddered, and was dead. I do not think I felt frightened, for the blow came from nowhere, an act of God, but I *was* sick with sorrow, with a sense of pathos: he had been in my platoon at Chelsea Barracks. I do not recall to what profession he had formerly belonged – by his appearance he might well have been a garden boy until lately: but I still recall his rustic grace, honest and young, and the burr in his voice when he spoke, like a young, gentle animal that has learned to express simple thoughts. (Who else living remembers him today, I wonder?) It was upon this night that a hatred of moonlight took possession of my mind, and it required a whole subsequent decade of peaceful years to free me of it: for several thousands of nights, every tree or bush that showed in the whiteness concealed the shape of a sniper, of the death which was every man's future, all our future.

Even here, in Flanders, cut off though we were by distance and by war, and albeit I was leading an existence the precise opposite of any that a young man could wish and, as a result, my mind was occupied with my own worries and troubles, nevertheless I still could not fail to distinguish the continuance of the two main threads woven into the web of my life at home by the Fates. For those who lived there now the shadow had grown to such dimensions that it stretched across the whole day as well as night. It filled the horizon for all these months. And just as pathos and ominousness had now hardened into something deeper, and more actual, so the humour of the situations had cheapened day by day into less and less realistic farce. To give a little the atmosphere of my home at this time, I will quote a letter from my brother, written from Renishaw at the beginning of the war, when he was aged sixteen.

This letter may bore you, but remember I am writing from the wilds of Derbyshire, surrounded by lunatics and octogenarians. Mother is at present carrying on a quarrel with almost every one of her acquaintance. And Father has been telling me about his system of taking the soap out of the eyes when washing. 'It really took me twenty years to discover it!' And it seemed like twenty to tell it! I have to pay for my own postage stamps, as he is too poor owing to the war. However, he is still going on with Barber's Garden, getting further plans from Mallows and altering the Golf Club. He now makes me walk about and carry a book on my head for twenty minutes a day. It's too infuriating, but exactly like him, isn't it? . . . That old ninny Aunt Florence has just been in to say how dreadful it is to curse one's parents. Even Turks and Mohammedans don't do that! . . .

Only one good thing for me, I believe, had come out of the interplaying forces at work in my home life: they had developed to the highest degree a sense of mutual confidence and interdependence among my brother, my sister and myself, from earliest years devoted to one another. We formed a closed corporation, whose other members wrote to me while I was at the war with the greatest regularity, so that I knew from them exactly what was happening, and how it was happening. I think no brother could have two more sensitive and percipient correspondents.

My mother also wrote at frequent intervals: as did my father, and for the most part kindly. Yet though primogeniture luckily afforded me my own *ex-officio* position in the universe, and though undoubtedly he worried about me, yet in a letter written to me at this time he announced that, finding himself compelled to reduce expenditure, and because, as he said, I was in the trenches and therefore could have no need of money, he had decided as a measure of economy to cut off my allowance. He was as good as his word, and proceeded to retrench in his favourite and familiar style. I did not know where to turn for money, but at the same time a certain ludicrous side to it, and perhaps a love of adventure, forbade me to take the matter too seriously – although I was resolved to give my father a fright and regain my allowance. Moreover, I had already learnt a lesson: always, in any disagreement with my father, to be inventive, to view the question in dispute from an altogether novel angle, and whenever possible to indulge in a high degree of fantasy. (This was a rule by which, more and more, in the coming years I guided my dealings with him, and it proved invaluable by its results.) Now a year or two before the war my father had started to farm in a small way, and had latterly expanded the scope of his operations, into which he had thrown himself with a kind of fury. Before long the area had amounted to no less than two thousand acres, and he had founded a company, of which, since some of the land it worked belonged to me, I had been made a director. He started, of course, with no knowledge of agriculture, but he was keen on fault-finding. I was away, and in the circumstances this new occupation afforded him the fullest outlet for it. He drove about, balanced on his British Museum air-cushion in a pony cart – a tub, smartly painted in green and yellow, and drawn by a skewbald pony –, criticizing to the top of his bent. Fortunately, Maynard Hollingworth, who made the plans and carried them out, was an expert in farming; and on his advice my father had particularly specialized in pigs and potatoes. I have mentioned that recently, where certain ideas, not political or esthetic, were concerned, he had rather unexpectedly shown himself liable to be very easily influenced by the press. Thus, in the years immediately preceding 1914, he had become an enthusiastic advocate of Standard Bread and paper-bag cookery, when those two objects or ideals were written up in rival daily papers. It happened that lately a correspondence had been published in *The Times*, concerning the possible benefits to be derived from reviving the medieval habit of payment in kind. My father had thoroughly enjoyed, and pondered on, these letters, and had determined that his approval of ancient ways should find a practical application. He had returned to Renishaw in January 1915, and late that month or early in February had sent a letter to my brother's housemaster at Eton, to intimate that, having been particularly hard hit by the war, he could not afford to pay the usual fees at the end of the term in money, but instead would deliver to their value pigs and potatoes. The housemaster was, it can be imagined, perturbed by the novelty of the suggestion and when the story transpired it created much interest. Sacheverell, whose life had been made by no whit easier as a result, appeared far from enthusiastic about the scheme when he wrote to tell me of it. His letter reached me at the Front, at about the same time as that from my father in which he had cut off my allowance, and from this conjunction an idea came to me. I was shortly due to proceed on leave and, after all, I remembered, I was a director of the Sitwell Farming Company!

I wrote to my father in the following terms, and without showing any sign of resentment.

MY DEAREST FATHER,

Thank you for your letter. I well understand your present position forces you to make economies, because I am obliged to do the same. I come home on leave in about a fortnight, and as I have no allowance now, I have been able to arrange, I am glad to say, with the guard on the leave-train to accept potatoes instead of my fare. – Ever your loving son, OSBERT.

In his reply to me, my father did not even permit himself to allude to the subject of my letter, and for a while I feared it had fallen flat: but not many more days had passed before, without a word of explanation, my allowance was restored in full.

On my return I learned more, and that my ruse had been successful: for Maynard Hollingworth described to me the following scene.

'One day Sir George rushed up to the office, waving a letter in his hand and shouting, "*What does the boy mean? They're not* HIS *potatoes: they're* MY *potatoes!*"

'I said to him, "*If you'd let me see the letter, Sir George, perhaps I might be able to help*". . . . He gave it me and after reading it, I said, "*It's nothing, Sir George; it's Mr Osbert's chaff!*" But he tore it out of my hand, and dashed out of the room, crying, "*Oh no, it's not.* HE *would do it!*"'

In the end it had only been by stressing the improbability of there being guards on trains near the fighting, and the difficulties I should undoubtedly encounter in securing the transport requisite for moving the crop from Renishaw to the Front, that Hollingworth had been able to allay, though not to dispel, my father's fears.

My leave was still some weeks – it seemed many weeks – ahead. At last the date was fixed, for March: at last intervening space dwindled until I reached St Omer, where I spent the night; at last Boulogne, and again England. But this period of a few days for which I had so greatly longed was destined to be one of profound misery. It was now that the shadow completed the process of taking substance to itself, and strode, a giant black figure, across our lives. I came back fresh to the situation, having had other things to think of: nor was I in any way prepared for what followed. Sacheverell being still at Eton, there was no-one in whom to confide, or with whom to discuss the likely outcome of the present lawsuit, a Crown Prosecution, and the climax of many other cases almost equally pitiful and degrading: no-one, that is to say, except my sister and Helen Rootham, both of them in the same predicament as I, for my father would never accept their advice, any more than he would take my own. Indeed, to be of help in any practical way was impossible. My mother's careless, impulsive nature, her total ignorance of even the most simple fact of arithmetic, my father's habit of refusing to see, when the using of his eyes might be painful or annoying, and his obstinate pride, proved too strong in their combination.

The London house he had taken at this time seemed to Edith and me to be full of a highly coloured, evil levity of spirit, so strong as almost to have a presence and become a haunting. When I arrived from Flanders, I was put in a bedroom on the ground floor, but entirely cut off from the rest of the house. It was dark and inconvenient, and I slept badly in it. I asked if I could be moved. My father, however, had read in the papers that the troops in the trenches were infested with lice, and he now explained to me that he had selected a room far away on purpose, in case I was acting as host to a pack of these vermin, since the distance made it less likely that they would attack him – for if they did, it might, he pointed out, entail very serious consequences! When I became angry, for personal cleanliness has always been something of an obsession with me, and protested that if thus afflicted I should not go to stay in any house and that it was a slur on me to suggest it, he fluttered his hand at me condescendingly, and replied, 'Not at all, my dear boy. It's no disgrace.

Any primitive form of life is most interesting!' As I was not a naturalist, this did not calm me. Though inwardly no doubt greatly perturbed by the turn affairs were taking, he behaved as though nothing untoward were afoot, and enlivened on several occasions luncheons and dinners of the most fearful family anguish by discoursing on *The History of the Fork*. That subject, which he had long had 'up his sleeve', always remained dear to his heart. It was impossible to make him talk of anything else, though at times I thought I could see in his eyes a look of perplexity and distress: but he quickly hid it. Nor was there any old friend in the house with whom to discuss matters. Stephen Pare alone remained of the servants among whom I had grown up, and though I could have perfectly well confided in him, he would not have wished it. He was too old, though he was only fifty, too sad, too blind to read the newspapers, too much shaken by the facts, usually reaching him in a confused form from other people, to say anything except, gently, 'Poor Lady!', as he polished the silver. It was singular that the final, appalling outcome – so utterly unforeseen by everyone, it seemed, but my sister and myself, who had long entertained doubts about the result of the suits, so absolutely unexpected by the victim herself until the very night before, when I sat up with her, trying to afford her some comfort, until three in the morning – affected Mrs Pare, who had been away from us nearly all my life (for I can only just remember her), more strongly than, outwardly, it influenced anyone else. The news of it somehow had filtered through to her poor mad brain the same night, and she contrived, because of her devotion to my mother and father, whose service she had entered when they had just been married, to break out of the asylum in which she had been for so long confined. From Lutterworth, she telegraphed at 9.41 the next morning to Turnbull, the agent and old family friend. The thirty-years-old form lies before me now, as I write. At the bottom is noted in pencil in Turnbull's hand, 'This must be from poor Mrs Pare. I did not reply, not knowing her address.' The message runs:

Turnbull. Sandybrook Hall Ashbourne Derbyshire. Could I go instead it must be cruel I promised his mother to stay with them can you help me Pare.

It was no wonder that Turnbull did not know her address, for she had, by the time he received her telegram, begun to tramp to London, through the howling winds and the rains of March. At night she slept on the gravestones in village churchyards. Eventually she was captured in London and taken back to her institution. But to me, the only radiance shed on those dark days is to be found, firstly in the courage and dignity shown by my mother, and secondly in the thought of this mad old woman driven to such lengths by a heart stronger than the brain, by her feelings of compassion and her sense of duty.

I left London, after going to see my mother, and then joined my father and Edith at Renishaw. Never have I known such storms as those which now battered the old house, until it seemed alone on its tableland in a world of fury. The tree-tops bent under gale after gale that, sweeping and tumbling over the moors, seemed to bring air from the distant battering seas, and the very smell of the waves could be detected. The wind moaned round the corners, and rattled the windows. It carried with it voices from a mile away – sometimes, I thought, from further. It swirled up the Chesterfield Approach, under the sombre trees, clumps of holly, box and yew, and brought with it to me an almost forgotten voice of prophecy, spoken, too, in an evil wind, but on a hot and sullen afternoon. In the day-time the gale seemed to dwarf the human figures, and thus bring relief. But almost I preferred the whistlings and scratchings to the sudden silences of the night, to its darkest, calmest caves, when your ears so nearly caught the sound of a sigh, or a footstep, or some commotion, faint now through centuries of repetition. But not only the distant past had its ghosts in these days and nights: the bones of many old pleasures came to life, the remembered laughter that surged up from the marble pavement in the garden, and floated in at my bedroom window when I was a child, and the strong smell of many flowers when the world was young.

Of our private calamity I will write no more, and but little further of the public catastrophe, the First German War. I wish to concern my reader with life, and not with death. The skeletons have jerked themselves for a moment out of their cupboards: let them never again *with my consent* be disturbed; let them now then return to darkness behind bolted doors, there to moulder until the ultimate trumpets call to universal judgement.

I did not return at once to the fighting, but was in London for some months – during which time, in May, my grandmother Londesborough died.

The second period of my service at the Front was from July 1915 until April 1916. The battalion to which I was posted trained for some weeks in Picardy, and then was used as a reserve battalion for the Battle of Loos. Never shall I forget the day before the attack, which was launched on a Monday. In the morning we had to attend Morning Service, with a long, meandering sermon on the immortality of the soul; and, after luncheon, while an air of deathly imported English Sunday still darkened the air, were given an address by an enthusiastic General, who explained how secret was our plan ('The Germans haven't begun to get an idea of it!'), and how novel it would seem to the enemy. (Taken together, the talks of morning and afternoon were like lectures delivered, surely, in the wrong order, on effect and cause.) Later in the day I talked to my old friend from Eton days, Peter Lycett Green, who had joined the Grenadiers soon after the outbreak of war, had lately been sent to France and now bicycled over to see me. We sat on a stone wall under some poplar trees and discussed the prospect, as we had done so often in the past, and I told him how profoundly the two talks, lay and ecclesiastical, had discouraged me. When next I saw my old friend, a month or two later, his leg had been amputated, for he had been wounded within a few hours of our conversation on that Sunday afternoon in September. But time was difficult to reckon, for each twenty-four hours seemed to contain a century. To my last moment, I shall consider the hours from sunrise to long past sunset that the battalion spent on the road, blocked and choked by other units, as affording the greatest sense of stultification I have ever known. Every half-hour or so, a staff-officer, in manner either over-languid or over-brisk, and talking in clipped, fox-terrier-like phrases, would ride past us, giving to those officers he knew information of a great mythical victory. The complete success of our action had come as a surprise even to our Staff, we were told. The Jerrys were in full retreat, the Boches were smashed, the Hun was on the run. And then, next morning at the earliest hour, we reached the battlefield. For many weeks the Germans had, of course, observed our preparations to attack them. They had been ready. Now the bodies of friends and enemies lay, curious crumpled shapes, swollen and stiff in the long yellow grass under the chicory flowers. A dry, rather acrid smell of death, just tinctured with tear-gas (this was the first occasion on which any gas had been used by the British), hung over the brown Rubens-like landscape. One scene I remember particularly well because of its irony. I saw it a week after the battle. We were quartered in the grounds of an immense château, almost entirely destroyed. The large park, situated among the cinder-heaps and primitive machinery of coal-mines, was full of the remains of temples, summer-houses, bridges, caves and grottoes; everything, in fact, had been pulverized – except a sham ruin, plainly erected a few months before a war which was to bestow upon the neighbourhood as many ruins as the most perfervid romantic could have craved.

Several of my friends had been killed during the five-day battle: more were to disappear into the desolate background of this region during the month that followed: this time, men even younger than my exact contemporaries (I was twenty-two). Among those I was never to see again was Ivo Charteris, who with his cousin, and my most intimate friend, Wyndham Tennant, had joined the Grenadiers at the beginning of the war, and had come out to France in August.

When the Battle of Loos eventually subsided, leaving the Germans in much the same position as when our attack had opened, the weeks again began to assume the monochromatic tones of trench warfare, a life penned in, pinned down, created solely, it seemed, for the tribes of rats and generals, who alone could benefit by it. Accordingly, I have not much to say, even if I felt inclined to dwell on it. There were, of course, episodes such as that which occurred while I was away for a few days in hospital: when my soldier servant, a charming natural character, who had been a navvy until the war came and he volunteered, drew the entire rum ration for the Company, and, with a chosen friend, drank the whole of it, and was as a result unconscious for forty-eight hours. Alas, I never saw him again, for the authorities were far from taking the same lenient view as that with which I regarded his escapade. But the reader would quickly tire of such typical events of our coffined life, and I will therefore confine myself to relating one incident that belongs to this time.

It was one evening in December 1915 that I saw, and spoke to, a ghost. We had been marched up at an hour's notice into the front line, to replace a Scottish regiment which had been so badly and unexpectedly mauled that the Staff had been compelled to withdraw it. It must be borne in mind that as a result we had been deprived of the usual few days' rest between spells of duty. It was, of course, dusk when I took over my portion of the trench, and after I had ordered the posting of the men I entered my dug-out. When I left it, a few minutes later, the evening had become already much blacker. In the corner of the bay opposite, I saw a private soldier, with his hands in his pockets, and noticed that his rifle was by his side, although it had long been an order that all the men should stand to, with their rifles on the parapet, at dawn and at dusk. I could not see his face very distinctly owing to the growing darkness: but

I swore at him for his carelessness, asking him what he meant by it. As I finished, with the words, 'I'm tired of having to tell you . . .', he was, suddenly, no longer there in front of me, and I was talking to nothingness. I took up the abandoned rifle, and carried it with me to the dug-out. It belonged to the regiment we had just relieved.

In the late spring I returned to England, suffering from blood-poisoning. Being rather seriously ill for some weeks, I was obliged during this time, while I was at Renishaw, to have a nurse: a fact which awoke the strongest feeling of competition in my father, who, through the course of his several-years-long breakdown, had come greatly to dislike not being the chief and most seriously afflicted patient in the house.

My views on the war began to make me feel in general uncomfortable in the company of those who did not share them, and grow intolerant of the fashionable world and its complacency: the manner in which it accepted the wholesale slaughter as just one more war (which must be fought to a finish) – whereas it was something different called by the same name; a massacre, and the sooner it ended, the better, if the fabric of European civilization was to survive. But, though the world held war still to be war in a medieval sense, it yet desired the end to be different from the end of medieval conflicts, when moderation always prevailed: now our aim was an uncontrolled, and uncontrollable, victory and the collapse of the enemy. For Democracy at war, and going to war, resembles a runaway bus: it cannot be stopped until it has come to a smash at the bottom of the hill. It is difficult indeed to estimate the difference to the happiness of the world had peace been made before the Bolsheviks came to power, had Russia become a progressive modern nation instead of a revolutionary state, and had Germany, instead of being ruled by Hitler – an inevitable development of its 1918, imposed democracy – developed into a constitutional monarchy. It is scarcely likely that the Kaiser or his son, after so narrow an escape as they must, in those circumstances, have realized that they had been granted, would again have risked war. But such speculations are without profit and merely sadden the survivors.

I had never been able to see beauty in war, which from the first had appeared to me as an endless foulness masquerading under an honoured but obsolete name. But now came a phase of active rebellion: though my feelings were based more, I believe, on intellectual than sentimental reasons. I could observe for myself that the war called out every bad feeling in man or woman, – while the good it was said equally to evoke,

I could not see as 'good'. Heroism has never been my favourite virtue: and still less do I sing the praises of 'taking it', the favourite merit, passive and uninspiring, of the Second World War. Who can help being fired at, bombed, or otherwise obliterated; of what use to panic, at such a moment, even if there were time? Is the pheasant brave, because it flies across in front of the guns on 1st October, or the oyster more than usually courageous when there is an 'r' in the month?

But while it can, I think, be denied that physical courage is a virtue, the fact remains that physical cowardice is so odious and unbecoming, if natural, a vice, that it ever makes us unthinkingly exalt courage un-allied to intelligence. Some people are brave in spite of themselves: it is a way of behaving, occasionally forced on us by the fact that there is nothing else to do, or no way of doing anything: or again as the result of a code or of inheritance. Thus in me there were currents of blood which ran against my reason, filling me with hatred of the Germans, with their clumsy cruelty, their forget-me-nots, their stupid cunning and their fondness for children and for home, and made me oblivious at times of my real tenets: that war, and not the conduct of those maddened by it, is the crime; that all wars and every war were inexcused and inexcusable, and that the politicians of any country who precipitated a war, or failed to end it at the first moment, were the true criminals. During the progress of the war, it became, further, clear to me that the only true heroism was to think for yourself, and then to act on your opinions; and, finally, that many conscientious objectors, though daily nagged at, and held up to ridicule and for hatred as cowards, in the contemporary daily papers, were, though often wrong-headed, as deserving of respect on this score as the greatest of military paladins. As for the voluntary stretcher-bearers and ambulance-drivers, their profession during war consituted a very high form, and needed a very high degree, of courage. To find the truth, and to state it unequivocally amid the general hysteria engendered by modern war, was, similarly, to perform a greater service to humanity and to your country than to hide it from yourself and stampede in one direction after another, like a sheep. Thus Shaw – almost the only famous writer who at this time did not betray truth, reason and his contemporaries and juniors in order to march with the band –, H. W. Nevinson and H. W. Massingham, with their calm protests concerning the war, and the conduct of it, became the men I chiefly admired at home.

Of Shaw and his work I had, indeed, long been a devotee. And I shall never forget the Sunday evening in the autumn of 1917 when I first met him at a dinner given for that purpose by Massingham and Nevinson. Nevinson's acquaintance I had made a little while before. Indeed I had become friends with the whole family. Mrs Nevinson most nobly came to support me at the election in 1918 – she was an accomplished and convincing speaker: and Richard and his charming wife Kathleen were already old friends of mine. Richard, with his dark, pugnacious, handsome, rather melancholy face, was a striking figure, then at the height of his fame as a painter of war. He had found in the painting idiom of the day a fitting manner in which to record its physical struggle; the endless, rhythmic repetition of trench life, of the roads that so fittingly led to it, and to the beginning, born in mud, of mechanized man. I had met Massingham through Robert Ross, that benefactor of many young poets, who had been responsible for submitting to him, as Editor of the *Nation*, the first of my series of satires, signed *Miles*, which subsequently appeared in his columns. I was twenty-four now, and still unused to meeting men of Shaw's genius. It seemed to me the culmination of all for which one could hope. The rest of us waited in the hall at Romano's until the famous playwright made his appearance, a few minutes late. He entered, a tall figure, broad-shouldered, with the easy, loose-limbed gait that marks him, and in his usual warm, rough suit, while, in addition, and rather unexpectedly, a white bandage encircled the crown of his head. I had never seen Shaw previously, though of course I knew him well through photographs, paintings and busts: but I had been unprepared for his genial presence, his fine manners, his great stature, and his typical Irish voice, generous and compelling. In spite of this last attribute, which should call out a responding fire in others, when we had gone upstairs and sat down at our table in the gallery, I remained for long mute, bound fast with wonder – with wonder, but not with awe: for Shaw's natural courtesy would have put anyone younger and less celebrated than himself at his ease. Merely, I wanted to listen, not to talk. He spoke much that evening of the great Duke of Wellington, a fellow-countryman in whose exploits and conversation he had always been greatly interested: he told us the story of how, on one occasion, when the Duke was asked by an admirer, 'How did you really manage to beat Napoleon?', he replied simply: 'Well, I'll tell you. Bonaparte's plans were made in wire, mine were made in string': a very good simile to convey strategic flexibility to a lay mind. When there came a silence, I had mustered sufficient confidence to say something. My eyes reverted to the bandage: it worried my curiosity.

'I'm sorry, Mr Shaw,' I observed, 'to see you've hurt yourself: I hope not badly?'

'Well, you see,' Shaw replied, 'I'm a teetotaller, and my wife got in a new kind of non-alcoholic drink for me to try. As soon as I'd had the first glass, I became intoxicated, and in going downstairs fell and cut my head open!'

What a feeling of relief it afforded, to find people in whose presence any idea, whether original or conventional, whether accepted or rejected by the world, whether condemned and derided or praised, could be discussed on its own merits, without anger. This, though an atmosphere entirely new to me, after my upbringing, and in the environment I had so far known, was one, withal, in which I felt immediately at home. Thus I was freed, and enabled to take my own line. Thus I spoke without fear. And, in the later war years, by which time I had formed my own opinion, I never hid my views. I was in a regiment of great traditions, I understood them and accepted the point of view of those in authority: it was only necessary to do one's duty. But the war was an evil, and should be brought to an end. And when Lord Lansdowne, later in the same month that I met Shaw, published his letter – first refused by *The Times* – in the *Daily Telegraph* and a storm of abuse, violent but innocent of thought, was launched against him, I went at once to the Guards Club and, from that military citadel, wrote – though I had never had the pleasure of meeting Lord Lansdowne – to congratulate him on his courage and sapience. And again, when Bertrand Russell came out of prison, to which he had been for expressing unusual opinions about the war in an article in the *Cambridge Review*, I organized a party for him the same evening, when Lady Ottoline Morrell took him to hear Violet Gordon Woodhouse play in her own unrivalled manner on the harpsichord the great compositions of Bach and Mozart. I do not believe that I have ever seen Lord Russell since that night. Another, but of my own generation, for whose courage I then was able to feel an admiration, was Siegfried Sassoon.

Apart from the abstract beauty of truth-telling, such as that of Bernard Shaw and the others whom I admired, there was no beauty, no virtue in war, as I saw it, but for a few scenes that remain in my memory. Thus it cannot be denied, I apprehend, that Ypres, caught in its whirlwind of iron and fire, was beautiful. For a week or more, the officers of my Company were billeted and messed in the cellars of the Convent of Irish nuns there. Outside, by day and by night, the heads of the gothic stone angels, with their hair curling upward at the ends, with narrow, smiling contemplative eyes which saw so much, and subtle, inward-looking smiles, were falling from great heights, from belfries and lofty, broken walls. One sculptured head I saw as I passed by, knocked off a figure high up on the Cloth Hall. Picking it up and carrying it in my arms to the cellar, I had it packed in a wooden box, and took it home when next I went on leave. The lofty stone buildings seemed to gain in height by their devastation; they towered up into the faint, misty, winter blue, where shrapnel burst with puffs of whiteness like a plaster cupid's cloud. So the broken and deserted city, the very capital of No-Man's-Land, extended its smashed streets and avenues of trees, black, angular shapes, sharp and ruthless, such as the contemporary gangs of Futurists would have wished to create had they been able to kidnap the God of Nature. The ruins possessed a special, a spectral quality, such as is to be noticed in the green, almost lunar towns, seeming to have been painted with verjuice and verdigris, that are sometimes to be found in the backgrounds of pictures by the great Venetian masters.

My life in the Brigade of Guards before the First World War may, looked back upon, seem to have been idle. It had been both too busy and too fragmentary to allow me to read with any intensity, still less to write. But now some instinct, and a combination of feelings not hitherto experienced, united to drive me to paper, this time to compose a poem: and never has anything astonished me more than to find how entirely I lost myself in the process, and yet was able to concentrate. Next ambition swelled up in me. It is, moreover, true that in one respect this first poem qualified me as an unusual poet: for through the good agencies of our friend Richard Jennings – who had sponsored the first poem of my sister's – these verses of mine were shown to the Editor of *The Times*, and shortly afterwards appeared under the title *Babel*, and signed with my name, in the columns of that great journal. This début, in the issue of the 11th of May 1916, must constitute, I opine, the sole instance of a first effort by a young author being printed in an organ of such national and international celebrity, so that, in so far as writing was concerned, it can be said that my muse was born with a silver pen in her mouth. Therefore I reproduce the poem in question here, so that the reader, with all indulgence, may judge of it for himself.

Babel

And still we stood and stared far down
Into that ember-glowing town,
Which every shaft and shock of fate
Had shorn unto its base. Too late
   Came carelessly Serenity.

Now torn and broken houses gaze
On to the rat-infested maze
That once sent up rose-silver haze
   To mingle through eternity.

The outlines once so strongly wrought,
Of city walls, are now a thought
Or jest unto the dead who fought . . .
   Foundation for futurity.

The shimmering sands where once there played
Children with painted pail and spade,
Are drearly desolate – afraid
   To meet night's dark humanity,

Whose silver cool remakes the dead,
And lays no blame on any head
For all the havoc, fire, and lead,
   That fell upon us suddenly,

When all we came to know as good
Gave way to Evil's fiery flood,
And monstrous myths of iron and blood
   Seem to obscure God's clarity.

Deep sunk in sin, this tragic star
Sinks deeper still, and wages war
Against itself; strewn all the seas
With victims of a world disease
– And we are left to drink the lees
Of Babel's direful prophecy.

From the moment of my beginning to write, my life, even in the
middle of war, found a purpose. To me hitherto work had always been a

bugbear, something wan and listless, like a ghost, to be avoided, haunting the end of every spell of freedom and pleasure. I had acquired through my education no ability to concentrate. My mind rambled dully if I sat behind a desk. In short, I loathed work with all my heart, whether at school or later, and whenever possible evaded it. But now I discovered my greatest pleasure – yet pleasure is not the correct term –, my greatest concern, an immersion and a transport, in this labour that had been revealed to me for my own. And the story of the next few years is necessarily one of increasing self-application, until within the span of a decade I was able to reach that point where the idea of a book lay so near me as to abide with me by day and night, returning to me at first waking, and permeating the hours with its particular scent and shape, until, indeed, I was able immediately to supply a lost page of my first novel, *Before the Bombardment*, because I knew the whole book by heart. But this pitch could only in time be attained to, and through being able to live quietly abroad with my brother for a large part of the year, during which periods I gave myself up entirely to my work, living for it; for in London I had only to appear, to find myself the centre of a whirlwind, a battle, and of many dust-storms raised by scrubby feet, as well as constantly being goaded by parents and becoming the victim of a thousand lesser worries. Moreover – and I believe it is a confession of weakness –, I am an artist whose ideas seldom come to him except when a pen is in his hand.

Already, even at the start, I realized the sacredness of my task: because, long before I had detected any capacity in myself, the artist had appeared to me as priest, prophet and law-giver, as well as interpreter: the being who enabled men to see and feel and pointed out to them the way. That I should myself prove to belong to this order at first constituted too great a happiness to credit – still greater, and rare, indeed, to find two such artists as my brother and sister, one on each side of me. Yet fortunate as I was in this respect, fortunate above all others in my generation, there was always hereafter a lurking duality: the excitement and interest to be derived from the lives we led, intellectual and devoted to art, and, underneath, the knowledge of the powerful enmity of many, the bitter loathing of the Philistine, and its continual symptoms in the press. For I was never under any illusions as to the hostility of the great book-hating public: a large and powerful body. All this I believe I understood instinctively, as well as from the results of experience, and better than most of my calling. I realized that everything I said or wrote would be misunderstood by a great many – and my heredity, coming as I do on all sides of stock that for centuries have had their own way, and have not been inured to suffer insolence passively, made it hard for me, and for my brother and sister, not to fight back: (so it was, I am inclined sometimes to think, as I survey the past three decades, that we gave as good as we got!). We knew, in addition, all three of us, that henceforth the sillier, more spiteful acquaintances of my father's and friends of my mother's, who never tired of mischief-making, would misrepresent every line we wrote and every opinion attributed to us, and that this would be reflected in our parents' conduct to us. (Already my father had invented his slogan, 'Edith's poems make *me* look ridiculous!') Continually they were working to kidnap us, and put a stop to our independent lives. Yet through all this, other more abstract things were more important, and the professional preoccupation of my mind, concerned with words, was my continual ecstasy as well as torment. And who can wonder at such an attitude? For in the beginning was the word, we have been told, and, albeit to the divine or to the usual layman this may seem merely an inaccurate translation, to the born writer – and I claim to be a writer born as well as self-made – it stands as the truth, the whole truth, and true in more senses than that in which it was meant to be interpreted.

CHAPTER THREE

Though the practice of his art may afford a writer his chief pleasure, no less than his principal and constant source of worry, though, too, a sudden inspiration may constitute his greatest luxury, yet a minute account of this, his real existence, would be – could only be – of but slight interest to the reader. How is it possible to picture for him the quotidian miseries and splendours of a life attached to the inkpot, the many months spent at a table, the hours when every disturbance is furiously resented, the other, more occasional moments when every interruption is welcome, the evenings when an author looks on his work and finds it good, or those frequent nights when it seems to him to have fallen unbelievably short of what he had intended, the inflations of self-conceit and the agonies of self-reproach, the days when everything grows to giant proportions because it has meaning, the afternoons when all dwindles to pygmy and shows none? What of the racked and sleepless hours before the dawn? Who would wish for a book composed of these? Further, though authorship is, in a sense, a peripatetic profession, since the Muses commune with an author often on long walks through woods, or on the top of mountains, and he is able after this fashion to conquer obdurate details, and albeit he can pack his fountain-pen and write anywhere so long as the place pleases him for writing, yet also it is the most static of careers, entailing for the majority of its practitioners a nearly monastic seclusion and regularity of life during a greater part of the year. Remember, too, when next you turn the pages of the book you have by your chair, that, if it be a serious attempt, it can scarcely have been completed in under eighteen months and may have taken much longer, and thus you touch the very essence of an author's time, as well as a solid block of it. This does not mean, of course, that he has been slave to the pen-wiper and the blotting-pad day and night for that whole period; but in the volume, notwithstanding, will be, I should hazard, twelve hundred hours of actual composing, writing and revising; that is to say, if it were concentrated, fifty days of twenty-four hours, without time off to eat or sleep. And in addition the book will have consumed countless weeks of indirect labour, and will have cost him the endless troubles provoked by forgetting to answer letters and keep appointments; because he has had something better to do, gentle reader.

If, for these among many reasons, it is useless to try very exactly to portray the life of a working author, nevertheless a consideration of one or two joys or sorrows peculiar to his calling may interest persons unacquainted with them. They resemble, I believe, those of no other profession. As a writer's fame increases, he is, for example, occasionally, though seldom enough, granted the singular sensation – almost I had written pleasure, but that is not an exact enough description to apply to the mixture of nervous apprehension, curiosity and gratification roused in him – of noticing, first that he seems unusually conversant with the book which the fellow-guest in the hotel, or fellow-passenger in an omnibus, is reading, and then, with a shock I have tried to define, of realizing why: that it is one of his own books.

Then, again, as an author grows older, he can read a book of his own, when it has become stone cold. This, I think, is one of the most extraordinary experiences he can professionally undergo, more unusual and stimulating than the first sight of a copy of his own first printed book. Before, he has seemed to be part of the volume, or has only read it with a view to correction and revision, while the body of it was still warm with his blood, and he could recall the particular difficulties he had encountered in one paragraph, or the unexpected ease with which the next had been completed. But now he can approach it, as he takes up other books, with the same wish to derive pleasure or an extension of experience from it, with the same casual eye for merits and faults, and with no memory of the processes of making it – though doubtless at the end of it he cannot help trying to reckon the loss and gain accrued in the intervening years. Thus last year I celebrated a private jubilee by reading *Before the Bombardment* twenty years after it had come out, and must confess to having greatly enjoyed it. It was most strange to be presented, after this fashion, between the lines, with the likeness of myself as a young author. There seemed to be no tie between us, yet plainly we were the same person.

Less rare, but none the less a pleasure, is the settling down in a new place for a long stretch of work, the happiness of unpacking, probably in a hotel bedroom, and of the technical preparations, the finding of a table that is steady, of a chair of the right shape, the purchase and spreading of the blotting-paper, the filling of pens. The room in which an author writes is of infinite importance to him, his whole world for those fifty periods of twenty-four hours. Light, heat and absence of noise are the first and most essential requisites: but the feeling of the room, the view from it, the way the light falls in it, are also of great concern to him. To speak less generally and more of myself, I love large apartments, richly furnished; but to rest in, and not for work. A great deal of my writing has been done in the barest of hotel bedrooms. *Before the Bombardment*, which I recognize as the corner-stone of the house I have tried to build, was begun and finished in two consecutive winters in South Italy, in the whitewashed cell of a hotel which had formerly been a monastery, with a fire of logs of orange-tree wood glowing on the hearth with its own peculiar green and yellow flame, or hissing and perfuming the dry air of the bitter mountain cold (which in winter descends to sea-level), and with a window placed so that from where I sat – often, as I thought, just looking out of it when I should have been concentrating (though that, too, had I known it, was an indirect part of the novel), – a view of sea, plumed like a peacock, and of distant ranges beyond, presented itself to

me, and seemed to stretch for ever into the innumerable and diverse
beauties of air and sky at that season. *Escape With Me!* – at least, the
second half of it – was written in a disused kitchen, domed and shaped
like a Moorish marabout, opening on a terrace, in the ancient ruined city
of Antigua, Guatemala. There, in tropical heat, the great prospect girdled
by volcanoes and the blue blossom of jacaranda-trees, I sat picturing
Peking, the while a sentry-vulture, posted at a small window, no doubt
by the order of his organization in case I should die during writing,
would, at intervals of about an hour, flutter a hideous blue-bottle-dark,
serrated wing in at the aperture or, more perturbing still, poke his bald,
carrion-coloured neck through it, to see if I were yet ready for him and
his band; when, with an accuracy of aim of which I should never have
dreamed myself capable, I would hurl my copy of the *Concise Oxford
Dictionary* at him through the narrow opening, and he would give a
squawk, which said all too plainly, 'As you know, duty is duty, and it's
only a question of time if you stay here long enough', and then flap
hungrily away, only to return a minute after I had gone out on to the
terrace to retrieve my invaluable missile: wherefore in time the lexicon
lost its cover, and on my return – for it is difficult to carry about the world
a book in this condition – I gave it away to the Estate Office at Renishaw;
but I could see that when I said to Maynard Hollingworth, 'It is only in
this state owing to my having been obliged to throw it regularly at a
vulture', the excuse sounded, and he thought it, far-fetched. To take
another instance, most of the poems in *England Reclaimed* were composed
in the bedroom of a hotel outside Syracuse, as was, a few years later,
Winters of Content, in spite of the many troubles, and the perpetual letters
that in consequence would assail me and had to be answered, relating to
a previous book over which a libel action was threatened. (The injured
lady, I recollect, gave an interview to a newspaper in which she said,
'Sitwell compares me to Madame Bovary. I do not know who she is, but
my friends tell me she is a French classic!') The volumes of *Left Hand,
Right Hand!*, so far as they have progressed, have been written at
Renishaw, in my small study enclosed within the thick walls of the oldest
part of the house. Here, among towers of books and accumulated papers,
are to be found many objects familiar to me since my earliest childhood,
for the room formerly served my father as his chief writing-place.

By now, I conclude that the truth of the statement made at the
beginning of this chapter has been established for the reader: that the
story of an author's pursuit of his profession can hold little of concern to

the outside world. The facts exampled above, slight and dull though they may be, are the chief I can muster. On the other hand, his, as it were, extra-mural activities (and the way he, as a writer, looks at them) can entertain and even, who knows, instruct the reader. Fortunately, my exterior adventures in the time of which I write were numerous and varied, and soon I return to one in particular. But first I must ask him to hold in the background of his mind for the remainder of this book, during most of which I talk of other things, the many long, often arduous but contented months devoted each year to writing; those vistas of days, for the most part unexciting and of a regular rhythm, spent usually abroad and in company with my brother Sacheverell, William Walton or Adrian Stokes, and other practitioners of the arts.

Possessed of many interests and, I am thankful and proud to write, of many friends, I found it needful, if I was to become a writer, to escape from them for long periods. The world was both too much with me and against me.

On the whole, then, so bitter had the long war made me, so full was I still of rage and despair, and of contempt for those who would not see, that I did not, in the years immediately following 1918, make new friends with the ease of the days before the war. But to this there was one glittering exception. Certain friends helped greatly, moreover, instead of hindering, and chief of these was my new friend, Mrs Henry McLaren, or Lady Aberconway as she is now. Indeed, any account of my daily life between the end of the First World War and the present day would be incomplete without the mention of her. I had been first taken to her house in 1916 or '17, and in 1926 I dedicated to her *Before the Bombardment*: so that it must have been somewhere between those dates, I think in 1920, that a mere acquaintanceship first sloughed its dull and torpid chrysalis, and soared as friendship: yet as sometimes happens in things important to me, I cannot be sure of the precise moment. I am, indeed, grateful to her, no less for her wisdom than for a rarer and opposite quality which transcends it; that is to say that she never hesitates to fly in the face of common sense should the most loyal and scrupulous principles of friendship she upholds demand the adoption of such tactics. Many of the most delightful hours of my life have been passed in her company. With the immediate impression she produces on entering a room, of delicacy of texture and sensitiveness of feeling, goes, too, at first sight and most misleadingly, what appears to be an unusual formality, this being produced by a natural precision of demeanour and speech, which, as one grows to know her better, adds an element of surprise to the effect of the discovery of her most unconventional wit and wits, in the same way that one finds out, too, before long, how her discretion covers an unusual and warm understanding of human beings. In addition, she permits herself the utmost bias on behalf of her friends, and there would therefore, I think, be no lengths to which she would not go to help them.

There were others, however, who made up for her unselfishness. There were many who wished to waste their own time, and many who wished merely to waste yours. Quite apart from attempts at forcible feeding, from requests to write prefaces or epilogues, or a few favourable words to be quoted on covers, to read manuscripts and send criticisms gratis, open – or shut – exhibitions, give interviews on any subject, autograph books, attend conferences, join clubs, sign letters of protest and manifestos, take part in symposiums, speak on the B.B.C. for infant fees, support every sort of society for the prevention of one, and encouragement of another – or sometimes the same – thing, write articles, celebrate centenaries, deliver lectures, and all those perpetual and ingenious schemes to make you catch colds and agues in a thousand different ways, and so prevent you from working for a time – or better still for ever; quite apart, then, from all this (which is the lot of every well-known English-speaking writer), my parents by themselves would have been sufficient to render impossible any serious and consecutive effort. To their children they constituted a profession in themselves, and one which wore out health and exhausted patience. You never knew what they might not do next. When, a few years later, I was at last, as will be seen, successful in persuading my father that he would be happier if he resided abroad, the paths of his children became a little easier: but until that moment it was out of the question to work untroubled and with ease at home in England. The letters from my father which rained in by every post, on subjects ranging from the composition of the atom to the best empirical methods of cutting your toe-nails, but, so far as I was concerned, for the most part relating to business and complaining of my lack or misuse of ability, concluded often with a *catalogue raisonné* of my faults of character and conduct, and were enough to oblige one to use up every scrap of energy in reply. My sister faced the storms in her own flat – even though, by coincidence, she was curiously liable to be away when my family came to London. My father's views on woman's place in the world – which were that she should be out of it – allowed her a little more freedom from his letters (on the other hand, my mother demanded her presence the whole time), whereas it was his duty as father, ancestor and descendant in one, to torment my brother, and still more myself in my character of eldest son, on every conceivable occasion. He liked to make plans, to inflate and deflate them at will, in the manner of a child playing with a toy balloon, and would plague an idea as a dog worries a bone. In addition, he must know exactly what we were doing or proposing to do. 'It is dangerous for you,' he used to point out, 'to lose touch with me for a single day. You never know when you may not need the benefit of my experience and advice.'

To combat this, first to obtain half of one's own life, and subsequently a still greater proportion, I was obliged to invent a technique. In this direction, success crowned my efforts – to such an extent that at one moment I had thoughts of opening a *Bureau for Advising Sons with Difficult Fathers*. The position nevertheless held continual possibilities of further trouble, for nerves became exacerbated and if somehow we tricked our parents into allowing us the time in which to write a book, the reviewers of the period would be sure to fall on it in the particularly insolent and vituperative manner then reserved for us. Hardly any other writers of the epoch incurred the same degree of obloquy. The works of the Georgian poets, for example, were received with acclamation. Thus – for the reader may doubt the truth of this, dismissing it as a symptom of that occupational disease of the artist, persecution mania – when *Before the Bombardment* appeared, one popular critic of a Sunday paper said that in it I spat on the whole of the Victorian Age and that the book should have been called *Great Expectorations*! 'It is not', this same sensitive being pronounced, 'so much a matter of taste or good breeding, as a matter of sportsmanship . . . I shudder at the vulgarities.' The *Outlook* pronounced that I was 'fussy' about the war, and through the general storm and roar of rage, the still small voices of the then Mayor of Scarborough and of the then Rector were heard to say respectively, through the medium of an interview, 'I have not read the book . . . it is in thoroughly bad taste', and 'It is a vulgar caricature. The best thing is to treat it with silent contempt.' Alas, the critics did not adopt the last, singularly original remedy recommended to them. 'Merely caddish', said the *Yorkshire Post*, the paper chiefly read by my mother's friends, who would, when they were in London, go round to see my parents, giggle in an embarrassed but jolly way about us, and confirm my father and mother in their view that as writers we possessed no talent and no future. ('You ought to stop it. It isn't fair on you two dear things!')

★

When in London – and the periods we spent there were now not so long, for, in addition to being obliged to seek sanctuary abroad while working, I was still prospective Liberal candidate for Scarborough, and had often to live there for a month or two – we liked to abandon ourselves entirely to its life. Though the years before August 1914 seemed now infinitely distant; though the whole inner consciousness of each of us who possessed a soul had been laid waste and tormented by the horrors which had taken place, the stories of torture, which might not be true, the mountains of dead, whom we had seen for ourselves, and the weight of whose sacrifice oppressed us still; though, too, the general hysteria engendered by democratic wars had envenomed our tempers, no less than the sight of suffering had embittered and saddened us; notwithstanding, we retained, as all of our age at the time must have done, a certain zest for life and an interest in it. The inner wounds would take many years to heal, but meanwhile the world was open to us, we could travel, make up for lost years, and observe what was going on round us. Part, at least, of the brilliant promise to be divined in the English world of art and literature in 1914, though all appeared to have withered at the breath of war, was now to be made good. The decade soon to open was one of the most brilliant in recent literary history, as a glance at the names of those writing will prove. There could be felt in the air of the great city much energy and a lively and pleasurable effervescence very different from the grey blight which lies over it after the Second World War: the kind of greasy, lethargic, puritan sloth which, I think, cannot have manifested itself again until now since the decade ending in 1660.

There were all kinds of amusements to be found or to be made, both large and small. One of them – but I forget whether in this year, or in one of the years immediately following – occurred with the return of Tetrazzini to Covent Garden. Sacheverell – already an ardent lover of Italian opera and singing – asked our friend Richmond Temple, who was a director of the Savoy, where the famous prima donna was staying, whether she would receive us, so that we could present to her a wreath of bay and myrtle as a tribute from the young writers of England. Madame Tetrazzini indicated her willingness, and it was arranged. The seven or eight persons who formed the deputation included Aldous Huxley, my sister, my brother and me. The night before, Aldous and Maria Huxley very hospitably entertained us to dinner, and afterwards, while Aldous was composing the speech for us, with Sacheverell – who it had been decided was to deliver it – at his side, Julian Huxley, I remember, walked up and down the room in a state of enchantment at the idea of the ceremony, offering to help his brother.

Eventually the speech was finished, and the next day, after luncheon, we assembled at the Savoy, and were conducted to the Tetrazzini's private suite. Her sitting-room into which we were shown had been converted for the occasion into a bower of white lilac: several journalists and a camera-man, with a towering camera and a flash-light assistant, were in attendance. All was ready for her to make her appearance. The bedroom door was now flung open, and the famous prima donna entered. Short, fat, ageing, wearing an over-elaborate brown *crêpe* dress, with much lace attached to it, she nevertheless had a captivating air of kindness and good-nature, and walked as one used to receiving acclamation. She advanced slowly, making a conventional theatrical gesture of greeting and pleasure, with her right hand to the poets, drawn up in line, and with her left hand to the camera-man, up his ladder ready to pull the trigger, and to the journalists, their pencils poised. The tall figure of Sacheverell, very young, – just over twenty – stood heading our number, with Aldous, over-topping him, just behind. Slowly, very slowly, she continued to move towards us. The camera-man was just giving the signal, when suddenly the great singer caught her foot in a rug and fell flat! There are those, I know, who hold that no fall, whatever the circumstances of it, can ever be funny. All I can say is that I disagree with them. Fortunately, she had come to no hurt, and still more oddly, seemed singularly undiscomfited by her misadventure. She was helped up, and straightened her dress: the poets straightened their faces: the camera-man again got ready: Sacheverell was just going to read our message, when, this time impelled I suppose by curiosity, Tetrazzini snatched the paper from him. Sacheverell, who dislikes speaking in public, was nevertheless determined to go through with it, so he snatched it back, saying at the same time in his deep voice, 'Prego, Divinissima', and began to read. The camera clicked – and so there a delightful occasion remains, enshrined in the dusty office files of newspapers.

Our chief extra-mural activity in 1919 – for my part-editing of *Art and Letters* counts as a professional – was the organizing of the Exhibition of Modern French Art at the Mansard Gallery at Heal's: of which Roger Fry, sponsor of the two great exhibitions of Post-Impressionist pictures in 1910 and 1912, wrote that it was 'the most representative show of modern French art seen in London for many years'. Associated with my brother and myself in collecting the pictures was a Parisian-Polish dealer, who subsequently became celebrated, Zborowski. With flat, Slavonic features, brown almond-shaped eyes, and a beard which might have been shaped out of beaver's fur, ostensibly, he was a kind, soft business-man, and a poet as well. He had an air of melancholy, augmented by the fact that he spoke no English, and could not find his way about London (to which city this was his first visit). The days before the opening of the Exhibition are memorable to me because of the interest of seeing the pictures unpacked, and of hanging them. During the war it had been for so long out of the question to see modern French pictures at all, except for a single specimen at some gallery, that considerable excitement now evinced itself. The July evenings were very hot, and after dinner, at about nine o'clock every evening, while my brother, Zborowski and I supervised the hanging, friends would come in from the Eiffel Tower restaurant and from Fitzroy Street near by, to watch. Among those present at these unveilings would be our hierophant, Roger Fry, who walked round from his studio. The Exhibition, though by no means enormous, included pictures by – among others – Othon Friesz, Vlaminck, Derain, Matisse, Picasso, Modigliani, Survage, Soutine, Suzanne Valadon, Kisling, Halicka, Marcoussis, Léger, Gabriel-Fournier, Ortiz, André Lhote, Utrillo, and Dufy, and sculptures by Archipenko and Zadkine. Derain and Picasso had both made their personal appearance in London that summer, when Diaghilev had produced the two finest ballets of his second period, *La Boutique Fantasque*, and *The Three-Cornered Hat*. I had been present at the first night of both performances, and shall never forget the excitement of first seeing truly modern works of scenic art upon the stage. Both ballets were exactly calculated to show the supreme qualities of satiric dash and comic audacity possessed by such great dancers as Massine and Lopokova, now at their zenith. Moreover Derain's drop-scene for *La Boutique* and Picasso's for *The Three-Cornered Hat* were probably the most inspired and original that had been painted for over a century. Picasso had, of course, long been the favourite of the *cognoscenti* of modern art, but Derain was a comparatively new star, and had much impressed them. And I remember one evening at the Mansard Gallery, as a glazed and framed canvas by this artist was being unpacked, and Roger Fry was admiring it, a friend drew attention to the fact that a currant had become wedged between the paint and the glass. A philistine was just going to remove it, when Roger boomed out,

'Better leave it alone. He probably placed it there intentionally. It makes rather a swagger contour!'

Indeed, so much esteemed that year was the French painter by those who knew, that it was said that all the cows on the home-farm at Garsington had caught the fever from Lady Ottoline and her friends, and, when they lowed in their green, daisy-sprinkled Oxfordshire pastures, could be heard now, instead of making their former pointless, vacuous sounds, to moo at each other, with the correct Bloomsbury accentuation, a purposeful *Doë-rain, Doë-rain!*

Sacheverell and I were very eager for the Exhibition to be a success, as much for our own advantage as for the good name of the English public of art-lovers. Sacheverell was most anxious to leave Oxford: but my father would not hear of his doing so, if he intended to devote his life to writing. To be a dealer was different. However, in the end, the idea of our starting a gallery broke down, for an enterprise of that kind needed capital, and we could find none: so, as matters turned out, it proved our sole joint venture in this field – though one, I believe, of which we can be proud. Rather than the great established names, and familiar masters, it was the newcomers, such artists as Modigliani and Utrillo, who made the sensation in this show. And my brother and I can claim the honour of having been the first to introduce Modigliani's pictures to the English public. It had been possible before to understand the beauty of his drawings: but the paintings offered a new and a greater revelation. The nudes, especially the reclining figure derived from Giorgione and Titian, manifested an astonishing feeling for the quality of oil paint: a technical mastery and exploitation strange in itself, because the artist had always wanted to be a sculptor, and only the cost of the materials prevented it. I was not in a position to buy as many of these canvases as I should have wished, but at least my brother and I were able to acquire a magnificent example – for the Parisian dealers who owned the majority of Modigliani's work in the Exhibition suggested, knowing our great admiration of this artist, that, as a reward for our services, we might like to select a single picture and pay them what it had cost them. Accordingly, we chose his superb *Peasant Girl*, for which we paid four pounds, the average gallery price for a painting by him being then between thirty and a hundred pounds.

Of recent decades it has, I know, been held that poetic and psychological understanding entering into a picture should not be allowed to prejudice the connoisseur in its favour: for esthetic value it must rest on pictorial qualities alone. And it must be admitted that even without such adventitious aids this would have remained a great work of art. Nevertheless, considered from the point of view of a poet, it was something more, just as were the canvases of Utrillo. After Modigliani it may be that Utrillo, who lacks the monumental sense present in the Italian painter's work, seems at first sight dull, with his apparently plain statements in paint of the most banal *banlieues* of Paris. With no man, no woman, no child in sight among those white peeling walls and dented, ribbed roofs, the lamp-posts showing diminutive in the clearing between sheer walls, where a building has been torn down and not yet replaced, or, on the contrary, rivalling in height the small, two-storey houses, with doors, windows, shutters surely too plain to diffuse any sense of emotion, these studies of the suburbs nevertheless exhale the most poignant miasmas of mind and spirit. Nothing moves, no leaf stirs. A finger lifted outside these stucco walls would alter, not only the surface of them, but the illumination of street and sky. The flat ceiling of clouds, the grey, clear light would themselves begin to flake and fall in powder. These canvases, full of exquisite morbidity, demonstrate that no tenements, no fag-ends of brick and plaster are too mean to be captured by art, and that man's habitations are porous, permeable by the human spirit. The sensibility and restraint of the painter, his indifference to all but his art, is here carried, like that of a Chinese landscapist, to its ultimate pitch. He is recording: he is not pronouncing judgement – yet that is in effect what he. *is* pronouncing, for these streets, waiting, empty, quiet, with a silence unbroken except for the barking of a pet dog, testify and cry aloud.

The opening day of the Exhibition, the first of August, proved that crowds could be attracted to a gallery even during the holiday season, then still rigidly adherent to a particular month. In order to prevent the public – who, it must be remembered, had seen no modern European painting for four years – from stampeding, we had persuaded Arnold Bennett, a friend of ours and a lover of pictures, to write the preface of the catalogue. We had hoped that his acknowledged common sense, his plain respect for competency and success in any branch of life, together with his high contemporary reputation as a novelist, would to a certain extent shield the pictures from the ugly display of abuse and bad temper which here greets every manifestation of art new to the country: but in vain!

We were fortunate enough to sell a good many pictures on the opening day. Arnold Bennett bought on my advice a splendid nude by Modigliani, and to someone else who consulted me I recommended another fine picture by the same master, and an Utrillo. For these two he paid a sum of about seventy pounds: within five years he could have sold them for at least two thousand six hundred pounds. The catalogue, with its preface by Arnold, was widely bought; unfortunately the beginning of the list of pictures in it carried the notice, '*This collection has been brought together by Osbert and Sacheverell Sitwell*'; which served to focus public rage on our two heads: though a considerable amount, on such occasions, was always, reserved for my sister, even when, as in this instance, she was in no wise implicated. My brother and I acted in the Gallery as shopmen in turn with our friend Herbert Read, selling catalogues, answering inquiries, and often quieting, or trying to quiet, protests – about the pictures. The table at which sat the one of us who had taken on the duty, had been placed in the middle of the Gallery, and below, by its side, stood an enormous wicker basket full of sheaves of Modigliani drawings from which the visitor could choose a specimen for a shilling.

Every day the public tantrums, whether inside the Mansard Gallery or outside it, in the columns of the newspapers, increased. For the most part the critics showed themselves impressed, at the lowest were civil: it was in the news and correspondence columns that riots and mutinies broke out. A notably irate series of letters, arising out of a favourable account of the pictures by Clive Bell, appeared in the *Nation*, and continued for six weeks, a fortnight after the Exhibition had closed! Throughout, the attackers maintained a strong moral note, and one of them declared that at one moment he had felt the whole collection of pictures to be 'a glorying in prostitution'! I think it was the Modigliani portraits which exacerbated the public. Especially the artist's manner of rendering necks annoyed – but that is altogether too mild a word – those unused to it. In the Gallery it was the same. 'Why does he paint people with necks like swans?' I used to hear asked, with passionate, venomous derision. And out of this rage I believe that it would have been possible at last to extract a mathematical formula, the heat of the anger seeming to be based on the number of times the neck of the given Modigliani could be multiplied to make the neck of the person protesting. Certainly, the thicker the neck, the greater the transports of its owner, and the thicker still would it become, swelling from fury.

Modigliani was nearing the end of his doomed life. Zborowski had undoubtedly been of great help to him for some years: but I cannot think him, kind and nice as he was, to have been the pure philanthropist-poet that he is represented to have been. Nor should it be regarded as a picture-dealer's business to be a philanthropist. Zborowski became a very successful dealer. It is in that guise that he must be regarded, as a man with a flair, and in that same capacity he would no doubt wish to be remembered. I recall how, during the period of the Exhibition, when Modigliani, recovering from a serious crisis of his disease, suffered a grave relapse, a telegram came for Zborowski from his Parisian colleagues to inform him; the message ended with a suggestion that he should hold up all sales until the outcome of the painter's illness was known. My brother, who was inexpressibly shocked at this example of business-men's callousness, showed me the cable, and Zborowski asked us personally to refuse to sell, if a possible purchaser should appear. As it happened, Modigliani did not immediately comply with the programme drawn up for him. He appeared to have regained strength, and did not die before the following year.

During the course of the following autumn, the terms on which we found ourselves with my father became less strained, and we determined to try to persuade him either to advance us the money to buy, or himself to purchase as an investment, a hundred or more pictures by Modigliani for which we were in treaty. Some of them were already in England, and the whole collection could have been acquired for between seven hundred and a thousand pounds. Though I had almost refrained from making such a suggestion for fear of the reception it would most certainly incur, yet when at last I ventured to broach the subject, and even after he had seen some of the pictures, which surely did not match his taste, my father showed himself inclined to agree to some arrangement. Still further to ease relations, and a little, perhaps, in order to pursue the point, my brother and I invited him to dine with us on the night of his sixtieth birthday, 27th January 1920, at our London house, 2 Carlyle Square.

The worst mistake we made on this occasion, and one we were bitterly to regret before the evening was over and for many years subsequently, was to ask my father's only friend, Mr MacTotter, the Silver Bore, to meet him. At first all went well; until the Silver Bore, who was as good-natured and, indeed, sentimentally friendly as obtuse (his continued friendship with my father must have been due solely to his never being conscious when he and his friendship were not wanted), brought out of his pocket a small package containing a birthday offering. After fifty years, the most elementary sense of psychology should have prevented him from falling into this error – for error it was, if he intended to please my father, to whom any present on an anniversary constituted an affront.

When the paper was undone, the parcel proved to contain a gilded snuff-box, big enough to hold cigarettes, and though, of course, in the best of taste, unquestionably a pretty and elegant object. When my father saw what it was – for he refused to touch it with his hands, as though he thought it might communicate some fever, and allowed the Silver Bore to rattle about among the tissue paper for him – he sank into a slow, sulky, smouldering passion, of ill omen to his sons' plans. The entire mask of *bonhomie* which he had prepared for the evening crumbled. He drew me aside at once, and remarked, 'A shocking waste of money, much better spent in other ways. Most selfish! *I* can't afford that sort of thing!' (In reality, he feared he might later have to give a return birthday present to the Silver Bore, and though not ungenerous with gifts, he liked to choose his own time for them, and on these grounds disapproved of festivals such as a birthday or Christmas. At hotels abroad, he would always try to wish the head-waiter 'A Happy Christmas!' first, before that smart and important recipient of presents could get it in, and if Robins, on Christmas morning, offered him his greetings, my father would snap out, in a tone of intense fretfulness, 'Yes, Yes, Yes, I *know!*') It took minutes that seemed like hours to restore any semblance of good-humour to him, but eventually we succeeded in coaxing him into a state of icy geniality, if such a contradiction in terms may be permitted. The dining-room itself aroused no particularly unpleasant comment, and he ate the meal with apparent enjoyment. Nor did he complain overmuch at having to climb upstairs to the drawing-room after dinner.

Arrived there, I took my father into the back part of the room, to show him our Modigliani, hanging over the fireplace. Being at the lowest a man of imagination and esthetic perception and, in some branches, of a liking for new ideas, he treated the picture seriously, and listened to all I had to say, until it seemed clear that he would at last fall in with one of our plans, and that in consequence it would reach fruition. Alas! at this very moment the Silver Bore, who entertained a neurasthenic dread of being 'out of things', and whose eyes always roved fitfully – and when I write *fitfully*, I mean it – away from the person to whom he was talking, in search of suspected hidden diversions, broke loose from the other room, where he had been prating and gibbering to my brother of tea-spoons and porringers, and stampeded up to my father and me. Noticing that we were looking at a picture, the newcomer turned his gaze in the same direction, and as he grimaced and quavered at it, a new tempo of indignation began to govern his trembling, which grew quicker and more convulsive. As Modigliani's peasant girl, monumental, posed for ever in her misty blue world, peered steadily out of her frame, through her thin, goose-like eyes, at the quivering, agitated, but well-tailored mass of the elderly gentleman opposite her, the struggle between them became – if only it had not been too poignant, because I already recognized that my fortunes and my brother's were deeply implicated in it – an interesting duel to watch. Inspired as MacTotter was by Good Taste, which inevitably blindfolds its victims, since it arms them for their battle against art with a system, if not of esthetic values, at any rate of academical respectability and decorum that can ostensibly be used on behalf of beauty, rather than, as in reality, against it, something in the painting before him clashed, I suggest, with the ideals upheld by the Queen Anne Coffee Pot: wherefore this was not and could not be Art. Personal prejudice, moreover, no less than principle, entered in. The quality of her immense and static dignity not only outraged the burgessdom of England, of which he was an incarnation, but offended more particularly against his own involuntary vivacity, bestowed on him by St Vitus. The peasant girl, he considered, had no expression, no movement. So intense was his emotion that at first it seemed as if he could not, for very anger, use his voice. But in the end all this agitation and waste of energy found their equivalent in sound, a high, defensive whinnying, long sustained. The peasant girl, immobile, held her ground. Not so, alas, my father. He would not look at the picture again: he was frightened out of it, by the force of conventional opinion as thus expressed.

A kind of sequel occurred some five or six years later. My brother and I returned to London after a prolonged absence abroad, spent in working at Amalfi. The evening after our arrival, a friend, himself a painter and a collector of modern pictures, came to dine with us. When later we were sitting in the drawing-room, he said, 'I've been wondering, by the way, whether you'd like to sell me your Modigliani. I'll give you a handsome price, eighty pounds!' He was aware that I had paid four pounds for it, and when I could not make up my mind what to do, for I both needed money and hated to part with the painting, he added, 'You won't be doing badly: you'll have made a profit of nearly two thousand per cent!' After reflection, and in spite of Mrs Powell's protests, I accepted his offer – only to learn a week later that the purchaser had resold it for two thousand pounds, while two or three months subsequently it was to be seen in the window of a famous Parisian dealer for the equivalent in francs of four thousand pounds.

The great rise in the value of Modigliani's pictures had taken place during the months we had been abroad, and out of touch with the world of galleries. It was evident now that when my father had permitted the Silver Bore to giggle and jiggle him out of his almost formulated intention to buy the collection of Modigliani's paintings, he had been laughed out of a fortune. Since money values constituted a standard that the Silver Bore admitted and understood, I decided to write to him and point out what he had accomplished.

CHAPTER FOUR

I must hark back to the short period I spent in hospital in the early months of 1919: for during those and the following weeks were planted many seeds which later were to germinate and flourish. In January of that year my brother and comrade Sacheverell had gone up to Balliol. It was a particularly listless moment in Oxford, as yet by no means recovered from a state of decayed emptiness, for war had hollowed it out. Sacheverell, though only twenty-one years of age, was already accustomed to something more lively, to London and the society of poets and painters which we there enjoyed. One day, when he came up to visit me, he mentioned, I remember, the sole redeeming point of Oxford for him: that he had met in a – as it seemed to him – leaden city, the only English musical genius it had ever been his lot so far to encounter, a boy of sixteen, called W. T. Walton – and that was the first time I heard the name. I did not pay much attention, since we already possessed among our friends an undoubted and more mature musical genius, Bernard van Dieren. Sacheverell, however, pursuing the topic, told me, I recall, that Walton's talent had first been discovered by the organist of Christ Church, Dr Henry Ley, and the late Sir Hugh Allen, and then fostered by Dr Strong, Dean of Christ Church for many years, and subsequently Bishop of Ripon and, later, of Oxford. Dr Strong had been so greatly impressed by the evident musical talent of this young boy from Oldham, who was in the Cathedral Choir School, that he had obtained a modification in his favour of the rules governing the qualifying age, so that Walton should be able to enter Christ Church as an undergraduate at an early age. Walton was said, no doubt erroneously, to be in consequence the youngest member of the University since the reign of Henry VIII. We must, Sacheverell continued, find some way of being of use to him, and of advancing his chances and genius.

In the end, perhaps, all that we were able to accomplish directly for him was to have prevented his being sent to one of the English musical academies and to have lent him, as a musician, what prestige we ourselves possessed in the world of art and writing at a time when he lacked supporters, and when, in consequence of our attitude, we incurred a certain amount of odium, both from those who did not believe in him and from those who did. Especially were we blamed by these last – and rightly – for being responsible for his not attending in London one of the two or three colleges officially provided for an academic training in music. These people worked in different ways but united in tormenting about it Walton's father, a well-known teacher of singing in Lancashire, and fortunately a man of character. On one occasion, they so well succeeded in their efforts that Mr Walton, very busy though he always was, came up to London especially to investigate, and failing to find my brother or myself, instead called on my aged Aunt Blanche, then rising eighty, who was speedily able to reassure him. The relationship between William and his father and mother, both of whom were fine musicians, was unusually happy, and it was said that almost the last words of his father were, 'Let William have his own way: he knows what he is doing . . .' Instead, then, of sending William to Kensington or Blooms-bury, we were able to keep him in touch with the vital works of the age, with the music, for example, of Stravinsky, and to obtain for him, through the kindness of our old family friend E. J. Dent, an introduction to Busoni, a modern master of counterpoint, who looked at some of William's compositions and wrote him a kindly polite letter about them. He also at times had the benefit of consulting Ernest Ansermet on various problems of composition. Moreover by travelling in our company in Italy, Spain and Germany, he soon acquired a knowledge of the arts, both past and present, belonging to those countries. It was noticeable from the first that he manifested an innate feeling for the masterpieces of painting and architecture, no less than of music: and inevitably the people, landscapes, festas and customs he observed increased the store of experience on which he could draw for the enriching of his work.

On leaving hospital towards the end of February 1919 I had gone to

Oxford, to be with my brother, and to see Siegfried Sassoon, who was living in rooms there. It was a very cold early spring, with long periods of frost that bit like iron into the flesh, and with the inevitable coal shortage that seems to be one of the jewels of the austere crown wherewith Victory likes to adorn herself in this country. Whenever, in these weeks, I saw Sacheverell, his hands, I recollect, were blue with cold, his fingers being too numb even to strike a match for the fire, ready laid and boasting a few precious pieces of inferior coal. He was very grateful, therefore, to Raymond Mortimer, who had come down to stay at Oxford, and who, although in those days we knew him comparatively little, would, with the genius of the Good Samaritan that he is, wordlessly materialize in the room, grasp the situation immediately, and, without being asked, at once rush towards the fireplace to set light to the sticks for him. Siegfried Sassoon was the first of our friends to have met Walton, through Frank Prewitt, the Canadian poet, who had lately left the Forces to go up to Oxford. Sassoon had taken my brother to see the youthful composer, and he now invited all four of us to tea.

We arrived at Christ Church in the early afternoon. The room was rather dark, blue-papered, with a piano opposite the window, and in the middle a table laid for tea, with, in the centre of it, thrown in for the sake of the almost ostentatious sense of luxury it would inevitably evoke, an enormous plate of bananas. Our host, not quite seventeen years of age, we found to be a rather tall, slight figure, of typically northern colouring, with pale skin, straight fair hair, like that of a young Dane or Norwegian. The refinement of his rather long, narrow, delicately shaped head, and of his bird-like profile showing so plainly above the brow the so-called bar or mound of Michelangelo that phrenologists claim to be the distinguishing mark of the artist – and especially of the musician –, even his prominent, well-cut nose, scarcely gave a true impression either of his robust mental qualities or of the strength of his physique. Sensitiveness rather than toughness was the quality at first most apparent in him. He appeared to be excessively shy, and on this occasion spoke but little, for I think he was rather in awe of us, as being his elders. Talk was desultory, though there were sudden determined bursts of amiably-intentioned conversation from his guests. The atmosphere was not, however, easy; music showed a way out of the constraint, and after tea we pressed him to play some of his compositions to us. Accordingly, he got up from the table and then sat down at the piano, the few steps between clearly indicating the burden of his hospitality, a feeling of strain, almost of hopelessness, combined with that of a need for intense concentration. As he began to play, he revealed a lack of mastery of the instrument that was altogether unusual, and as a result it was more difficult than ever to form an opinion of the music at a first hearing. He played the slow movement from his *Piano Quartet*, later published by the Carnegie Trust, and other compositions which have no doubt disappeared. It was, indeed, as impossible that afternoon to estimate his character or talents as it was to foresee that for the next seventeen years he would constitute an inseparable companion and friend, and an adopted, or elected, brother to Edith, Sacheverell and myself.

Sacheverell and I went for the Easter vacation – he had joined me at Biarritz – to Spain, where I fell ill. On our delayed return to England, he went back to Oxford, and I to Scarborough; where I found waiting for me a welcoming letter from my father. It began:

You show a lack of judgement – you allowed the Military Authorities to put you, when run down, into the influenza ward: then, though warned of the necessity of keeping quiet, you rushed about Spain till you got jaundice.

Later in the summer, I returned to Swan Walk, where Sacheverell joined me at the end of June; for the first time accompanied by William Walton. The young composer seemed still more shy and silent. Most of the summer days he appeared to spend in his room at the top of the house, where he sat by the window for long periods, eating black-heart cherries from a paper bag, and throwing the stones out of the window, down on to the smooth brown-tiled pavement outside the door. Swan Walk was so quiet that there was only to be heard a distant booming of traffic, and nearer, this dry, staccato rattle of cherry stones.

Soon a piano was hired for him, and in consequence he remained in his room for longer periods even than before, at intervals being peered at cautiously through the door by Mrs Powell, 'to see he was all right'; for she had quickly become attached to him, and possessed great faith in his talent. For the next twelve years, until her death, she looked after him also with much imaginative tact and consideration. The piano, though he attacked it so often, was seldom, through some process of personal magic, heard downstairs. If it were, I would sometimes advise him to have a dumb-piano to practise upon, when he would grow very indignant. He had, it may be noted, always to be near a piano, though his playing of it, I apprehend, never very much improved. And this was curious, for one of the first things a stranger would have observed about him was his manual dexterity: he could do almost anything with his hands and by his ingenuity, so that often, for example, I would, when a key was lost, ask him to pick a lock for me. The instrument, however, continued to exert a powerful fascination over him and, in example of this, I recall his despair when, on his arriving one August some years later to stay with my brother, it was found that the ancient, rather rickety wooden staircase leading to his room was too narrow to allow of a piano being carried up it. Six men from the warehouse attempted it in the morning but failed: it was a plainly impossible task. Meanwhile it was arranged that the piano should be left on the first-floor landing at the foot of the stairs, until some two days later, when the men would come back with a trolley and crane and hoist it into the composer's room through the window. In the afternoon my sister and brother and I went for a motor drive: William – still grieving for his piano and the forty-eight hours that must be lost – asked to stay at home. When we returned, the enormous instrument was safely in his bedroom. Often in the days which followed we implored him to reveal how, single-handed, he had accomplished this tremendous feat of skill and strength: but he could only explain, 'I did it with a bit of string.' Indeed we were never able to elucidate the mystery in any way, or find out more about the no doubt most intricate mechanism that his daemon, in conjunction with his own extreme inventiveness and acting through his considerable muscular strength, had devised.

It would be, perhaps, accurate to say of him that he was wordless rather than, as I have written, shy, but the difficulty he appeared to find when he was a very young man in communicating easily with his fellows no doubt militated against his making friends rapidly at that time. Nevertheless, at Oxford he possessed several; notably Roy Campbell, then eighteen or nineteen years of age, and only lately arrived from South Africa. In this respect resembling William, he exhibited in his appearance a curious mixture of strength and delicacy. He also was inclined to be rather silent at first, but the unusual intensity of his appearance, his pallor, the clearness of his eyes and gaze, and their suggestion of tautness and of interior life, as well as his evident passion for poetry, set him apart as a strong personality. I remember, too, how we would always try to persuade him, when he came to see us, to say a few words in Zulu, for the clicking sounds were fascinating and required a true virtuosity to render them.

Later William came to make friends with greater facility: but at first he chose them principally among musicians. My brother, my sister and I already counted van Dieren and Berners among our friends, and a year or two later we added to them Constant Lambert, at the age of seventeen a prodigy of intelligence and learning, and gifted with that particularly individual outlook and sense of humour which, surely, were born in him and are impossible to acquire. William had soon adopted these friends and been adopted by them, but in addition he possessed others among composers who were solely his own.

The first work of William Walton's I heard given in public was a piece of chamber-music which had been chosen as the only English contribution to the International Festival of Modern Music in 1923, held that year at Salzburg. To be present at it, the composer, Sacheverell and I travelled to the Austrian city. The quartet was an incursion into atonal music, and was not too successful, though the second movement showed considerable mastery. Walton had scarcely as yet, I believe, emerged with his own style. I had recognized at once his lyric and elegiac gifts, but it was not until the rehearsals of *Façade* that I fully realized his genius.

In the past twenty-five years, *Façade* has been given many times. At its first public performance it created a scandal and involved all connected with it in a shower of abuse and insult. But it was actually first given on the night of 24th January 1922 in the drawing-room of Sacheverell's and my London house, 2 Carlyle Square – which William was sharing with us –, and the rehearsals for it also took place there. It is not easy to describe *Façade*, nor to explain the kind of entertainment it provides: but its history is not without fascination, and that I can give you, together with an account of the details of which it was built up. First, however, I must emphasize that its primary objects were to exalt the speaking voice to the level of the instruments supporting it, to obtain an absolute balance between the volume of the music and the volume of the sound of the words. Another chief, equally difficult, aim to achieve was the elimination of the personality of the reciter, and also – though this is of lesser consequence – of the musicians, and the abolition, as a result, of the constricting self-consciousness engendered by it. Towards our purpose, the instrumentalists were secreted behind a painted curtain.

Façade has, in the course of its strange career, had three curtains designed for it: the first by Frank Dobson, used for the private and public performances of 1922 and 1923, and also in 1926 at the several perform-ances at the Chenil Gallery; the second, for the International Music Festival at Siena in 1928, by Gino Severini; the third by John Piper, for the Aeolian Hall in 1941. Because of its function, an enormous mask occupied the centre of each of the three of them, but in the first and second the round, open mouth was filled by the receding hollow cone of a trumpet, whereas in the third this has been replaced by a microphone. (The trumpet-shaped instrument to which I refer was a megaphone of a kind invented some years before by a former singer in Grand Opera, and an authority on voice production, who had in the first place devised it to help his own performance in the rôle of Fafner. In time, however, the Admiralty took it up, and it was widely employed during both wars, and during storms at sea when the captain had to shout orders from the bridge through a bellowing wind. The Sengerphone – the inventor, Senger, had named it after himself – triumphantly preserved the purity of the tonal quality it magnified.) Thus the audience saw no-one speaking. The painted curtain was provided instead for it to look at, and it heard the human voice speaking, not singing – but speaking at last on an equality with the music. We had, in short, discovered an abstract method of presenting poetry to an audience.

The idea of *Façade* first entered our minds as the result of certain technical experiments at which my sister had recently been working: experiments in obtaining through the medium of words the rhythm of dance measures such as waltzes, polkas, foxtrots. These exercises were often experimental inquiries into the effect on rhythm, on speed, and on colour of the use of rhymes, assonances, dissonances, placed outwardly, at different places in the line, in most elaborate patterns. Some of the resulting poems were sad and serious:

> Said King Pompey, the Emperor's ape,
> Shuddering black in his temporal cape
> Of dust: 'The dust is everything –,
> The heart to love and the voice to sing,
> Indianapolis,
> And the Acropolis,
> Also the hairy sky that we
> Take for a coverlet comfortably . . .'

Others were mocking and gay:

> When
> Sir
> Beelzebub called for his syllabub in the hotel in Hell
> Where Proserpine first fell,
> Blue as the gendarmerie were the waves of the sea . . .

All possessed a quite extraordinary and haunting fascination.

Otherwise, apart from this general origin in the words, it is difficult to say which of us thought of the various parts of the production, for we were all four continually in one another's company, and as soon as the initial idea had somehow or other entered the air, it had filled us with enthusiasm. The title itself, *Façade*, was taken from the remark – it had been repeated to us – of a bad artist, a painter, with the side-whiskers of the period but with a name which, as it proved, has not attached itself to the epoch. He had passed judgement on my sister in the words, 'Very clever, no doubt – but what is she but a Façade!' This had greatly delighted us, since what can any poet hope for better than to constitute a façade for his poetry? It seemed an admirable summing-up, and the very title for the sort of entertainment we wanted to present. William was of course to compose the music. I remember very well the rather long sessions, lasting for two or three hours, which my sister and the composer used to have, when together they read the words, she going over them again and again, while he marked and accented them for his own guidance, to show where the precise stress and emphasis fell, the exact inflection or deflection. For the rest, I had thought of the manner of presenting *Façade*, of the curtain and the use of a mask, Sacheverell had found the Sengerphone, and he and William went up to Hampstead by bus to interview Mr Senger.

The rehearsals for the first performance dwell with an ineradicable vividness in my memory, and there prosper with their own warmth, kindling even the bleak prospect outside. The drawing-room is of the usual L-shaped London type. Three windows look out on the square, and one, at the back, on to a tall sycamore, the branches of which in this peculiarly bitter February weather looked black as night, except where hoar-frost lay on them, so that the whole tree took on the glitter and flash of a tree in a Hoxton tinsel-print. The instruments formed a sextet: flute, clarinet, saxophone, trumpet, 'cello and percussion. The players sat at the wide end of the room, near the three windows. Through these poured the implacable whiteness derived from the snow-covered ground outside, from which beat up a pure and alpine vibration under a green-white sky. Inside, the room, with its tones of pink and blue and white and violet, seemed filled with polar lights from windows and tropic lights from fires: for all the glass objects, of which there were so many, and the doors lined with mirror, glittered with redoubled vehemence. As the strange new sounds shaped themselves under the hands of the rather angry players, the evening outside began to envelop the world in a grape-bloom blue, the lights had to be turned on, and the pictures glowed from the white walls. I say the players were rather angry, and so at first they were: irate with the young conductor who seemed to know his way about in this new and difficult world he had evolved. He stood there, holding his baton, with something of the air of an elegant and handsome snipe – for in the last three years his appearance had grown more stylized –, or, if there was a hitch in the music and a pause had to ensue, he came, as I often told him, to resemble a famous animal music-hall star of the period, the Boxing Kangaroo. But William possessed persistence as well as genius, and led his players safely through. Soon they became interested, if puzzled, then amused and pleased. I remember the clarinet player inquiring, during a pause of the composer, who was conducting:

'Excuse me, Mr Walton, has a clarinet player ever done you an injury?'

In spite of the two piled-up, blazing fires of Derbyshire coal – it had been cut deep under the park at Renishaw – the room remained at freezing-point; but soon Mrs Powell appeared from downstairs, carrying a tray on which stood glasses and two gigantic straw-covered Chianti flasks full of sloe-gin which she had made in the autumn, bringing back the berries from her native Herefordshire uplands, and as, like Ceres in a late-Italian picture, she dispensed it in generous measure, the instrumentalists warmed to their work, and the long afternoon itself began to glow, to possess its own perfumes, its own atmosphere, unique, never to be recovered. I had, of course, always comprehended the genius of the words, but as I heard the music I understood, too, its genius, the incomparable manner in which the composer, who was not yet twenty years of age, had played with every idea, and matched, underlined and exhibited the words. This music was full of the feeling of the growth of animals and green things, of crude bird song, of breaths of a world of felicity forfeited, of a tender melancholy, and in some numbers, of the jauntiest, most inexplicable gaiety.

The performance took place the following evening at 9.30. The programme, typewritten, bears no date, and the cover carries the words:

'FAÇADE'

Miss Edith Sitwell
on her
Sengerphone

with accompaniments,
overture and interlude
by
W. T. Walton.

Then follow the titles, and the poems, in this order:

(1) Overture.
(2) Madame Mouse Trots.
(3) The Octogenarian.
(4) *Aubade.*
(5) The Wind's Bastinado.
(6) Said King Pompey.
(7) Interlude.
(8) Jumbo's Lullaby.
(9) Small Talk (1)
              (2)
(10) Rose Castles.
(11) Introduction and Hornpipe.
(12) Long Steel Grass.
(13) When Sir Beelzebub.
(14) Switchback.
(15) Bank Holiday (1)
              (2)
(16) Springing Jack.
(17) En Famille.
(18) Mariner Men (Presto.)

After the final poem comes the notice:

'FAÇADE'

All these poems, and some additional ones, will appear in a book called 'Façade' which Miss Edith Sitwell is publishing privately in a limited edition with a special frontispiece in colour by Gino Severini – at the Favil Press, Kensington.

The front part of the room was so densely packed with thin gold chairs, it was scarcely possible to move. Across the narrow opening where had been the conventional double doors, now stretched the Dobson curtain. Painters, musicians and poets, of whom a large proportion of the audience consisted, were naturally enthusiastic in their reception of *Façade*, for it was essentially an entertainment for artists and people of imagination. But it must be admitted that in the comparatively small drawing-room of Carlyle Square, the sheer volume of sound was overwhelming and that many of the more orthodox friends whom we had invited to be present were so perturbed by a performance unlike any other they had seen or heard, and for which they could not pick out from the repertory of party-experience the correct label, 'Charming', 'My dear, we *loved* every moment of it!' or 'It reminds me of old days at Covent Garden!', that they did not know what to say, or where to look. We had fortunately arranged for an ample supply downstairs of hot rum punch, an unusual but efficacious restorative. It had been brewed after an old recipe supplied by our friend Barclay Squire, the learned archivist and historian of music, and included among its ingredients, as well as rum, I remember, green tea, sherry, China tea and the juice of a fresh pineapple. This served to revive quickly those who had lost their bearings on a voyage of discovery, and had arrived back feeling somewhat confused, concussed and self-conscious.

Fifteen months later, we gave *Façade* at the Aeolian Hall, at 3 o'clock in the afternoon of 12th June 1923. During the space of time that had elapsed, we had striven to smooth out the imperfections of the entertainment. I have not been able to obtain a copy of the programme, but I remember the wording ran: *Osbert Sitwell presents Miss Edith Sitwell in 'Façade'*.

The press – or rather that section of it now defunct, the gossip-crew, which cherished a deadly parasitic hatred and fear of all work, manual or intellectual, but more especially artistic – had been engaged for days past in trying to whip up the public to pretend to feel rage and resort to insult. Many hours before the curtain rose – or, more precisely in this case, was lowered – the air had grown so tense that I recollect how it rendered my brother and me ill at ease to the extent of being unable to eat any luncheon. From 1 o'clock, therefore, we sat silently within the Burlington Fine Arts Club's demure precincts – at that hour deserted, for they included no dining-room – until it was time to walk the short hundred yards or so to the Aeolian Hall. A large audience had already assembled when we arrived to join my sister in the Artists' Room. I proceeded on to the platform first, walking in front of the curtain to make a speech describing the novel elements in the performance, and attempting to explain its aims. After acknowledging the applause, I went behind the curtain to announce the various items of the entertainment through the mouth of the mask, smaller than the principal head in the middle. Then the fanfare which heralds *Façade* sounded, and the fun began.

On this occasion the entertainment took full effect, though not in the manner we had expected, or at least had hoped for: without apparent reason now infuriating a house that, twenty years later, was to wax to the same degree enthusiastic. The front rows, especially, manifested their contempt and rage, and, albeit a good deal of applause countered the hissing and indicated interest and enthusiasm in certain quarters, nevertheless the atmosphere was so greatly and so evidently hostile that at the end of the performance several members of the audience came behind the curtain to warn my sister not to leave the platform until the crowd had dispersed. For several weeks subsequently, we were obliged to go about London feeling as if we had committed a murder. When we entered a room, there would fall a sudden unpleasing hush. Even friends avoided catching one's eye, and if the very word *Façade* was breathed, there ensued a stampede for other subjects and for safety. In fact, we had created a first-class scandal in literature and music.

The morning following the entertainment, 13th June, brought indeed a black, bleak dawn for us in the press. The fun, the wit, the tunefulness, the beauty, to which qualities, when three years later the performance was repeated at the Chenil Gallery, Mr Ernest Newman was to draw attention in the columns of the *Sunday Times* – he was not present at the first performance in the Aeolian Hall –, on this occasion completely escaped the critics. All the papers except the *Daily Mail* combined in attack. The mask on the curtain was characterized as a 'meaningless, crudely-painted moonface', the music as 'collected from the works of the most eccentric of the ultra-moderns', while the words were dismissed as 'drivel'.

The consequences of *Façade* were several: one was that the notion, difficult to dislodge, now entered the Philistine public's head that Edith, Sacheverell and I were continually declaiming our poems through megaphones in order to call attention to ourselves: whereas the whole point of the procedure we had adopted was, as I have explained – and even explained on the day of the performance – precisely opposite in its intention, which was to conceal the reciter and abolish his personality. The idea, however, still persists or recurs from time to time in the more dusty sections of the press, and in little technical treatises on poetry written apparently by plumbers for their mates. I have, I may say, met people who even have convinced themselves that they have been present in the flesh at such gatherings, that they have heard and seen us read through megaphones – have watched us, with trumpets clamped to our lips, spouting.

CHAPTER FIVE

My sister, in the years immediately following the war, had been responsible for drawing attention in England to the work of Miss Gertrude Stein, then greatly neglected here, and in the summer of 1929 Edith and I accompanied Miss Alice Toklas and Miss Stein to Oxford, to hear that gifted writer deliver her celebrated lecture under the auspices of my friend Harold Acton. We had seen in the motor how nervous she was, albeit as I watched her on the platform, while the chairman was introducing her before her speech, I found it hard to credit, for always in her pose as she sat, there was something monumental, as if she were sitting to a painter who was making a record for posterity: the body turned to stone from flesh, but more powerful, in no way dead, and her massive philosopher's head had the eagle-lines of a Red Indian warrior's. When she stood up – and always, because of the latent force to be divined in her, one expected her to be taller than she was – she showed a mastery of her audience, and her address, though couched in her accustomed style, proved a consummate piece of lucidity. I remember, however, a certain commotion arising and some accompanying laughter, when towards the middle of her discourse she remarked, 'Everything is the same and everything is different!'

Many undergraduates had come to the hall to amuse themselves after the lecture at the expense of a writer widely and angrily derided, her work dismissed as the 'stutterings of a lunatic'. But in the presence of this obviously distinguished woman, the wiser of them recognized that there was not much to be done in this line. At the end, two young gentlemen, not so easily discouraged, shot up to heckle her from positions widely apart in the audience: but they asked an identical question.

'Miss Stein, if everything is the same, how can everything be different?'

In a most genial, comforting manner, Miss Stein replied:

'Well, just look at you two dear boys!'

Everything, then, in this ultimate chapter is, similarly, the same, and yet different from how it was in the scene with which the whole work begins.

What has altered? In these thirty years which have passed, the hedges have grown – perhaps it is that which makes the figure of the man who planted them look smaller. Certainly he complains that he cannot see over them. What else has altered? A whole world has just perished, and the lawns are greener. There have been great and general catastrophes to the nations; and private calamities in the family. The lawns are softer and more smooth.

This is again the month of August, full of green pride. There is a pomp, not only in the full-weighted trees, but in everything, in the clouds, which resemble huge tufts of feathers, or float with the majesty of icebergs in the bursts of sun unloosed by these clouds, in the vanity of the occasional golden weather, when the spangles of the heat dance everywhere above the ground, in the colour of flowers, glossy, coruscating under the light, in the scent of carnation, rose and stock. All is full, over-sweet, over-ripe. At this season, in the decade following the war, we entertained nearly every year a large house-party. Some members of it were invited by my father and mother, others by me, who acted as host. Among my guests was often Constant Lambert, who came on his first visit to us in August 1925, when there were about twenty persons staying in the house. He arrived in time for dinner, at which my father, whose acquaintance he had yet to make, was not present. Constant was only eighteen, and since this was his first large house-party, was very alert and rather nervous. In consequence, he was punctual to the minute in coming down to breakfast at nine o'clock in the dining-room. He found it empty, though the table was laid and the air was full of the savour of breakfast dishes. A plume of steam hovered in the air from a Viennese coffee machine on a sideboard. An almost electric tension brooded in the emptiness, as if anything might occur at any moment. The young musician, however, concentrated on eggs and bacon and coffee, and sat down, with his back to the chimney, and facing the sash windows. Suddenly, the strange happening for which subconsciously he had been waiting occurred: for, looking towards the window opposite him, he was amazed to see the distinguished, bearded, medieval face of an elderly gentleman, crowned with a large grey felt hat, pass just outside, in a horizontal position, – as if he had fallen prone and was about to raise himself – and holding a malacca walking-stick in the mouth. The vision of this venerable figure proceeding on all fours was startling in its unexpectedness, and strongly recalled to the mind of him who beheld it Blake's picture of Nebuchadnezzar, though it is true that the Babylonish king was notably less spruce in appearance, and that his counterpart was plainly English and lacked those memorable nails shaped like the claws of birds. Constant hurried to the window, looked out – and realized what was happening. It was – it must be – my father, at work, and carrying his cane in this unusual manner in order to observe the views and measure from the new level – for he intended to drop the lawn three or four feet, and so, in his present position, was at the height of a man standing at the altitude he planned. But even though Constant knew in his heart who it must be, he was too bewildered to mention what he had seen to the other guests, who now came into the dinning-room, filling it with their chatter.

The atmosphere of the house was gay, this August and in the years immediately preceding and following, for at last we were in full peace, and those of my generation had recovered their spirits and again shed the whole decade that war had added to the age of most of them. But I must emphasize that though I greatly enjoyed the twenties, the years of struggle in my career, when it was necessary to fight, and yet, for all the fury, years too of accomplishment, as well as of travel and pleasure, I never, notwithstanding, felt I belonged to them as did those who could only remember adult life after the war: I was conscious of other claims on my loyalty; I belonged by birth, education, nature, outlook and period to the pre-war era, a proud citizen of the great free world of 1914, in which comity prevailed. Nevertheless, with health restored, and energy in consequence renewed, it was easy to relish the days, possible even to be ready for the perpetual traps my father laid for us.

During several years, and until as late as 1923, he had seven sitting-rooms in his own occupation as studies, and in three or four of these stood a specimen, straddling a sofa, of the desk he had designed in order to enable him to write more easily when lying down. All his papers he kept on the floor, so that each resembled a drift of dusty snow, or a beauty spot after a public holiday. The majority of documents, some of them folded and done up with red tape, others overflowing from boxes or, again, just loose and ready as an angel's wings to float up to heaven on any casual draught, related to the law-suit he was conducting against the coal-lessees: the rest were concerned with his customary interests, pedigrees, household economies, heraldry, decorative furniture, sum-maries of his financial transactions with me, or consisted of notes on *Practical Farming*, on the *Use of Ceremony in Byzantine Court Life*, on the *Origin of the Medieval Romances*, the *Buildings of the Emperor Frederick II in South Italy*, or the *Black Death* – of course –, and on his own *Inventions*, possible and impossible.

In these he had recently been taking a renewed interest. Earlier in the summer, when he was staying in London, he had sent for me to see him one afternoon on an urgent matter. When I entered his room, he rose from his bed, in which he had been resting, locked the door so as to be sure we should not be interrupted, and then went back to bed again. In a low voice, he confided in me:

'You know, Osbert, I sometimes have an idea with money in it.'

'Yes, Father.'

'Well,' he gave a long dry laugh like a cackle, 'I've just produced an egg.'

He waited a little to allow me to look astonished, which certainly I did – sufficiently, even, I think, to satisfy him.

Gratified, he continued, 'It's a breakfast egg . . . The yolk will be made of smoked meat, the white of compressed rice, and the shell of synthetic lime – or a coating of lime. It will be delicious, will last for ever, and be ready at any time. It wouldn't matter where you might be, in the desert or on a polar expedition, all you'd have to do would be to boil it for two or three minutes, as you wished – and there would be your breakfast, ready for you, and very nourishing and sustaining. You'd feel wonderfully fit after it, ready to do a real hard day's work. It may make the whole difference to explorers!'

'What a good idea! You ought to patent it at once.'

'As a matter of fact, that's why I want to consult you. I would like to make a little money for Sachie after I am gone – but how am I to place my egg on the market? I thought perhaps I'd see Selfridge's about it – they seem very go-ahead. But whom shall I ask for, and how shall I announce the reason for my visit? I daren't trust my egg to anyone else – it might be stolen.'

'I should ask for Mr Gordon Selfridge himself. Tell the commissionaire to take you up in the lift, and just step into Mr Selfridge's sanctum, saying, "I'm Sir George Sitwell, and I've brought my egg with me!" '

'Capital idea! That is what I will do. Thank you so much, dear boy: I knew you would help me.'

Accordingly, he set off for the Oxford Street shop the next morning at eleven: he was dressed in a silk hat and a frock-coat, an article of dress already, even then, nearly extinct, and carried a bundle of papers, with diagrams on them. He was very late for luncheon when he returned, and though his eye seemed to rest on me with a certain coldness, he never explained what had happened during the interview, if it took place. My mother did not like to ask him, nor subsequently did he ever refer to the egg again. Yet it had in no whit discouraged him, for I noticed on the floor of one of his studies that the sheaf entitled *Inventions* had grown much more bulky of recent months.

It was, as he often explained, delightfully convenient to keep everything on the floor. 'I know exactly where to find what I want, and can put my hand on it at any moment!' he would say. So that now, when the coal law-suit had just been settled out of court, it was with regret that he began a retreat, and rather ruefully de-requisitioned one sitting-room after another, surrendering them again to the use of the family. But though circumstances obliged him to do this, for he had grown to like many guests to come to the house in August and September, and otherwise there would have been nowhere for them to sit, nevertheless in no least respect did he modify his ideas, moderate his conceptions or abate his flights. Indeed latterly he had coined several new slogans to express his individual sentiments, at last developed to their utmost capacity, and when, having risen from his bed to come down after dinner, he sat by himself, in full evening dress, white tie and waistcoat, in the ballroom in the middle of his Regency sofa, very long, and supported by a carved and painted lion at either end, so that he resembled a Byzantine Emperor on his throne, he would often at this hour, and always to the delight of his children, enunciate his favourite command disguised as a request:

'*I must ask anyone entering the house never to contradict me or differ from me in any way, as it interferes with the functioning of the gastric juices and prevents my sleeping at night.*'

Albeit I tried to persuade him to have this notice printed on cards, and to cause one of them to be placed on the chimney-piece of each room in the house, my efforts, though they came very near success, ended in failure.

During the particular August in question, a distinguished archaeologist was staying in the house, being engaged in excavating for my father the problematic site of the Norman Manor of Eckington, held by the Estoutevilles. The place having been arbitrarily selected, not one stone remained above ground, or was found under it, to suggest that such a building had ever existed. Even Professor Voxall, I apprehend, was surprised when one morning he dug up a bottle of truffles and a tarantula-spider set out on a board; objects which my brother and I, tired of this futile exercise of my father's and of its expense, had, the day before, buried there for the expert to discover. While at Renishaw, this learned man was afflicted with a return of malaria, from which he suffered, having contracted it in the East during the war. When I went to tell my father that his guest was indisposed and would be obliged to stay upstairs for dinner, I found him in bed resting. I ended with the words, 'I only hope he's not dangerously ill. It's *malaria*!' The reaction was immediate. Plainly my father was taking no risks. Almost before I had finished speaking, he had whisked out of bed and rung the bell, and when it was answered he said curtly, 'Robins, bring me my mosquito-net!' Thereafter for a month he slept under it.

My mother, who had quickly tired of her guests, spent much of her time in her bedroom: for she had now a Swiss maid, and had to her delight learnt that Frieda could yodel. One of the endearing traits in my mother's character was that she could never have enough of a good thing, and so she was continually sending for Edith, Sacheverell and me to help her to persuade her maid to perform. The entertainment delighted her, and she would sit in her chair, her face creased, her whole body shaking with laughter, though her brown eyes were still full of melancholy. The Swiss girl did not notice, for she was very shy, and would only consent to perform for us if hidden by a screen: but once installed behind her Japanese panels of black embroidered with bumpy storks in gold thread, she would tirra-lirra her heart out. My sister was usually successful in inducing Frieda to yodel to us, for she was her pupil, taking yodelling lessons every day. So we would all gather there, in my mother's room with its gay but faded paper of bunches of flowers, and its niche and eighteenth-century cornice; my mother in the armchair, near the wide-open window, where the sun-drenched scent of the sweet green leaves she loved came in at her. My sister would be sitting on the bed. Now a person of the utmost distinction and beauty, with her long slender limbs and long-fingered hands, and the musing but singularly sweet expression which always distinguished her, she belonged to an earlier, less hackneyed age, in which the standards of Woolworth mass production did not exist: (in fact, as an American is said to have remarked in front of her portrait in the Tate Gallery, 'Lord, she's gothic, gothic enough to hang bells in!'). My mother, who had so cruelly ill-used her, had come to love her society, her wit and perception, and it was symptomatic of Edith's fineness of character that she responded and, now that my mother was growing old and her spirits flagging, set herself, at a great waste of her own energy and time, to amuse her – and there was little else one could do for her.

Edith, then, would be sitting on the bed: while on a very straight Chippendale chair, but thrown backward and supported in front by his own two long legs, Sacheverell would balance his tall frame. His appearance at that age – twenty-five or six –, his very handsome head, with hair curling at the sides, and with its cut and contours so Italian in essence, but so northern in colour, translated perfectly the strange power and intensity that have always been his, the generous warmth of his temperament, so genial and impulsive, the passion of many kinds that burns in him – passion for people, for books, for learning, for works of art, for old lamps that can be lit again at his fire –, the wit, distinguished and apt, which he despises in himself and does nothing to cultivate, instead preferring the jokes of others which he so immensely enjoys: the flash, deep as bright, of his anger, large as the scale of his mind and frame, but never enduring, breaking down eventually into a smile, though by no means an easy smile. Meanwhile, I, with my rather heavy mask and build, would be seated in an armchair opposite. Frieda's shelter was in front of the door, and sometimes, just as her voice had reached to the top of a high mountain, and was preparing to receive answer from another, my father, attracted by the sound, and always liking to know what was going on, would bolt in and find himself enclosèd with her behind the Japanese screen. He was tall enough for his bearded face, which recalled more vividly every day the Italian paintings of the Renaissance – he was at no great distance from the portrait of Cesar Borgia or of the Grand Turk by Bellini, and from the heads of effigies of the same, or of an earlier, epoch on tombs –, to show just above the top of the screen with an expression of extreme and dignified distaste. He would say nothing – indeed he could not make himself heard, for the maid had not noticed his entry and continued her song until, a few moments later, she suddenly saw him and stopped. Standing on tiptoe, and blushing, she would then peep over the barrier, and say, 'Please, m'lady, I cannot go on with my music'. My mother, still laughing, would say with an effort at control, 'I wish you wouldn't always interrupt, George. You're just like an *auguste* – must always be in everything!' He would go out, with that particular lowering of one shoulder that meant that he would not forget and would think out counter-measures for use later on. Meanwhile Frieda's peaceful, innocent mountain-music would soon again drown every other sound.

Though such incidents continued whenever my father paid me a visit at Renishaw, yet, looking back, 1925 appears to me to have been unequalled. Perhaps it was because the object for which I had striven so long was near to attainment. I had persuaded my father to emigrate – to Italy. Himself was always far happier there, and I had long realized that he was one of the fortunate few whose energies and wish to control those round them increase and strengthen with age – he was now sixty-five. Though I realized that my parents, of course, would continue to visit me from time to time for long periods in England, and I should have to stay with them in Italy, yet their residence abroad would induce a new feeling of rest and freedom in the air. As an inducement to him, there was Montegufoni, with its enormous house and garden just waiting to be 'improved'! He liked the idea; 'I shall be known as the Italian Sir George,' he remarked – though I never could make out by whom. In addition, he was able to furnish for his own consideration and enjoyment historic precedents and parallels: he thought of the Emperor Charles V and his renunciation of two worlds, and then of his own ancestor, Walter de Boys . . . But in the interval he would abandon himself to nostalgia and heart-searchings. It was hard, indeed, to be obliged by your care for the future, and by your selfless devotion to your children, to abandon the old home in the autumn of your days: for his inner thoughts on subjects of this kind were now, I fear, always couched in such set phrases – as is nearly always the case with someone who is sentimental without being affectionate. Meanwhile there was much to be done. He shut up Wood End and from there moved all the furniture, which he had brought from Italy, to Renishaw, sorted the pieces, added to them others he had imported similarly to Renishaw, and then sent the whole lot back to Italy. The same patient frieze of workmen whom we saw in *The Scarlet Tree* plodded by impassively with articles of furniture, backwards and for-wards, or placed and extended their ladder, to the same music of my father's perpetual 'No, no, no: all wrong!' Sometimes a guest lying in bed would be startled by my father, at the head of his troupe, bursting in and proceeding to remove all the furniture. Neither he nor the workmen would heed protests, and the poor victim, as my father went on remorselessly, inexorably, to dismantle the room, would begin to believe himself invisible and inaudible, indeed almost to doubt his own existence. At last he might be able to get through some remote hint, as though it were a message in a bottle, to my mother, who would at once stop Frieda yodelling, send for my father, and say, 'George, you can't do that!'

'Somebody has to do the work, Ida. I don't know how it would get done without me! It is a great strain on my health.'

My mother repeated to herself softly the refrain of a famous clown's song: 'A Terrible Lot To Do Today, To Do Today, To Do Today. A Terrible Lot To Do Today, To Do To Do Today.'

'You ought to take things more easily,' she would urge.

'But how can I? Everybody on the place sometimes has a holiday. But I can never afford to take one!'

'Nonsense, George.'

'Well, what would happen to you all if I did?'

He went on to explain that he was winding up his interests at Renishaw as fast as he could: but some things he would be obliged to leave unfinished. There was Barber's house, the two Golf Club Houses, and the Manor in Warwickshire I had lent to my Aunt Florence for her lifetime, and which my father had been for many years restoring.

'And none of the work is for myself,' he pointed out. 'It's all for others!'

'Yes, but you know,' I interposed, 'that in most cases the people you are doing it for have asked you not to do it.'

'I'm afraid I can't help that! It's the *right thing* to do – and now most of it will have to wait until I'm able to visit Renishaw – if I'm spared!' And a look of dejection spread over his face, as he thought of how he was setting out to make his way in the world all over again.

On the eve of his departure for a new home, I offer a brief summary, by another hand, of his various activities during the previous decade. The reader, familiar with them already, will find, I trust, that by the addition of this bird's-eye view to my own he will obtain a solid, almost stereoscopic vision of them. These extracts which, short as they are, disclose, moreover, a glimpse of a fascinating personal, or impersonal, relationship, are taken from the Estate Correspondence, and were addressed by the agent to his former chief, Peveril Turnbull, whose pupil he had been.

Jan. 9, 1911. Sir George writes every day. He has taken over Plumbley Railway, and is going ahead with the carriage drive through it.

Jan. 16, 1911. I have just received a letter from Sir G. wanting all sorts of particulars re bringing water from the Eckington Woods to the Lake by piping through the Railway Cutting. I will find out the cost of pipes and that may frighten him.

June 7, 1911. You kindly ask me how I am getting on, but I don't know, for we've just had my pet nuisance (Sir G.) here for a week. I have over 40 men, 11 horses and a traction-engine working, the rent audits begin tomorrow. I am busy getting particulars for this year's land auctions and Merry went to the Auditor to ask when he can come here to go through the accounts. Sir G. wants the rates on woods appealing against etc. etc. etc.

Nov. 21, 1911. We are worrying at a plan for a gardener's cottage. Sir G. alters it every five minutes.

Dec. 21, 1911. We have had Sir G. here all this week (rather a nuisance when one wants to get rent audits squared up). I think I drove him away by developing a bad cold. He is worrying about the gardener's house, alterations to Barber's, and great alterations to the Far Landing.

Jan. 4, 1912. Sir G. is here since Tuesday. We are laying out Barber's garden: and lifting the turf on the lawn at Renishaw, taking out the subsoil and putting in 18 inches of good soil. We are altering the Golf House (at Renishaw), and building greenhouses, etc.

Feb. 19, 1912. I am quite well myself but horribly sick of drawing plans forty times over for Sir G. and continually falling out with him over them.

July 4, 1912. He (Sir George) gets frightfully angry when the slightest thing goes wrong, such as the fact of the loganberries being ripe, and its not being reported to him. He considers everything can be foreseen and arranged. All my time is taken up with going about from one job to another, for we have about 60 to 70 men working all over the estate . . . My wages are £230 per annum and house.

Jan. 11, 1913. I find it very difficult to get money out of Sir G. to pay for the various works . . . We are now making a golf-course for Rotherham. We are just about to spend £2,000 on the Golf House at Renishaw.

Jan. 14, 1913. Sir George sends me a long list this morning of things I have done wrongly through not consulting him. In future, I am to consult him about everything. I want to build a new earth-closet for Staniforth's cottage, but I suppose Sir G. will tell me to wait until he has had time to consult Lutyens about the best form to build.

March 20, 1913. We have C. E. Mallows, the architect, on with Barber's garden and are delving furiously so that Sir G. may see how it looks before he goes abroad. We are also constructing turrets in plaster to give him the effect of ones in stone. These are for the entrance gates.

Oct. 13, 1913. I've been offered the job of road-surveyor for this district. It's the sort of job I've always wanted, so I'm astonished to find myself not at all anxious to take it on. I don't like leaving Sir G. while he has so many irons in the fire . . . A good row with Sir G. now would help me to decide. The gardens here looked very wonderful last month but nobody was here to see them.

Feb. 4, 1914. Wages this week £110. We have 80 men, a traction-engine, a steam wagon and 21 horses working. There appears to be no sign of pulling up . . .

Sept. 8, 1914. Sir G. wants us to take over all the poor pasture on the Estate and plant with wheat. We are to plough up the South Park and no end of a job it is on the top of our work.

March 20, 1915. I had a go at Sir G. this morning, and think I have screwed him up to £300. He sticks at making it permanent, and thinks it should come down again if the cost of living comes down, but I'm hanged if I'll ever do it for less.

May 12, 1916. Sir G. is here, and insists on wasting labour on Barber's garden still.

March 29, 1917 . . . Sir George has given all the Warwickshire tenants notice, and intends to take their farms in hand. This in spite of your warning letter. He would have taken all the Mosbro' and Eckington Woods valley farms, had I not turned very stupid about it.

Feb. 17, 1918. We have over 500 acres of wheat in on the various farms. Thinking of harvest is like a nightmare. Sir G. says I have not enough work to justify a permanent assistant!

Feb. 13, 1920. We are still chucking money away on the old black-and-white house at Long Itchington at the rate of £35 a week.

April 19, 1920. Sir G. came to terms with the Colliery Company on Saturday. I thought it a jolly good thing at the time, but am beginning now to doubt it. All the stored-away plans for gardens, garden-terraces, etc. are being hauled out ready to go on with this summer. I look like having my hands full.

June 17, 1922. (Farming) losses make it very difficult to get any pay out of Sir G . . . I was a fool for turning down that road-surveying job!

Before emigrating, there was much business to be transacted, much writing to be done. He composed and sent letters, identical in terms, to the Chancellor of the Exchequer and the Archbishop of Canterbury. In them he pointed out that it was a hard thing for an old man to be driven out of his own home by the burden of taxation: but there it was, in future his dear son would pay, and he was setting out, with the capital sum he had acquired in his lifetime, to make a new career for himself and his descendants in Italy.

By now, he had fallen badly into the mock-gothic idiom, and later, when he had reached the Castello, he made the following entry: 'In mid-September, 1925, the Lady Ida and I set out, with fair wind, for France, and thence to Italy, to make a new home for ourselves. Before leaving, I had divided my lands and goods between my two sons, and collected the rents and debts due to me: those which I could not collect, I forgave: we propose to settle in the ancient Castle of Montegufoni, which I purchased in Osbert's name in 1906.'

My mother took the change philosophically, except for her fear that she would not get the English newspapers punctually.

'The Government muddle everything,' she would remark.

Certainly it was a new life for my father and mother. The first night was to be spent at Boulogne, because a long journey, he averred, tired his back, and probably too because, an ancient town, it had lain on the old pilgrim route – a fact which always now greatly influenced the direction of his travelling. Our adventures, which ranged in tone from tragedy to farce and back again, started on the cross-Channel steamer, where my mother sat on deck, near a couple of parents who were on their way to visit the grave of their son, who had been killed at the Battle of the Somme in 1916. On the boat the poor father had a heart attack; his first one. My mother, with a kindly impulse to help, said, 'I've the very thing! The doctor has given me some stuff for the heart. Call Frieda, and tell her to get it out of my bag!' Unfortunately, the action of my mother's heart was fast, that of the traveller slow: the medicine at once further retarded it, and he grew rapidly worse. At Boulogne, an ambulance had to be called to meet him at the quay. My father sat near by, watching, and remarking from time to time, 'One day your mother will be the death of someone!' or 'Poor man, you'd have thought having to go to see his son's grave was enough!' I never heard whether he recovered.

Meanwhile it was found that my father had told his servant to register all the luggage through to Paris, where we were not going: there was no way of obtaining it until the next day, and we were doomed to pass a miserable night without our belongings at Boulogne, in a large seaside hotel with interior walls of paper-like thinness. By the time we arrived at the hotel my father, unprepared for the brand of gothic discomfort with which he was thus faced, was in a far from good humour. My brother and I went upstairs to see our bedrooms, and as we came down the double staircase, mean in its Louis XV hotel pretensions, we could hear my father indulging in the curious buzzing-like humming we knew so well, for he always made this noise when irritable or angry. He was walking up and down the hall with a rapid, impatient gait, just outside the dining-room.

'It sounds exactly like a bluebottle,' I remarked to my brother.

At that moment my father approached, and looking in the direction of the dining-room, said at once, and in character: 'I was just wondering which table to settle on!' That we laughed – and it was difficult not to do so – made the atmosphere still more uneasy.

Baveno, on Lake Maggiore, was always my father's first Italian stopping-place, and we set out for it the next day, going straight through on the train-de-luxe, while Robins and Frieda came on by a cheaper train. Directly Robins arrived he went up to my father's room. It was about two in the afternoon, and he found the old gentleman resting. He was in bed, as usual with the head of it turned against the light, so that he lay facing the door, and he was wearing a coat over his pyjamas. As Robins came in, his master looked at him severely, and remarked:

'You've again forgotten my keys, Robins! I've told you repeatedly not to let me travel without them.'

Robins crossed behind him, and taking up the keys, which were lying on the dressing-table beside a heavy gold watch and chain, as they had been taken out of his pocket by my father when he had undressed, said, 'I knew I hadn't forgotten them. Here they are, Sir George, with your watch!'

Without looking round, my father said, 'No they're not! And by forgetting them, you've put me to a great deal of trouble and expense. I've had to force the locks of all the luggage.'

As he finished speaking, pandemonium broke loose in the passage outside. There were sounds of sobbing and shouting, even screams. Robins rushed from the room and found two ladies, the manager, valets and porters and maids in furious altercation. He remarked, too, what he had not observed when he came in, all my mother's and father's luggage lying there, and at once noticed that there seemed more of it than usual. At this moment the quarrellers united and attacked him in a body. What did he mean by it? Had other people's property no value for him? They would call in the Carabinieri: he would soon be shut up in a cell. It was a scandal! Other phrases of the same kind poured out. The explanation of all this disturbance was that my father had not only broken open his own luggage and that of my mother, but also two large trunks which had been lying near it, outside neighbouring doors. These had been placed there, packed and locked, ready to be taken to Baveno station, in order to be registered to Paris by the train-de-luxe, in which the owners of the two boxes were travelling. The train was due to start in an hour's time. Indeed, the two ladies had just been leaving in the omnibus, when they looked for their luggage and discovered what had occurred. The locks were destroyed beyond repair, the contents in disorder, turned upside-down as if a Customs-House officer had been running wild through them.

Robins escaped back into my father's room, and told him what had happened. My father calmly bolted the door, and said:

'I'm afraid I really can't help other people's troubles!'

Eventually the manager found two other trunks (my father refused to contribute a centime to the cost), and the two poor ladies hurriedly repacked and, still in a woebegone condition, just caught the ordinary passenger train, on which, no doubt, they were compelled to sit up all night.

Even after this, the new life did not move at once into an easier rhythm. The weather was unexpectedly bad. It rained without ceasing: and we sat silent at luncheon, in a bay window overlooking the lake. It was like being in an aquarium – sky, lake, land, were all water. And we had to drink water, too – for thus embarking on a new career had increased my father's attention to economy, and we were not allowed wine, though it was the beverage of the country. At least, however, my father's decorative sense never deserted him and one particularly cold, wet day, after sweeping aside the waiter's suggestion of a bottle of red wine, he remarked with the familiar flutter of his hand, as water was brought in a light-blue jug:

'That's always been my theory: water should be served in a glass jug, with just a touch of blue in it.'

To which my mother added, in a melancholy but rather angry tone:

'Yes, George – and a gold fish!'

All these superficially humourous incidents were, of course, only the minor episodes of a life in many directions tragic, and certainly unsuited to its times: they gained their humour from the often grave and always resourceful character of the man, and the dignity of person against which they were displayed. Such was the strength of will my father exercised that argument on any point with him was outside the bounds of possibility. One could only protest, make a gesture, or ridicule; he would never listen to reason now, and, as ever, that he could be in the wrong was inconceivable to him. Thus even such occurrences as I have just narrated produced an extra sense of frustration in those who shared in them.

Montegufoni was now a very different place from what it had been when my father bought it. The courts had been cleared of their accretions of buildings, so that vistas of other rooms or of courtyards could be obtained from every room in the house. The vegetables, lettuces and Indian corn and tomatoes, had been removed from the terraces, and Tuscan roses bloomed month by month in their place. The oleander, in size a tree, which had been moved, flowered now in the middle of a small box parterre my father had made in the Cardinal's Garden: but in spite of alterations, the main changes were still to come. This vast labyrinth of a building, in which for the past thirteen years, since he had bought it, there had been perpetual discoveries and openings-up, and renovating and repainting, was in the next fifteen years never to know an hour's rest from structural repairs and decoration: it was being continually carried back, pinned down to a past that – like the present – only existed in my father's mind. During this period, both my mother and father were to find a comparative contentment, even happiness, they had never yet known, for my mother liked the climate, and the life in Florence, and my father enjoyed the absence of life in the house. Another rhythm and tempo had been substituted for the Renishaw comedy, those of the *Commedia dell'Arte*. The old play of my father's aloofness, and lack of interest in people, the largeness and smallness of his mind, with its contradictory layers of intense nonconformity and yet of respect for the conventions, against my mother's unthinking, easy, unfailing sociability, and complete want of intellect or esthetic understanding, was acted once again in this new setting, still more grandiose, romantic, and yet in a sense derelict (for it was without life and belonged only to the theatre), so that the action had now the fullest sweep and scope. My mother, for example, would ask twenty people to luncheon, and forget to tell either my father or the butler or chef; indeed it would pass from her mind altogether. Suddenly, just as my father was having a quiet early luncheon, the guests would arrive, tired and hungry after their long mountain run – that was the sort of incident which would occur regularly, affording, as it were, a theme for variation. As for my father, nobody, when he was out of his study, would know where to find him, though he would be in the house or on the terrace: one moment he would be inspecting the well in the cellars; the next, peasants, wandering below, would be astonished to see Il Barone at the top of the tower, with his glasses to his eyes. Sometimes they would think they descried him there after dusk, high up under the sky, outlined against it in the lily-like opening, until they began to believe that he was an astrologer practising his craft, telling the course of the future. Actually, he was more concerned with the earth than formerly. He began, too, almost to *like* people in the excitement he derived from showing them the Castello, and what he had done to it.

Many of the visitors were distinguished in the arts, but my father and mother never knew who they were. Sometimes, therefore, when I was in England, my mother would, if she remembered the names, write to me, to make inquiries concerning the identity of her guests, or to give me a description of them. And I found that my mother's pen-pictures were always more vibrant and full of point than my father's. 'A Mr D. H. Lawrence came over the other day,' she wrote, 'a funny little petit-maître of a man with flat features and a beard. He says he is a writer, and seems to know all of you. His wife is a large German. She went round the house with your father, and when he showed her anything, would look at him, lean against one of the gilded beds, and breathe heavily.'

As my father grew older, he plainly lost his bearings and ceased to know any longer who was alive and who dead. I have already described how he invented a novelist who did not exist: now, in somewhat similar but more macabre fashion, he planned to give a party.

'I thought next May, I'd give an Artists' Party, Osbert,' he announced to me; for artists were still a tribe, like the Levites, set apart. 'May is always the best month here. And it would be nice if you two boys could come out to join me. We'd get some really interesting people together, who could be relied upon to entertain one another – far less tiring for the host!'

'Who would you ask?' I inquired cautiously, well knowing already that he would not, of course, ask any of our own friends among painters, and was, indeed, quite unaware of their names or profession when they arrived to stay at Renishaw: nor would he be likely to ask the older masters we admired, of whom Picasso was the chief. But I was startled when, as he reeled off for me the list, I comprehended both how thoroughly he had thought it out, and that all of his proposed guests, Whistler, Degas, Renoir, Rodin, Lalique, Sargent, at least possessed one thing in common: they were all dead!

My father occupied as his study a room in a good strategical position, for it was situated right in the middle of the Castle. From this room, directed the alterations, usually in company with a character known as Il Professore, whose duty it was to superintend the scraping and restoring and faking that was everywhere in progress. It was difficult sometimes to tell what were the improvements on which the workmen were engaged. Once, for example, I remember my father taking me into a room where six plasterers had been employed for a fortnight, from early morning till dusk, scratching the walls like a mischief of monkeys.

'Do you notice any change here?' he asked.

And when I replied, 'No, none,' he said with an air of intense gratification, 'Good, that's just what I've been aiming at!'

Henry Moat – who had come back to look after my father – took to life at the Castello with joy. Now he presided with a still more immense dignity over my mother's luncheon parties, and the sound of his tread as he came to announce a guest was equivalent in stateliness to a procession. He liked the red wine, the peasant girls, the sunshine, the sleepiness. Apart from occasional attacks of the gout from which he now suffered, this period formed a long Indian Summer for him, as it did for my parents. While my mother was in Florence, and my father resting, Henry would retire to read in his small room upstairs, which rather resembled a cabin.

He would call my father at five and bring him breakfast not long afterwards. My father would then read *The Times* of two days before, and other journals and letters, till seven, when he would get up. At eight he would go round the Castle in detail, telling all the workmen to stop what they were doing, and do something else instead. Then he would consider the garden, interfere with the gardeners, and go back to write in his room, probably various severe letters. If he intended a letter to be really disagreeable, he would pen it many times, at each correction infusing into it a fresh but icy venom. After this fashion he would both perfect it, and also be able to keep a copy. He would have luncheon, usually by himself, at 11.30; then a siesta till three, when he would get up again, and go the rounds of the Castle once more, this time informing the men that they were gravely at fault, had misunderstood what he had said earlier, must undo everything they had done since, and go back to what he had stopped them doing in the morning. The Italian plasterers and painters, in their round caps made of newspaper and their light overalls, with their faces covered with fine dust from the walls, seemed thoroughly to enjoy all this.

My father and Henry still had differences of opinion. Thus one winter night when my father was travelling in Sicily, Henry entered his master's bedroom, to tidy it and to take his clothes away, rather later than usual – very late, according to my father's standards, it being about 8 p.m. My father was already in bed, with the light out, and a sharp altercation followed. In the course of it Henry remarked that he did not like having his 'head bit off'. He then left the room, slamming the door behind him; only to find himself in complete darkness, for in the passage the lights had been turned out by an economically-minded porter. Too proud to go back and open the door, or to ask my father's help, he proceeded on his way, blundered with all his immense weight into a piece of furniture with sharp corners, and for a full week subsequently carried about with him the mark of this misadventure in the shape of two black eyes.

My father was greatly delighted at the turn things had taken, and told me all about it when next I saw him.

'Henry burst into my room late one night in Taormina,' he related, 'and was very insolent . . . I suppose the charitable thing would be to think that he'd been indulging in those heavy Sicilian wines (such a mistake! He's getting on, and should be more careful!). But I'm glad to say, when he left the room, the great man forgot to turn the light on outside, fell against a cupboard, and completely knocked himself out. You never saw such black eyes! Like Turner sunsets. He's been much more civil since . . . Of course, I haven't mentioned it to him!'

Henry, for his part, complained that during his own long absence my father's manners had deteriorated. He had, his servant averred, abandoned his former dignified choice of language. Previously he had never even been known to use a single colloquialism: but whether owing to my influence – to that knowledge of modern slang which he sometimes alleged I possessed –, I do not know, Henry asserted that now, when he approached his master one morning and politely asked for the settlement of an account, long overdue, my father sidled towards him, and slowly bringing his face very close to that of his servant, pronounced clearly, in quiet but menacing tones, the words, '*Shut your ugly mug, can't you!*'

'Believe me, Mr Osbert, you could 'ave knocked me down with a feather, when I 'eard 'im demean 'imself like that,' Henry added.

On learning this, I decided to make use of the reputation with which my father had endowed me, of being a master of modern slang. The worst of it was, I knew so little of it. Almost less than my father, of whose customary innocence in this respect, I produce, as prelude to what followed now, an example from a year or two earlier. One afternoon in London, I had gone to see him and found him lying on his bed, with a pleased and meditative expression. He at once remarked to me:

'Dr Borenius called on me this morning. It appears he wishes to give me a present. Very kind of him, I'm sure. But I don't like putting him to the expense.'

'What sort of a present, Father?'

'A ring – one of those Merovingian rings, I presume. He knows I'm interested in such things, and has lately written on them in the *Burlington* or some other paper.'

'I'd like to see it some time.'

'Well, he said he'd send it to me on Thursday . . . So any day after that . . .'

There seemed to me something odd about the matter, but it was not until I related to William Walton in the evening what my father had said, that the explanation struck him, and he elucidated it for me; as our friend Borenius himself later confirmed to us.

'Of course what Borenius said was that he'd telephone! "I'll give you a ring, Sir George, on Thursday!" '

I think that my father, though in general, as we have seen, he disliked receiving presents, was in this instance disappointed. At any rate, he remarked to me a few days later, but without any indication to whom or what the remark applied,

'Such a pity to promise people things, and then forget about them. It is most inconsiderate – really, inexcusable.'

So, at Montegufoni that autumn, I decided to experiment. Having first taught my father to substitute for 'If I should pass away this month', a favourite phrase of his, the less formal, more intimate, 'If I should pop off', which, pronounced with great dignity and pathos, was most effective, I was encouraged to more spectacular flights. He did not always notice things at once if you wanted him to, and so, to make sure, I pronounced in very clear tones to him, for several evenings running, the word *blotto*, saying, 'I don't know why, but I feel completely *BLOTTO* tonight'. Finally he remarked it, and asked me what it meant. I replied, it meant tired – very tired.

'A term of military origin, I presume, Osbert?'

'Indian, I should say, Father, like tiffin and mufti, and perhaps muffin.'

'Very interesting.'

After that he adopted the new expression, and, a few days later, when two ancient American men came over to luncheon, remarked at the end of the meal with genial condescension, 'I've had rooms prepared for you for a siesta after lunch, in case you feel *blotto*. I'm completely *blotto* myself!' The two Americans looked astonished, and on their return to Florence complained to their friends that it was not the sort of thing they expected a dignified English gentleman like Sir George to say to them.

My mother, though she could not talk the language, made many friends among Florentines and our Tuscan neighbours. They appreciated her simplicity and impulsive kindness, and could sympathize with, or at any rate understand, her rages. The large rooms, the flowers, the warmth, suited her. She would join in the Comedy both consciously and unconsciously, by continually providing situations in which my father's contradictory qualities – the mainspring of character comedy – were given full play. Through the many autumn hours of sunshine, he would recline on a long wicker chair, aloft in the Cardinal's Garden, planning and scheming as though death did not exist: and my mother, if she were not in Florence, would sit in a low comfortable arm-chair just inside, by the central window – which was also a door – of the Gallery. As I entered, she would look up from her rattling cloud of dismembered English newspapers, and would remark – it was one of her favourite labels for him – 'Your father's pretty preposterous today!' She habitually ran the alliterative syllables into one word, and added an extra 'r'; *pretty-preprostrous*. Then she would gaze, with her large melancholy brown eyes, at the hedge of verbena, the golden mounds of sweet geranium, the scent of which filled the house, just as the bumping and buzzing of large winged beetles and bees outside filled it with the lazy sound of their droning. Occasionally, too, a huge butterfly or some immense droning insect would enter the long room, and flutter or rise and fall under the coved and painted ceiling. Outside the oleander flowered now, its branches and green-grey leaves sprinkled with rosettes of pink blossom, and the few surviving song-birds that the Italian sportsmen had so far failed to shoot found their voices again. The entire parade of light, sound and scent conjured up a vista of endless and immortal summer, fuller perhaps than summer itself, a different season with a rind of gold, and ripe as the ripest fruit. But though she enjoyed all these things, she regarded them as a peasant regards them; and she disliked the conscious display of semi-esthetic pleasures, such as when my father would call, 'I'm just going to the lower terrace, to observe the sunset'.

'Don't, George! I advise you not to,' she would reply, in a voice of discouragement. 'I know a lunatic who used always to do that!'

But my father, at this moment, is still sitting in the Cardinal's Garden, at about four o'clock. The sun has turned the colour of the stucco of the Castle to a rich yellow, and the supports of the Cardinal's coat of arms over the door seem almost to swim in the light, for they are full of baroque action. For a time, he pondered deeply on the details of a new lay-out, placing them in his mind against the principles of garden design which he had formulated and rediscovered. He looked at the parterre he had recently created. People were very stupid over such things. Only the other day a visitor had suggested that it would improve the borders to it if there were more flowers in them; they could not understand that the brown of the earth was an important element, forming a background for the colours of the stocks and ranunculus! Now he changed the line of his thought, stroked his beard, and gave his mind to his descendants – ideally different, in his imagination, from his children –, and the financial edifice he was devising for their advantage increased in intricacy. With age, his will-power had hardened, and his plans became more and more involved. Nor did he ever detect the evident error in his calculations: that when he died, and his death set in motion the involved and secret machine he had created, the one person who understood it and could work it would automatically have ceased to exist. After half an hour or so spent in reading the chart of the future – which he saw always more clearly than the present, and with a delusive perspective that rendered it almost as vivid for him as the past – he began to wonder what the workmen were doing. He looked at the face of his large gold watch. It was almost time for him to go up and give them the benefit of his advice based on a lifetime of experience – or if it were the spring or autumn, my brother and Georgia, his wife, and Edith and I, would often be visiting him for a few weeks, and he would feel it his duty to advise and guide 'the children': for such we remained to him.

The rather painful fun that my parents in combination so continually evolved became more rapid in action every year: though the stage grew to be less crowded. Gradually my father's contemporaries, and those others who had made part of his life, were receding. The Silver Bore died early in the thirties. Poor Pare was dead. My Aunt Florence was dead. Henry retired in the spring of 1936, and took lodgings in Scarborough.

In July of this year, the decline in Henry's health, which had caused him to retire, became more emphatic, and he wrote to Maynard Hollingworth:

> I have to undergo an operation which I fear will prevent me coming to Renishaw this August. Captain Osbert asked me and I had been looking forward to that treat The hospital are waiting a special instrument I have been X-rayed four times and nothing showed. Then they put search lights inside me in fact I was floodlit I told the doctor who is a jolly chap if he found any anchors or scrap to fetch them up as scrap is a good price.

However, with his great strength, he made temporarily a good recovery.

In the summer of 1937 my mother died in London after a short illness at the age of sixty-eight. To her last days, she remained in part child, with a child's impetuosity and humour, and in part older than her years, though she did not look more than fifty-five, and was as straight as though she had been a young woman, retaining her particular carriage of the head, so distinctive to her. She always told me that she entertained a great horror of old age. Indeed, as I drove round in a taxicab at six o'clock on a July morning to break to my father in his hotel – she had been removed to a nursing home – the news of her death, there came back to me, unbidden, but perhaps with a certain cruel relevance typical of the way the human mind works on very mournful occasions such as this, a fragment of conversation from many years before. It had taken place in the dining-room at Renishaw, at luncheon, on a fine August day. Only my mother, my father and myself had been present. My mother, who had been silent, suddenly observed:

'How much I should hate to live to be old!'

This remark, harmless as it seemed, pierced my father's armour, and he replied, but addressing his words to me, and in that unnaturally placid voice which in his case sometimes heralded a storm:

'I think all *intelligent* people would like to live to be old, wouldn't they, Osbert?'

My mother then interposed, 'But I should hate to feel I was being a trouble to anyone.'

And I, answering her, said, 'But *really intelligent* people don't mind that, Mother!'

My father had glowered at me, and had fallen back on one of his favourite rebukes:

'Rude without being funny!'

That had been fifteen years ago, and now I was on my way to tell him she was dead.

In the autumn, my father returned to Italy. He seemed happiest at Montegufoni, which he seldom left: happier I think than he had ever been, though he still, I know, greatly enjoyed his rare visits to me at Renishaw. Ernest de Taeye had, alas, died in 1934, and a new but able chief reigned in his stead over the flowers. I recall that my father, one morning during his last stay, entered the hall in an obvious state of exhaustion.

'What have you been doing?' I inquired.

'Just been showing the gardener round the garden,' he replied, bestowing on this task of supererogation an air of indefinable patronage.

To a certain extent his advancing years had compelled him to cease from continual active interference in the plans of his children, for he grew tired more easily. He now relied more on a sole weapon: *will-rattling*, as

Samuel Butler has described it. He continually altered or threatened to alter this document, and made a different one with several firms of solicitors. He liked from time to time, too, to stage a death-bed scene, when he would summon out for the occasion from England the ancestors of his descendants – that is to say his children. When thus sent for, I would always ask if I might see his doctor, and I remember the despairing voice of the celebrated Florentine doctor he consulted, as he said to me:

'Such an illness as Sir George lays claim to is a matter of X-ray plates, and not of faith. Sir George has *not* got it. I am twenty years younger, and he may outlive me by many years. He is an old man, but if he does not get pneumonia, he may live for twenty years.'

When I returned from Florence to Montegufoni, I found my father in bed, awaiting the end, and looking extremely melancholy.

'How long does he give me?' he gasped out.

'Another ten to twenty years,' I was able to reply. This cheered him up. And usually his fears – or at any rate the same fears – did not last long. He had too much to do, and he could not combine a perpetual death-bed scene with giving orders to the workmen and countermanding them. Besides, in some ways he liked change (indeed one of his favourite maxims was 'one ought to ring the changes more often') and before very long he would believe himself to be – or with part of his brain would believe himself to be – in the grip of another mortal illness. (It must be noted that, when genuinely ill, he always showed courage and stoicism.)

In the winter of 1937 I went out to Montegufoni to warn my father that in my opinion Italy would before long be involved in war with Great Britain. For my trouble, however, I was dismissed with an outsize flea in my ear. 'There won't be a war!' he maintained with an air of omniscient finality. I countered this, for I was worried about what might happen to him, by saying:

'All right, there won't be one, then – but if one *was* to occur what would you do?'

In the manner of Robin Hood, he replied, 'I should take refuge in the mountains!'

When I could not help adding, 'I suppose to look for the mountain-ash berries', he was annoyed, but I do not think he knew what I meant, or remembered that fragment of conversation of long ago to which I was alluding.

The same kind of life he had always led was continuing at the Castle. He was still at work, entering notes, writing long books, tracing pedigrees. He had just completed a new garden lay-out beneath the old rampart ('Between ourselves,' he observed to me, 'I believe I'm the only person living who could manage that double axis properly!'), and had recently disclosed a new vista of small, high rooms, painted and furnished in elaborate, but very individual pseudo-gothic. He had been delighted at the surprise people who knew the Castle well displayed when these apartments were shown them, for no one hitherto had been aware that they existed. His views on life had not much changed: though in one respect he had modified them. He attached more importance than formerly to the effect of the mother's heredity upon the children. In talking to our friend Francis Bamford, who stayed at Montegufoni for a considerable time at this period, he expatiated on the fact that it might be the blood of his Irish mother and Scottish grandmother mingling with that of the English Sitwells which had been responsible for producing so remarkable a character as himself. He added, 'Sacheverell probably acted wisely in choosing to marry a Canadian: it may be Nature's attempt to reproduce *me*!' I do not think he was lonely, his time was more than fully occupied, and as Henry once remarked, 'Sir George always liked to know where people *were*!, and now he knows they're all in the cemetery.' None of them now could contradict him, or interfere with his plans. He was undisputed lord of his own territory in space, time and imagination. He had grown more than formerly to *like* seeing people; though he still seldom knew who they were. Sometimes he gave large luncheon parties (I always wondered on what principle he gathered the guests, and how it was arranged), and when I was staying with him he would preside at a table in the vaulted dining-room, while I would be in charge of a smaller table in the hall beyond. And I recollect being struck by the pathos and symbolism of a remark he made to me one afternoon, after the guests had gone: 'I don't know how it is, but always it seems to me that I hear more laughter in the next room!'

In August 1939 my father came on a visit to England, but towards the end of the month hurried back to the Continent. As soon as he arrived in Italy he set to, and began to renovate the stucco statues of gods and goddesses and peasants in the seventeenth-century grotto, the finest in Tuscany. The domed and painted ceiling had become so fouled by weather and so obscured by dirt that the mythological personages and symbolic emblems portrayed upon it were unrecognizable: now, however, with washing and a little judicious aid from an expert in this line of work, they had become plainly identifiable. In his enthusiasm at these results my father wrote me a letter of, in a sense so abrupt, and certainly to prying eyes so mysterious a kind, that it was not delivered for a full two months: during which period, no doubt, the officials of the English Censorship, their gaze then directed towards the Mediterranean nations, were busily trying to interpret the cryptic message they were sure it must contain.

DEAREST OSBERT,
   The figure of Athens, under the Crown, is now clearly visible rising from sea, at the moment when Aurora's chariot is topping the horizon. She gazes in the direction of Rome, behind whom are to be distinguished the figures of Mars, the God of War, and Neptune, who governs shipping. Egypt, in the guise of a priest, looks on in dismay, wondering what her fate may be. And, in the right corner is an owl, the attribute of both Athene and Minerva. Ever, dear boy, Yr affectionate father, GEORGE R. SITWELL.

   After this, for many months, the letters which arrived for me from my father were stained with acid, and had obviously been subjected to a thousand tests of one sort and another. It looked to me, further, as if the Italian authorities were also on the track, for out of one letter fell a scrap of paper with *niente* scrawled on it in pencil.
   For my father's eightieth birthday, on the 27th January 1940, I sent him a telegram of congratulation, adding Henry's name to that of others still living who had been in his employment on the Renishaw estate. I wrote to inform Henry that this had been done.
   I received one morning some weeks later a letter from him in reply. It was headed 7 Cliff St, Whitby, and dated 23rd February 1940.

DEAR CAPTAIN OSBERT,
   It did me good to see your fist again, and really you write a good hand now. Thank you for adding my name to the telegram that proves you think of me and I must ask you to forgive me for not writing before to answer your letter but I have had ten days in bed with pleuresy, but it has left me weak but getting better slowly.
   There was an anxious time here on Feb. 3rd a German bomber was chased right over the town and land by three Spitfires they brought him down just above Ruswarp. 1½ miles from here he was riddled with bullets and one of the German crew had his head, chest and arm perforated at about 9 p.m. a Belgian ship came on the rocks 6 of her crew being drownded and two of our lifeboatmen fine fellows. It was the blackest night I ever saw and (as) there is no navigation light along the coast it is most difficult and dangerous. The two dead german airmen were to be buried at the cemetery here but rumour got about that the fishermen

had been bombed and machine-gunned there looked like being trouble so they were taken to Catterick near Richmonc in the middle watch and buried there. I had a nice letter from Sir Geo which I will send you on by reading between the lines he has every hope of living a good many years yet if he is going to see the perfection of his new gardening scheme at the Castle he often told me he would like to see 80 I now think he is heading for 100. I was rather tickled about him going into the Blue Nuns Home for fear of hurting their feelings I don't think it is habitual of him considering others feelings.

Now dear Sir, with all my very best wishes for you and Miss Edith from your obedient servant HENRY MOAT

P.S. I often think Mr Hollingworth ought to have been a gunner on a Spitfire. He would have brought them down like ninepins.

The night before my receiving this letter, I had been startled several times by the sounds of a heavy tread down below, and by bumpings in the pantry, which for nearly forty years, on and off, had been the principal scene of Henry's professional activities. In the morning, my sister, who slept in a distant part of the house, had complained similarly and independently of having been woken up on three or four occasions in the night by ponderous footsteps moving about. Later in the day I received the letter reproduced above, and an hour after that a telegram came informing me that Henry had died the previous afternoon. He had written his letter to me on the morning of his death.

Soon, in the middle of May, I was going to visit my father. The opportunity offered itself in this fashion: the British Council asked me to lecture in Milan, Florence, Rome, Naples, Palermo and other cities. I could take the opportunity of spending a few days with him on my way from Florence to Rome. I arrived in Milan, and the following evening delivered the first lecture – and the last: for as a consequence of the anti-English feeling being so carefully organized and exploited, the war which Italy was planning against us had drawn so near that one could almost feel the ferine breath of the God Mars, as, his armour covered with the verdigris of centuries, he rose from the ruined Roman temples and tombs, and strode towards us. Outside the station, that vast monument to Fascist power, large and heartless and cosmopolitan as the buildings of ancient Rome, an edifice made for triumphal banners more than for men, crowds of students sang vivacious anti-English songs, and any shop with an English name had to be guarded. Every day tension increased, and the morning after my lecture I was advised to abandon my tour and to return home. I therefore never reached Florence or Montegufoni.

The trains to the frontier were crowded with English invalids, retired governesses, and old people living on small pensions, who had spent whole decades in Italy and were now obliged to abandon the homes they loved, and the people they liked. To reach French soil seemed like stepping on dry land: everything appeared still secure, unthreatened; but another sound from the armoured footsteps in Italy was nevertheless to be detected here, that of a faint but terrifying creak, the preliminary, almost imperceptible shifting of a mass about to fall. In a day or two the Germans would reach Dieppe, and the thrasonic discourses on the radio, by democratic politicians almost already in flight, were due to begin. Every day the trains from Italy arrived at a later hour, and were more crowded; few English remained in that country, few even in Florence, for centuries their chosen city. But my father stayed on, in his Castle that was at the same time objective and subjective, a very solid structure, floating on its little hill, its towers surrounded by the pennons of the Italian skies, and a delicate edifice created out of long and often painful dreams; a fortress that was simultaneously physical, emotional and mental. Surely this triple stronghold would prove impregnable?

He never listened to the radio, and I was told that when in the morning he heard the news that Italy had declared war on England, he climbed the tower of the Castle – with some difficulty, for he was over eighty and had been ill for a long time – and remained up there for an hour or more. It was still early on a June morning of delusive trembling shadows, and already the air was dancing, spangling with motes the enormous expanse of tiled roof patterned with circular lichen, shaped like the patches of water-lilies on a pool, in silver, almond-green and gold, that lay below him. Under these again were the areas of stone, the paved courtyards, dark green, with a sparkle of glass in their darkness, and the organization of terraces and buttresses by which the great building was held up. Round and outside that, for miles the landscape was visible, lying as it were in folds and mounds of crinkled, wrinkled silk and sweeping up to a horizon pricked by the battlemented towers of other castles. Here and there in the sheen of gold and green was a patch almost black, where a cypress wood lay: within the cloistered, aromatic peace of which the nightingales still sang all the day long, as well as all the night: sang, they say, even when, three years later, the tanks came pounding through these same odorous groves.

Aloft, then, at the top of his tower, at the summit of his eighty years, my father was contemplating the view: but in spite of the clearness of the day, the view was indistinct. He wondered where best to place the belvedere: but, he realized, with the war in progress, it would be difficult and very expensive to build now. A war always unfortunately sent up the cost of materials and labour. Usually he found it easy to concentrate; but today the prospect before him kept dissolving into other scenes; the sheen of sun and shadow, the cups and hollows, the extreme width and undulation of the Tuscan landscape would merge into another, that was, though distant from him in time and space, still more familiar. The hollow of the stream below turned into a lake, the terraces into other terraces, the fountain into other fountains, the clumps of cypress into tall, antlered deciduous trees. Then these gardens, now themselves ancient, with the stout green walls that he had with such virtuosity contrived, melted into still earlier shapes. The vast bulk of a battlemented house, looming against its background of trees and of tangled vapours from sky and earth, was muffled in darkness, just as the winter skies were obscured by smoke from the giant furnaces recently established: everything seemed muffled in grief and darkness; and his mother, similarly, was swathed in black Victorian weeds, a young widow. She was struggling with the accounts for a large part of the day, trying to understand the losses that had fallen on the family; the echoing rooms, through which he ran by himself, seemed all the more immense for the emptiness. Somehow the exterior seemed more real, more bound to existence, than the inside of the house; he ran outside. There were the formless lawns, that yet had exercised a fascination by their glossiness; beds, carefully regulated and planted out with flowers in geometric patterns, vases, trees, the Gothic Temple, and the view; the great view as one day he would present it. Women in dark vast crinolines, in little bodices and bonnets, swayed over the green lawns with a curious sailing motion. He returned to the present, and wondered what had made him think of that; the clouds that hung over Montelupo, he supposed. Then the present collapsed again: he was playing croquet with Ida on the new lawn, and the dull clatter of the wooden balls and mallets mingled with the cooing of doves in the summer air; they were playing, four of them, the men in tight coats and trousers, and with boaters on their heads, the women with leg-of-mutton sleeves and straw hats. The laughter floated up among the flutter of leaves. He hadn't played croquet – in Italy they never seemed to play it! – for years, he reflected: not since Sargent had come down that time. He was afraid the surface of the group showed signs of deterioration: but there it was, artists were all alike, and refused to consult him as to the correct methods of making the pigments they used. He could have given them several valuable hints. Fortunately he had insisted on having his own way with the grouping of the picture, and on choosing the clothes for it. Ida, standing beside him, but a little distant, in a sequined white evening dress, with a hat with a transparent brim (a clever idea), and a scarlet feather (it needed just a touch of red): the two boys on the Aubusson carpet, playing with their toys. And Edith, with his arm round her shoulders. (Fathers should always stand in portraits, with their arms round their daughters' shoulders.) A pity that her nose was the wrong shape. But it seemed to him, looking back, that in life things often turned out like that. The whole group, he thought, showed English family life at its best: but much had changed since then: he had forsaken politics for literature – and by the way, Edith and the boys had taken to writing, too (such a mistake!). The children were not round him now, as they had been in the group, and he wondered where they were – missing his advice and guidance in these difficult times, he had no doubt, wherever they might be! It was singular: a man called Lawrence had been over to call, two years before, who had heard of all three of them as writers. That poem of Edith's about the half-witted girl waiting for her lover by the stream was quite interesting: but he wished she would consult him about rhythm. When he had spoken to her about it, she had merely denied that she had ever written the poem: but he remembered it well. Literature and painting had gone downhill, he was afraid. There was no-one equal to Sargent nowadays, though there had been an improvement in popular taste, in furniture and clothes. But the decline elsewhere was evident.

Though it was better not to think of it, yet, as he looked northwards, he could not help wondering what was happening behind the barrier of mountains. *La Grande Nation* was tottering to collapse. He was not surprised. Democracies were essentially selfish: now he feared they would sink into the ground drenched with their own blood. The papers said the roads were crowded with motors, all going in the same direction towards the sea: all the vehicles moving at the same pace – that was democracy all over! – slow as a man walking. Modern progress ended there, in great cities burned and whole races enslaved. At least the chivalry of medieval times would have prevented that! The innocent would have found sanctuary in the cathedrals, and the ladies of the castle and their children would have been safe within their massive walls of stone (as for the villeins, with whom he felt little sympathy, they enjoyed watching other people – especially their masters – go to war and not return). He thought of the splendid cathedrals in Normandy, of his long visit there a few summers ago, when he had stayed at Valmont to study the ancient holdings in land and the fortresses of the Estoutevilles and of the Sacheverells; castles which had already, centuries ago, dwindled to broken mounds of stone.

It was difficult to know how to divide up the day: for the poor workmen had most of them been mobilized (amazing, when he thought how much more valuable was the work they had been doing for him than that on which they were now employed!). He must have been up here quite a long time. He looked at his heavy gold watch, which he had presented as a boy of thirteen to his grandfather, the Waterloo veteran, who had at his death kindly left it back to him. He remembered, again, how the old gentleman had told him, as a boy of four or five, that he was to be a poet when he grew up. (Singular that all the children should be writers!) Ten o'clock, just after. (The second hand was slightly crooked, and it was difficult now to get anything mended.) He looked over the edge towards the court – already you could feel the intense heat coming up from the pavement, the tiles, and the terraces. Everything was very quiet, except for two hens that had escaped into the court from outside, and a pigeon that flapped and cooed out of the cote (he thought of Ida's pigeons at Renishaw, which the white owl had dispossessed). Somewhere below a man was whistling *Giovanezza*, the Fascist Anthem, as he watered the lemon-trees, and there was a sound of raking going on among them. Certainly it was peaceful up here. A tower made a great addition to a residence; one ought always to insist on breakfasting up it, but now, with the labour shortage, servants jibbed at a hundred steps even. Twenty people could easily breakfast here; it would be delightful. One's friends would enjoy it. Sometimes he wished he had always lived in a tower – indeed, almost felt as if he had done so. (No doubt, if he had, poor Henry would once again have given notice. Still, looking back, there was something to be said for him. He was always cheerful. If only he'd taken the advice given him, he'd have been healthy – most probably still here – and sometimes it was difficult not to wish he were!) Every country house should have at least one tower: better still, two. It had been a mistake not to build those two square towers at Renishaw, on the north front. They would have been most useful to Osbert, and Hollingworth could have a really modern office in one of them. In war-time, the roofs would have been invaluable, too, for watching – or spotting: and how much the sentinel – what did they call him – roof-spotter? – would *enjoy* being up there on a nice, fresh, frosty night!

He must go downstairs now, and begin work: he had got on well with the last chapter of the family history, and must really try to finish it. He began slowly to turn towards the steps: but now he noticed that in spite of the purity of the air a white cloud of dust hung over the road far below. Troops, he supposed. Well, he must be going down – as he descended into the darkness, he wished, all the same, that he could foresee what would happen. He'd like to know what his English acquaintances in Florence thought of the position – but he'd forgotten; they'd all gone! He was alone at last.

Meanwhile, I had left Italy and returned home, without being able to visit him.

I never saw him again.

Envoy

It is difficult to know the end of the world when you reach it. There are no signposts to tell you where you are. The sky is still there, the light shines down, from heights canopied or azure. In the shapes of the clouds, in their groupings and shiftings, you can still read visions of fortune as easily as a disaster. You think in the same way. Moreover there is the cruel physical, or animal, persistence. You sleep and eat – eat with the same movements of jaws and hands. Nothing comparable to the collapse of the West, which we are witnessing, has happened since the fall of Constantinople to the Turks. They too, however, those of them who survived to see the next day, were by habit and necessity compelled to eat and sleep, and in time to work.

Since I began to write this autobiography, in 1940, the world has again changed out of recognition. Some dangers have disappeared, and others, if possible more stupendous, have tumbled into their places. In the last few years tens of millions of human beings have perished in circumstances of execrable torture, by the ragings of war, the wastings of peace, the malice of man. For this the actions of no person or group of persons are solely to be impugned. No-one can read the chart of the future, even if it exists. However, it is permissible to blame the selfishness of those who lived in upholstered towers constructed to last only until their death. To these my father, of whose tower I have so often written, had never belonged: the materials he had used were of fine quality, and its design was individual, fantastic but complete. Moreover the future – as he saw it – was ever in his mind, and the edifice was dedicated to it, to house countless impersonal generations, armies of descendants. No: I refer to those who mouthed in first-class railway carriages the comfortable Edwardian slogan, 'It will last my time!' or the equivalent, in trams and buses, 'Why worry?' For myself, I had never expected the world I knew to endure, and this, perhaps, gave a sharper edge to my vision, to my living. From my earliest youth, I had, I believe, an unusual sense of time, of the recession of the present into the past, and its emergence into the future. Even as a child, I had tried to fix in my mind scenes that I wished to stay with me, so that I could enact them again in memory. And so it was that later I set myself to record them, and to fuse with them into a work of art the story of the development of three artists.

We cannot peer across at the future, though its people can gaze at us with a cool and detached curiosity from across the chasm. But it is well that we are thus curbed, since it is unlikely that we either should see much that would please us or hear much good of ourselves. Even if we could foresee the events of a few years, we should not, I believe, add to our contentment. It was happy for my father that when, as I have just described, he climbed the tower at Montegufoni, and remained there for a while, looking out, he did not understand then the present state of affairs. My father often in years past had pointed out the error in my literary outlook. I was pessimistic, he said. A book should always have a happy ending. Tragic things, he was glad to say, seldom happened in real life. Yet, had he now been gifted with the power of prognostication, what a vista of miseries, individual no less than terrestrial, would have been disclosed to him! A man of eighty must know that Death is not far away in the wings, is already hovering for his cue: but my father would have seen, as well as his own end in Switzerland, some three years ahead, in utter isolation, in a house in which he could see no-one, and send and receive no letters, the ruin of all he planned for, through the vicious cupidity and deceit of those who pretended to serve him; a result that had come to pass because of his own continually increasing blindness to character.

An omniscient being, again, posed high in a refuge on the mountains and looking out from it, would, if well disposed towards humanity, have perceived little that could gratify him. The second instalment of the atrocious cataclysms of the twentieth century, which no statesman had foreseen, were on the point of being realized, and would soon reach a new culmination. Gifted with an eagle's vision, he would, on the same day of June, have perceived the prostrate body of Europe crawling with grey German armies like lice. Just over the border of the morrow, he would have seen France, for centuries the light of Europe, vanish for the space of four years, to emerge in a new guise, and beyond that, Italy, Mother of the West, crawl out from the wreckage with a broken spine. As a child, I used to be depressed by the Jewish doctrine of vengeance, of an eye for an eye, and a tooth for a tooth: but now Christian nations recognized it as insufficient and out of keeping with the age. The Germans attacked London, and reaped their reward in cliffs of desolation, in angular mountains of rubble, taller and more obsolete than the Aztec pyramids, which had been their great cities, and which now choke and encumber the survivors. The Japanese bombed Pearl Harbor and paid for it with a gigantic totem-pole of smoke, surely fated, in the same fashion as the story of the Flood, to become a legend for savage men in the future. That monstrous shape rose over Hiroshima, a city which for an infinitesimal fraction of time glowed with such a light as man on earth had never seen; a light which, though in itself it was Western Man's final tribute to Darkness, seemed more potent than the radiance which had once attracted the Three Kings to the Manger, and, indeed, its shadow still lies over the future of the world. But what the price may be that will one day be exacted from the whole of humanity for that devil's picnic in the flower-sprinkled isles, we can still as yet only comprehend at times in the dumb and sable corners of consciousness, where a knowledge of the future and a terrible awareness of justice abide.

At last, then, total peace came with the stridency of a scream in the night. It possessed the violence of a nightmare. Europe turned turtle, and half of it was submerged, cut off from view, but the democratic statesmen continued to play their games. They chose this solemn moment of death and exhaustion for a frivolous strutting among the ruins. The enemy was perforce utterly silent, but our masters of the East and West shouted at one another across the champagne, through the fumes of vodka and cigar-smoke, their impious threats or partial acceptance of abominable bargains. Each in turn, with faces sly or swollen, fitted the clown's cap to his head and grimaced at the spectres marching towards them, in mobs and armies and hordes, from past and future. The English celebrated the world's end with neither a bang nor a whimper, but with their old traditional booby-trap, a general election. Nevertheless, a change in them was evident.

Issuing victorious from a long war waged with stubborn heroism by the whole people, they now dingily begged only to retain a few dehydrated or reconstituted eggs, a once-a-week dusting of tea, and a banana for the children. Clear or prophetic sight became, in the new code, a treachery to patriotism. A novel democratic folly possessed the educated, making them praise virtues that did not exist: the very faces of the former rulers had altered, softened, lost force, while a creeping wave of envy about small things seeped into the homes of the people. The Americans, who had first emerged as a people out of the fight against tradition, were thus now left, together with the Republic of Switzerland, and the Principality of Monaco, as the sole defenders of it. Meanwhile, the world's engines turn, and the greatest of cataclysms, which we can all foresee, and none seems able to prevent, prepares itself. Beyond that, who knows, who sees – I had almost written 'who cares'? I care, most certainly.

I, a Citizen of the Sunset Age, an Englishman, who saw the world's great darkness gathering, salute you, Stranger, across the Chasm. I strain toward the dawn of a new age, and offer you the story of events and persons in a day when the light flared up before it failed. I have tried, by such art as I could capture in my sum of days, to transmit to you almost the physical sensations, the feeling of our hours of warmth and cold, I have summoned to my aid every power I possess of evocation, to paint for you the life of which I was part, the places I saw, the people, the absurdities, cruelties, immensities, virtues and comic lapses of man's character, the incomparable capacity for joy and sorrow of that paragon of animals. I have tried to prove how a child is the centre of experience and light, from which the limbs and souls of men and women grow, radiate like the petals of a sunflower, and into which, like flowers, they die back. To achieve this, I have called into service not only hand and head, but the heart and the nerves of my whole body. I have endeavoured to make you feel what it was like to be alive before the world fell into the pit. I have not wanted to justify or explain, but to make a statement, to record; this is how it was for one of my origin, experience and temperament. Those of my generation obtained an end to our world in 1914. We scarcely expected the second and more fatal. Be warned, Stranger, that the fool returns to his folly, and that kindness and good feeling, and the sense of a kinship to nature which is their fount, should be cultivated as well as intelligence and the ability to make, or take, or distribute money. Above all, my message is that the world could only have been saved – perhaps still can be – through the spirit of man, especially through art, its noblest and most important manifestation. Alone of men – though with the farmer, the gardener, and the sailor following him at a distance – the artist exercises a profession that is entirely beneficial, and creative in itself. He unlocks for others the gates of the mind, the senses and the soul.

This I can tell you, Stranger, from things observed in my world: but what of yours? I cannot see your face, neither its colour nor shape, nor hear what tongue you speak. It may be – who knows? – some dog-English, learnt from old scripts and used as a general language, variously pronounced as dog-Latin in the Middle Ages (for the English language, whatever else is in decay or collapse, remains, as I have essayed, too, to show, magnificently alive, its possibilities unexhausted). I must content myself, then, with such facts as are clear, and build on them my own edifices. The sky and earth will be the same, though the planets are conquered, and men's loves and jealousies and follies. The vast panorama of the heavens, offered to me now, will be what you will behold also. I stare out of window, trying to conjure up the metropolises of the future, when men have again crept out of the ground into which they will have been forced. Once out of their burrows, they will build with renewed vigour and aspiration. As the reader knows, who has had the patience to accompany me so far, I have indulged in sciomancy and the magic of clouds all my life, and I see vast cities, palaces and domes, spires and arches, rise up, reform, as the clouds tumble like children upon the hills. Towards the apex of the sky are whole clusters now of gigantic towers, crowned with the sun, and through the vast thoroughfare of the firmament run rivers and torrents and cascades of light. On walls huge as hills, and undulating like the Great Wall of China (which once I saw) are set giant images, gods or demigods, drenched in light, the reflections of the times in which the states and cities were born. Among the golden rush and swerving of the clouds, maned like horses, from the vaulted halls where sit in conclave the ancient philosophers, with their grave eyes, wide-open as those of statues, and with their white beards flowing in the spectral, polar winds, while they listen to music or ask questions of the past, I hear voices, reaching to me faintly. What was the world like before it fell, they ask: was there deep sorrow? No, there was a peculiar sadness in the air, a feeling of hundreds of days leading up to this particular day, and every now and then the breath of a change to come as when the great airs of summer move under August trees: only that, and a surge of vanity in man. It is difficult to know the end of the world when you reach it.

INDEX